A Match on Dry Grass

A Match on Dry Grass

COMMUNITY ORGANIZING AS A CATALYST FOR SCHOOL REFORM

MARK R. WARREN, KAREN L. MAPP, and
The Community Organizing and
School Reform Project

OXFORD
UNIVERSITY PRESS

OXFORD
UNIVERSITY PRESS

Oxford University Press, Inc., publishes works that further
Oxford University's objective of excellence
in research, scholarship, and education.

Oxford   New York
Auckland   Cape Town   Dar es Salaam   Hong Kong   Karachi
Kuala Lumpur   Madrid   Melbourne   Mexico City   Nairobi
New Delhi   Shanghai   Taipei   Toronto

With offices in
Argentina   Austria   Brazil   Chile   Czech Republic   France   Greece
Guatemala   Hungary   Italy   Japan   Poland   Portugal   Singapore
South Korea   Switzerland   Thailand   Turkey   Ukraine   Vietnam

Copyright © 2011 by Mark R. Warren and Karen L. Mapp

Published by Oxford University Press, Inc.
198 Madison Avenue, New York, NY 10016

www.oup.com

Oxford is a registered trademark of Oxford University Press

Library of Congress Cataloging-in-Publication Data
Warren, Mark R., 1955–
A match on dry grass : community organizing as a catalyst for school reform / Mark R. Warren, Karen L. Mapp, and The
Community Organizing and School Reform Project.
    p.   cm.
Includes bibliographical references and index.
ISBN 978-0-19-979359-4 (cloth : alk. paper) — ISBN 978-0-19-979358-7 (pbk. : alk. paper) 1. School improvement
programs—United States. 2. Educational change—United States—Citizen participation. 3. Educational accountability—
United States. 4. Community organization—United States. 5. Community power—United States. 6. Social action—
United States. I. Mapp, Karen L. II. Title.
LB2822.82W364   2011
371.2'07—dc22   2010054553
ISBN-13: 9780199793594 (cloth), 9780199793587 (paper)

5 7 9 8 6 4

Printed in the United States of America
on acid-free paper

The Community Organizing and School Reform Project is located at the Harvard Graduate School of Education. The project
is led by Mark R. Warren and Karen L. Mapp and consists of Keith C. Catone, Roy Cervantes, Connie K. Chung, Cynthia
J. Gordon, Soo Hong, Ann Ishimaru, Paul Kuttner, Meredith Mira, Thomas Nikundiwe, Soojin Susan Oh, Kenneth Russell,
Amanda Taylor, Mara Casey Tieken, Anita Wadhwa, and Helen Westmoreland.

We dedicate this book to community organizers and leaders—the parents, young people, community residents, teachers and educators—who are working long and hard to transform schools and communities in pursuit of educational and social justice.

Contents

Conclusion: Lessons for School Reform and Democracy Building   249

Preface and Acknowledgments

The Community Organizing and School Reform Project came together as a joint team of faculty and graduate students at the Harvard Graduate School of Education. We wanted to contribute to building the foundation for a new field of research on the role of community organizing in education reform. We firmly believed that real progress in transforming public education in low-income communities and communities of color would only come when parents, young people and other leaders from these communities themselves became active participants in shaping reform processes. By studying community organizing efforts that were making a significant impact on improving public education, we hoped to build a broader and deeper understanding of this emerging movement among researchers, educators and the broader public.

Mark Warren and Karen Mapp, the two faculty members, provided overall leadership and took overall responsibility for the research project. Fifteen graduate students formed teams to study the six organizing groups represented in this book:

- Ann Ishimaru, Cynthia J. Gordon and Roy Cervantes studied PACT in San Jose
- Keith Catone, Connie K. Chung and Soojin Susan Oh studied One LA in Los Angeles
- Meredith Mira, Thomas Nikundiwe and Anita Wadhwa studied Padres y Jóvenes Unidos in Denver
- Kenneth Russell and Mara Casey Tieken studied Southern Echo in the Mississippi Delta
- Soo Hong studied the Logan Square Neighborhood Association in Chicago
- Paul Kuttner, Amanda Taylor and Helen Westmoreland studied the Northwest Bronx Community and Clergy Coalition in New York City

Soo Hong and Mara Tieken served, at various times, as project coordinator and provided leadership to the group as well.

The project turned out to be a very powerful experience for all of us. In many ways, it was a unique experience for an academic research project. We conducted our research with the most rigorous academic standards. However, we also shared our deeply held beliefs and values and our own personal journeys into and through the project. By trying to implement principles of organizing within our project, we formed a community.

The research teams formed particularly tight bonds through their shared experience out in the field. Many of us were new to field research and this collective approach created a powerful learning process. Those of us with more research experience were pushed to grow and develop in new ways.

Meanwhile, we endeavored to make all decisions collaboratively in the project as a whole. Indeed, our meetings were marked by lively discussion and sometimes heated debate. We learned to work together, value both our commonality and our diversity, and build the kinds of relationships often missing in university settings. We started as teachers and students but we ended as colleagues.

As a result of this collaborative process, we have created a synthetic, co-authored book, not an edited volume. We conducted the research project and wrote this book together. The names of the team members for each of the case studies are listed on the case chapters; they are the primary authors of those chapters. Mark Warren is the primary author of the introduction, chapter 1, chapter 8 and the conclusion. All project members, however, contributed to the analysis presented in those chapters and, indeed, in all the chapters.

Meanwhile, although fifteen Harvard students formed the research teams and participated in all aspects of the project, an even larger number of students contributed in some capacity to the project, mostly in the stage of research design and the construction of research instruments. We would like to thank these students and colleagues: Tiffany Cheng, Sarah Dryden-Peterson, Zenub Kakli, Carolyn Rubin, Sky Marietta, Dulari Tahbildar, Phitsamay Sychitkokhong Uy, Kerry Venegas, and Malia Villegas. In addition, Carolyn Rubin participated in all team meetings throughout the duration of the project; she helped organize cross-case themes and assisted the group in reflecting on our collective process. Paul Kuttner produced the graphic design of our tree image featured in chapters 1 and 8.

We would like to thank the Harvard Graduate School of Education for creating a supportive home for this project. Dean Kathleen McCarthy, Academic Dean Robert Schwartz and Associate Dean Daphne Layton offered concrete assistance and smoothed the way to keep the project moving forward. The school's sponsored research and finance teams, including Helen Page, Nadija Mujagic, Tiffany Cott, and Pat Varasso, helped us raise funds and keep track of our complex accounts. Our staff assistants Melita Garrett and Jon Whichard helped coordinate travel, payments, and so many details that arise in a project of this size and scope. The research librarians at Gutman Library, Kathleen Donovan, Carla Lillvik, Marcela Flaherty and Leila Kocen, were always helpful and efficient. Gino Beniamino and Kristin Lofblad assisted us in managing our Web site and Information Technology needs; Jason DeWaard, Robert Sheffield, and Jonathon Womack helped us with communication.

We would also like to thank our friends Anne and Udo Kuckartz at Max-QDA, and also Ray Maietta, for making the qualitative data analysis software available and helping us to use it efficiently. Barbara Alihosseini and the folks at New England Transcripts took great care in transcribing our interviews. Meanwhile, Maria Tagle transcribed Spanish interviews and Maria Isabel Hernandez translated these interviews into English for us. We appreciate the assistance of all these people.

We received financial support for this project from a number of sources. We would like to thank Harvard's Center for American Political Development and the Edward W. Hazen Foundation for seed grants that helped us get the project off the ground. Lori Bezahler's enthusiasm and support helped us expand our resources. We would like to thank the Charles Stewart Mott Foundation, the Ford Foundation, the Spencer Foundation and the Carnegie Corporation of New York for their generous support for our research. In particular, Cris Doby at Mott and Cyrus Driver and Jeannie Oakes at Ford provided thoughtful advice and asked good questions that helped push our research forward.

A large number of colleagues participated in various discussions of our research as it developed and helped us focus our data collection and sharpen our findings. We would like to thank Kavitha Mediratta, Seema Shah, Sara McAlister, John Beam, Julie Kohler, Charles Payne, Jeannie Oakes, Shawn Ginwright, Richard Elmore, Susan Moore Johnson, and John Diamond. We would especially like to thank John Rogers, Jean Anyon, and Rob Kleidman who read the entire manuscript and offered constructive suggestions.

This project developed at the same time that many of us were establishing a new Special Interest Group on community and youth organizing in the American Educational Research Association (AERA). Discussions with our colleagues in this new group also helped inform our research and enabled us to better see how our findings could inform this larger field. We would like to thank JoAnn Trujillo Hays, the principal of Academia Ana Marie Sandoval, and her staff for hosting our session at the AERA meetings in Denver where we reported the findings of this project. We also thank Rosa Linda and Oscar Aguirre and their staff at Rosa Linda's restaurant where we celebrated after the session.

We would like to thank James Cook, our editor at Oxford University Press, for his wholehearted support of our book project. He helped shepherd us through the editing and production process with efficiency and good humor.

We would like to offer our profound appreciation to our families and friends who enthusiastically supported us through the process. We spent many weeks away from home, conducting field research at our sites. We spent far too many hours in meetings and in writing and re-writing countless drafts of the manuscript. Our spouses, partners, children and friends believed in us and wanted to support our efforts to contribute to educational justice and a more democratic society. They shared our excitement about the possibilities for transforming public education and building power for communities to shape their own futures. We simply could not have completed our project without the help and encouragement of this broader community. We would particularly like to thank Roberta Udoh, Sade and Imoh Udoh-Warren, Donal Fox, Darshan, Varinder and Dev Wadhwa, Seth Dewart, Wim and Quinn Taylor, Zack, and Mika and Jani Semke, Mikio and Vickie Ishimaru, Hyunkyung and Eunsim Oh, Yon W. and Yung H. Chung, Leah Okimoto, Edwin, Lauren and Christopher Choy, Young Hong, Bob, Mary Ann and Megan Mira, Michelle, Izaac and Akenna Nikundiwe, Carla Shalaby, Dulari Tahbildar, Nikki and Mikaila Russell, Mary Alexander, Wade Westmoreland, Priscilla Little, Rebecca Craft, Erika Kreutziger, Elaine, Peter and Mike Kuttner, Sandra and Donald Tieken, Courtney P. Gordon and, in memory, Kurtiss J. Gordon.

Finally, we would like to thank the organizers and leaders of the community organizing groups we studied: PACT, One LA, Padres y Jóvenes Unidos, Logan Square Neighborhood Association, Southern Echo and the Northwest Bronx Community and Clergy Coalition. We also appreciate the assistance of all the teachers, educators and other folks with whom they work for welcoming us into their schools and organizations. They shared with us their stories and their passion, their critique of public education and their hard-nosed political analysis, their dreams for their children and their visions of a more just and caring society. We have learned tremendously from their work and we deeply value our relationship with these committed organizers and leaders.

We conducted this project as researchers attempting to advance the new field of the study of community organizing for education reform. Yet we know that building a movement for educational justice will require many different kinds of people finding ways to work together. We hope our project contributes to this broader effort by helping researchers, educators, policymakers, organizers, and community leaders learn from each other to advance our common mission of educational and social justice.

A Match on Dry Grass

Introduction

A New Movement for Equity and Justice in Education

Down south, five hundred African American parents, young people and community residents gather from across the Mississippi Delta for a conference at Mississippi Valley State University on "Dismantling the Achievement Gap," where they strategize to advance their campaign to dramatically increase state funding to African American schools in poor, rural communities. On the West Coast in Los Angeles, a school principal and her staff work with Latino parents and neighborhood Catholic churches to close down the dump across the street from the school, which is causing such high levels of asthma and other health conditions that children seem to spend more time in the health clinic than the classroom. Up the coast in San Jose, parents, teachers and principals design new small autonomous schools where parents are full partners in educating children in schools which value the culture and traditions of the Latino community. In Chicago, one hundred and fifty parents graduate every year from a leadership training program sponsored by a community organizing group; all work to support teachers in the classroom and many go on to become school-community leaders, initiating campaigns to open community learning centers, launch "Grow Your Own Teacher" programs and lobby for affordable housing in the neighborhood. In Denver, Latino youth take the lead to reform a failing high school at the center of their community, working with parents and other community residents to lobby for college prep courses in the school, restorative justice disciplinary policies across the district, and affordable access to state universities for undocumented immigrants. On the East Coast in New York City, Bronx high school students and educators lead a local politician through their overcrowded school building, in the process cultivating an ally in their effort to increase much-needed classroom space in terribly overcrowded schools.

In low-income communities across the country, parents, young people and educators like these are finding new ways to work together to improve quality and address equity in public education. They are joining community organizing groups in building a new movement committed to transforming public education and working for social justice. Rather than remaining passive victims of an unjust system, through community organizing, parents and young people are becoming active change agents in their schools and communities. In this book, we examine this new movement by presenting case studies of organizing groups that have made significant impacts on public education in communities across the country—in New York City, Chicago, Denver, San Jose, Los Angeles and the Mississippi Delta. We bring their voices to light so that we can better understand why these parents and young people have devoted their precious time and energy to working for school reform and what their aspirations and goals are for their children. At the same time, we identify and analyze the key organizing processes through which low-income communities are working to improve quality and promote equity and justice in education and beyond. In the end, we show how building powerful forms of family and community engagement in schools can play an essential role in creating desperately needed reform in public education and contributing to healthier communities for children and young people.

Inequality, Power and the Failures of Public Education

Despite great attention to reforming public education in low-income communities, significant progress has been slow to come. Test scores have risen in some categories and in some localities, but it remains unclear how much of this increase reflects real improvements in learning. Some individual schools have had notable success. Overall, however, the crisis of public schooling continues. Fully half of all black and Latino youth continue to fail to graduate high school with their peers, with the proportions even greater in large, urban and poor, rural districts.[1] Many of those who do graduate are not prepared to succeed in college. Only about 13 percent of Latinos have graduated from college—and this at a time when a college degree is becoming essential to economic well-being. Meanwhile, the results of the failures of our educational system can be devastating. Most children of color who do not graduate high school are destined to lives of poverty and economic hardship, excluded from mainstream participation in American life. Many, especially black and Latino young men, will end up in prison.[2]

In other words, the failures of public education represent a profound and perhaps the most important social justice issue of our day. Indeed, many have called education *the* civil rights issue of our time. Large proportions of low-income families and children of color continue to find access and opportunity to the social and economic benefits of American life denied to them because of the lack of good education.

In communities where parents are well organized and politically influential, such poor performance is not normally tolerated nor allowed to persist. Yet parents in low-income communities typically do not have the political clout to effect change. The difference in power and resources across communities means that American public education is strikingly unequal. We spend twice the amount on education in whiter and more affluent communities than in some poorer districts right next door. More affluent students attend better resourced schools with state of the art equipment and textbooks and highly qualified teachers; meanwhile, low-income students of color tend to go to under-resourced schools in older buildings with less—or even unqualified teachers. Few today might charge American elites with intentionally keeping black, Latino or poor children down, yet the results are remarkably similar.[3]

In our view, the disempowerment of low-income communities provides a key part of the reason that the educational systems in these communities are failing and are allowed to persist in failure. Pedro Noguera has shown how urban schools operate in what he calls "captured populations" who lack the resources to pursue alternatives. As school districts move from one reform effort to another, change seems more symbolic than real. Schools in low-income communities, both urban and rural, lack a political constituency of those most affected—parents with children in schools, who can demand real improvement and hold public schools accountable for results over a sustained period of time.[4]

Many people recognize that the problems of public education are embedded in unequal power relations and social and economic inequality in the larger society. Indeed, many teachers in poor communities become frustrated because, however hard they work in the classroom, they know that the conditions students face outside of schools have an enormous impact on their ability to learn. Ever since Jonathan Kozol decried the "savage inequalities" of American public education, we have seen a steady stream of research and writing that ties educational failure to the effects of poverty and racism. Yet most educators have no idea what to do about that. Indeed, many educators and school reformers ignore issues of power and carry on as if this reality does not matter.[5]

Community organizing offers a fresh approach to addressing educational failure as part of a larger effort to build power for marginalized communities and tackle issues associated with poverty and racism inside and outside of schools. As we will show in the pages of this book, organizing groups help build a political constituency with the power to demand school improvement and hold systems accountable. Yet organizing groups do not just demand change; they also work to organize parents, young people, community residents and educators to contribute to change efforts. Indeed, most organizing groups are strongly committed to finding avenues for collaboration with educators as constructive—and powerful—partners. At the same time, organizing groups are multi-issue organizations. While they work to improve education, they also address the range of issues affecting low-income families, like housing, health care and neighborhood safety. As such, community organizing offers a critical contribution to school reform efforts, while at the same time it works to connect education reform to efforts to address structural inequality in America, that is, to broader social justice goals.[6]

The Emergence of "Community Organizing for School Reform"

Twenty-five years ago, one would have been hard pressed to find many organizing groups undertaking sustained work on school reform. In the seventies and eighties, community organizing groups concentrated their efforts on community development issues like affordable housing, job training and neighborhood blight. During the nineties, however, community organizations increasingly came to appreciate the central importance of education to the future life prospects of young people in low-income communities. Many began to experiment with school reform work as an important part of their broader agenda. Estimates of the number of groups undertaking education work by the turn of the century placed the number at somewhat more than two hundred groups. A recent estimate suggests that there are now as many as five hundred organizing groups engaged in work around public education in urban areas alone.[7]

More and more people have started to encounter organizing groups active in their communities. These groups work primarily at the local level and so have stayed below the radar screen of national politics. With the election of Barack Obama to the presidency, however, the term community organizing entered the national political discourse.

Yet despite the growing acquaintance with community organizing, few people understand what organizing is or how it works. If anything, the American public and most educators understand community organizing to be a set of techniques that rally people together behind some cause. There are techniques to organizing for sure. At times, organizing groups do mobilize large numbers to rallies or other events. But community organizing involves much more than this. Organizing groups do the patient, long-term work to build the capacity and leadership of people to create change in their communities and schools. They teach people the skills and knowledge necessary to bring residents of their communities together, identify issues of pressing concern, research those issues to develop an agenda for action, build alliances with other groups, negotiate with public officials, and collaborate with educators and other institutional agents to create and implement new policies and practices.[8]

The Community Organizing Paradigm

Community organizing can be distinguished from more commonly known advocacy and service paradigms. Organizing groups do not advocate "for" parents or communities; nor do they provide services to them. We have many advocacy groups, like the Children's Defense Fund, which do important work promoting changes in law or policy to better meet the needs of children and their families. These professionally led groups typically have mailing-list type memberships and concentrate their activities on lobbying legislative bodies or pursuing legal cases. Organizing groups, by contrast, concentrate on building active participation and leadership at the ground level. As they organize, people may collaborate with professionals and policy advocates to lobby for their issues and agenda, but the core work of organizing groups rests in building the capacity of community members to create institutional and policy change on their own behalf.[9]

There is now widespread recognition of the importance of involving families in the education of their children. Family-involvement programs typically take a service orientation, where schools provide parenting classes or other programming to help parents better support their children in school. Although community organizing groups do work to involve families, their approach represents quite a different paradigm from traditional parent-involvement programs. Dennis Shirley was one of the first researchers to distinguish parent involvement from the kind of engagement that occurs in organizing. According to Shirley, "Parental *involvement*—as practiced in most schools and reflected in the research literature—avoids issues of power and assigns parents a passive role in the maintenance of school culture. Parental *engagement* designates parents as citizens in the fullest sense—change agents who can transform urban schools and neighborhoods." In other words, organizing groups are primarily political, albeit normally nonpartisan, organizations focused on institutional change.[10]

The Purpose of this Study

In response to the rise of these groups, a new body of research is starting to document the accomplishments of community organizing groups in the field of education. In an important recent study, researchers at the Annenberg Institute for School Reform were able to show that community organizing, when pursued in a district over time with intensity and at sufficient scale, is positively related to improvements in student outcomes. They found that schools engaged with community organizing groups had higher student educational outcomes, including higher attendance, test score performance, high school completion, and college-going aspirations. They also were able to document the effects of community organizing on creating equity-oriented change in school district policy, practices, and resource distribution. At the level of individual schools, the authors showed how organizing strengthens school-community relationships, parent involvement and engagement, and trust.[11]

We wanted to design a study that would build on this research while going deeper and broader. We undertook our study in order to identify and examine the key processes through which organizing groups work to bring parents, young people, community residents and educators together to build the capacity for change. As such, the purpose of our study was not primarily to document results but rather to dig deeply into organizing processes. We sought to create rich descriptions and complex analysis of *how* community organizing groups work to create equity-oriented education reform.

At the same time, we wanted to conduct a study that would reflect the diverse world of community organizing for school reform across the country. Previous studies had largely focused on the organizing tradition rooted in the work of Saul Alinsky and represented today by the Industrial Areas Foundation (IAF) and the PICO National Network, among others. Indeed, the best-known example of education organizing is the Alliance Schools strategy developed by the IAF in Texas. We wanted to include these traditions but also others that looked more directly to a Civil Rights movement tradition or that blended different traditions to create new hybrids. By looking across our in-depth studies of each case, we planned to identify important similarities and differences in the way organizing groups pursue education reform.[12]

A Multiple Case Study Design

We believed the best way to examine organizing processes was to develop careful, richly detailed case studies of significant organizing groups. We selected groups that have marshaled significant resources to education organizing, that have sustained their focus on education for a number of years and that have achieved some significant accomplishments. We believed that education reform presents a challenging arena for organizing groups. Weak and sporadic efforts are not likely to produce results. Therefore, we decided to study strong forms of organizing as the ones capable of making a substantial impact on the institutions of public education. These groups are not necessarily well-known outside their localities but are nevertheless doing hard and patient work to transform the culture and practice of public education and civic engagement.[13]

Because we believe that community organizing for school reform is emerging as a national phenomenon, we wanted our study to be truly national in scope. So we selected organizing efforts from across the country, in New York City,

Chicago, the Mississippi Delta, Denver, Los Angeles and San Jose, California. This selection also provided us with a variety of local contexts—historical, demographic and institutional—so we could explore the impact of context on the development of organizing. We also decided to select groups that follow different organizing traditions and that work with a variety of demographic groups. We were especially concerned to include organizing efforts with African Americans, Latinos and newer immigrant groups.

The six cases we chose include: the Northwest Bronx Community and Clergy Coalition in New York City, the Logan Square Neighborhood Association in Chicago, Southern Echo in the Mississippi Delta, Padres y Jóvenes Unidos in Denver, One LA-IAF in Los Angeles and People Acting in Community Together (PACT) in San Jose, California. In selecting the six groups, we were not able to capture all the possible variety in education organizing, nor all possible communities and local contexts. We do believe, however, that these cases provide us with a very good selection of some of the most significant organizing initiatives for education reform across a variety of important contexts in the United States.[14]

Collaborative Research within a Single Project

An exciting and unique feature of this research project was the collaborative process we developed. Under the overall leadership of faculty members Mark R. Warren and Karen L. Mapp, fifteen graduates students at the Harvard Graduate School of Education worked together to conduct this project. We developed a conceptual framework as well as a common research design with which to begin investigation in each of our cases. Once the initial research design was developed, the core work of the project consisted of the case studies. Teams of two to three doctoral students formed the case study research teams and they were empowered to enter the field and shape a research process authentic to each locality. They spent a year traveling to the research sites, interviewing participants, observing activities in schools and communities, and collecting relevant documents like organizational reports, newspaper articles and statistics on school performance.

Meanwhile, we created a dynamic process where case teams constantly reported back to the faculty leaders and the other case teams. Every step of the process occurred in dialogue with the entire research project. As the teams analyzed their data and wrote up the case chapters in this book, findings and analysis were shared across the whole project in order to stimulate deeper analysis of each case. In the final phase, we worked as a project to analyze and compare our findings across the six cases to create a synthetic account of the transformational work of community organizing for school reform.

We believe our collaborative approach created a highly rigorous research process. This approach was particularly relevant to our goals. By empowering each case team to respond authentically to local context, we were able to develop richly detailed and contextually grounded case studies of each organizing group.[15] By pursuing a common research design across the cases and by working together on the overall analysis, we were able to identify the similarities and differences in the way groups organize for education reform. We present further details about our research methods in the appendix to this book.

Plan of the Book

In chapter 1 of this book, we present a framework for understanding how strong forms of community organizing work for equity-oriented education reform. We trace the historic roots of contemporary community organizing in various organizing traditions and stress how local groups find their roots in the shared histories and identities of local communities. We identify the core processes of organizing as relationship building to develop the power to create change, even as organizing groups respond to local context, that is, the opportunities and constraints in the larger environment. We emphasize that organizing groups pursue education reform as part of a broader process where parents, young people and other residents of low-income communities develop the power to influence the social and political processes that determine their fate.

In the case chapters that follow, we trace the reasons for each organizing group's entrance into the work of education reform, the key processes through which they build capacity and power for low-income communities, and their experiences engaging with educators and other reform actors in the hard work of school reform. We also look carefully at how local context shapes the way organizing groups engage with education reform. Each chapter focuses on an important campaign through which we develop a narrative that reveals and analyzes core organizing processes.

We start the presentation of our case studies in chapter 2 on the West Coast with People Acting in Community Together (PACT) in San Jose, California—an affiliate of the PICO National Network. In the Alum Rock school district, Latino parents were concerned that their children were failing in large, impersonal schools that were disconnected from the children's community. We concentrate on PACT's use of the PICO organizing cycle to build a campaign to open several new small autonomous schools. We show how PACT helped build schools with deeply relational cultures and strong partnerships between educators and parents, schools that have become among the most successful in the district.

In chapter 3, we travel down the West Coast to Los Angeles. We examine the work of One LA, which is working to apply the Alliance School strategy developed by its parent network, the Industrial Areas Foundation, in Texas. In Los Angeles, however, IAF organizers faced a massive, sprawling city where parents felt completely disconnected and excluded from public schools. We examine how One LA dug deeply into individual schools where it developed the capacity of school leaders—including parents, teachers, and administrators—to build relational cultures within and across institutions as the foundation for school improvement. We show how this strategy was used to build a powerful alliance to close a local dump creating health problems for children and to reorient professional development to improve instructional practice.

In chapter 4, we examine the organizing work of Padres y Jóvenes Unidos (PJU) in Denver. Growing out of the Chicano and Civil Rights movements, PJU organizes parents and youth in Denver's Latino community around education, immigration and other issues. With its 38 percent drop-out rate, North High School, located in the heart of the Latino community, served as a powerful symbol of the failure of public education. We show how young people at North High School, through working with PJU, emerged as leaders of a reform effort at the school. Through leadership development efforts centered on political education, we trace the efforts of young people to build a powerful alliance among parents, other community residents, and the district superintendent to create a meaningful reform process at the school.

In chapter 5, we move south to examine the work of Southern Echo in the Mississippi Delta. The denial of education dating back to slavery has long served to disempower African Americans in rural Delta communities. We show how Southern Echo draws from the Civil Rights movement organizing tradition to address issues of systemic racism and inequality in the public education system. To combat the isolation and fear felt by African Americans, the network combines strong local organizing with efforts to bring rural communities together across counties. We examine the key processes through which Southern Echo organizes by focusing on a critical local fight to stop the opening of a segregated public school in Tunica and on the network's historic campaign to dramatically increase state funding to public education in African American communities.

In chapter 6, we examine the work of the Logan Square Neighborhood Association (LSNA) in Chicago. As rapid immigration transformed Logan Square into a largely Latino community in the 1980s, new families became profoundly isolated from the neighborhood schools their children attended. In response, LSNA created a model parent leadership program that has trained over 1,200 parents across eight neighborhood schools to go into classrooms to support teachers. We examine how LSNA organizing processes build not just broad parent participation but leaders who created a broad range of educational initiatives that met their needs, even as they emerged as leaders addressing health and housing issues in the communities surrounding the schools.

We close our cases in chapter 7 with the Northwest Bronx Community and Clergy Coalition in New York City. The Coalition organizes parents, youth and community members around a variety of community issues through congregations, neighborhood associations and schools. In responding to the tremendous diversity in its neighborhood, the Coalition has developed a reputation for flexibility and creativity in organizing approaches. We focus on the Coalition's efforts to address severe overcrowding in Bronx schools, where the group confronts a massive and notoriously unresponsive bureaucracy in the city's department of education. We trace the Coalition's effort to engage parents and young people across the Bronx and to build a powerful alliance with unions and other groups to demand the construction of more schools and the creation of more classroom space.

In chapter 8, we draw from across our cases to synthesize our understanding of the methods, processes, and capacities through which community organizing works to create and support equity-oriented school reform. Despite their differences, we show how the organizing groups in our study follow a set of central processes common to all. These groups build relationships and power for transformational change in communities and schools. We highlight transformational processes at the individual, community, and institutional levels and discuss the power that comes from their interrelationship. We also discuss how context and tradition shape the different ways these transformational processes develop in each group.

In the concluding chapter, we elaborate the lessons from our research for educators and the broader public who care about advancing quality and equity in American public education. We argue that organizing's process-oriented approach has much to offer to a school-improvement paradigm that is too often narrowly expert driven and imposed on schools in a top-down manner. We highlight the value of strong forms of engagement of families and communities in school change processes and the importance of linking school reform to efforts to address the broader set of issues that prevent the healthy development of children in low-income communities. We conclude with a discussion of the power of organizing to revive the democratic promise of public education in an America that faces profound and growing inequality.

In analyzing the organizing strategies of the various groups in our study, we are not necessarily endorsing any particular school reform initiative that a group undertakes. Generally, we believe readers will be sympathetic to the efforts of these groups to grapple with deeply entrenched social justice issues. Some, however, may be troubled about particular initiatives that seem to ally with larger, sometimes neoliberal reform agendas; other readers may support these agendas. One of the groups we studied worked for the creation of small, autonomous schools and even charter schools. Another called for a high school reform initiative that required teachers at the school to reapply for their jobs. None of the groups, however, have fully embraced larger, national reform agendas, neoliberal or otherwise. Rather than judge these efforts from the standpoint of national debates, we invite readers to understand the experience of families and communities who are suffering from a failing educational system and attempt to comprehend how and why they came to build the campaigns they did. The purpose of our research was not to prove the effectiveness of any particular school reform strategy. Rather, it was to analyze how organizing works. Organizations that bring the voices of those long excluded from participation in the process of education reform do not necessarily have all the answers, but we believe that they do have a vital and essential contribution to make to improving public education and advancing social justice.[16]

1

How Community Organizing Works

Organizing groups build capacity and power for communities so that they can increase equity and improve public education as well as address the range of issues confronting families in low-income communities. In this chapter, we set out a framework for understanding how they pursue these goals. We draw upon a broad research and theoretical base in a variety of fields as well as from the analysis we developed through our research. Although we have used some illustrations from our case research, we have written this chapter in a way that can be read first, that is, before the case chapters to follow. Thus, we hope readers will benefit from having this framework in mind as they proceed to read the case chapters.

As noted in the introduction to this book, we focus on strong forms of community organizing as the kind of organizing capable of making a difference in public education. Our framework may not fit all groups who carry the community organizing mantle, particularly those that are short-term or episodic. We would argue, however, that this framework helps us understand how organizing groups grow, build capacity, and sustain their organizing over time so they can have a significant impact on equity and justice in public education and beyond.

How Does Organizing Work?

Figure 1.1 presents our understanding of how strong forms of community organizing work. We chose the metaphor of a tree for several reasons. First of all, this metaphor suggests that organizing is a phenomenon that grows and develops. Indeed, organizing efforts take time to mature, and they need to be intentionally cultivated and nurtured. Second, strong organizing efforts have deep roots. These roots lie in various organizing traditions, but they are also found in the shared histories and identities of particular local communities. Although these roots set the direction for any particular organizing group, organizing efforts also respond to their environment, that is, to the opportunities and constraints

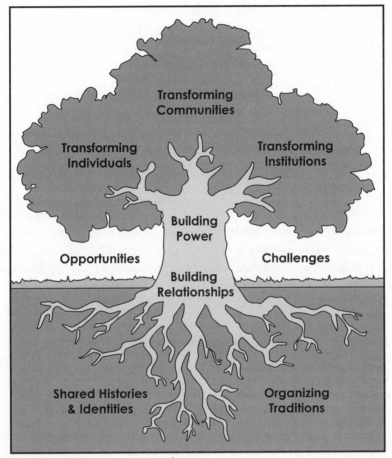

Figure 1.1 How community organizing works.

presented by changing political and educational contexts. As a result, organizing initiatives can develop in the diverse ways that we will examine in the case chapters to follow.

At the same time, strong organizing efforts do share fundamental features. We show these core processes—building relationships and power—in the tree trunk. By enacting these processes, organizing groups work to transform communities, individuals, and institutions. In the following sections of this chapter, we elaborate on each part of this framework. In the case chapters of this book, we trace how particular organizing efforts sink deep roots and develop in certain contexts as they build relationships and power. In chapter 8, we draw across our cases to elaborate on the ways organizing works to transform individuals, communities, and institutions.

Though we take examples from our research on community organizing efforts at education reform, it is important to remember that community organizing groups are multi-issue organizations. Organizing groups work to improve education in the context of building the power and capacity for communities to address a wide range of issues. Consequently, our framework is not limited to education organizing; we believe it is applicable to any strong form of community organizing.

The Roots of Contemporary Community Organizing

The groups and networks involved in community organizing for school reform today draw from a variety of organizing traditions. Indeed, organizing has a long tradition in American democratic life. Theda Skocpol and her colleagues have described nineteenth- and early twentieth-century America as "a nation of organizers." Religious ministers fanned out across the country and built churches and networks of faith organizations. Organizers were active building many diverse movements like populism, settlement houses, and labor unions. African American organizers also built a rich network of fraternal associations, anti-lynching campaigns, and the early NAACP, while women organizers formed groups like the National Congress of Mothers, which later became the PTA. Community organizing today represents a modern form of our country's rich organizing tradition, a promising contemporary strategy for building participation in civic and political life and creating a more just and democratic society.[1]

Although the roots of community organizing can be traced to these earlier movements, community organizing began to be formally established as a distinct practice through the work of Saul Alinsky in Chicago in the 1930s. Just as unions were organizing workers in industry, Alinsky sought to create organizations through which working people could build the leadership and power necessary to create change in their neighborhoods. Alinsky became famous for his brash tactics; he once claimed to have fed baked beans to a group of community residents and led them to a "fart-in" at Rochester's symphony hall to protest Eastman Kodak's discriminatory hiring practices. But Alinsky was also serious about the difficulties of political change and worked hard to professionalize the field of organizing. He founded a training institute called the Industrial Areas Foundation (IAF), which has grown to become one of the largest organizing networks in the United States.[2]

The Alinsky organizing tradition has a number of distinctive features. First of all, Alinsky focused on the social institutions that structured community life, especially those of faith—like religious congregations. Alinsky sought to strengthen these congregations as mediating institutions through which working people could develop power. Religious faith also brought values of social justice and community care that provide a foundation for building and sustaining organizing efforts. Alinsky was a radical because he built power for poor people. But he emphasized pragmatism over ideology as he sought to organize the "middle" of the American polity. Alinsky saw the American political system as fundamentally an open one. Working people could organize through their institutions and build the power to be heard.[3]

The social movements of the sixties also shaped the field of community organizing in a variety of ways. The Civil Rights movement had roots in a long tradition of local organizing, often led by women. Leaders like Ella Baker, Fannie Lou Hamer, and Septima Clark worked closely with local people, developing political consciousness and action from the ground up and tying local organizing efforts to the national movement. While public attention focused on national leaders like Martin Luther King Jr., Baker emphasized training local people, and she mentored the young organizers conducting the early lunch counter sit-ins and later campaigns in the Student Nonviolent Coordinating Committee. Clark worked with the Highlander Center to form the Citizen Education Program, which combined literacy teaching with personal growth and collective activism. The Highlander Center helped connect organizing to the practice of critical social inquiry developed by Paulo Freire.[4]

One of the distinctive features of the civil rights organizing tradition, which has become an integral part of many modern community organizing groups, is political education. The struggle for access to quality education and the struggle for liberation have been fundamentally interconnected in the African American community. The Chicano movement has also shared this focus on education for freedom and liberation from oppression. From this perspective, the American political system may ultimately be opened, but only as part of a struggle against systemic exclusion and racial oppression. Organizers have often relied upon black church culture to unite and inspire people to struggle against racial oppression. Political education helps people situate their personal and contemporary situation in a larger historical and collective narrative while developing the tools to critique structures of inequality.[5]

The women's movement broadly and the organizing efforts of women of color in particular have also influenced community organizing. The feminist tradition brought to the field a number of distinctive features. First, it brought recognition to the particular role that women play as leaders of community struggles, even if they do not hold formal, institutional positions. While men dominated the formal positions, as pastors or national movement leaders, women often did the hard day-to-day work of supporting communities, and they built the local networks that moved folks into action. Second, feminism offered a stronger and more explicit appreciation of the importance of these networks, that is, of relationships in organizing. One of the hallmarks of contemporary organizing is the distinction made between a leader who is embedded in relationships and the individual activist who speaks out at a meeting but is not connected to the broader community.

Third, the feminist tradition, drawing especially from the traditions of women of color, emphasized an ethic of caring as the foundation for organizing efforts. If Alinsky stressed hard interests as the motivation to participate in organizing, and if the civil rights tradition emphasized social justice values, then feminism recognized that women often became politically active out of their work as community caregivers. Feminism, by stressing the connections between personal and political life, has inspired organizing groups to take a more holistic approach to working with local people, helping them to develop as whole persons in their personal and professional lives, and not just as public actors.[6]

The new immigrant and labor movements of the eighties and nineties also contributed to the field of contemporary community organizing. Although Alinsky had been inspired and influenced by union-organizing drives, the worlds of labor unions and of community organizing groups developed largely in separate spheres. Moreover, as community organizing groups grew, unions began their long membership decline and most lost their organizing mission. In the decade of the nineties, however, a re-energized labor movement began collaborating with churches and community organizations to undertake new kinds of organizing campaigns, like the Justice for Janitors efforts in localities across the country. These campaigns often focused on organizing workers who arrived with the new waves of immigrants entering the United States after immigration reform in 1965, many of whom were undocumented. Unions began supporting immigrant rights and allying with new immigrant-rights movements that fought deportations, sought avenues toward citizenship for undocumented people, mobilized to preserve bilingual education, and lobbied for access to public colleges and universities for undocumented students. In these ways, the new movements brought issues of language, culture, and citizenship to the fore in community organizing.[7]

In the case chapters of this book, we locate the roots of different organizing groups in these traditions. Some groups are very explicit about the traditions they engage. One LA and PACT both identify primarily with the Alinsky tradition, while Southern Echo and Padres y Jóvenes Unidos grow more directly out of the civil rights tradition. Nevertheless, we do not try to box groups into specific traditions. Although some groups clearly take more explicitly from one tradition that another, many represent a blend of influences. Indeed, to some extent all contemporary organizing has been influenced by these different traditions.

Some scholars stress the differences in organizing approaches but we take a different perspective. We find that these kinds of polarities can often result in stereotypes that fail to do justice to the complexities of any one approach, let alone the mutual interactions that occur between approaches. We believe that organizing groups capable of making significant and sustained contributions to school reform share underlying similarities in core processes. We will show how organizing groups emphasize different traditions. However, in the end, we find we can best understand the field of community organizing for education reform through a more integrative approach.[8]

Strong organizing groups do not spring out of thin air; rather, they find their contemporary roots in historical social justice and democratic movements. Despite their differences, all of these organizing traditions emphasize a set of common goals. They strive to give voice to the voiceless, build the participation of local people, increase the power of historically marginalized communities, expand citizenship and democracy, address the profound inequalities of American society, and work to transform our public institutions to make them responsive and accountable to poor and working families.

Shared Histories and Identities

The "community" in community organizing is not well understood. Some people see organizing as a set of techniques that can be applied to bring *individuals* together for some purpose. But strong forms of community organizing engage people through their shared connections. They do not approach people as isolated individuals. Rather, organizing taps into—and grows out of—the shared history, culture, and identity that already exist among people, however nascent. That is, they organize *communities*.

Sociologists have struggled with defining community. By one count in the mid-1950s, sociologists employed over ninety definitions! Perhaps one reason for this diversity of views is that there can be different kinds of community. We can think of community defined by geography—which could be a local community or a national community. We can think of community defined by ascribed or other shared characteristics like race, ethnicity, or religion. We can also think of communities of interest, as in a professional community. Furthermore, these types of community are not always distinct; they can overlap and this perhaps complicates the defintional issue even further.[9]

However we define it, though, for people to constitute a community and not just a collection of individuals, they need to be connected to each other and to recognize those connections as significant in their lives. The interconnections between people can be understood as the social structure of community life, which Robert Putnam and others have called social capital. The relationships and connections between people, especially those mediated by trust, provide an essential foundation for community life, and we treat these issues at greater length later in this chapter.[10]

However, while connections between people are necessary for community to exist, these connections are not sufficient to define it. As Robert Fowler put it, community suggests "a sharing of life that is meaningful to members." People in community share a history and set of experiences that creates a degree of common identity and culture. They have a sense of shared fate, however nascent, a belief that "we're all in this together." Indeed, this sharing of experience, particularly at the hands of oppression and injustice, can orient people toward social justice.[11]

By community, then, we mean a group of interconnected people who share a common history, a set of values, and a sense of belonging—in short, a culture and identity. This is a different approach than taken by most scholars of community organizing. In fact, perhaps surprisingly, studies of community organizing rarely define what they mean by community. Implicitly, if not explicitly, however, most define community by local geography, typically the neighborhood.[12]

We think local connections are critically important to organizing because they provide the primary place where people can build face-to-face relationships. Indeed, community organizing groups do their work primarily in local areas. The quality of local and neighborhood institutions—the schools, the parks, the libraries, and the level of safety on the streets—matters greatly to people, especially to families raising children.

While local ties are important, however, they do not always provide the most salient form of identity. African Americans in one locality, for example, might feel a stronger sense of belonging and shared fate with a national African American community than with white neighbors who live down the street. Moreover, as people develop the capacity to connect with others across the nation and even the world, we cannot take for granted that geography determines community identity.

People can be members of several communities. Someone might identify as an African American, a Christian, a New Yorker and an American, among other possible identities. Some of these identities can overlap; for example, black culture and Christianity have been tightly bound historically. In that sense, organizing groups can engage people around one or more salient forms of connection.[13]

The various organizing traditions previously discussed engage people as members of different kinds of communities. The Alinsky tradition, especially in its modern form, engages people primarily as members of faith communities. The civil rights tradition engages people's identities and shared history as members of racial communities like African Americans. The feminist tradition primarily engages people as women, while the newer movements we discussed organize people as members of immigrant communities. Therefore, we think it important to investigate the ways organizing groups define and engage communities. As will be seen in the case chapters, organizing groups draw upon various types of community membership, only some of which are based in local geography.

Communities can have different degrees of shared values, and individual people can have different levels of attachment to those values. Indeed, our discussion so far has portrayed a rather idealized community with a high level of shared identity. In reality, many of the communities that organizing groups engage are somewhat tenuous or fractured; often not much of a sense of "shared fate" exists prior to organizing. In some ways, organizers can be seen as acting to increase the level of attachment and to make more salient people's sense of connection to the traditions of their community. Richard Wood and MaryAnn Flaherty, for example, have shown how faith-based organizing does not simply recruit people out of faith institutions into organizing efforts. Participation in organizing also strengthens people's sense of connection to their faith as they find organizing a meaningful way to live out their faith values in practice.[14]

To emphasize the shared features of a community does not imply that communities are monolithic identities. There can be important differences of opinion and even cleavages within a community. What binds a community together can be contested and subject to change. Community implies some level of consensus, but healthy communities are dynamic. They feature argument and debate over values and how to live them out. New challenges emerge to which people respond. As a result, the consensus can change gradually and sometimes dramatically over time.[15]

In the end, we understand community as a historically shaped and emergent phenomenon, not a static one. Organizing groups become an active agent in this historic and ongoing process, providing a vehicle for people to build the capacity of their community. From this point of view, we can better understand that community organizing is not about applying a set of techniques to mobilize individuals. Strong organizing groups dig into and emerge out of a community's historical tradition. They engage with people around their shared culture and identity. They mobilize a community toward action with a sense of purpose that aligns with their traditions. They help craft a new chapter in a community's story as they expand and reorganize relationships while people work to put into practice dynamic understandings of their deeply held values.

The Importance of Context

Context matters to organizing in a variety of critical ways. In fact, we understand community organizing as a phenomenon deeply rooted in and responsive to context. Organizing is not a one-size-fits-all strategy that can be applied everywhere in the same way with the same result. Although most studies of organizing describe the local context, a surprising few have examined context closely or stressed its importance. Yet we cannot fully grasp how organizing works without attention to context.[16]

Using our tree metaphor, any particular organizing effort takes root in certain kinds of soil, shaped by local social and political history. Groups that follow similar organizing traditions will grow differently depending on these local contexts. This is because organizing groups start where people are. Organizing groups bring people together to share their concerns as well as their desires and passions. All of these factors are historically shaped. Of course, at a broad level there are important similarities across contexts. In terms of education, all of the communities where organizing focuses suffer from school failure. Almost universally, people want a better education for their children. But communities in different regions face important differences. For example, educational inequity in the Mississippi Delta is rooted in a deep history of racial exclusion. Southern Echo organizers, as discussed in chapter 5, face a context where whites have often abandoned the public school system for private academies yet continue to control spending for the education of rural black children. Meanwhile, African Americans bring their experience as members of rural communities that are small and isolated, where challenging the racial system can lead to threats, violence, and loss of jobs. Strong forms of organizing respond to these kinds of particulars in local historical context, and, as a result, they vary across localities and regions of the country.[17]

Local communities are dynamic entities and, therefore, organizing groups also have to respond to contemporary demographics and community makeup. As a wave of new immigration entered the United States, for example, many neighborhoods like Logan Square in Chicago experienced rapid demographic changes. When the Logan Square Neighborhood Association (LSNA) was founded in the 1960s, the neighborhood was largely composed of white Americans from a variety of European ethnic groups. During the seventies and eighties, Latino migration into Logan Square quickly transformed the community, so that by the nineties the neighborhood schools were almost entirely composed of Latino students. As we will see in chapter 6, LSNA developed a parent mentor initiative that proved highly successful in responding to the situation of the new Latina mothers in the neighborhood, providing them with an opportunity for connection and creating an organizational culture in which they could thrive.

The development of the organizing process depends not just on the context of local history and demographics but also on the contemporary environment surrounding the group, that is, on the opportunities and constraints posed by public and private institutions. We show this in figure 1.1 as the environment around the tree that affects its growth. In the field of public education, one critical factor is the responsiveness of educational institutions to organizing initiatives and the willingness of educators to collaborate with organizing groups. As we will see in the chapters to come, organizing groups demand change, but most see a need to collaborate and contribute to the capacity of educational institutions to improve. That does not mean, however, that organizers will find willing partners. Organizing groups develop their own agendas that may or may not align with the plans of district officials or school principals, who, in addition, may not see the advantages of sharing a degree of power with community-based organizations. In one well-known case, Kavitha Mediratta and her colleagues show how the Oakland Communities Organization proved able to ally with district officials and work together to build a set of small schools. The number of small schools has now reached more than forty, and the collaboration has transformed the way education is provided in the district. On the other hand, when one of the groups in our study, PACT in San Jose, tried to work with a local school district to follow a similar plan and open new small autonomous schools, they were met with resistance. District officials had their own reform agenda based upon centralizing control over schools and standardizing curriculum and instruction across the district. As a result, PACT has had to struggle to find a set of educational allies with whom they can work to implement their vision.[18]

Another important contextual factor lies in the constellation of these available allies. We know that most social movement organizations are finely tuned to the world of alliance building. When organizing groups seek to influence large institutions or pursue reform goals on a large scale, they often require allies that can broaden their base of power. Whether groups succeed in forming broader alliances will therefore affect how organizing efforts grow and develop. For example, the Logan Square Neighborhood Association proved able to ally with a broad range of organizations to lobby the Illinois state legislature to pass a Grow Your Own Teacher (GYO) program, which, in turn, helped stabilize funding for their own teacher-training effort.[19]

The broader policy environment also influences organizing. The initiatives of some groups align with policies promoted by larger policy networks that can often provide support and resources to organizing. Oakland's small schools movement, mentioned before, benefited from a national policy environment and resource-rich foundations interested in small schools or in transforming large schools into small learning communities. At the same time, innovative organizing initiatives can also spread to the broader policy community. The Illinois Grow Your Own Teacher program that found its origins in the work of LSNA has helped inspire GYO efforts across the country. In the end, organizing groups both creatively adapt to the policy context and apply their strategies to shape education reform discourse.[20]

This context can shift over time so that organizing groups continue to move in new directions. None of this is to suggest that groups abandon core values or goals espoused by their members. But neither are organizing groups entirely self-contained entities. The relationship between organizing efforts and larger, sometimes controversial, policy movements in education is a complex one. For our purposes, we emphasize that organizing groups are best understood as relatively open systems interacting with their environments. They find themselves in ongoing dialogues and relationships with a variety of actors, and they move and change in response both to internal processes and external relationships. Meanwhile organizing groups influence external actors and institutions, so even the context faced by groups is best understood as dynamic rather than fixed.[21]

Building Relationships

If community organizing groups have deep roots in communities and traditions and respond to historical and contemporary context, we understand the core processes through which they work to influence public education as building relationships and power. We place these processes in the trunk of our tree metaphor because they are so central to how organizing works. Despite differences in organizing tradition and emphasis, we find that strong forms of organizing share these core processes.

Organizing starts with relationships. Organizers seek to connect people to each other for the purposes of taking public action. They build what scholars have called social capital. Social capital refers to the resources inherent in the relationships between people that help them achieve collective aims. Where financial capital and human capital are in short supply, as they are in many low-income communities, social capital often provides a particularly critical resource.[22]

As discussed earlier, organizing groups start out by engaging preexisting connections in communities. They work to strengthen these connections and move them into action. Out of these relationships develop core groups of community leaders with the capacity to act together in the public arena. When necessary, these leaders can tap broader social connections to demonstrate public support in rallies, demonstrations, and accountability sessions with public officials. In this way, social capital provides the key source of power for community organizing groups. Organizing groups leverage social capital to change the power dynamic in conventional relationships between public institutions and low-income communities.

Building social capital among parents is particularly important to education organizing because studies have shown that working-class parents, unlike their middle-class counterparts, are not typically connected to each other around schools. Some organizing networks have formalized strategies for building relationships, centered on one-to-one meetings between participants. However, all organizing groups work to build relationships in one way or another. Relationship building starts with conversation. Community residents often gather in small groups at house meetings where they share stories and identify common concerns; in these more intimate settings, they reveal the private hurt that results from institutional failure and oppression. As people connect through these stories and identify the commonalities in their situation, leaders begin to identify issues that can be actionable.[23]

In this way, organizing groups build and leverage what scholars call "bonding" social capital, that is, connections between people who are alike in significant ways—as Catholics, as African Americans, or as Latina mothers, for example. Standing alone, parents and other residents of low-income communities are less likely to engage in civic matters. Coming together in community organizing efforts, people can find mutual support among people who have similar experiences and face similar challenges. In this way, they can build the confidence necessary to enter the public arena as powerful actors.

Bonding social capital is insufficient on its own, however, to build the kind of capacity necessary to create educational change. Isolated and marginalized, low-income communities may lack the resources to be successful. Organizing groups also build what scholars call "bridging" social capital, that is, connections between dissimilar people.[24]

If we think of bonding social capital as located within a community, we can understand bridging ties as those that connect diverse communities. New ties across communities expand the base of resources and power available to organizing groups, even if they are sometimes difficult to create. Some organizing groups work intentionally to cross lines of race, bridging black, Latino, white and sometimes Asian American communities. They may also work to cross lines of class, bridging low-income and more affluent communities. Indeed, faith-based community organizing groups have been identified as representing some of the few venues where participants from communities deeply divided by race work together for common goals. Engaging each community first around its particular faith identity as bonding social capital, these organizing efforts work to identify common values and concerns across race and faith lines to build a broader sense of shared fate as people of faith.[25]

The effort to build bridging capital involves deep cultural work. Our discussion here of bonding social capital runs parallel with our earlier discussion of engaging the cultural narratives of community. As groups build bridging ties, they redefine the boundaries of community. Through involvement in Southern Echo, for example, African Americans in one Mississippi Delta community strengthen their ties and sense of shared fate with other communities across the state. Working with Padres y Jóvenes Unidos in Denver, Chicanos gain an appreciation of the commonalities they share with the struggles of other people of color and the broader struggle for human rights.

In the end, organizing efforts start out rooted in where people are at—in their communities and social networks. But they do not remain there. Organizing groups work to expand people's social ties and help them develop a larger sense of community, common identity and shared fate.

Relationships and Power in Education Organizing

There is another type of bridging tie that is particularly relevant to organizing work in education, that is, ties that connect parents, youth and community residents on the one hand to educators on the other. Because teachers in low-income communities, particularly those in urban areas, typically come from outside the communities where they teach, we see the creation of bridging social capital between organized communities and educators as particularly critical to educational change. With bonding social capital, that is, organized "on the outside" as it were, groups can demand change and even work to hold systems accountable for change. However necessary this approach might be, it is insufficient to fundamentally improve the education provided to low-income children and children of color.

Education is not like the other institutions that organizing groups have tried to influence. Many groups cut their teeth in organizing campaigns related to community development issues. They pushed city housing authorities to enforce codes, forced banks to end redlining and to lend in inner-city neighborhoods, and lobbied city governments to get a variety of services improved. When they turned to education, many organizing groups initially took the traditional approach of marshalling their base to build the political will to get schools and school districts to meet community demands. Organizing groups quickly learned, however, that traditional approaches proved inadequate to the task of transforming education. Public schools often lacked the resources—the funds, the qualified teachers, the modern school facilities—to respond quickly to demands to provide a high-quality education. Moreover, public schools in many low-income communities struggled with the social capacity to improve, because low levels of trust and cooperation among the teaching staff—and sometimes factional divisions and outright racial hostility—undermined improvement strategies. Consequently, organizing groups discovered they had to find ways to collaborate with educators, to push for change but also to contribute actively to the financial resources and social capacity available for public schooling. Forging these collaborations requires new kinds of relationships.[26]

There is another important reason that organizing groups need to work to build new relationships between organized communities and educators. Groups cannot simply demand that educators teach well and expect results. This is partly because good teaching cannot be forced and partly because many teachers may not know how to do what communities are demanding. In the end, organizing groups have to win over the hearts and minds of teachers. Jeannie Oakes and John Rogers have cogently argued that poor teaching practices are often rooted in prejudices and stereotypes on the part of educators toward students of color. If teachers do not believe that students of color can achieve at high levels, they are not likely to teach at that level. If they do not understand the culture of the communities out of which their students come, they can misinterpret behavior. Through new relationships, educators can come to see the strengths and capacities of adults and young people in communities of color. They also can learn more about community cultures so they can develop a more culturally responsive pedagogy.[27]

Bonding and bridging social capital may well influence each other. Low-income parents may need the collective support of other parents to develop the confidence to enter the educational arena as equals to college-educated teachers. At the same time, reluctant educators may be more likely to try collaboration when pushed by organized parents or young people.

As organizing groups build relationships, they also pay explicit attention to building power. Unfortunately, the conceptual tools we have for understanding the kinds of power groups build are limited. Most people understand power as the ability to influence others. One person or group has power if they can get others to do their bidding. This kind of power can be understood as unilateral power or power "over" others. Organizing groups do build this kind of power, which is best represented when they rally large numbers or demonstrate to push institutions to change.[28]

Organizing groups also try to build a different kind of power, one that can be understood as relational. Given our analysis of the importance of relationships to school reform, this kind of power is particularly critical to organizing work in education. Organizers like to point out that the Latin root of the word "power" means "to be able." This kind of power resides in the capacity to take action. If unilateral power involves power "over," relational power emphasizes power "with" others, or building the power to accomplish common aims. Unilateral power is zero-sum, but relational power represents a win-win situation. In other words, organizing groups build power to influence education reform, but they are also looking to build power with educational institutions to cultivate and achieve shared objectives whenever possible. Relational power requires mutuality, a degree of reciprocal influence, and an exchange of views and interests. These qualities can only be accomplished through the development of relationships.[29]

Educators do not typically like to talk about power. Most feel disempowered themselves. There is certainly some truth behind that perception. Teachers often struggle to maintain some degree of autonomy in their classrooms. Their curriculum and increasingly their teaching practices are set by district or state mandates. Principals feel under pressure to deliver results in terms of standardized test scores and many feel little autonomy in their role. In that sense, the promise of organizing to expand everyone's power through collaboration can be appealing to educators.[30]

More broadly, Americans typically think of power in negative terms. Organizing groups stress that it is the abuse of power that is harmful. They try to get people to see power, especially relational power, as a good thing. Power as the capacity to act is something necessary and important for communities to build. To counter the possibility of abuse, organizing groups work to keep power accountable to community interests and values.[31]

In their relationships to parents and young people, educators do hold an unequal power position, and organizing proposes to change that. Teachers have the advantage of a college education, while most low-income parents do not. They have expertise in curriculum and instruction, while parents typically do not. They have the institutional authority to grade children and determine whether and how they advance in school. From the parents' point of view, that gives educators quite a degree of power over their children. Organizing groups challenge educators to examine their own positions and these power relationships.[32]

Parents and educators have historically had complex relationships, but in our current period this relationship is shaped profoundly by race and class. Many studies have shown that teachers hold "deficit" views of the families of the children they serve, often based in racial or class stereotypes. In an important study, Erin Horvat and her associates showed that parents in middle-class communities can act powerfully in their children's schools because they have relationships with each other centered on the school, and because they possess the education and other resources that give them the confidence to relate to teachers as equals. By contrast, working-class parents are not typically connected to other parents at the same school, and these parents often lack the education and status to feel they can stand up to school authorities as equals and advocate for their children.[33]

In order to build relational power in the context of inequality, organizing groups place high priority on building knowledge among parents and young people in low-income communities. They do this in several ways. They help leaders study educational processes, including school financing and budgeting, curriculum and pedagogy, and disciplinary procedures—indeed the whole range of educational reform issues as they are relevant to the concerns and

issues identified by community members. Groups also strive to foster knowledge of how larger systems operate. For some, these are systems of oppression
that work to maintain poverty and racial inequality in education and the
economy. All groups train emerging leaders in the operation of political systems
so people can develop strategies to effect change. Using political education or
other means, organizing groups also help leaders place their current struggles in
the context of larger historic efforts within their community, whether as people
of faith committed to social justice, as African Americans struggling for freedom, or in other ways.

Organizing groups try to avoid a top-down educational process that simply
delivers information to participants; rather, they utilize a more popular education approach and embed knowledge building in the active participation of parents and young people. In other words, leaders in organizing efforts learn about
educational processes as they conduct research relevant to issues they have identified and as they put their ideas into action. As community leaders build knowledge and connections, they develop the capacity to reorient power relationships
and become powerful actors in alliance with educators and others.[34]

As parents and young people build knowledge and develop campaigns,
there may well be cases in which parents and educators disagree about how to
best educate children. Strong leadership and collective action by parents
therefore have the potential to lead to conflict with educators. Taking a more
relational view of power, parents and educators can look to their shared interest in advancing the education and well-being of children to help them
work through inevitable differences and conflicts. When they work closely
with educators, community organizing groups can act as go-betweens in this
difficult process to help parents and educators equalize power and create a
truly collaborative process.[35]

The dynamic tension between conflict and collaboration in organizing is an
enduring one. We will see many examples of this tension in the chapters to
follow. At the beginning of their efforts, groups often have to marshal enough
power to be recognized and to gain a seat at the table where their voices are
heard and included. They may need to mobilize their supporters at various times
to push their campaigns along. However, as discussed previously, groups will
need to find some way to collaborate with educators if they want to transform
the operations of educational institutions.[36]

By building relationships with educators, organizing groups create new
forms of accountability for schools to the communities they serve. Accountability is not simply imposed from the outside, as it often is in state systems
based on standardized test scores, but developed in a more face-to-face manner.
Organizing efforts bring sometimes disconnected and remote public officials
into closer relationships with the people they are meant to serve. In this way,

organizing groups press upon public officials that the concerns of the community should be placed at the heart of public office.[37]

Transformational Work

We understand the work of community organizing groups as transformational. By that we mean that these groups are not just out to win a particular campaign objective. They are trying to build leadership and community capacity to transform power relations. In our view this transformational work occurs at three levels: individual, community, and institutional. We place these processes in the branches and leaves of our tree metaphor. Our multilevel analysis of transformational work will be developed in greater detail in chapter 8, but we will sketch our ideas briefly here. At the heart of all of these transformational processes lies action. Transformation occurs as organizing groups bring individuals, communities, and institutions into relationship and action.[38]

At the personal level, organizing groups transform individuals as they build leaders through action campaigns. Community organizing groups have long been recognized for their attention to leadership development. In the Alinsky tradition the main job of the paid community organizer is defined as recruiting and training leaders. These volunteer leaders then take responsibility for leading the group—running meetings, speaking in public, and making organizational decisions. Any participant in the organizing effort is called a leader, in recognition of their potential. The civil rights organizing tradition, perhaps best symbolized by the work of Ella Baker, also prioritized the development of local leaders in contrast to the attention placed upon charismatic, national leaders like Martin Luther King Jr.[39]

During organizing efforts, leaders develop through various components of participation in collective action, like conducting research, building relationships, organizing meetings, and designing reform initiatives. Organizing groups help leaders develop the skills and knowledge to become meaningful actors in the processes of educational change, some of which are highly technical. As leaders come to build relationships and power with others to take action, many undergo profound experiences of personal transformation. Organizing groups offer the opportunity for parents and young people to develop as leaders and provide scaffolding and support to that process. Many participants and leaders find this to be a powerful and transformative experience, as we will see in the chapters to follow.[40]

Organizing groups root themselves in community culture and identity, and they work toward transforming communities by bringing them into action. It may be helpful here to appreciate the difference between latent and active social ties.

People may be connected to each other in a way that provides a potential resource, what can be called latent social capital. Perhaps those ties provide important sources of assistance or social support, helping people "to get by." Organizing groups move these latent connections into action, and that sometimes requires shaking up old ties and building new ones. As many organizers put it, "all organizing is reorganizing." Through action, people build new relationships and expand the boundaries of their community.[41]

Organizing groups build on an historical narrative about community. But they also work with communities to reshape that story into a contemporary narrative concerning who they are today, what they are organizing for and why their cause is just. Scholars of social movements have termed this process framing. These "collective action frames" help to mobilize supporters and position the group to engage with the broader world. In our view, though, the concept of framing presents the process in an overly instrumental manner, implying that organizers freely pick and choose among frames to find the one that will work. Rather, we believe organizing efforts develop out of and are shaped by traditions. Organizing groups are products of historical movements as much as they are strategic actors in contemporary settings. For example, as we will see in chapter 4, Padres y Jóvenes Unidos grew out of the Chicano social movement of the sixties and sees itself as part of the effort to write a new chapter in that historic struggle. The frames it employs grow as much out of that standpoint as they do from the group's calculation of strategic or tactical advantage.[42]

The building of community and the development of leaders contribute to institutional change in public education. More specifically, organizing groups work to transform the relationships between organized communities and the institutions of public education. Partly this occurs as groups build the capacity of communities to demand change. But deep relational work is also involved. These new relationships break down the disconnection between educators and low-income communities. They begin to shift the balance of power and create many opportunities for new collaborations and united effort on behalf of children.

Looking Ahead

Transformational work by organizing groups takes a variety of forms, as we will see in the case chapters to follow. We find that there is no single way organizing groups work to improve education and increase equity. Our tree metaphor helps us understand why. Organizing groups draw upon different organizing traditions and engage different kinds of community identity and values while they respond to opportunities and constraints in the local context. Indeed, organizing represents a process-oriented approach to education reform, not the implementation of any particular program of reform, a subject to which we return in the conclusion of the book.[43]

We have placed the three transformational processes on an equal plane for an important reason. Community organizing groups do not engage in school reform solely for the purpose of improving public education. They work to improve public education as part of a larger process of developing leaders and building power for communities to address the full range of structural imbalances that combine to create poverty and marginalization. From this perspective, no particular reform goal will matter in the long run if parents, young people and other residents of low-income communities do not develop the capacity to influence the social and political processes that determine their fate.

This view represents a different paradigm from the typical approach of school reformers who are focused sharply, some might say narrowly, on improving schooling outcomes. We do not want to be misunderstood. Certainly, community organizers and parent leaders care deeply about improving education and educational outcomes for their children. But that is not their only goal, nor do they think such improvement will occur outside of processes that cultivate individuals with the capacity to shape their lives and contribute to empowering their communities. That is why we describe community organizing as transformational work. We reveal the dynamics of transformational efforts at each of three levels in the case chapters to follow and elaborate on their interrelationships in chapter 8.

2

"A Match on Dry Grass"

Organizing for Great Schools in San Jose

PRIMARY AUTHORS: ANN ISHIMARU, CYNTHIA J. GORDON,

AND ROY CERVANTES

On a Monday night in the spring of 2009, the pews at St. John Vianney Catholic Church were filled to capacity.[1] Over seven hundred community members came to hear commitments from their elected officials on the Alum Rock Union Elementary School Board in East San Jose, California. Predominantly Latino parents and children from the local Rocketship Mateo Sheedy Charter Academy poured out of buses, joining parents, students, and community members from the neighborhood. Parents held the hands of young children and hushed older siblings, while white-haired grandmothers and older men quietly entered the church. Many families wore yellow T-shirts with "70%" stickers, representing the percentage of district eighth graders who scored below proficient on state tests in reading and math.

Art Meza and Junior Muñoz—local parents and the meeting's co-chairs from the community organizing group PACT (People Acting in Community Together)—called for the crowd to settle down as they opened the action, titled "Saving Our Children with Excellent Schools." Art stated the purpose of the meeting—to create real solutions and partnerships with elected officials. Junior asked the crowd to stand up together and then asked everyone but the first three rows to sit. Junior stated that these few left standing represent the meager 10 percent of students in Alum Rock who will eventually graduate from college if things do not change.

PACT leaders came to the podium to provide research and testimony. Veteran leaders Dianne Doughty and Beth Gonzalez discussed PACT's hope to launch a strategic partnership with the school district to "keep what is working and create more [small district and charter] schools that work." Current ACE

33

(Achievement, Choice, Equity) Charter School parent Blanca finished her testimony in tears after hearing her son talk about his experience feeling safe and secure at the ACE Charter School, and how he now hopes to go to college someday and eventually become a doctor.

Finally, long-time parent leader Elizabeth Alvarez came to the microphone and recounted the history between PACT, the district, and the small schools. Elizabeth noted the numerous instances since 2001 when the district saw small schools as the enemy. She talked about the district's hostility towards PACT-organized parents, the struggle to develop and pass a small schools policy, and the ongoing fight to maintain the small schools' budgetary, curricular, hiring, and scheduling autonomies. Elizabeth then reflected on the recent successes in Alum Rock, such as the small schools' high state-standardized test scores and the recent openings of the ACE charter and other charter schools.

Elizabeth then turned and addressed board trustees Gustavo Gonzalez and Esai Herrera directly and asked: "Will you lead the district towards a new strategic partnership with PACT and successful charter schools in Alum Rock?" Community members who had struggled over the years to envision, create, and maintain the small schools joined other local parents, students, and neighbors as they turned to the board's trustees to await their answer.

For People Acting in Community Together, a multiethnic, interfaith community organizing group, this moment represented the culmination of years of effort to ensure high-quality schools in the Alum Rock Union School District of East San Jose, California. As a member of the PICO National Network, PACT works with parents and members of religious congregations to initiate change in their community and schools.[2] In this chapter we chart the group's journey toward new small autonomous schools within the Alum Rock Union Elementary School District, charter schools outside of district control, and an empowered community in San Jose more broadly.

In order to create systemic change in any policy arena, PACT follows the PICO organizing cycle, a four-step process that proceeds from listening to research and action to reflection. (See figure 2.1)

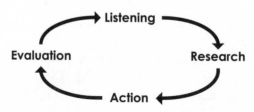

Figure 2.1 Four step PICO organizing cycle.

The organizing cycle guides PACT's work to build relationships, develop leaders, and build power in a way that is responsive to the particularities of new situations, people, and challenges. Indeed, the story of the Alum Rock new small autonomous schools reveals how each turn around the organizing cycle is a unique process that responds to a dynamic context while also building towards a longer term goal of empowering "regular folks" to make change in the community. Throughout the cycle, PACT's work maintains a laser-sharp focus on developing leaders who together form an empowered community. In the context of organizing for educational reform, however, PACT has discovered that the cycle must be especially flexible, leaving time for developing and transforming the culture of schools to institutionalize change.

In this chapter, we trace the efforts of PACT organizers and leaders to organize parents and community members according to the PICO organizing cycle in the Alum Rock small schools campaign. We discuss how PACT first began to engage parents and people of faith in the Alum Rock school district through intensive one-to-one *listening*; through this process they built relationships and identified education as a pressing issue and small schools as their campaign. We then examine how PACT utilized these relationships to develop "regular folks" into leaders through the processes of *researching* and creating three new small autonomous schools within the district. We show how the design team process for the small autonomous schools in Alum Rock helped create a new kind of school culture focused on developing parents as leaders who take ownership and have influence in decisions about their school. We consider how the context of organizing within a sometimes contentious district influenced PACT's campaign for small schools and how planning and staging public *actions* at critical moments enabled PACT leaders to enact and speak to power by defending the small schools. The final part of the chapter follows the *evaluation* and development of PACT's strategy to maintain the small autonomous schools, as well as found additional charter schools outside of the district. In the end, we conclude that PACT's use of the PICO organizing cycle has enabled them to reach their mission of cultivating relationships between "ordinary" people to drive the development of "extraordinary" leaders who take ownership over and positively impact their schools and communities.

PACT Enters the Community of Alum Rock

For many years, the corner of King and Story Roads has been notorious for gang violence in the predominantly poor and Latino Alum Rock neighborhood of East San Jose, California. The neighborhood is so tough that locals nicknamed it "Sal si puedes" (Get out if you can). This likely play on words echoes Cesar

Chavez's and Dolores C. Huerta's rallying cry to farm workers—"Sí, se puede" (Yes, it can be done)—making an ironic label for the Latino neighborhood where Chavez first started organizing. It was in this neighborhood in the mid to late 1970s that Jose Carrasco, one of the founders and first organizers of PACT, started speaking with leaders and members of several prominent Catholic churches to find out what issues were important to people living there. These questions sparked the beginning of a long journey in which PACT organized to empower people of faith to act collectively around their common concerns.

The journey started when community leaders and clergy from a group of Catholic churches in East San Jose asked Jose Carrasco if he would help them get organized. Jose, a second-generation Mexican American with a direct style of communicating and a compact, commanding presence, had organized with the Industrial Areas Foundation (IAF) in Texas and Los Angeles and had also been deeply involved with the farm workers and Chicano movements. After Jose agreed to assist them, leaders at many of the twelve churches started to hold house meetings and listening campaigns. St. John Vianney parishioners and veteran community leaders Lily and Rudy Tenes recall gathering small groups of people in homes to study the scripture and learn about their concerns. From these house meetings, new leaders emerged who began to speak with members of the broader community. Residents raised concerns about the quality of education, traffic safety, graffiti, road ditches, and gang violence. Lily remembers that one of their earliest campaigns got a traffic light installed on a nearby street.

As the numbers of people involved in each of the individual churches increased, Jose noticed they were identifying similar issues across their congregations, so he encouraged them to work together. Around 1980, they chose the name People Acting in Community Together to use when they worked on common issues, and PACT became a federation of local congregations and parishes. Each church retained its own identity within this federated structure through *local organizing committees* (LOCs) focused on their own congregation's issues. People from each LOC met together as PACT to discuss and work on citywide issues. Though they might have been working on a host of different issues, from safety to youth concerns and health care to immigration, PACT leaders were unified by a shared understanding of themselves as people of faith whose responsibility was to act on their faith values by making positive change for the common good. From the very beginning, Jose emphasized the importance of church dues providing a stable financial base for the group and the centrality of scripture, self-reflection, and moral accountability to provide a deep foundation for organizing.

Early on, PACT distinguished between two types of roles in the organization. Following the Alinsky tradition, they used the term *organizers* for the paid staff who find and cultivate growth and development in community leaders.

<u>Leaders</u> were volunteers, ideally "indigenous" community members, who share a common self-interest with their followers and whose concerns drive the organizing. Some leaders held official (unpaid) positions in PACT, but we follow the group's practice in referring to all volunteer participants as leaders.

Throughout the eighties and nineties, PACT worked on many local, citywide, and even state-level initiatives such as health care and gang violence prevention. PACT scored several major policy victories, including its most high-profile win to date, the passage of the Children's Health Care Initiative in 2000. This initiative guaranteed funding for every child in Santa Clara County to receive high-quality health insurance. Together with other PICO organizing groups, PACT subsequently helped expand this model statewide. PACT also had many early victories in education, such as securing funding for homework centers throughout the city of San Jose, building a youth center in Alum Rock, and gathering support for alternative education high schools. As one of several organizing groups in San Jose, PACT leaders decided to invest their energy into improving public schools and ramped up their focus on education issues in 2000.

From Real to Ideal: Organizing for Education in Alum Rock

In 2000, PACT parent leaders in the Alum Rock school district were working on a campaign to train teachers how to do home visits with their students' families, an approach pioneered by PACT's sister organization in Sacramento and supported by the state through the Nell Soto Home Visitation grants made possible by PICO's efforts. When Matt Hammer arrived as PACT's new executive director that same year, PACT had already begun developing relationships with teachers and families in several Alum Rock schools. A thirty-something white man of Jewish heritage and the son of a former San Jose mayor, Matt was no stranger to politics and pushing for change. When he was fresh out of college, he cut his teeth in organizing with Southern Echo, a community organizing group in Mississippi discussed in chapter 5, and later became an organizer with Oakland Community Organizations (OCO), another PICO affiliate. During Matt's five years at OCO, the group successfully organized to get the school district to open new small autonomous schools to address unequal access to quality education by low-income families in Oakland. OCO helped design and open the schools, which eventually numbered forty and completely transformed the structure of public education in the city.[3] Matt played a central role in this effort and, as part of the intentional sharing of ideas across the PICO network, brought his experience in organizing for small autonomous and charter schools with him as a potential resource to PACT.

After Matt's arrival, organizers and leaders took on several small campaigns at Chavez, Ryan, and Cureton elementary schools in the Alum Rock district. Matt recalls these first campaigns:

> We started helping people begin to develop a priority list of issues that they wanted to work on. It really took off like wildfire. It was very much like throwing a match on dry grass. I don't know that anybody had ever been in that neighborhood asking these kinds of basic questions about what are your dreams for your kids and what's going on at the local public school, and what do you think about building an organization that would have the power to deal with some of these problems?

Matt and other PACT organizers began to work with parents to identify and vocalize the differences between what they saw in the schools their children attended and what they wanted—to differentiate between the real and the ideal. A veteran PACT leader, Maritza Maldonado, participated with Alum Rock parents in those trainings. Maritza, a Mexican American woman, grew up in East San Jose and attended the church where Cesar Chavez organized. Her commitment to organizing came from her Catholic faith and from her experiences as a young girl attending house meetings with her mother and watching the community picket in front of the grocery store as part of the farm workers' famous grape boycott. She describes the PACT training Matt conducted for the parents in Alum Rock this way:

> PACT does a fabulous training on "real" versus "ideal" and one of the first trainings Matt did with parents was put up Ryan School and say, "What's real here? What's happening here?" And they always start off with the physical surroundings—dirty bathrooms, the water fountains don't work, the lack of pencils, the lack of textbooks, all of that stuff. And it's always fascinating to me to see the ideal because most parents can't see beyond what's the reality. And it's always harder to move parents to the ideal. And it only takes one to start dreaming. "So what would you really want your child to experience? What is it that you want?" "Oh, well, I would love them to have drama. I would love them to have music." So why is it that we can't have that ideal for each kid in Alum Rock? Why can't that be the reality?

PACT organizers began to work with parents on the issues they identified: dirty bathrooms, lack of textbooks, and their schools having long-term substitutes rather than permanent staff. Through this process, parents built up their leadership skills as they pursued issues for which they could create solutions and win. By the end of 2000, they organized and led an action at Our Lady of Guadalupe that filled the church with about one thousand people and success-fully pressed the Alum Rock Union School District superintendent to commit to either hiring a permanent principal and staff for Chavez Elementary, pro-viding textbooks and basic materials, and getting the bathrooms cleaned or coming out of the district office to the school to do those things himself. All the while, PACT encouraged parents to explore the relationship between the ideal and the real and to develop their vision of what a great school for their children would look like.

A Campaign for High-Quality Education Options in Alum Rock

After the success of that action, organizers pushed parents to ask deeper ques-tions about what was going in Alum Rock schools and whether students were receiving the kind of high-quality education they needed and deserved. The Alum Rock district was comprised of over 13,500 students, about 77 percent of whom were Latino; 60 percent of students were English-language learners and 89 percent were eligible for free or reduced-price lunch.[4] Unlike other large cities with a single public school district, Alum Rock Union Elementary School District was one of nineteen different public elementary and high school dis-tricts serving students in the city of San Jose. Amid this fragmented, crisscross-ing network of districts, Alum Rock had a reputation as one of the worst districts in the city. From 2000–2008, the district had *seven* changes in superin-tendents. In 2000–2001, when PACT organizers and leaders began asking questions about the quality of education the district was providing, state-standardized test results revealed that only 31 percent of district eighth graders scored proficient in English/Language Arts and 33 percent scored proficient in mathematics.[5] Parents in the area were becoming increasingly anxious about sending their children to the local schools and worried about their children's prospects for graduation.

LISTENING TO BUILD RELATIONSHIPS AND NEW LEADERS

To determine how best to proceed in Alum Rock, PACT organizers realized they needed to broaden out to include more parents in discussion about their hopes for their children's education. Jose Arenas, a PACT organizer who grew up in the area, began a series of one-to-ones, meeting first with his cousins Laura and Van-essa Gonzalez. These face-to-face meetings focused on listening to their con-cerns, sharing personal and sometimes painful stories, and talking about building

PACT as an organization with the power to address their shared concerns. Jose asked how Laura's kids were doing at Arbuckle (an Alum Rock elementary school) and about her desires for their education. Laura was excited about her son's teacher Preston Smith, who really engaged parents in their children's education; "I wished everyone was like that—this is what it should be like!" Jose asked her, "Wouldn't you like this every year?" Meanwhile, Jose and Vanessa discussed Alum Rock's terrible reputation, how schools were above capacity and how kids moved around because there was not enough room; Jose ended the conversation by suggesting that they shouldn't settle for a low-quality education just because their parents did. Jose got referrals to more parents and began to hold one-to-ones beyond his own family and friends.

Using one-to-ones and relationship building in this way, PACT initiated a new organizing cycle with an extensive listening campaign at Our Lady of Guadalupe and St. John Vianney churches. The new listening campaign revealed that many congregation members at Our Lady of Guadalupe—like Laura, Vanessa, and long-time PACT leader Maritza Maldonado—were indeed highly concerned about education in Alum Rock. Maritza and other PACT leaders used the relationships they had in place through their church and social lives to begin to build a group of people ready to work toward high-quality educational options in Alum Rock.

As the Our Lady of Guadalupe LOC focused on the need for high-quality schools for the children of Alum Rock, PACT organizers and leaders continued listening and extending their relational networks to seek out more potential leaders. For example, Maritza, both a PACT leader and teacher at Ryan Elementary School, approached the parent of one of her students, Carmen Rodriguez, an immigrant mother of three and a monolingual Spanish speaker who had lived in East San Jose for almost twenty years. Maritza set up a one-to-one with Carmen and then invited her to a meeting to discuss her children's educational experience with other parents. Carmen attended this meeting because she knew her daughter deserved the best in school but did not know how to ask for it. PACT organizers and Maritza worked with Carmen so that she could share her concerns about her children's education with other parents, listen to their concerns and interests, and start to talk about what they could do together about it. Once Carmen found parents with shared interests in education, she invited them to larger group meetings. This original group of five eventually grew to ten, then thirty, and finally fifty parents coming to meetings to talk about better schools.

Though Carmen may initially have begun her involvement in this campaign based on her own self-interest for her children, she gradually developed a stronger sense of the collective stake the whole community shared in demanding a quality education for everyone's children. Through this process, Carmen developed skills PACT considers fundamental to leadership—being able to listen and conduct one-to-ones to build relationships and the capacity to develop a "following" based on those relationships. This kind of relationship building through listening begins with organizers who are tasked with conducting 20 one-to-ones a week with leaders and potential leaders. These leaders in turn are trained to do their own one-to-ones, and, in this way, the base for PACT's organizing expands outward. "A leader is any volunteer who shows up," explains PACT leader and board member Joan Cotta. "It's immediately empowering to call someone a leader because if you appoint someone a leader, you become what you're told you are." Whether she had known it or not, Carmen was considered a PACT leader even before she began filling up the room with more parents interested in creating great schools.

Eventually, the listening campaign reached a turning point. The one-to-ones had revealed education as a prevalent issue for the community to build a campaign around. Organizers and veteran PACT leaders had identified a sufficient group of new leaders such as Carmen to take bigger roles in the campaign. Meanwhile, with facilitation from PACT organizers, parents and congregation members had begun to reach a consensus that they wanted more than the gradual improvement of failing schools; rather, they wanted to push for creating new, great schools for their children. With a steadily growing base of parents and leaders, PACT began to take steps to make great schools in Alum Rock a reality.

RESEARCH TO DEEPEN LEADERSHIP

While PACT continued to build relationships and new leaders through listening, parents and community members like Laura, Vanessa, Carmen, and Maritza entered the research phase of the organizing cycle to identify potential "winnable" solutions to the problem of low-quality education in Alum Rock. Identifying solutions was a collaborative process in which organizers brought input from educators and other professional organizers while parents and community members contributed their expertise on local needs and desires of the community to investigate possible reforms. Matt talked about his experience with OCO in creating high-quality educational options in Oakland like small autonomous and charter schools. Parents responded strongly to these ideas and wanted to learn more. They read Deborah Meier's book *The Power of Their Ideas*, about the development of small, high-quality schools in neighborhoods similar to theirs. Because PACT parents felt alienated from the large schools their own children attended, they liked the notion behind keeping schools small enough— ideally between 100 and 400 students—so that each child could feel individually known by adult staff.[6]

In 2001, PACT took parents to Oakland and New York City to see what actual, "living and breathing" small schools looked like. This was an eye-opening experience for many of the parents who, like Carmen, were originally from Mexico and had otherwise never traveled outside of California. They learned firsthand about small schools reform, saw students no different from those in Alum Rock thriving in a culture of close relationships and high expectations, and began to perceive how their "ideal" might become "real." The parents became convinced that the creation of new schools was necessary to generate the kind of wholesale, rapid change needed in Alum Rock. From parents, teachers, and administrators at the other schools they visited, the group also began to learn about the importance of school autonomies that would enable the new small schools to develop a structure, curriculum, and teaching practices that would create a culture of strong relationships and shared decision making among *all* members of the school community. According to Matt Hammer and the parents themselves, they came back from the small school visiting trip "fired up," determined not to settle for anything less than the best for the children of Alum Rock, and focused on developing a plan that would meet their specific needs.

Powerful forces like the Gates Foundation were pushing for small schools and small learning communities across the country. PACT was happy to learn from and gain support from this broader movement without, however, having to embrace it in its entirety. For example, PACT was aware that the broader small schools reform movement was yielding mixed outcomes in terms of student achievement.[7] But PACT believed that its approach—creating new elementary and middle schools owned by parents and supported by the community—contrasted with many of the funding-driven, district-mandated initiatives to break larger, comprehensive high schools into smaller schools.

PACT parent leaders began talking with district officials about the possibility of creating new small autonomous elementary and middle schools within the Alum Rock Union Elementary District. In this stage of the research phase, parents gained knowledge about the Alum Rock district and its political dynamics as they met with the superintendent and board members to talk strategically with them about the reform. The meetings aimed to build relationships with public officials while also educating PACT leaders about the school system and developing their political skills. "Research meetings with decision-makers are where you find out where the real power is," explains organizer Karen Belote. Through their research and meetings, PACT parent leaders remained focused on creating small schools within the Alum Rock district, as well as deciding to press the district to approve the application of one charter school.

PACT was disappointed to find, however, that these initial efforts were met with hostility by the district superintendent and other officials, who were focused on their own reform agenda and expressed no interest in working with organized parents on theirs. Undeterred, PACT leaders continued their efforts to organize for new small autonomous schools, but the superintendent's opposition evolved into a personal backlash with "wounds" that PACT leaders would still feel keenly nearly a decade later. The superintendent fired or eliminated district positions held by PACT leaders and made public accusations about PACT's nonprofit status, even referring to them on television in one instance as "Parents Acting Like Fools." PACT leaders spent months embroiled in a vitriolic battle with this superintendent before deciding to address the issue with school board members. After a large action at Our Lady of Guadalupe church, school board members launched an investigation into the superintendent, which eventually led to his departure for issues related to fiscal mismanagement.

Under a new, more amenable superintendent, PACT leaders resumed the process of contacting and meeting with district officials. They were told that a new small autonomous school *policy* must be in existence before any small schools could be approved and created. Consequently, PACT leaders began organizing for such a policy, while continuing to build a strong base of shared leadership.

This shared leadership was cultivated and enacted in the regular local organizing committee (LOC) meetings. In LOC meetings, leaders rotated responsibilities such as chairing meetings, leading reflections, conducting one-to-ones, scheduling meetings with elected officials, and facilitating those conversations. PACT leader Elizabeth Alvarez describes this process:

> It's very important for there to be shared leadership and for every person to know how to lead a meeting. When we do the meetings with board members and others, it's one of us that leads the meeting. It's not the organizer and it's not Matt. It's the parents or people in the community that are actually leading those meetings, and so you move up. You learn how to lead a meeting, how to feel that sense of ownership and that sense of empowerment that you didn't have before.

These responsibilities were an intentional means through which PACT developed leadership skills, such as public speaking and political strategizing, built leaders' ownership of the work, and eventually created a sense of empowerment for the leaders.

Exercising such political and leadership skills was new and often intimidating to the vast majority of the parents engaged in the Alum Rock small schools organizing, and individual leaders often required a "push" to develop to their next level of learning or growth. PACT leader Laura Gonzalez talks about how one of the organizers, Alicia, would always push through her initial resistance to get her to do challenging things:

> It's not that I didn't want to do it—it's just that public speaking just terrifies me. Since being with PACT, though, I've chaired some meetings and things that I never would have done before. I've done meetings

at the school where it was just me and other parents that were running the meeting and presenting, and that was something I would never have done before PACT. So as a person I've grown and as a mother and as a student—I went back to school—and that was something they would always talk about and so little by little, I took some classes here and there, and I owe it all to PACT.

Many PACT leaders shared these kinds of personally transformative experiences, from Elizabeth Alvarez, mother of five, now working on her master's degree in urban planning, to Cristina Ortiz, an immigrant from Mexico, who testified at school board meetings in support of the small school proposals, and to Art Meza, who challenged the superintendent and school board members to clarify district administrative policy at a public meeting.

In 2002, persisting in their efforts to win a small autonomous school policy, PACT leaders held another big community meeting at St. John Vianney Church. This was a momentous action at which PACT leaders' efforts finally paid off; they got a commitment from the Alum Rock school board to pass a policy allowing for the creation of new small autonomous schools and support for the charter school it backed. The new small schools policy was to include autonomy over hiring, scheduling, budgeting, and curriculum. PACT believed that the various autonomies would be critical in allowing the would-be new small autonomous schools to form a culture distinct from that of other district schools; the autonomies would also enable the new school leaders to include strong family and community participation in the new schools. As a result of continued PACT engagement, the school board finally passed the policy in 2003, committing itself to the creation of six new schools. At long last, the ideal schools, previously only part of parents' dreams, would soon become a reality in Alum Rock.

THE DESIGN TEAM PROCESS FOR IMPLEMENTATION

In 2003, PACT parent leaders joined with educators to form Small School Design Teams for what it saw as the first three of the six schools. These teams would begin the challenging process of envisioning, designing, and advocating for the new Alum Rock small autonomous schools. To bring in additional technical and professional expertise, PACT hired Marty Krovetz and Dennis Chaconas to coach the teams through the planning and proposal writing process. Marty Krovetz was a San Jose State University professor of education and head of the LEAD Center, an emerging Coalition of Essential Schools (CES) affiliate. Dennis Chaconas was a former Oakland Unified School District superintendent. Both Dennis and BayCES (the CES affiliate in Oakland) had been key partners in small schools creation in Oakland.

With PACT support, parents and educators on the design teams visited other small schools, interviewed school leaders, other parents and community leaders, and learned about parents' rights, curricular issues, and school budgeting. They also learned about California's Academic Performance Index (API), the state's system of standardized testing through which the new schools' success would be measured. While each of the design teams' learning processes were similar and they all shared a vision of schools enriched by highly engaged parents and small, personalized environments, the three teams each developed a different focus for their school proposals. For the elementary school L.U.C.H.A. (Learning in an Urban Community with High Achievement), the design team envisioned an extended day, featuring a full-school gathering to kick off each day, monthly community meetings, and the goal of developing college-bound students and conscientious leaders for a global society. The bilingual educators and parents on the Adelante Dual Language Academy design team crafted a K-8 language immersion program where Spanish would predominate in the early years and English would be gradually phased-in each year; parents would come to read with students every week and students would be immersed in cultural learning. The teachers and parents on the Renaissance Academy design team envisioned a middle school focused on project-based learning around social justice, science, and the arts, featuring exhibition nights to engage the entire community in student learning, block scheduling for greater depth, and teachers who looped with the same students throughout middle school.

For all three teams, the design process emphasized parents as the primary educators of their children and leaders in the school community. Parents' ideas and experiences shaped the designs as much as educators; they helped write parts of the proposals and they spoke at district school board meetings in support of their designs. Carmen Rodriguez highlights learning about the power of parents acting collectively through this process (translation follows):

> Descubrimos que teníamos mucho más derecho que ellos que eran los directores y los maestros y eso nos dio como mucha fuerza y mucho poder. Entendimos que si nos uníamos, unidos más personas, muchas personas teníamos más fuerza. Aparte era aprender a hablar con las personas que están ahí, cómo hablar con ellos, no pelear, sino hablar . . . con las palabras correctas y exigir lo que realmente debíamos exigir, lo que merecíamos, lo que merecían nuestros hijos, lo que no nos estaban dando.

> We [parents] discovered that we had much more right than they who were the principals and teachers, and that gave us a lot of strength and a lot of power. We understood that if we joined together, more people joined together, we were stronger. In addition, it was learning to speak out to the people who are there, how to speak with them, not to fight,

but rather speak out . . . using the right words and demanding what we really had to demand, what we deserved, what our children deserved, what they weren't giving us.

The design teams included potential principals and teachers for the new schools, recruited through existing relationships with PACT leaders and organizers. While parents lent their expertise to design the vision of a school culture that engaged them as true partners in supporting student learning, teachers and educators lent their expertise in pedagogy, curriculum design, and instruction. The design team process helped deepen relationships between the parents and educators. Kristin Henny, a teacher on a design team (who later became principal of the school she helped to design) highlights the deep connections she forged with the L.U.C.H.A. parents involved in the design team:

> I have those parents who were on the design team who I have probably the deepest relationship with because we went through so much blood, sweat, and tears. So for those parents, it's a friendship. We've crossed that line between I'm their school principal and I'm their friend to "We've worked together on a professional level."

Matt explains that the design team process was purposeful about relationship building and meant to illustrate to the would-be principals a model for enacting leadership in their new schools. Indeed, Kristin credits the design team experience for getting her started thinking about parents as empowered leaders who can impact school cultures. Armed with knowledge about the power of organized parents and shared leadership, the parents and future school staff culminated the design team process by proposing three new small autonomous schools to the Alum Rock Union School District.

And they were successful. In the spring of 2004, PACT leaders, parents, and teachers celebrated a major win when the school board approved the three new small autonomous school proposals. The schools were scheduled to open the following fall for the 2004–2005 academic year, and the process from plan to implementation was hectic and rushed, by all accounts. In a major push that spring to recruit students to fill the new schools, the design team members spoke at masses at all the local Catholic churches, went door-to-door in the neighborhoods, and even stood at the entrance to Mi Pueblo, a large local Mexican grocery store, to catch parents and convince them to enroll their children in the new schools. Parents responded enthusiastically, and all three schools opened their doors that fall.

To translate the design team plans into their ideal visions of actual schools, parents and educators had to continue to find a way to work together. In the next section we examine one of the new schools closely and show how parents and educators at L.U.C.H.A. began to develop a new kind of school culture.

A New Kind of Culture: Organizing Meets Small Schools

The buzz of over a hundred 5 to 11 year-old voices fills the outdoor basketball courts and concrete playground at L.U.C.H.A. Dressed in black pants, collared shirts, and dark sweaters and sweatshirts, students wait in groups, some standing and talking, others playing with balls, and still others running and chasing each other. Principal Kristin Henny seems to know everyone there, greeting each child and parent by name as she walks around. Teachers greet children and parents as more arrive, and many mothers—and a few fathers—with younger siblings in tow stand off to the side chatting in Spanish, waiting to watch the "L.U.C.H.A. launch."

The principal blows a whistle, and the children organize themselves into lines of about twenty. "Good morning L.U.C.H.A. leaders!" Kristin's voice booms to the crowd. After the Pledge of Allegiance, Kristin leads the L.U.C.H.A. creed. Teachers and students, and even a couple of the parents, loudly and enthusiastically declare together, "I am a leader in my home, in my school, and"—pointing at the neighborhood all around them in a large circle—"in my community." Together they recite a promise to each other to be responsible, respectful, compassionate and—pounding their small fists into their hands enthusiastically—"to work hard every day!"

Following announcements, Kristin inserts a CD into a portable player, and a volunteer from each class comes to the front to help lead. The Jackson 5's "Blame It on the Boogie" blares out over the playground and students start spinning, clapping, pointing left and right, up and down, and running in place. The kids are smiling as they dance, and teachers and City Year volunteers join in as well, everyone moving to the rhythm of the song.

As the last notes ring out and the tinny speakers fall silent, Kristin announces it is time for class. Students leave in an orderly fashion. Mothers gather up toddlers for the walk home; some checking first with Laura Gonzalez, the school's administrative assistant, to see if there is any work she needs help with. The launch is over and another day at L.U.C.H.A. has begun.

This scene at L.U.C.H.A. exemplifies the vibrant culture of the school. The many parents who stay to watch the L.U.C.H.A. launch and offer to help afterward typify the school's high level of parent engagement. The parents talking with each other and with Kristin before the launch begins are a testament to tight-knit relationships at the school. The reciting of the L.U.C.H.A creed is an explicit recognition of the values—leadership, responsibility, respect, compassion, and hard work—that guided the founding of the school during the design team process. Now they guide teachers in their interactions with students each day. In this way, educators and parents at L.U.C.H.A. have created school structures and strategies that support a new kind of school culture, a culture that L.U.C.H.A. parents and educators believe is a big part of the reason for the school's high performance and success.

TEACHER ORIENTATION AND HOME VISITS: BUILDING RELATIONSHIPS

Before L.U.C.H.A. even opened its doors that fall, teachers attended staff training and development designed to build relationships. The principal, Kristin, explained that it was important to "have that time for team building and having staff know each other well before they're even interacting with the community because . . . we want to build a cohesive group of teachers who know each other and have those relationships as well." This intentional relationship-building process created a cohesive team of educators who were ready to reach out to parents when the school year started.

Just as the goal in PACT's organizing cycle is to constantly strengthen and grow a network of relationships, teachers at L.U.C.H.A. wanted to build relationships with *all* parents at the school to support every child. So, in the first month of school, teachers conducted home visits with all families. Home visits, as pioneered by PACT's sister organization in Sacramento, entailed teachers going to their students' homes to meet students' families or caregivers, introducing themselves, and learning about students' academic and emotional needs from their families. One teacher, Melissa McGonegle, explains that the home visits gave the families

> a sense of how much the teachers care and a chance to clarify any expectations or questions about the year. I think it's just really a chance to spend that time talking about the student one-on-one and not worrying about "they got a 75 percent on this math test," but really, "what are your hopes and what are your dreams for your child?" I feel like it's been successful if it's a new family to L.U.C.H.A. and they leave excited about whatever upcoming event there is, and if I get a sense from the parents about how I can best support them with any kind of behavior issues and then what they're most proud of their child for, so that I can really be on the lookout for how I can help develop that over the school year.

These home visits played a role similar to the organizer's one-to-one meeting. Just as an organizer views each person as a potential leader and expert on their community, teachers at L.U.C.H.A. viewed parents as experts about their children and potential leaders in the school community. Similar to organizers, L.U.C.H.A. teachers asked about parents' ideals in terms of their hopes and dreams for their children, looking for ways to involve parents in the school community.

VOLUNTEERING AND COMMUNITY MEETINGS: ENGAGING PARENTS

In addition to home visits, the design team also sought to facilitate parent engagement by requiring participation through a commitment of thirty volunteer-hours of service for the school. While at first, this volunteer work generally took the form of more traditional parent *involvement* (such as field trip chaperone duty, paperwork support, or help with food for events), these activities and subsequent trainings enabled parents to become more proactively *engaged* with student learning and school-wide support (such as classroom assistance, homework checking, creating and planning school activities, or advocating for the school at the district level).

L.U.C.H.A also built parent engagement through monthly community meetings. These evening gatherings were an opportunity to build community between parents, teachers, administrators, and students and engage them in the key activities and decisions affecting the school. In contrast to parent meetings at traditional schools elsewhere in the district where only a small handful of parents participate, about 70 percent of the parents (150–175) attended L.U.C.H.A. community meetings every month.

One such community meeting exemplified the high level of engagement and ownership parents at the school felt. The principal, Kristin, had asked, in both English and Spanish, for parents' feedback on a summary of their school that was to be part of an award application. A Latina mother raised her hand and pointed out a sentence in the summary that read:

> A plethora of events take place throughout the year to encourage that parents are involved and informed and able to positively contribute to not only their own child's progress, but the greater development of the entire community.

The mother objected to the wording of this sentence, saying that it sounded like the school was trying to get the parents to come and be involved, but instead, she said it was the "parents who create the events that parents participate in."

TEACHER TEAMS AND PARENT-TEACHER PARTNERSHIPS: COLLABORATING FOR STUDENT LEARNING

In order to fulfill the design team's vision for L.U.C.H.A., the growing relationships between teachers and the deepening parent engagement in the school needed to be focused on student achievement. As a result, the principal and teachers opened their classroom doors and worked to build authentic professional collaboration to improve instruction. Kristin hired teachers who were interested in building a collaborative culture and consistently emphasized this goal in orientation and other activities. She explained that the teacher who thrives at L.U.C.H.A. is a "team player that wants to learn and develop as a teacher, and learn from their peers, and work with their peers on a regular basis." Once the school opened, teachers collaborated on curricular issues in weekly staff and grade-level meetings, reviewed data to strategize how to help struggling students, observed their peers regularly in the classroom, and reflected together on their teaching practice. Once the structures for collaboration were in place, Kristin found that "people end up going above and beyond, because they see how beneficial the collaboration is." This ongoing process of collective reflection and improvement dovetailed with PACT's organizing approach in which individual development fuels organizational learning and action.

Meanwhile, teachers at L.U.C.H.A. began to draw upon parents as resources and key partners in educating students. As Matt Hammer explains, a teacher who is thinking like an organizer is a good listener and will "think about parents as co-educators of their kids, and as resources, rather than as standing in the way of some ideal education plan that the teacher has for the kid." The culture of parent engagement with learning has become so strong that one L.U.C.H.A. father explains that the primary focus at the school is not on parents supporting the teachers, but rather on the teachers supporting the parents. L.U.C.H.A. teacher Carlos Ponce concurs:

> Parents are the most important teachers, and we have students for a year, and then they go on to another class. Their parents are going to be the most important example and teachers in their lives, so we really value their opinion and their help, and their ideas.

PARENT TRAININGS AND DECISION MAKING: DEVELOPING LEADERS

As parents became engaged in collaboration with teachers around student achievement, L.U.C.H.A. staff and PACT organizers held trainings for parent leaders to help them develop skills and knowledge about resources to support their children's learning, begin to help them prepare for college, and handle discipline and motivation issues. Principal Kristin explains that "it's not just that we expect the parents to be leaders, but we help them to tangibly receive those skills and shape their leadership through trainings and workshops." These skills helped parents to take part in shared decision making and leadership at the school. According to Matt, this shared leadership means

> always looking for opportunities for people to take on leadership and that that leadership is about being in a relationship with other people, representing their interests. It's who's in control and who's making all the decisions, so just as much as possible, creating . . . shared leadership, democratic decision making and a relational culture inside a school.

Teachers and parents were consistently involved in making decisions at L.U.C.H.A., and the monthly community meetings provided a key forum for these processes. For example, Kristin used community meetings to inform her hiring decisions. Myong Chang, a new L.U.C.H.A. teacher, recalls interviewing for her position first with Kristin. She and other prospective teachers were then interviewed by small groups of parents at a community meeting, and their subsequent feedback to Kristin informed whom she hired.

Shared leadership and the use of school tasks as leadership development opportunities at L.U.C.H.A. paralleled organizing principles. Both parents and teachers were framed as leaders, and this expectation also extended to students. The emphasis on student leaders is most clearly illustrated in the L.U.C.H.A. launch, the ritual described at the beginning of this section. The L.U.C.H.A. creed, in which the students pledge "I am a L.U.C.H.A. leader," is not only recited each morning at the launch, it is embodied in the way teachers think of and teach their students. Teacher Carlos Ponce explains how and why they view students as leaders:

> We want to set them up for success and we see it as fostering leaders, people who are going to be of value to their community, and leaders outside of their home. And so that's why we call them L.U.C.H.A. leaders. To us they're more than students. They're the people that are going to be leading our country one day, and so we want to prepare them for that.

"OUR SCHOOL": A SENSE OF OWNERSHIP

Over time, L.U.C.H.A. appeared to be producing empowered students, teachers, parents, and community members who, in the words of Matt Hammer, "deeply own the school." In such a culture, according to PACT, the success of students and the school becomes a shared responsibility of everyone, so parents are more engaged, teachers are more committed, students are more motivated, and everyone moves together toward shared goals. Veteran PACT leader and former Alum Rock teacher Maritza Maldonado emphasizes how this organizing culture resulted in a sense of ownership at L.U.C.H.A. and the other small schools. "That's what makes it work. A sense of everyone moving in the same direction, that this is our school. It's not the principal's school. It's not the teachers' school. It's our school."

Through building a culture of engagement and shared responsibility for student learning, PACT organizers and leaders felt that L.U.C.H.A.'s high academic standards for all students started to produce solid results. They point to the fact that, by the end of its first school year, L.U.C.H.A. had an Academic Performance Index (API) score of 753 (out of a total possible 1000). In 2005–2006, L.U.C.H.A.'s API score rose to 834, the highest in the district (excluding the KIPP charter school), and in the third highest decile for similar elementary schools in the state. Proud parents and organizers pointed out that Renaissance Middle School, one of the other new small schools, became the highest performing district middle school (excluding KIPP) that year as well. As one L.U.C.H.A. parent said in a community meeting, the PACT organizing process helped the community create a vision and the result was that the school was "el trabajo de todos los padres" (the work of all the parents).

Small Autonomous Schools at Risk: Responding to Shifts in Context

As the new small schools established cultures of engagement and began demonstrating strong student performance, hostility and suspicion arose from teachers and principals at other schools. Principals of nearby schools felt they had students "taken" from them, other teachers thought small schools were being given special treatment and more money, and some thought the small schools were "creaming the crop"—taking the best students from other schools. Meanwhile, the originally supportive union leadership changed, and the new officials no longer wanted to allow small school teachers to work an extended day. The new small schools shared facilities with larger, traditional schools, and there were administrative tensions over common space usage, and even animosity between students at the two schools at the middle school site.

Many parents and community leaders involved with the small schools believe that a lack of communication across the district about what the small schools were, how they would operate, and how students would be enrolled, contributed to these tensions. This lack of communication came in part because of turnover in district leadership. During the 2004–2005 school year in which the small schools opened, a new superintendent and board of trustees took leadership of the district. The new leadership was far more interested in district-wide standardization than site-based autonomy for new small schools. Tensions were heightened when the new superintendent created a Small Schools Taskforce that excluded PACT leaders, despite promises to include them. This taskforce discussed what it called "unfair" budgetary autonomies, and that led small school proponents to feel their autonomies were under attack.

A number of dynamics may have contributed to the new district leadership's lack of support for the new small schools and their autonomies. First, the district office and PACT leaders appeared to have diametrically opposed theories of action for what would improve educational opportunities for Alum Rock Union Elementary School District students. The district favored a uniform approach across the district, featuring standardized curricula, direct instruction models, like Open Court reading and Saxon mathematics, and greater centralization of administration. In contrast, PACT organizers and leaders believed student achievement would be improved by creating school cultures that fostered parent engagement and strong relationships, and by giving schools the flexibility to make their own decisions around hiring, curriculum, and budget. Secondly, the district appears to have perceived PACT as an outside group, without educational expertise, that was activating parents, publicly exposing the district's problems, and providing unsolicited solutions. Indeed, a number of individuals, including a former Alum Rock Union Elementary School District board member and government agency staff outside of the district, noted the district's insular tendencies and resistance to "people coming in from the outside and telling them what to do," particularly noneducators.

Despite these tensions, the original small schools policy passed in 2003 had outlined the creation of six new small autonomous schools, so PACT set about recruiting and supporting two additional design teams for the next round of school proposals. Since PACT believed that education-specific assistance to schools was not its core mission, PACT created the ACE (Achievement, Choice, Equity) Public School Network as an independent organization to provide this kind of technical support. Although at this point PACT was more focused on creating in-district small schools, it wanted to keep its options open, so ACE was also planned to be a locally rooted, charter-management organization for future potential charter schools.[8]

Meanwhile, the prospects for the two new school proposals began to feel politically uncertain as the superintendent and board began to publicly voice concerns about the schools. PACT leaders continued to push for their approval using tactics that may have heightened tensions with district administrators, such as showcasing the shortcomings of the district's traditional schools and writing letters to school board members expressing disappointment with the superintendent's actions.

ACTION FOR POWER

Energy began to vibrate in the room as more and more people streamed into the Mexican Heritage Plaza and greeted one another on a warm, spring evening in 2005. The group of over seven hundred Alum Rock residents was largely Latino but included a smaller number of whites and Asians, and people of all ages: families juggling babies in strollers, laughing teenagers, elderly church ladies helping each other navigate the stairs, and quiet older Mexican men with work-hardened hands. PACT distributed translating equipment at the sign-in tables, so Spanish speakers could listen to simultaneous translation of the action. Reporters arrived and TV cameras began to circulate through the crowd, while organizers engaged in frantic negotiation with facility staff to let the overflow crowd squeeze into the room. At the front of the room, a table faced the audience, and Alum Rock school board members Tanya Freudenberger and Kim Mesa were seated behind the table. Large, white poster-boards with the PACT logo and a list of questions sat on easels behind them.

Fearing that the school board was retreating in its support of the new small autonomous schools reform, PACT leaders staged this major public event, billed as an Action for the Future of Alum Rock Schools. PACT was able to turn out such large numbers of people because of the relationships that the leaders had built in their communities. As Darcie Green, a staff person to a state assemblyman and a former PACT leader, says: "The reason they're able to turn out two hundred people, three hundred people to a meeting is because it wasn't just in a flyer. Everybody knows somebody else and it's one-on-one relationship based." These people represented votes, and their numbers would serve to hold officials accountable to promises for small schools. Meanwhile, media coverage of the event expanded the arena to an even larger potential audience. Veteran leader Lily Tenes puts it most succinctly, "People are power."

This action illustrates PACT's organizing approach. An action team of PACT leaders and organizers carefully planned each detail; leaders took specific roles in the meeting, from chairing or time-keeping to giving what the group calls the "credential" (outlining PACT's mission and accomplishments), or asking the officials to commit to positions on the issue. Each of these roles enabled leaders to gain new political or public speaking skills, while organizers worked behind the scenes, prepping and supporting leaders, coordinating logistics, and facilitating media access. In this way, in addition to bringing the issues to a head in the public arena, the action was a key leadership development opportunity.

When the hundreds of parents, children, and community members finally found their seats at the 2005 action, the PACT leaders chairing the action welcomed the crowd and outlined the ground rules, noting: "This is not an open forum. Any speakers must be acknowledged by one of the chairs." A local priest offered a prayer, followed by a PACT leader who gave the PACT credential. PACT leaders then delivered a research report, using a PowerPoint presentation, to describe the creation of the small schools and frame the need for continued commitment by the Alum Rock school board, so that superintendent turnover would not threaten the small schools.

PACT leaders then gave testimony to bring, as the group says, "our pain and passion" before the public officials. These stories were deeply personal and moving while articulating the need for high-quality education options like the new small autonomous schools. Youth shared their feelings of helplessness and fear at a stabbing at their school and their hurt and indignation at a teacher's scornful reaction to their Mexican accent; mothers talked about the renewed hope they had for their children now as students at one of the new schools.

Tension mounted when PACT leaders "spoke truth to power," as the group says. The chairperson pointed to the large poster-board covenants sitting on easels at the front of the stage, saying, "As a people of faith, we take covenants very seriously. As PACT leaders, we believe in accountability." A panel of parent and community leaders lined up in front of the table. Each, in turn, stood at a microphone facing the school board members and asked a yes or no question designed to "pin" the school board members to a concrete and public commitment that they could be held accountable for in the future. For example, PACT leader Vanessa Gonzalez asked:

> Will you continue to champion autonomy as described in the district
> policy and lead on decisions that support the spirit of autonomy and
> site-based decision-making, especially budgeting?

Both school board members had been given the questions prior to the action, so there were no surprises, but PACT leaders "pushed back" until the official clearly stated yes or no in front of the entire congregation. PACT seems to be both feared and revered by politicians and decision makers for this kind of public confrontation between the power of position and authority and the power of people during an action.

In the end, Alum Rock school board members Kim Mesa and Tanya Freudenberger did not agree to all of the commitments proposed by PACT leaders. According to organizer Alicia Ross, the board members bowed to last-minute pressure from the superintendent who insisted they make no substantive commitments, and "we won about half of what we wanted." The board members committed to helping maintain the site-based budgeting autonomy of the small schools and agreed to look at facilities issues, but they did not agree to support the proposals for two additional new small schools or to persuade the union to approve extended days for small school teachers.

Despite the few tangible wins and continued uncertainty about the fate of small autonomous schools in Alum Rock, the action was both a transformational personal experience for many PACT leaders and an opportunity for those gathered to experience their *collective* power in pressing elected officials to respond to their concerns. As Executive Director Matt Hammer explains:

> It's really an action when people hopefully come to see their power to get something done. Typically up to that point, we've been calling people leaders: hopefully coming out of an action, people are calling themselves leaders.

PACT organizer Marie Moore highlighted Art Meza's individual development over the course of the small schools campaign as a prime example of the "win" of personal transformation that results from organizing and culminates in an action. Art, a parent of five with a child in each of the three small schools, was not involved in the design teams, but enrolled his children in the new schools in their first year. A local high school graduate and life-long resident of East San Jose, Art has a reserved and unassuming manner, as well as a familiar ease with many parents and teachers at the schools.

When we first met Art, he described himself as "more of a soldier and a body out there." When we asked him whether he was a leader, he said, "So I feel that I'm lacking in that area but one good thing is that I know that there are some parents that will be out there. We all serve a nut or a bolt in this machine." But later, after participating in many more one-to-ones, research meetings, and helping to lead an action, Art talked about how he had learned a great deal and relied on PACT to help him with public speaking, political strategy, and understanding how to network and build relationships with other parents. We asked again if Art considered himself a leader and he reports, "Yeah. I do my best. That's one word that I can actually say and tell you, I'm a PACT leader, and a parent, even if the district doesn't like it—they're just going to have to live with it."

Art's humble demeanor belied the vast knowledge of complex educational policy that he had learned in the past year, from standardized testing and district administrative policies to average daily attendance funding formulas and California state law regarding confidential government meetings. Once too intimidated to talk with his children's teachers, Art became one of three parents who called a meeting with the superintendent to discuss site-based budgeting and pressed the issue when the superintendent nearly took away control of the meeting and denied them the opportunity to speak. As a man who previously felt he couldn't speak in public, Art eventually went on to chair the major PACT action that opened this chapter. In the end, Art's participation in PACT transformed him from a private parent to a public leader willing to act collectively with others to face the district and push for high-quality educational options in Alum Rock.

"Death by a Thousand Cuts": Defending Autonomies

Despite the continued organizing, PACT leaders faced major disappointment at a subsequent meeting when the Alum Rock school board voted to deny the proposals for additional new schools on the grounds that a facilities assessment was needed. As for the three existing small schools, the district continued to chip away at their budgeting, hiring, scheduling, and curricular autonomies in an ongoing battle characterized by PACT organizer Alicia Ross as "death by a thousand cuts." For example, the schools were now required to pay 25 percent of their budget back to the district in overhead, a portion PACT considered unreasonable.

PACT leaders and organizers cared so much about autonomies because they connected these autonomies with the flexibility to develop a school culture like L.U.C.H.A.'s that is essential to the ensuing academic success of students. Maritza explains that it wasn't just the school's size or their principal, but rather their culture that mattered so much:

> So it's what we know, right? That you have to change culture. The culture of the school has to be different—when you have autonomy around curriculum or around budgeting and around staffing, wonderful things can happen.

Indeed, these autonomies appeared to be connected with the successful L.U.C.H.A. practices we described above. The autonomy around hiring meant that school leaders had the freedom from district procedure to engage parents in finding and hiring teachers who were willing to put in the extra time and effort needed to improve students' academic performance. The autonomy around budget-making decisions meant that parents could develop leadership skills and give valuable input at community meetings about how to make the best use of the school's discretionary funds. The autonomy around curriculum meant that teachers could collaborate about how best to supplement the district curriculum to meet the needs of their individual students. It was through these autonomies that principals could extend leadership opportunities to teachers and parents, who in turn developed the leadership to demand these opportunities for themselves.

In addition to threatening school autonomies, the district appeared to disrupt the new schools in other ways as well. For example, the district issued mandates preventing PACT organizers and ACE school coaches from stepping onto school grounds, which forced them to hold meetings in the parking lot and at other off-campus locations. Also, the superintendent instructed the small school principals not to have any contact with PACT, implying that their job security was at risk if this directive was ignored. In December of 2005, the school board rewrote the "new small autonomous schools" policy into a more generic "small schools policy" to eliminate specific mention and description of any autonomies. Meanwhile, tensions among small school principals, PACT, and ACE arose when ACE was unable to follow through on all three years of seed money originally promised to the small schools to help them cover their budget as their enrollment was increasing. Preston Smith, founding L.U.C.H.A. principal, predicted that in such a contentious environment, "the district will [eventually] swallow and eat and crush those schools."

CHARTER SCHOOLS IN ALUM ROCK: REFLECTION AND STRATEGY FOR A NEW CONTEXT

Certain that the district would not consider or approve any further small autonomous school proposals, PACT leaders debated internally about how to provide more high-quality educational options quickly. Some parents, focused on the need for immediate change from the entrenched cultures in failing schools, proposed focusing more of their resources on establishing charter schools. Although PACT had been supportive of the creation of several charter schools in Alum Rock, its organizing up to that point had focused on the creation of small autonomous in-district schools. Many long-time PACT leaders in fact felt conflicted about supporting charters and wondered if charters undermined public education. But the district's intransigence toward small schools and deepening commitment to standardization via Open Court and Saxon math curricula eventually convinced PACT leaders and organizers that moving to open a charter school would be the only way to regain leverage in the district. PACT decided to propose a charter school that could instill a culture of success on its own terms, like the current small schools, but would be guaranteed the autonomies that the small schools were struggling to maintain. Furthermore, PACT leaders and organizers believed that when the district began to experience the financial impact of the competition of funds and students going to the charter instead of the district schools, Alum Rock Union Elementary School District administrators and board members might eventually become more amenable to additional small autonomous schools within the district system. Although there is little evidence that such competition had created change in other districts, PACT remained hopeful that this strategy would work in their specific local context.

California charter laws require an organization to propose a charter for a school to the district in which it would be located. PACT's first charter proposal was developed by parents in a design team process similar to that for the district-sponsored small schools, but the proposal was eventually denied by the district. A second proposal, written this time primarily by new ACE director Greg Lippman was denied twice by the district despite a protracted effort to work collaboratively with them. Since California law allows charter proposals denied by a district to be considered by the county, ACE, with PACT's active support, took its charter proposal to the Santa Clara County Board of Education. Despite heated testimony from Alum Rock district administrators against the proposal, the charter was unanimously approved by the county, and the ACE Charter School opened its doors to academically struggling middle school students in the fall of 2008.

As the future of Alum Rock's three small schools continued to hang in the balance, PACT Executive Director Matt Hammer became increasingly interested in working with the larger network of charter school management organizations in San Jose. In addition to ACE, the other charters in the area included Rocketship Education (co-founded by Preston Smith, L.U.C.H.A.'s founding principal), Downtown College Prep (co-founded by ACE director Greg Lippman), and KIPP Charter Schools. Matt referred to the combination of small autonomous and charter schools as a "new schools movement" in Santa Clara County. PACT did not necessarily embrace charter schools as *the* answer to public education across the country, as many in the emerging charter movement claimed, but the group believed that charters represented an important option for creating great schools in Alum Rock.

Though PACT planned to continue organizing new parents in Alum Rock and supporting existing small school parents in their struggle to maintain their autonomies, the ACE charter represented another opportunity to instill an organizing culture in a school at its outset. ACE lacked the design team process so critical to L.U.C.H.A., so PACT provided an organizer at the school site to work with parents and the principal to develop a culture of parent engagement and leadership opportunities. As a result, it appeared that ACE had several characteristics consistent with the organizing culture at L.U.C.H.A.

ACE Charter School Principal Vanessa Sifuentes valued parent engagement in the school community and believed in shared ownership of the school. In their first year, the ACE Charter School started a Parent Leadership Group with the help of Marie Moore, a PACT organizer. Vanessa describes the group:

The Parent Leadership Group consists of a really strong core of invested parents. I'd say it's probably between fifteen and twenty really, really strong families who plan our monthly meetings. They coordinate the agenda and then they tell me when it's my turn to speak. It's really helpful for me but ultimately, it's helpful for the parents because they get a sense of ownership over what's happening at their school, and they can plan things whenever they want.

Two ACE parents, Enriqueta Archundia and Graciela Díaz, explain why they come to the meetings:

In other schools, there are groups for informing parents—maybe five parents will come out of three hundred or five hundred children at the school. We only have one hundred children here, and each month we have more than half of the parents come to the meetings. We come because we feel connected like a family. The principal is talking with us, with the students, and they tell us about the developments of the children; they tell us right away. Whenever there are problems, they solve them.

In addition to helping plan the monthly meetings, ACE charter parents were engaged in teacher-hiring decisions and in a number of other ways, appeared to be growing the leadership skills to be able to collaborate with teachers and the principal to collectively develop solutions to school problems.

However, the school faced high levels of teacher turnover in its first year, with only one teacher slated to continue into the second year. In that context, it was perhaps not surprising that ACE charter teachers did not emphasize parents as partners or leaders to the extent that teachers at L.U.C.H.A. did, and that only one of the teachers we spoke with was familiar with PACT beyond Marie, the organizer at the school. Yet many of the elements of an organizing culture were present at the ACE charter. At the time of this writing, it was too soon to report the academic success of the school as measured by test scores. But the principal, organizer, and key parents were working hard to build an engaged community of parents and teachers who take collective responsibility and leadership for high levels of student learning and achievement.

"THE TIDAL WAVE AT ST. JOHN VIANNEY": ACTION TO REACTION

In March 2009, PACT held the action titled "Saving Our Children with Excellent Schools" that opened this chapter. The action followed the 2008 election that resulted in a new school board more open to small autonomous schools and led to the departure of the superintendent who had so opposed them. When veteran PACT leader Elizabeth Alvarez addressed board trustees Gonzalez and Herrera directly and asked, "Will you lead the district towards a new strategic partnership with PACT and successful charter schools in Alum Rock?" the response from board members was "YES!" This declaration echoed through the church as over seven hundred community members erupted into applause and shouts of joy.

As the action continued, a mix of veteran and new PACT leaders and parents received numerous commitments, one after another, from the newly elected members of the Alum Rock Board of Trustees, commitments that would have been unheard of a year earlier. Board members pledged to provide or extend current leases on district facilities for the current charter and district-run small schools. The trustees also promised to ensure that new principals for both L.U.C.H.A. and Renaissance Academy had staff and community support and committed to hiring a superintendent supportive of small schools and charter schools. Finally, the board agreed to recommend a stronger small school policy that included budget, personnel, and curriculum autonomies. As action co-chair Art Meza read the last of these commitments, the crowd began to clap once again, leading to a standing ovation for all the work leading to this moment; the work not only of current PACT leaders at that action, but of those who participated throughout the almost decade-long Alum Rock small schools campaign.

As the last of the crowd left the church, PACT leaders, parents, and organizers filed into a small room behind the altar for the initial debrief. PACT organizer Marie Moore began with congratulations all around, from action co-chairs Art and Junior to all the "pinners" and parents providing testimony. Veteran PACT leaders, Beth, Dianne, and others commented on the strength of this action and the importance of making sure board members followed through with their commitments. Matt Hammer framed the wins as commitments from district officials who "saw the tidal wave at St. John Vianney coming and wanted to get ahead of it." He then reminded everyone about the organizing principle that the importance of the action is in the reaction. Leaders would need to reflect on and evaluate whether officials followed through on the commitments they made and if, in the end, they were achieving their goal of great schools for all of Alum Rock's children.

Conclusion: From Ordinary People to Extraordinary Leaders

Across many years and twists in the journey, the Alum Rock small schools campaign illustrates how PACT utilizes key strategies and processes to create an empowered community and high-quality schools. The PICO organizing cycle (listening, research, action, and reflection) is fundamental to PACT's strategy for change, as it enables the organizers and leaders to maintain core organizing processes while responding to shifting contexts and challenges. We have presented particular phases and strategies within the organizing cycle as though they are discrete and easily categorized, but PACT's organizing is more dynamic and multilayered than any simple prescriptive set of steps. For example, as we have seen, there is really never a point at which one-to-ones cease and the focus on relationship building disappears. Similarly, constant reflection and learning are built into every stage of the cycle.

We found that enacted through this dynamic organizing cycle are three core processes—building relationships through listening, developing leadership through relationships, and building power through organized leaders in action. *How* PACT approaches these activities in the specific context of East San Jose is critical to the outcomes they produce. First, in the Alum Rock small schools campaign, building relationships through listening involved one-to-one meetings between parents and PACT organizers to understand community members' deep concerns and dreams for their children. Leaders and organizers together identified small schools reform as a "winnable" solution to the problem of poor education and alienating school environments.

Second, PACT develops leadership through relationships simultaneously at both the individual and group levels. PACT organizers understand empowerment as a developmental process, such that both individual growth and community collective power must be carefully cultivated and supported over time. Organizers develop deep, trusting relationships with individual leaders in order to "push" or challenge them to take the next steps in their personal development. Individual growth fuels the empowerment of the community of leaders and organizers that make up PACT through the building and maintaining of relationships among a network of people. In the Alum Rock campaign, the research process also enabled leaders—many of them mothers who had not previously been active outside their homes—to deepen their leadership by equipping them with knowledge about the educational system, skills in public speaking, facilitation, and strategic thinking, and the confidence to build public relationships with district and county education decision-makers and policy-makers. For PACT, this is the kind of leadership necessary to build power to make change in the world.

According to PACT, power comes through organized people, the third key process the group uses in its work. The 2009 action that opened and closed our chapter was a classic example of the way PACT leaders built power, showed their power, and spoke to power, leading to public commitments by Alum Rock school board members. This show of more "unilateral" power by PACT leaders is also balanced by ongoing attempts at building "relational" power in which leaders try to meet and work with public officials to move a particular issue forward outside of actions. As we saw, PACT cannot completely control the willingness of district officials to collaborate. But the group never gave up its efforts to push officials to support small schools and its offer to work together for that goal.

THE CHALLENGES AND COMPLEXITIES OF PACT'S EDUCATION ORGANIZING WORK

These strategies and processes have enabled PACT to make significant progress in improving education for San Jose children. Nevertheless, the group faces considerable challenges in sustaining its current work and reaching its larger goal of providing high-quality education for all of San Jose's students. First, developing the ongoing relationships so essential to PACT's organizing can be challenging when one organizer leaves and a new organizer joins PACT's staff, and this kind of turnover has happened often at PACT in recent years. Many long-time leaders were on their third PACT education organizer in the span of the Alum Rock small schools campaign, and we heard a weary note as small school educators and PACT leaders contemplated the need to start over in developing those relationships with a new organizer. Moreover, although no PACT leader explicitly mentioned it, having only a few bilingual Spanish-speaking organizers may also have made relationship building more challenging, particularly with the many monolingual Spanish-speaking Alum Rock parents. Despite this organizer turnover, however, PACT leaders appear to continue growing, first in relationship with one organizer and then another, to develop their individual leadership skills. New organizers can even bring different strengths, experiences, and, as one outgoing organizer suggested, fresh perspectives and less attachment to old wins, which can be advantageous in long-term, complex education campaigns.

A second challenge PACT staff and leaders face in their education organizing work is the complexity of shifting the culture within the institution of public schools. In fact, Matt Hammer considers PACT's nationally recognized Children's Health Care Initiative a comparably easy "win" for the organization, since it involved "simply" changing a policy and shifting funds from one place to another. The education organizing process, by contrast, is much more challenging due to the protracted nature of the campaigns required to change the way the institutions of public education operate. PACT has found it needs to build a new culture within schools as part of an effort to shift the larger educational system. In education, PACT has had to create design teams and build a coalition of charter school management organizations, activities that do not fit neatly within any phase of the organizing cycle, but have proven to be necessary for PACT to navigate the changing educational context in Alum Rock. PACT has also been engaged in long-running efforts to improve alternative education for community youth and stem the high dropout rate in East San Jose. The alternative education organizing has been similarly multifaceted, ranging from policy work with state legislators to change state alternative school funding to collaboration with county administrators to revamp the county alternative education system.

Nevertheless, PACT and their allies have demonstrated that, by using an organizing approach, cultures of engagement and achievement can be established at new schools. Yet the organizing paradigm and the emphasis on autonomies suggest that each school needs to create its own authentic design process, rather than simply replicating the same version. Indeed, from the morning launch and shared decision-making practices at L.U.C.H.A., to exhibition nights at Renaissance, and Friday morning reading with parents at Adelante, the small autonomous schools' cultures each had characteristics that were distinct to their context and undoubtedly part of their success. More deeply, though, the small autonomous schools had in common a culture based on building relationships, developing leadership across the community, and sharing decision making and power to create a sense of ownership over the school. Thus, education organizers face the challenge of balancing the time it takes to support community-driven design processes to build school cultures appropriate to each context, with the reality that individual processes for every school may not be the quickest path to creating high-quality education for the greatest number of students.

Another challenge of education organizing in Alum Rock is staff turnover at the new schools. Principals, like organizers, are particularly central to relationship building, but, like organizers, they are in short supply and have proven hard to keep. Many strong L.U.C.H.A. educators, including principals Preston Smith and Kristin Henny, have left the school to lead new Rocketship charters. This challenge is buffered by parent leaders who exercise ownership and strong and deep levels of parent-teacher collaborations. As a result, these kinds of school cultures may well outlast the active involvement of a key principal and even of an organizing group in a school. Additionally, new charter schools led by educators who helped create the original small autonomous schools, even without the active partnership with PACT, may spread this new school culture even further.

However, PACT is not satisfied with creating strong cultures of academic success at individual schools; they aim to create high-quality educational options for *all* of San Jose's children. "This work is not just for one, two, or three children. We're trying to create change in the whole district," explains PACT parent leader Elizabeth Alvarez. PACT leaders and organizers like Matt Hammer reason that if small autonomous schools and charter schools in Alum Rock illustrate that children in these neighborhoods can succeed and excel academically, then parents will likely move their children to these schools and organized parents will demand the creation of similar schools. Meanwhile, if the Alum Rock Union

Elementary School District has to compete to maintain student enrollment and the associated per-pupil funding from the state, then the district will be forced to improve the overall quality of Alum Rock schools. Whether this theory of change will be borne out in San Jose remains to be seen, however, because it depends in the end on how district officials choose to respond to this competitive pressure. In addition, the growing influence of the larger charter school movement may well shape developments in Alum Rock. PACT remains hopeful that it might benefit from these pressures while, at the same time, concerns remain that some students might be left behind in the rush to charters.

The story of the Alum Rock parents, students, community members, and their schools is not over. PACT continues to engage both veteran leaders and new parents and community members in each successive phase of the PICO organizing cycle to build relationships through listening; develop leadership through these relationships; and build power through organized, educated, and empowered leaders. In the case of Alum Rock, these processes helped to develop ordinary parents and community members into extraordinary leaders capable of demanding and creating high-quality educational options not only for their own children, but for all the children in their community.

3

"An Appetite for Change"

Building Relational Cultures for Educational Reform and Civic Engagement in Los Angeles

PRIMARY AUTHORS: KEITH C. CATONE,

CONNIE K. CHUNG, AND SOOJIN SUSAN OH

On a Sunday afternoon, in the midst of a record-setting heat wave in Southern California, nearly five hundred people representing seventy different faith, labor, and education institutions from across the Los Angeles metropolitan area are packed standing-room only into a gymnasium at Crenshaw High School in South Central Los Angeles.[1] Schoolteachers and administrators are seated among Catholic priests, labor-union representatives, and community-organization leaders right behind a row filled with Korean, Latino, and Jewish members representing religious congregations. The room buzzes with energy as people of diverse ethnic backgrounds, faiths, and ages greet old acquaintances, meet new ones, and experience an afternoon full of workshops and talks from national experts on a variety of topics, including housing, safety, jobs, health, and education. The gathering is the plenary session of the One LA Economic Summit, an event organized by the members of One LA-IAF, an affiliate of the national organizing network, the Industrial Areas Foundation (IAF).

As the room settles down, the southwest regional director of the IAF, Ernesto Cortes Jr., exhorts the attendees that knowledge drawn from their life experiences is invaluable to solving the problems facing their community. A winner of the 1984 MacArthur "Genius" Fellowship that recognized his organizing work with the IAF in Texas, Cortes is at once both approachable and intimidating. He intersperses his incisive remarks with sharp humor and with excerpts drawn from the numerous books on economics, politics, and history he voraciously reads. He then invites one of his many colleagues and friends, Dr. Robert Moses, the civil rights leader and the founder of the Algebra Project, to say a few words. With august bearing and with decades of demonstrated commitment to education as a civil right that lend special weight to his words, Moses observes to the audience that "Education is . . . the experience of the total person applying intellectual and physical energy to solving problems." He then invites the crowd to recite the Preamble to the Constitution with him. As Moses' quiet and steady voice leads the chorus of people, the slow recitation of the Preamble becomes a liturgy:

> We the People of the United States, in Order to form a more perfect Union, establish Justice, insure domestic Tranquility, provide for the common defense, promote the general Welfare, and secure the Blessings of Liberty to ourselves and our Posterity, do ordain and establish this Constitution for the United States of America.

In the solemn silence that descends on the crowd, the reminder of their common civic purpose touches a chord, and a few people wipe away the tears that had come to their eyes. Moses softly observes, "The Preamble begins with 'We the People'—not 'We the Congress,' 'We the Supreme Court,' or even 'We the Citizens.'" He charges the leaders of One LA that it is their responsibility to continue to work toward the democratic goals outlined in that visionary document.[2]

Moses' call to the audience to press for "a more perfect union" is poignant, especially being spoken in the context of Los Angeles, a county of 9.8 million people speaking 224 different languages, with nearly 2 million residents living below the poverty level. Indeed, the diversity of member institutions gathered at the One LA Economic Summit—a broad spectrum of organizations that includes churches, synagogues, unions, community nonprofits, and schools—reflects not only the diversity present in the Los Angeles metropolitan area, but the multifaceted and broad-based nature of the organization One LA works to create.[3]

Since its beginning, One LA has been building a strong base of institutions like schools, churches, and unions, through which its organizers have been recruiting and training leaders to build relationships and power for sustainable social and economic change. What often unites leaders from diverse communities and institutions are shared values rooted in their different faith traditions. One LA is not a faith-based organization per se; it calls itself a broad-based organization that includes both faith-based and non-faith-based institutions like schools and unions. Moses' civic liturgy at the Economic Summit, nevertheless, echoes the religious rites familiar to many One LA leaders. Cortes follows Moses' words with a reminder that they are not only "people of the Constitution," but also are "people of the Book . . . people of the Covenant."

Cortes artfully alludes to Abraham receiving the Covenant at Mount Sinai—a common father of faith and a Biblical story familiar to all Jewish and Christian congregational members. Cortes, moreover, likens the audience to Biblical "strangers" who persevered in faith for the promised land yet to come. His words infuse the work of organizing with spiritual meaning and illuminate a greater purpose behind their collective struggle for justice. The group leaders are called to continue their "slow and patient work" to form a more perfect union—their promised land.

The implementation work of translating the energy generated by Cortes and Moses into concrete actions planned and executed by the IAF leaders falls on the shoulders of One LA organizers. Sister Maribeth Larkin is a senior organizer who directs the day-to-day work of the organization and supervises a staff of approximately eight other organizers. Also a member of the national staff of the IAF network, Larkin is a former parish social worker who has been organizing for more than thirty years in Texas and California. She left social work to become an organizer upon realizing that she wanted to be *intentional* about "building peoples' capacity to exercise their own power and their own agency on behalf of themselves and their families, and [learn] how to take the power of institutions like churches and schools and others—and use that as leverage to challenge and change systems." Her slender frame belies the strength of conviction that fuels her words when she speaks about organizing and about the respect and attention she feels are deserved by the communities with whom she works.

Reflecting on the Economic Summit, Larkin identified the purpose of the action as a public event—to build constituency and knowledge while renewing the political energy and public will necessary to impact educational practice and policy:

> Sunday was about building a constituency and helping people under-stand . . . what . . . it takes to create a different kind of public will and public policy. . . . We're not going to be able to do what we need to do to rebuild an effective public education for K through twelve . . . in Los Angeles or anywhere else in the state unless we get a lot of people clear about why that is in our interest, and then clearly acting to challenge and change the public policy.

Indeed, Larkin repeatedly stressed that the organizers see their primary work as building relationships and power among people who have common interests and "want to have real conversations and take real action about the quality of public life that they are all embedded in and invested in, day in and day out." Because education is a primary concern to One LA leaders, and more broadly defined, serves as a primary means to build informed citizenry, Larkin said it will always be part of the group's work, although never its sole focus.

Larkin further articulated this intentional focus on building adult and institutional relationships as part of One LA's theory of change to improve the quality of public education:

> We need to help reinforce the understanding that this work in schools is successful when we create these adult partnerships, and we get institutions talking to each other and working together and identify a broad enough political force that needs to be taken seriously . . . that overcomes some traditional . . . barriers. What's evident is the energy that comes out of new relationships that crosses those barriers, and the sort of creative ideas and solutions that emerge when that happens . . . You can't do that in isolation.

In the case study that follows, we highlight this emphasis on building relationships between leaders and institutions as well as developing leaders among parents, school staff, and community members. Perhaps because of this holistic attention to addressing community needs and building community leaders, our case study shows that through One LA's organizing work, not only do schools improve in performance and quality, but schools also can become a different place where other community concerns can be expressed and acted on.

While One LA actively engages with multiple issues facing their constituents, this case study only draws on one part of One LA's work—organizing schools in metropolitan Los Angeles. We begin with a brief summary of the origins of the IAF's education organizing work in Texas, the founding of One LA in Los Angeles, and an overview of IAF's organizing principles as they pertain to education. We then focus the remainder of the chapter on One LA's efforts at two sites: Fernangeles Elementary School and Harmony Elementary School. We conclude with a discussion of lessons learned from One LA's organizing work at Fernangeles and Harmony, including the promise that its approach holds for transforming schools on a larger scale.

Origins of One LA's Education Organizing Work

One LA's education organizing approach can be traced to the Southwest IAF's work in Texas. Founded in 1974 by Ernesto Cortes Jr. and by a group of pastors and lay leaders in San Antonio's Mexican American Catholic community, Communities Organized for Public Services (COPS) is the oldest Texas IAF organization. It first entered the world of public education in the early 1980s, after it had been organizing among faith communities for nearly ten years. COPS successfully compelled the San Antonio Independent School District to make its budget transparent to the public and organized to defeat a local referendum that would have directed $1.6 million toward the construction of a new administrative building when children were attending school in dilapidated temporary classrooms throughout the city. These victories encouraged the Texas IAF network to begin focusing more intently on educational issues and led to its helping to pass House Bill 72 in 1984, which increased per pupil expenditures, improved student-teacher ratios, and increased teacher salaries.

While these city- and state-level victories for public school funding were important, the Texas IAF saw the need for reform to happen at a deeper level—a reform that challenged and transformed less visible yet critical dimensions of public schools. With an intensive implementation of the IAF organizing strategies focused on relationship building, leaders and organizers were able to help predominantly black Morningside Middle School, the lowest performing middle school in Fort Worth, revitalize its school community. As a result, parent involvement increased dramatically and student achievement scores moved from last to third in Fort Worth over the course of just two years.

Based largely on Morningside's success, Texas IAF leaders lobbied the state legislature to approve a pilot "Alliance Schools" program in 1992. The Alliance Schools network grew rapidly from 21 schools to 120 schools across Texas, and Alliance Schools became official institutional members of their local IAF organizations. Alliance Schools broadly adhered to the idea that a school should be a "community of learners." No single strategy was put forth for school reform. Rather, the Alliance Schools placed an intense focus on building relationships and developing local leaders within schools. Organizers worked directly with principals and teachers, who would become organizational leaders along with parents and community residents, working to change the culture of schooling in each school. In addition, the IAF created alliances between schools and other institutions like congregations to build the power necessary to impact educational issues and address community concerns at the city or district level. With organized school communities working together for change, Alliance Schools began to show significant improvement. As a result of these successes, the Alliance School model and Ernesto Cortes Jr. became nationally recognized for their contributions to education reform. In reporting his study of the Alliance School network in Texas, Dennis Shirley observed that "a host of teachers, parents, administrators, and community leaders credit the Alliance School network with revitalizing their schools and neighborhoods."[4]

Building IAF's Presence in Los Angeles

In 1998, Ernesto Cortes Jr. was asked to come to LA to rebuild IAF's organizational presence in Los Angeles. Though Cortes had founded United Neighborhoods Organization (UNO), the first IAF organization in Los Angeles, in the 1970s, and though IAF's presence had grown to include three additional affiliates that organized four distinct urban neighborhoods in Los Angeles, the IAF ultimately faced difficulty in finding an effective model for organizing such a diverse and vast area. Having four separate organizations meant each one was too weak to build the power necessary to address community concerns. Furthermore, while the need for power and resources was common across all areas of Los Angeles, some neighborhoods were not able to raise as many financial resources as others. Cortes reflected that the organizations "didn't do enough organizational building. They went too quickly and to big campaigns . . . but they never really paid attention to the intensive development of the infrastructure of the organizations."

To address these challenges, experienced IAF organizers like Sister Maribeth Larkin and Ken Fujimoto came to Los Angeles from different southwest IAF organizations in 1999 to help with the effort. They established LA Metro as a sponsoring committee and spent 1999 to 2004 raising the money and interest necessary to build an institutional base for the new organization. One LA had its founding convention in 2004 with 12,000 people in attendance, representing over one hundred institutions. The name "One LA" was chosen by leaders to represent their desire to unite the diverse geographic and demographic constituencies of Los Angeles. Although Latinos figured prominently in membership, One LA succeeded in attracting participation from African Americans as well as from some Asian American communities and a number of white communities in more suburban parts of the county.

Given the challenge of organizing in the wide geographic expanse of Los Angeles, the new organization divided its one hundred institutional members into eight geographic clusters, with an additional ninth cluster specifically created for labor unions. Still, with only about eight organizers on staff, One LA struggled for a strategy that would allow it to build both deep and wide. Larkin recognized the tension between building a large network for breadth and developing individual leaders and institutions for depth; she observed that if enough attention is not paid to the base, the organizers will always run the risk of the relationships becoming too thin. Indeed, organizing a place as vast as Los Angeles was an ambitious, if not audacious, effort.

Education Organizing in the Context of Los Angeles

When it began its education work in Los Angeles, the IAF not only faced the challenge of balancing breadth and depth of organizing, but it found itself confronting the second-largest public school system in the country, serving approximately 800,000 students in twenty-six cities. The Los Angeles Unified School District (LAUSD) is an $11 billion operation with each school board member representing close to 200,000 constituents. The large operational size and geographic expanse contribute to a lack of transparency and accessibility; families, educators, and community leaders attempting to promote meaningful change within or across schools quickly encounter institutional barriers and systemic inefficiencies. Eloise Metcalfe-Lopez, the director of Center X, UCLA's Program for Teacher Education and a member institution of One LA, also points to LAUSD's penchant for constant reform as being disruptive to building sustainable relationships:

> Once you think you have made some progress in building relationship with the district, you find yourself at ground zero because there's a high turnover with school administrators, district personnel, and managerial changes . . . They renumber the districts, reorganize students into different schools, or appoint a new local district superintendent and new principals. We constantly have to build that relationship again.

Following the Alliance Schools strategy that worked so well in Texas, One LA first began its work in Los Angeles by reaching out to the school district to form collaborative efforts, which included working with the superintendent of LAUSD and the teachers union, United Teachers Los Angeles (UTLA). The efforts that began under Superintendent Roy Romer's leadership, from early 2001 until about 2005, seemed promising for a time. For example, Principal Robert Cordova at Trinity Elementary School worked with One LA and district administrators in 2001 to address a district funding schedule that placed students in one of the tracks of the year-round school at a significant disadvantage. While the district budget schedule did not release funds until the fall, the students in this particular track would start the school year in the early summer, and the discrepant funding schedule would rob the students of academic resources and support systems such as tutoring and supplemental services. When Trinity parents, teachers, and community members successfully organized to alter the LAUSD budget timetable to close this funding gap, it positively affected more than 250,000 students in the district. One LA also believed collaborative relationships at the district level were critical for recruiting principals to join the organization and deepening its work at the school level.

Such promising potential to build relationships and bring district-wide change was lost, however, when Mayor Antonio Villaraigosa made his widely publicized move to take over the school district. Larkin recalled that the tug-of-war among public officials "turned into a very high-profile battle between the superintendent and the mayor and the members of the school board lined up on one side or the other." With changes in district leadership and competing objectives for the teachers' union, One LA's reform efforts targeted at the district level proved difficult to maintain.

Key IAF Organizing Principles

As their collaborative efforts at the district level stalled, at least momentarily, One LA prioritized sinking deep roots into individual schools and smaller school districts. This local work was always a key part of the Alliance School strategy. Indeed, One LA's Education Plank states that the quality of education in Los Angeles suffers, in part, because of a thinness of public relationships or a "lack of a political constituency."[5] One LA organizers believe that they can build a network of institutional relationships of trust among students, parents, teachers, principals, clergy, business, community leaders, and local residents that responds to the weak existing culture in schools often characterized by distrust, fear, and blame. The success of schools, in part, depends on engaging parents as critical stakeholders in cultivating a culture of inquiry, reflection, and collective action. In identifying, training, and developing these leaders, One LA hopes to grow a "new political constituency" for public schools and public education sustained by "deep, trusting relationships among and between schools."

In practice, the principle of "power before program" means that One LA generates its organizing agenda from listening to its leaders' experiences and needs instead of imposing a one-size-fits-all organizing program as a "silver bullet" for schools and communities. In fact, because One LA focuses on identifying and drawing on the strengths of a particular institution, its context and its needs, schools and communities develop different reform strategies. The intentionality and flexibility of One LA's organizing model are further articulated by Larkin:

> We don't go in there with formulas . . . The organization doesn't say here's the structure that's going to work for you. The organization says

what do you all think? You're the education experts; you're the local community. What do you think you want to try? And then, how do we help you get that in place, by removing district obstacles, or getting the right people in the room to help you get permission?

Larkin believes that creative energy and innovative solutions emerge when parents, teachers, religious leaders, and school administrators transcend traditional barriers to collectively develop a learning community. One LA sees its work as distinct from "generic organizing" that mobilizes people around an issue. Rather, according to Larkin, One LA's work is "about changing a culture of the way people operate. One LA's work always moves in two directions, action and culture change, simultaneously, and with equal intent." As people learn relational skills, they are able to apply these skills to transform their place of work and living, or school and neighborhood.

In recruiting leaders, One LA invests in people who have what they call an "appetite" for leadership. In particular, the group looks for those who are, according to Larkin, "most relational, most interested in developing their capacity to be agents of relational power." One LA organizes "the middle," which, again, is different from what Larkin perceives as "traditional" organizing. Larkin explains:

> We're looking for people who are moderates. We're not looking for flaming left wingers, and that's a departure from a lot of social activism— because our power is built on numbers, the ability to bring people together, and the majority of people are in the middle. They're not at either political fringe. So we're not going to be controlled by [neither] a radical left-wing agenda nor a radical right-wing agenda.

Pragmatic in its approach, One LA builds a broad constituency on the ground to create the political space to initiate change strategies and build the power to hold people accountable for their public commitments.

Larkin notes that there are two extremes in education reform. Some people develop a boutique or museum model program that works in one school regardless of its applicability to the majority; others adopt a one-size-fits-all reform to impose on all schools regardless of local conditions. One LA tries to strike a balance between these two key strategies—developing relationships between institutions while building relational cultures within institutions. One LA's theory is that if the effort is organized on a small scale and then taken more broadly, there is a greater chance for success. The emphasis is on having real and tangible impacts at the local level while building relationships across the district so that local school communities can learn from successes and apply them flexibly to their own contexts.

In the following sections, we discuss how these organizing principles have been applied in two school communities. We want to emphasize that both parts of One LA's strategy—cultivating institutional relationships and building relational culture—are present at both schools. However, we have chosen to highlight one aspect for each school to fully capture how the organizers and the leaders of One LA use these strategies. The first story begins with One LA's work in the neighborhoods of Fernangeles Elementary School, illuminating the theme of building institutional relationships to develop power. The second story centers on One LA's work at Harmony Elementary School, illustrating the theme of leadership development and establishing a relational culture inside schools.

Civic Power through Institutional Relationships at Fernangeles Elementary School

When IAF organizer Joaquin Sanchez came from Texas to work for One LA, he was assigned to the San Fernando Valley, northwest of downtown Los Angeles, one of One LA's nine clusters. A UC Berkeley-trained engineer, Sanchez got introduced to the IAF when he volunteered as a youth minister at his church in Austin, Texas. Sanchez eventually became an IAF organizer and came to Los Angeles as an experienced senior organizer. His unassuming and respectful manner paired with a sharp and practical intelligence quickly endeared him to One LA leaders. "Joaquin learns *with* you," said a district administrator, reflecting on how she saw Sanchez working with rather than condescending to parents. He was now asked to take these talents to Sun Valley, a predominantly immigrant, largely Latino, working-class neighborhood where 95 percent of the student body at the local Fernangeles school qualified for free or reduced-price lunches.

IDENTIFYING THE ISSUE AND BUILDING AN ORGANIZED CONSTITUENCY

In order to understand the concerns of the residents in the Fernangeles community, Sanchez began with face-to-face meetings with community members to talk with them about their values and interests. In IAF parlance, these meetings are called one-on-ones. A one-on-one is a personal conversation, usually between an organizer and a community member, designed to learn about the community member's values, pressing concerns, level of interest in organizing, and the resources the person is able to offer. The organizer also shares some of his or her own "story" during this time, and the two people discover meaningful connections and begin to develop trust as a result of such a purposeful encounter.

After holding a one-on-one meeting with Principal Karen Jaye and asking her for a suggested list of potential school and community leaders, Sanchez also organized a series of "house meetings," where groups of people could share their personal experiences, find common interests and values, build trusting relationships, and determine steps for action around an agenda collectively owned by those engaged in dialogue. House meetings are a strategic tactic employed by One LA organizers and leaders alike to capitalize on already existing networks of social capital and to develop them into authentic and sustainable relationships moving toward action.

At the initial house meetings with parents at Fernangeles Elementary School in 2003, Sanchez asked basic questions about their experiences at the school and in the neighborhood and the challenges and pressures they faced as families. As one parent spoke about her son waking up "with a bloody stain on his pillow from a bloody nose," other parents began to nod, and they realized that six out of the eleven children of the seven parents present at the meeting had asthma and other respiratory problems. In Sanchez's words, there was a "recognition that a number of them were going through the same things, but they'd never really shared that burden with each other." Indeed, the group would later find that the neighborhood's children had twice the national rate of asthma.

When the group spoke with Principal Jaye about the issue, they found a sympathetic listener. An effective communicator and a vocal advocate for her staff, students, and parents, Jaye makes sure that her office door remains open to welcome unforeseen requests and unscheduled conversations. In response to the group's observation about health issues, Jaye shared her experience of having to buy extra cabinets to house all of the asthma medicine she needed for the students. As Jaye puts it, she had to make the decision, "Do we just keep buying cabinets, or do we try to figure out how to do something about this, because there seems to be an interesting number of kids that were developing asthma?"

It turned out that the cause of the problem was not hard to find. Sun Valley was home to more than thirty auto dismantlers, eight recycling sites, several concrete material plants, and thirty-four landfills. One of these active landfills, the Bradley Landfill, had grown to one hundred feet above ground level while receiving up to ten thousand tons of garbage per day from businesses and apartment buildings throughout Los Angeles. It was located two and a half blocks from Fernangeles Elementary School. To Josh Stehlik, an attorney at the LA County Neighborhood Legal Services, a One LA member organization, the concentration of industrial complexes near low-income residents is not a mistake:

> I've always been fairly angry that somehow Sun Valley has to shoulder
> this obligation that . . . the city should really deal with at a citywide level
> so that the burdens and the benefits of waste management throughout

the city are equitably distributed. One thing we did . . . was to map out where the brown fields in LA County were located. They tended to map very closely onto low-income communities, particularly in South Central and the Northeast San Fernando Valley, which were two of the most concentrated areas.

The group's identification of the asthma problem coincided with Waste Management, the landfill owner, requesting a permit to raise the height of their landfill another forty-three feet, potentially creating what would become the equivalent of a fifteen-story building of trash. Waste Management also wanted to build a permanent trash-sorting facility near the school.

Given what they deemed a winnable, concrete issue that concerned their constituency, One LA leaders decided to begin a campaign to stop the issuing of the permit. As house meetings continued over the course of more than a year, organizers were able to identify a core group of leaders willing to develop a plan of action. Meanwhile, the group reached out to other institutions and people, allies who could bring resources and their own networks to support the campaign.

One of these allies was Father Richard Zanotti of the nearby Our Lady of the Holy Rosary Church. When he was approached by Karen Jaye and Maria Sooy, outreach consultant and support services coordinator at Fernangeles, he realized, "We were talking about the same people. A lot of our folks send their kids to Fernangeles Elementary, so we had something in common. I realized that if we would work together, we would have much more of a say than if I just came out on my own" against the landfill. Overcoming the isolation of institutions and building these new alliances is a central part of One LA's strategy. According to Sanchez, "We're trying to build an organization that wants to understand power, wants to understand politics, wants to develop leaders, and wants to connect with a mix of institutions."

Fernangeles Elementary School teacher Ricardo Loredo used the IAF parlance of "organized people and organized money" when he recalled their identifying the need to create an "organized people" in Sun Valley to counter the "organized money" of Waste Management Inc.'s $11 billion operation. Loredo, who was a part of the core team at Fernangeles during the Bradley Landfill campaign, saw One LA's key assets as "giving the community an opportunity to have a voice." According to Loredo, One LA's ability to build alliances was one of the reasons he found them effective and what made them different from other groups. He observed:

> Having a group like the neighborhood council support One LA is a big deal because it makes the base broader. More people will listen if these

people are with us. I think that's the difference—One LA reaches out to all these different groups and joins them together.

Loredo sees this kind of broad base building as "essential for big companies and politicians not to walk all over low-income communities."

USING PUBLIC SPACES AND CONDUCTING A STRATEGIC CAMPAIGN

The core team leaders understood that in order to win the campaign, they needed to research the facts and educate the public about the health consequences of the landfill; consequently, they spoke with the press, collected signatures on petitions, and organized public meetings with PowerPoint slides that outlined the major health risks of continuing to add to the landfill. They also persuaded Waste Management to produce an Environmental Impact Report on the proposed changes. Because nearly 25 percent of Sun Valley residents speak little or no English, leaders also successfully lobbied for the report to be translated into Spanish and held public meetings in Spanish with English translations.[6]

The core team leaders also met with city councilpersons and other politicians to voice the community's concerns regarding the landfill and to ask publicly for support to stop the expansion of the landfill. One such public action was held at Mary Immaculate Church in Pacoima just before the 2005 mayoral elections. In order to prepare for the action, Father Jim Fee, the senior pastor at Mary Immaculate, and other priests spoke about the issue in their Sunday sermons, put notices in the church bulletin, and prepared lay leaders who would tell their stories at the action. One LA organizers helped these leaders think about how to plan the event so that the mayoral candidates would not take control of the meeting and make it a campaign event; instead, organizers insisted that One LA leaders maintain control of the meeting so that the politicians would listen to people's concerns.

The One LA leaders turned out an impressive one thousand people to the action on February 15, 2005. Among them were stakeholders, including community members and representatives from Waste Management, as well as the mayoral candidates. Although Waste Management representatives did not speak during the spirited meeting, they lined the side and back rows of the sanctuary holding picket signs. One LA leaders not only presented research on the link between public health and education, but they also told personal stories about how the dump affected their families.[7] In the end, the mayoral candidates, including Antonio Villaraigosa, who would go on to win the election a few weeks later, committed themselves to fighting the expansion.

Gaining the commitment of the future mayor was a big win. However, the event was also significant because it challenged traditional notions of the appropriate use of spaces in churches and schools. Father Jim Fee, the senior pastor at Mary Immaculate, recalls the action as being "dynamic and significant" not only because "it was so public and a big meeting" but because it was "using the particular space [of the church], which is defined in another way for another purpose." Similarly, Ricardo Loredo remembers that Waste Management tried to influence the school district leadership to prevent Karen Jaye from holding meetings regarding the landfill at the school, claiming that they were not a legal use of a public school space. Father Jim found that his parishioners at Mary Immaculate were energized by the new use of the church space, a result of both deliberate preparations and the success of the action.

As the community came together through these faith and school institutions, ideas about what their actual space could represent in terms of civic engagement shifted. Anna Eng found the following to be true in her experience as an organizer for the IAF:

> The organizing . . . offers the local schools political clout and political cover . . . to be able to push for a variety of items that are in their interest, that they could not, politically or otherwise, do on their own . . . There are so many external things that impact education . . . and being a part of a broad-based organization like One LA allows you the breadth and the power to be able to address some of these issues.

This use of institutional space to organize for civic power is a key aspect of One LA's organizing strategy. Bringing public actions to these institutional sites affirms that churches and schools are community spaces, built not only for religion and schooling, but also for the development of civic capacity, and ultimately, for the vitality of democratic engagement.

HOLDING PUBLIC OFFICIALS ACCOUNTABLE

After Mayor Antonio Villaraigosa's 2005 election victory, One LA and the core team at Sun Valley worked to press him to fulfill his campaign promise to stop the landfill's expansion. One way they sought to hold his attention on Sun Valley against competing interests was to get him to come out and visit the area to see with his own eyes the issues that face parents, schoolchildren, and other community members. Sanchez discussed the goal of bringing Mayor Villaraigosa out to Sun Valley:

> One was just to teach and educate the mayor firsthand about the issue. There also is always a difference when the public officials actually see it for themselves firsthand, versus just being told about it in an assembly.

Hearing a story. . . . can be a powerful experience but not the same thing as . . . having to drive there and getting stuck behind a trash truck, or hearing from somebody who's living right next to it and actually being at that person's house.

To accomplish these goals, the core team planned a bus tour for the visit, where the mayor would visit different community members' houses and also spend time on the bus in conversation with leaders from the community.

One LA's attention to detail and organization was evident in the days leading to the tour, as the core team in Sun Valley held four planning meetings with the mayor's staff; the mayor himself attended the last meeting. Before the visit, the core team planned the bus route, selected whose houses the mayor would visit, and made dry runs of the tour. Indeed, as One LA leader and Pastor Julie Roberts-Fronk observed about IAF events, "Everything is scripted, down to the second."

As the mayor rode the bus with twenty-five community leaders, Sanchez recalls, he began to ask questions like, "What other kind of improvements do you want?" The mayor's questions were answered as they made four stops at different people's homes to hold short house meetings with fifteen to forty people at each one. Antonia Lamas, a house meeting host and a Fernangeles parent, recalls what she appreciated about the event: "We were able to explain to him our situation, what the community is going through, the problems we have, what we need, what we lack . . . he came to see with his own eyes."

Fernangeles Assistant Principal Alma Flores also notes the kind of opportunities that One LA's work with the parents created:

They create a safe place for parents to express themselves to say . . . "These streets are horrible. We feel that we're invisible. We feel that no one pays attention to us." It really gives the community a voice. It validates their concerns and they realize that they're not alone, that there [are knowledgeable] people who have their interests in mind who are going to speak out for them.

Indeed, the parents' involvement may even affect children, as they see their parents speak up for themselves and emerge as leaders. Fernangeles teacher Mayte Acuna explains:

Sometimes the parents feel, "Well, we could say all this, but what's the point? Nobody's going to take us seriously." But as we noticed something would pop up in the newspaper about one of the meetings . . . they noticed that their kids actually were paying attention to what's going on. And . . . we'd see some of the kids say, "Oh, you know, my mom was at the meeting," being proud of what was going on with their parents, and . . . the students were starting to realize that "My voice is important."

As Larkin observes, "Every success in organizing is . . . never about getting the speed bumps in, or the stop signs, or the crossing guard, or the dump closed. That's the means to create the kind of partnerships that people take each other seriously." By rebuilding civic capacities to tackle environmental hazards affecting children's health, school attendance, and academic performance, One LA redefined "educational issues" more broadly thereby summoning those involved to understand that the conditions for learning extend beyond classrooms.

WINNING AND LEVERAGING THE RESULTS

After four years of campaigning by One LA and the community members of Sun Valley, Waste Management dropped its bid to expand the dump in December 2006, and the residents celebrated as the landfill received its final load of trash on April 15, 2007. The campaign against the landfill expansion was a big victory and helped build a broad and newly active constituency in the community. The campaign galvanized a strong relationship between three major community institutions, Fernangeles Elementary School, Holy Rosary Church, and Mary Immaculate Church, and displayed to teachers, parents, and other community members that, if organized, their voices will be heard. Ricardo Loredo stresses the major outcome of the Bradley Landfill effort as building "an infrastructure in the community where we can get word out to community members. We can . . . stand up for people and stand up for things that we believe in."

In fact, Principal Karen Jaye, Father Jim Fee, Father Richard Zanotti, and other institutional leaders continued to meet every other Friday to share concerns and work together.

Not only are Father Richard and Father Jim institutional leaders from whom she receives support, but Jaye also finds them to be resources for the community. As principal, she finds herself providing "a lot of health and human services." Jaye says:

> Sometimes it's really beyond us. It's beyond the school—I'll be honest—and I have on several occasions called over to one of the priests and said, "Please help this family—I can't." And they do. Likewise, they will call and say, "This child is having a problem at this school. Can you call the principal for me?" And I will make a phone call, and we help one another out in that way.

The students' response to seeing their principal collaborate with the clergy is electric, according to Jaye:

> When Father Jim comes here, or Father Richard comes here to a meeting the kids go berserk-like, "Oh, my God, the priest is in the school!" I told Father Jim and Richard that they can come anytime, actually—the kids do better when they're here . . . It's very cute. One kid tried to get Father Richard to give him communion, so Father Richard had to say, "No communion today, son." We've had some funny experiences. The kids are floored that the clergy know me, and I know them.

Students have the opportunity to see adults engaged in learning communities, that is, in relationships of care, and working together to solve the issues that impact their health and well-being. Father Richard comments on the unusual nature of these relationships between school and churches, saying:

> A lot of times the school is over there and the parish is over here and . . . what we are trying to say is, this is one community . . . and we need to work together on this. So it is a challenge, but I think things like One LA helps us to get a little bit beyond our own immediate concerns.

ONE LA AND THE ACHIEVEMENT ACADEMIES: CAPITALIZING INSTITUTIONAL PARTNERSHIPS FOR PARENT EDUCATION

Institutional relationships forged by their collective work on the Bradley Landfill issue also led to a collaborative partnership between Jaye and Sister Maria de los Remedios Aguilar, principal of the Our Lady of the Holy Rosary School, the private Catholic school that is a part of Father Richard's parish. As Jaye and Sister Remedios shared concerns about their schools, Sister Remedios learned about Achievement Academies organized by One LA at Fernangeles. The academies are a series of workshops designed to inform parents about the school system and the curricular content taught in class so that they can provide academic support for their children; the workshops are intended to empower parents to be advocates for their students. Sister Remedios described the academies this way:

> The Achievement Academies . . . empower the parents, to be involved in the education of the children, especially the immigrant parents. They are familiar with the system in their own countries, but not the system here. So sometimes they don't question teachers because questioning the authority is not part of the culture. So it empowers the parents to be

more involved, and know what the children are supposed to know by each grade level, to make sure that the children are placed in the right place. Unfortunately, many children, because their last name is in Spanish . . . are pushed to the lowest ranks. So it gives the power to the parents to say, you have to fight for your children's future.

Designed initially by Joaquin Sanchez as he worked in the Boyle Heights neighborhood, the academies, just like any other One LA organizing strategy, look different in different schools, depending on the needs of the parents. However, they all address college entrance requirements to some degree, including a visit to nearby college campuses, and coach parents on how to express their concerns to teachers.

Using the existing Achievement Academy curriculum as well as the district's third-grade standards, Fernangeles Assistant Principal Alma Flores led a series of sessions for parents. The Fernangeles Achievement Academies focused on teaching parents about the literacy standards for third grade so that they would be able to work with their children at home. She found these opportunities provided academic enrichment, strengthened educational partnership between home and school, and created an inviting space for marginalized parents:

> Some of the parents that came to the Achievement Academies are not our regular parents [who are involved in the school]. In planning, we asked, "How do we reach out to those parents who, for whatever reason, stay away from campus?" So . . . we had a nice goal of bringing them in, making them feel comfortable. There was always refreshments. There was always time to question, little time to socialize again. The no blame thing, and I think often parents feel that if their child's not succeeding, then they're going to be blamed or that school is not a safe place. So I think we really succeeded in making Fernangeles a safe place where they could come and ask questions . . . I think that they definitely feel more welcome, more apt to kind of see us as regular people who really have their interest and the interest of their students in mind.

Indeed, to make the school a welcoming place for parents, Fernangeles takes care to hire staff that are fluent in Spanish and conduct parent classes and meetings in both Spanish and English.

As significant as the victory in stopping the landfill expansion was, perhaps more importantly, the process of the campaign created an unprecedented kind of public space and thickened public relationships in which people could "really talk as equals—because up to the point . . . the people in the community were not seen as equals," according to Loredo. It turns out that the organizing and civic empowerment strategies used in Fernangeles are found across the One LA landscape. Associated Pomona Teachers President Morgan Brown observed that One LA offers teachers and parents "training about power and about how to engage in the school, not just as a volunteer that cuts paper . . . but actually as a leader who can sit down with the principal and go through a budget and express their hopes and fears about where their kids are headed and where this community is headed." Harmony Elementary School teacher Mauricio Escobar echoes these comments, noting that One LA "helps people discover that they do have power, and organize." When a group of Fernangeles parents were asked what they had learned through their involvement with One LA, one of the parents responded: "That united, we make a difference."

Relational Culture and Leadership Development at Harmony Elementary School

One LA strategically embraces storytelling by training leaders to declare their personal narratives publicly and powerfully. When Robert Cordova, the principal at Harmony Elementary School in South Central Los Angeles, recollects his first involvement with the IAF, he articulates it as crisply as he dresses—in freshly pressed suits and neatly cuff-linked shirts. Now a seasoned educator, Cordova begins his story with his first year as the principal at City Terrace Elementary School in East Los Angeles. There he faced a challenging group that he came to refer to as "pesky parents," who were quite vocal in their criticisms of the school. Cordova soon found himself caught between these parents and district supervisors who were telling him, "I don't care what you're doing; you make sure that this person [a pesky parent] gets appeased." Faced with these challenges, Cordova began to search for successful educational models working with similar populations. He discovered the Alliance Schools in Texas, which were collaboratively partnering with predominantly Latino populations similar to those in East Los Angeles:

> I was investigating some of the schools in Texas that had some real success and . . . some of them were IAF Alliance Schools . . . I said, well, I'm going to investigate this and I went to some of the IAF trainings and began to learn about their strategy of working with the community, not just the parents . . . I started to do it and I saw the power.

During Cordova's participation in IAF trainings in Texas, he encountered Alliance School principals, and decided he wanted to work effectively with the community like they did. "You can do these other things, you can make yourself look good, and you can get promoted, but are you really going to do something that's meaningful? Are you really going to have the power to do something that's meaningful?" To invest in discovering what "meaningful" work would look like in his school, Cordova began listening to parents in a new way—learning about their interests, concerns, hopes, and dreams for their children. With the mentoring and guidance of One LA organizers, Cordova helped City Terrace teachers, parents, and community members begin to talk in purposeful ways to discover their shared concern for all children's well-being. Intentional listening deepened trust between parents and teachers, and stronger relationships provided a basis for building power. It was not long before parents and teachers convinced the city to install a traffic sign at a dangerous intersection that had been a safety hazard for students and families walking to and from school. This early victory inspired parents and teachers, solidifying their confidence that together they could positively change their community. Consequently, Cordova became further convinced that relational organizing comprises the core of principal leadership: building trust with parents and teachers by mobilizing around their shared interests and concerns for their children, school, and community.

When Cordova was transferred from City Terrace to Trinity Elementary School in South Central Los Angeles, he brought with him the skills and sensibilities he had gained as a One LA leader. At Trinity, Cordova used the same IAF organizing strategies to lead a combined effort of parents and teachers to convince LAUSD officials to change the funding schedule, not only for Trinity students, but also for the benefit of over 250,000 students in greater Los Angeles—work that was highlighted earlier in this chapter. Cordova was then asked to open a new elementary school called Harmony just a few blocks away from Trinity.

Cordova came to Harmony with a vision for a school community with a relational culture that develops leaders among the faculty, parents, and other community members. Even before Harmony opened its doors in July 2004, Cordova organized a staff retreat where teachers could start building relationships by talking about what was important to them and what drove them to teach. In fact, when he recruited teachers and staff for Harmony, Cordova had shared his own public story that made clear his vision for a school built on a relational culture. At the retreat, he encouraged staff members to focus on aligning the expectations, norms, and practices to the relational culture they had committed to build. When the school opened, portions of monthly staff meetings continued to be devoted to teachers engaging in dialogue—sharing new stories about students and families, reflecting on their daily instructional practice, refining their shared vision, and developing concrete action steps to improve the quality of education for Harmony students.

One LA organizers facilitated some of these sessions, and parents were invited to learn alongside the staff. Harmony's Title I Coordinator, Kelley Budding, reflects on the use of organizing strategies at these sessions:

> We did a Tuesday staff development with teachers and parents at the same time. And that's pretty radical. That's just not happening at other schools, where you actually have the teachers' staff development occurring along with parents. The staff development was on how to lead house meetings and have these public conversations. Other schools will talk about parent involvement, but not really. Holding house meetings is a strategy . . . this is a way that you can have conversations and build power within your community.

Cordova found that relational organizing requires an artful navigation between relational and unilateral power. Communicating the complexities and nuances of organizing concepts and strategies to his staff required time and patience, at times, leading to tension when managing his staff in different situations. During one of the faculty discussions on Bernard Loomer's article about the two types of power, some teachers openly challenged what they perceived to be an ideological contradiction.[8] Teachers would say, "Oh, he talks about being relational. How is he relational when he is giving us the bottom line and telling us what needs to get done?" In Cordova's view, he learned from One LA to capitalize on the relational power that results from two parties building an intentional relationship to act upon a shared self-interest, sometimes referred to as "power with." Nevertheless, Cordova believed there were situations that warrant executive decisions—or unilateral power. With his measured practice in both unilateral and relational power, Cordova tried to cultivate a learning organization at Harmony. While maintaining his authority as a principal, he worked to create a safe space for openly constructive dialogue among teachers.

DEVELOPING CORE LEADERS WITH THE IAF MODEL

While cultivating a relational culture amongst faculty, Cordova simultaneously conducted one-on-one meetings to identify and mentor a group of core leaders among his staff. Just as an organizer would do, Cordova utilized one-on-one meetings to listen—to learn about their personal backgrounds and experiences, to discuss their interests and passions, to follow-up with hard questions all the while providing new leadership challenges. Once leaders were identified, training and mentoring provided safe space for learning and reflection. Cordova first learned from Ken Fujimoto, a senior IAF organizer who started working with him at City Terrace, that mentoring is an ongoing process that creates room for thought-provoking questions to agitate a leader to think about important issues while supporting them in taking on new challenges. Fujimoto has been an IAF organizer for twenty-three years, and his experience stretches back to his organizing work with the United Farm Workers in the mid-1970s. He sees every conversation as an opportunity for mentoring and training: "You have to take every opportunity; every conversation you try to weave into it, some kind of training."

Early on, Cordova purposefully directed his energy to support Tommy Welch, the English Learner (EL) Program coordinator, and Kelley Budding as key potential leaders. Welch, whose energy and effervescence are contagious, gradually developed his leadership as he moved from being a classroom teacher to becoming the EL Program coordinator:

> I slowly was involved, because I was still a new teacher. I would do the community walks—we'd go around the whole neighborhood, and we'd be assigned streets, and ask, "Who lives where? What resources are here? What church is here? What store is here?" We'd go talk to a store owner, and go talk to the parents . . . Cordova would give me small leadership roles. When I was the testing coordinator, I changed the whole way we did it, and when I went to get my national board certification, I did all my projects for the EL Program . . . So, very slowly I started increasing my leadership role.

Over the years, Welch has come to see his relationship with Cordova not only as professionally valuable but also as personally meaningful; he likens it to the kind of trust and comfort shared between "father and son."

Cordova infused faculty meetings with principles and techniques he learned from One LA organizers and trainings. He prioritized funding to send approximately thirty key teachers and parent leaders to local and regional One LA training sessions. Budding, who developed into a respected school leader with a knack for relating closely to parents and teachers, credits One LA training as "pivotal" in her growth as an administrator:

> One LA has helped me see things not just as a program . . . to connect with people first to connect them to the program. It happens through the relationships and the connections with people and trust. So, I think they've been pivotal in that. They offer a way to act on theory that we've read about, offering concrete suggestions like when you have a conversation, this is what you look for, or in thinking about what other people's interests are . . . I don't know that I would have had that vision before I'd come into working with One LA.

Leaders like Budding found that discussions deconstructing the concept of self-interest or responding to carefully selected readings further opened up space for them to build genuine connections and empathy toward each other.

BUILDING TEACHER GRADE-LEVEL TEAMS

As teachers built more trusting professional and personal relationships, they began to see how the organizing approach could impact their instructional practice. In many urban schools, teachers often see administrators and instructional coaches as unsupportive and even absent, while administrators seldom include teachers in key decision-making processes. At Harmony, however, teachers were seen as critical stakeholders in improving instruction. For example, when Welch took the lead for Harmony's EL Program, he facilitated a collaborative process with teachers to rewrite the mandated district curriculum to enable the school to track the progress of English-language learners from unit to unit and year to year. Cordova supported this process by arranging for release time for teachers to meet together. In the end, the model that Welch and the teachers developed together not only was implemented effectively in Harmony classrooms, it became a sought-after model in other LAUSD schools.

Meanwhile, Harmony instituted grade-level team meetings that deliberately incorporated One LA strategies such as the one-on-one relational meetings. For example, rather than directly jumping to technical and logistic tasks, these meeting often began with time for teachers to get to know one another as people not simply as colleagues. This attention to team building helps busy teachers take the time necessary to build the kind of mutually supportive relationships necessary to create highly functioning grade-level teams and caring school communities. As third-grade teacher Mauricio Escobar explains: "We have a culture here, we teachers. I have [teacher] friends in kindergarten, first grade, fifth grade, because we have a relationship. We had our one-on-ones that make us more understanding of each other, and supportive of each other." Amparo Navarro, a fifth-grade teacher, notes how these relationships would also enter into grade-level team meetings:

> The grade-level meetings have to be the most personal moments . . . you can sense the person having a bad day and there are the little candies or . . . Kelley bringing in vitamin waters in our meetings . . . little things like that . . . the human connection we need every day by greeting each other, saying, "Good morning! How are you? How's it going?" We do the same things with our grade-level team; we talk to each other.

At these meetings, teachers of the same grade level, sometimes with an administrative coach, openly discuss issues with which they struggle in their own classrooms, and engage their colleagues for insight, inquiry, and practical advice. Grade-level team meetings, for Escobar, provide relevant and enriching professional learning opportunities:

> We analyze grade-level data weekly. For example, my lowest bar [in the graph displaying standardized assessment results] was vocabulary. I thought there was something wrong with my printer [laughter]. It was zero. Not one kid met the benchmark. But we share these results within grade-level teams, and then we share with other grades, and ask, "Hey, what are you doing that's working?"

The high levels of pretense, blame shifting, and judgment that often creep into these kinds of meetings in many schools rarely penetrate through the thick relationships teachers have built together at Harmony. With the foundation of a mutually supportive community, teachers find it easier to be vulnerable and confront difficult issues necessary to improve their practice.

CONNECTING WITH PARENTS

The collegiality and camaraderie shared among Harmony teachers extend beyond grade-level teams. From the beginning Cordova encouraged teachers to build strong relationships with parents. Starting at the initial faculty retreat, Cordova stressed the importance of welcoming parents' perspectives and incorporating parental leadership at the school. Harmony faculty spent time identifying potential parent leaders—starting with parent volunteers helping in classrooms or with school events, and also reaching out more broadly.

Previously, at Trinity, Cordova had secured outside funding to compensate teachers for conducting home visits during after-school hours. At Harmony, Cordova continued his effort to sustain the home-visiting model because he and the staff believed in the importance of having the kinds of conversations with parents that can only happen outside of school space. At parent-teacher conferences in school, teachers typically do all the talking—providing a one-sided perspective on student academic performance and behavior. Cordova and his teachers, however, believed that students' academic engagement and school adjustment can only improve when parents and teachers have a mutual conversation which can lead to an educational partnership based on trust:

> Teachers need to talk to them [parents]. They need to have a relationship with them . . . be a partner with them. That requires certain behaviors from the teachers who sat as a staff and said, "If we truly believe parents are partners, what does that mean our behavior needs to be?"

And we came up with this: We need to make house visits . . . We need to make sure that we have the one-to-one conversations with them. We don't talk about academics; we talk about who they are, where they came from, and what they hope for their kids. That's shared— that's reciprocal.

Entering an authentic dialogue disrupts the unequally distributed power relationship between parents and teachers. In such space, teachers are able to listen as parents share their stories. Cordova notes, "It's one thing having the principal stand in front of the teachers and say the number one concern is . . . It's another thing to have a parent sitting next to the teacher saying I want a teacher who cares for my kid looking into their eyes. It's a big difference."

Cordova encouraged his staff to be intentional about building parent-teacher relationships in all their interactions. Many teachers applied the one-on-one and house-meeting strategies they had learned from staff trainings during parent-teacher conferences and back-to-school nights. To more fully accommodate nontraditional work schedules or varying levels of comfort, teachers often met with parents after school as in the home visits. The conversations with parents included a wide range of issues affecting children and their families, from neighborhood safety to academic concerns, from family hardship to cultural adjustment for the parents.

The core leadership team also played an important role in solidifying the relationship between parents and the school. Cordova, Welch, Budding, and Harmony teachers supported the establishment of a vibrant parent center where parents enroll in English classes, learn about providing academic support for their children, take on volunteer opportunities, and share various community and neighborhood resources. Parents are involved in running a Parent Teacher Student Association and the Safety Valet Program—directing morning school traffic during arrival and dismissal; they also serve on various leadership committees for the school concerning administrative and budgetary matters.

IDENTIFYING PARENT LEADERS

Indeed, the core leadership team made intentional efforts to mentor parents to expand their leadership capacities not only on school-related issues but branching out to concerns shared by a broader community. Living in a residential neighborhood that was situated between two busy South Central thoroughfares, parents worried for their children's safety when walking to and from school. Fast moving traffic outside the school was a problem, according to Harmony teacher, Cynthia Fraire:

One parent shared her story where her daughter got run over by a car, and we also wanted to get a safety guard, so we were organizing for that . . . Anna Eng, the One LA organizer, wanted more of the parents to be involved as opposed to the teachers because the teachers already had a lot on our plate. Anna wanted us to contact Jan Perry, our councilperson, and the Newton police station, and all these other people from the community . . . We started off and the parents took a more active role . . . We got the speed bump and we got the crossing guard. Yes, that was a great thing that we were able to accomplish.

The successful safety campaign was what Eng would call a "teeth-cutting" issue, one that is both important to community members and winnable with concrete results. Parents could see the physical presence of the speed bump and crossing guard and know that their organizing efforts had made an impact. The campaign was also a process through which parent leaders learned organizing skills.

Harmony parent and teacher leaders were able to capitalize on their new organizing skills to tackle other persistent neighborhood safety and violence concerns. In fact, at least five times during the 2007–2008 school year, Harmony had to close its campus, locking the outside gates until the police indicated that the area was safe and secure. One lockdown in particular occurred after a shooting incident at a nearby bus stop that injured five local middle school students and made the local headlines. Harmony leaders, including parents, moved into action and asked for a meeting with the local police. Because Harmony leaders had been working to build a relationship with the local LAPD, Budding already had scheduled a meeting with Newton Station Senior Lead Officer Diaz and later heard from Councilperson Perry that she wanted to attend. About twenty-five parents and a handful of teachers attended the meeting that quickly became contentious as Diaz and Perry reacted defensively to the questions and requests posed by the community members.

As they planned the next meeting, Luz Benitez, a Harmony parent with four children, stepped forward. Benitez volunteered at the school in her son's classroom and served as the leader of the school's Safety Valet Program. In preparation for the next community meeting, Benitez suggested that they focus on welcoming the participants and emphasize that they "were not attacking the officials because they wanted their help." With more time to prepare and with word getting out about the controversial first meeting, the next meeting held in the Harmony auditorium attracted nearly two hundred people from eleven different institutions, including teachers, parents, and administrators from other area schools. Benitez opened up this meeting and recalls her participation in the event:

Entonces como esa fue idea mía, yo tuve que ir al micrófono y pedirle a la gente que si tienen preguntas, que hablaran uno a la vez y que no gritaran, que les habláramos con respeto para que ellos nos contestaran con respeto y nos escucharan.

Since it was my idea, I had to go to the microphone and ask the people who had questions to speak one at a time, not yell, and speak to them courteously so that they would answer courteously and listen to us.

Representatives from the mayor's office and LAUSD then made opening statements, after which people broke off into small group house meetings facilitated by Harmony teachers who took notes on chart paper from the ensuing conversations. The mini-house-meeting structure invited parents and community members to voice their stories and come to a common understanding of broadly shared issues. The representatives from the various public offices circulated through the room, listening in on each of the meetings and reading the notes. "It was fabulous," according to Budding, "because they got to see a ton of ideas and see how everybody was working together, and at the end each group shared out."

Organizer Ken Fujimoto took notice of the leadership displayed by Benitez and approached her after the meeting to schedule a one-on-one relational meeting. At the next community meeting at Harmony, held about three weeks later with the mayor's Gang Reduction and Youth Development (GRYD) task force, Benitez took on even more leadership; she and a fellow Harmony parent, Armando Villanueva, told stories about community concerns of confidentiality when reporting illegal activities to the police.

Harmony parents and teachers continue to work on issues of neighborhood safety and violence; there appear to be no quick solutions and the issues require intensive and sustained focus. But these campaigns serve another purpose. Through community meetings and planning sessions, Harmony parents like Benitez step forward and demonstrate the kind of desire and temperament One LA looks for in leaders. Harmony staff and organizer Fujimoto identify these parents and focus their energy on developing them as leaders.

BUILDING PARENT LEADERSHIP

Sensing an opportunity to capitalize on the emerging appetite for leadership displayed by parents after the controversial meeting with Diaz and Perry, Fujimoto and Budding recruited and planned for a series of Parent Leadership Academies. Twelve parents signed up for these trainings and met with Fujimoto for about two hours each Saturday. One LA organizers and Harmony leaders had identified needs at the school that were different from those addressed by the Achievement Academies held at Fernangeles. At Harmony, the Parent Leadership Academies were designed to build the skill and knowledge parents needed to be leaders, addressing issues like relationship building, leadership, power, and organizing.

Parents collectively identified a new issue while talking with each other and with the Harmony staff during these Leadership Academy training sessions. Harmony, like many overcrowded schools in LAUSD, was run on a year-round calendar, which presented a number of challenges. First, children from the same family were sometimes assigned to different "tracks," causing them to have different vacation schedules and posing unnecessary childcare burdens upon their family. Meanwhile, city-provided youth services are planned on the basis of a traditional school calendar—often leaving children in nontraditional tracks with very few extracurricular and recreational options during their untimely school vacations. Finally, in a school like Harmony that embraces collaborative practice across classrooms, teachers in the same grade-level teams but on different tracks have difficulty meeting to discuss their instructional plans and strategies.

Fujimoto, Budding, and the parents decided that the 12th Annual LAUSD Parent Summit, which featured a full Saturday of workshops and forums hosted by LAUSD for parents throughout the city, would provide a venue for parents to practice their leadership skills. Budding and Welch brought five Parent Leadership Academy leaders to the summit where hundreds of parents and school officials from across LAUSD packed the LA Convention Center. There were over fifty different workshops with over one hundred presenters and an array of topics that could be overwhelming to any summit attendee. The Harmony parents, however, had a singular objective that they had developed in a planning meeting with Fujimoto and Budding earlier in the week: to voice their concerns about the year-round calendar to LAUSD board members. In preparation for the Summit, Fujimoto and Budding printed photos of each LAUSD board member to familiarize Harmony parents with the faces of targeted leaders, focusing especially on Board President Monica Garcia and Harmony's district representative, Richard Vladovic. Budding had previously learned that the session entitled "Conversation with LAUSD Board Members" would be the only time when parents could publicly voice their concerns to board members. Armed with scripts prepared by Budding based on conversations in their planning meeting, the parents quickly recognized Garcia from her picture and eagerly introduced themselves even before the session began; they then proceeded to take seats at the front of the room.

Soon after the floor was opened for questions, Luz Benitez went up to the microphone. Benitez first tried to ease the tension she felt in the room by saying how stressed the board members looked and told them to relax, saying, "Tranquilo, tranquilo." There was some soft laughter in the room. Benitez spoke clearly and calmly to the board members, never looking at her script. She briefly discussed the negative consequences of the year-round tracking schedule. Moreover, she invited district representative Vladovic to come to Harmony to meet with parents for further conversation. Unlike many parents from other schools at the summit who simply expressed complaints or raised questions, Benitez strategically targeted a key leader, offered suggestions for follow-up, and demanded a public response. In response, Vladovic said he was familiar with Harmony and Principal Cordova, suggested that Harmony was only 140 kids over the student quota necessary to run on a traditional school calendar, and asked an assistant to schedule a time for him to meet with the parents to discuss the matter further.

This display of empowered leadership from Harmony parents was the direct result of their participation in the Leadership Academies. Indeed, with one daughter in college and another in high school, Dora Orrego has been an LAUSD parent for over twelve years, but it was not until her son enrolled at Harmony in pre-kindergarten five years ago that she got involved with one of her children's schools. "Now," says Orrego, "since I'm more involved, I have more courage; before I didn't even have the courage to speak up ... Now, I know my rights." She speaks about the concept of "agency" she learned from Fujimoto at the Leadership Academies and explains how she had not seen herself as having political agency before the Leadership Academies, but that now she perceives herself to be an agent of change.

After the parents spoke out at the summit, things started to fall into place. In contrast to the previous lack of support from the district for a calendar change, Cordova found himself sitting at a table with parents and representatives from the UTLA teachers union and the school board, all supporting the change. What made the difference? According to Cordova:

> One LA helped us with building the attitude in the parents that they're the boss, this is their school, and they have a right and a responsibility to organize, and to know what it is that they want from the school. So that was all part of it, that when they went there [to the Parent Summit], they were ready to speak to them [the School Board] about what is it that they wanted for their school as parents.

Harmony elementary started with one school leader's vision of a school with a relational culture, strong teacher and parent leaders, and the power to provide excellent learning opportunities to children in a neighborhood historically failed by the educational system. With the assistance of One LA organizers, school leaders and dedicated parents have worked hard to organize a school community with strong relationships, reliable leaders, and the power to teach, learn, and effect change. The Harmony Web site now proudly declares:

> After four colorful years, Harmony Elementary is transitioning onto the Traditional Calendar thanks to the organizing efforts of the parents, the staff, and the community. Teachers can settle into classrooms to call their own and families can establish firmer connections as all 800 students will attend continuously for 180 days beginning in September.

Harmony was the only school out of ten in its local district cluster to meet federal, state, and district annual academic targets for the 2007–2008 school year, and it exists today as an example of the potential for One LA's approach to build a relational culture in schools in a way that makes a difference for children and their families.

Conclusion

One LA's organizing work at Fernangeles and Harmony Elementary Schools uncovers the promising potential for schools to function as vital civic institutions in transforming classrooms, families, and neighborhoods. Their stories invite us to bear witness to what our schools can be as they beckon us to reimagine schools not as factories in the mere business of test score production but as vibrant and welcoming spaces where education for democracy can begin. Their stories further illuminate how organizing principles can be employed to build the institutional capacities of schools to address community concerns. By organizing schools alongside other community institutions, One LA builds the leadership of principals, teachers, and parents to develop the deep relationships and sustainable power necessary to create new school and community cultures. Moreover, organizers and leaders at both Fernangeles and Harmony embody the multifaceted and intentional nature of One LA's organizing approach. Through engaging a cross-section of stakeholders—parents, administrators, public officials, clergy, and teachers—to build relational power across traditionally isolated constituencies, One LA works to break down the conventional boundaries often erected between various community members and their institutions.

At Fernangeles, a deep commitment to immigrant families and a philosophy that "school does not stop at the sidewalks," demonstrated how a public school can build powerful institutional relationships to take on an issue that seemed too large and threatening for any of them to tackle alone. Their "David and Goliath story," as school administrator Maria Sooy calls it, exemplifies how One LA intentionally sought to build relationships among local institutions to present a collective political force capable of challenging a large corporate power.

Harmony, on the other hand, began its organizing work by first focusing on developing leadership and building a viable relational culture among the principal and staff before mobilizing parents. If Fernangeles worked through cross-institutional partnerships to agitate and mobilize a strong constituency, Harmony capitalized on internal relational networks to identify, train, and mentor leaders with a hunger and an appetite for change. Whereas the organizing at Fernangeles revolved around a concrete issue that imposed environmental and health hazards on students and their families, Harmony prioritized a less visible yet chronic concern—the absence of genuine relationships and trust in urban schools—to improve instructional quality and family engagement.

Both schools, however, relied heavily upon the organizing principles of One LA to frame and strengthen their work. Both stories reveal the larger agenda One LA aims to achieve in birthing civically engaged individuals and communities. They attest to the creativity of One LA leaders and organizers in adapting broad organizing strategies to build the structures and relationships necessary for effective work that responds to local needs and draws from local expertise.

The Challenges Ahead

As noted earlier, One LA has set for itself the daunting challenge of influencing educational change and civic life across the vast expanse of Los Angeles County and LAUSD. The organization made important gains in sinking deep roots in local institutions and demonstrated its capacity to build organized communities committed to change. Nevertheless, it continues to search for ways to expand its reach on a larger scale. In doing so, its strategy faces some important challenges.

First, One LA is committed to identifying and developing institutional leaders, and in schools this means first working with principals. Principal leadership is necessary when cultivating relationships with other community institutions as well as building a relational school culture. Principals Karen Jaye and Robert Cordova both grew as leaders through One LA training and mentorship on the part of organizers. Further, each sought to develop multicultural competencies for working with low-income, immigrant families by seeking to understand and draw upon parental values and expectations in educating children. In the end, these principals came to believe in the critical role of schools as civic institutions that foster engagement and empowerment of communities as the bedrock for rebuilding democracy.

By relying so heavily on institutional leadership, however, One LA is faced with a challenge in urban school contexts where principals are under pressure to demonstrate immediate turnaround by raising test scores, and where leadership turns over at high rates. Principals like Cordova and Jaye have found the space to work with One LA, even without official support at the district level. Yet Cordova is already leading his third school in the short space of time he has been with One LA. He took his toolbox of One LA organizing strategies with him, but had to start over each time. Meanwhile, the schools he left behind had to struggle to maintain organizing without his leadership. One way to meet this challenge is to build a relational culture among the school community that is deep and strong enough to survive principal transition. Nevertheless, expanding the number of principals engaged with One LA, especially without a district-level partnership, and sustaining school-based organizing through turnover remain important challenges.

Furthermore, One LA starts with relationships not programs, and prioritizes process over outcomes, and this is profoundly counter-cultural to most educators and education reformers. As the starting place for organizing in Harmony and Fernangeles, dialogue opened up channels to humanize the disempowered and the voiceless: those in power came to understand their burning questions and deep-seated frustrations as well as aspiring hopes and dreams. Within this broad strategy is an unstated faith that when put into conversation and relationship with each other, those closest to the issues—principals, teachers, and parent leaders—will build together the knowledge and relational power necessary to address community concerns. A reliance upon and trust in the local knowledge and expertise of those closest to the ground empowers parents and teachers who are "experts" in their terrain, generating knowledge and skills unique to their experiences and contexts. One LA leaders and organizers also place value in actively cultivating opportunities to pause and reflect as they build an authentic change process in their school communities.

This approach contrasts sharply with more mainstream education reform that seeks to implement single-focus reform strategies without much attention to how to build support for their implementation in individual schools. Instead of searching for a silver bullet reform strategy that works for everybody, One LA relies upon local knowledge and expertise to develop a custom fit. One LA is attentive to research that identifies effective approaches to teaching and learning. Senior organizer Sister Maribeth Larkin reiterates that One LA does not have "a one-size-fits-all reform strategy."

> Our strategy is get the relationships going, get people comfortable with being in a relationship, help them build that capacity to be talking to each other and . . . deepen that culture within schools and across communities as a public institutional effort . . . Because we are always about building relational power, building a culture of conversation and

relationship and accountability for what's our public purpose here. And then how do you build a relational culture that deepens and reinforces itself at every possible place?

Indeed, this is the flexible and creative side so central to One LA's model of organizing.

Nevertheless, although One LA empowers the school and surrounding communities to define locally driven agendas, it also has a larger vision of a unified "One LA" organized broadly across the entire city. One LA would like to effect district-wide, systemic change, but as an organization that drills so deeply into specific school institutions, it struggles to find a strategy that could build change across a district as large and diverse as LAUSD, especially with limited resources. After all, One LA has only about eight organizers on staff. It is here that the unique stories of Fernangeles and Harmony are paradoxically instructive. While each school had a different focus for its organizing and different manifestations of identified issues and actions, each also had impressive increases in parent involvement and improved relationships among parents, teachers, and community stakeholders. In other words, in two different neighborhoods over twenty miles apart, One LA's broad-based organizing strategies enabled two schools to address their uniquely identified issues in ways authentic and specific to their locality and led to school improvement in both cases. Thus, with a focus on going deep, One LA offers an approach to school improvement that is at once custom fit and widely applicable.

At the end of this study, One LA continued to experiment with ways to expand its work at the district level. In partnership with the Algebra Project spearheaded by Bob Moses, One LA built relationships with two large LAUSD high schools—Franklin and Crenshaw—along with Occidental College to provide rigorous math curriculum for cohorts of students who would otherwise not have access to honors and advanced courses. Another promising avenue for the group's impact at a district level can be seen in the Pomona Unified School District, about an hour east of Los Angeles. One LA partnered with the Pomona teacher's union to sponsor a campaign to pass a $235 million education bond as well as to lobby against state education budget cuts.

These developments demonstrate the flexibility of One LA's organizing approach when faced with new issues and contexts. Further, their approach shows promise for implementation on a larger scale. In pursuit of uniting Los Angeles's diverse collective as one, One LA's commitment to revive a democratic spirit by directly engaging local citizens across isolated institutions still continues—with the group's goal to form a more perfect union, that is, *E pluribus unum*.

4

"Our Strength is the Power
of Our Community"

Political Education and the Continuation of the Struggle in Denver

PRIMARY AUTHORS: MEREDITH MIRA, THOMAS NIKUNDIWE,

AND ANITA WADHWA

Prelude: "They have us on lockdown"

Located on a quiet street in Denver, West 33rd Avenue, Rosa Linda's restaurant is a small, red and white brick building with large windows and brightly colored canopy umbrellas shading a few outdoor tables.[1] Inside the restaurant, framed accolades and philanthropic awards adorn the sand-colored walls. Sunlight spills onto cacti and wooden tables and booths flanked by brightly colored paintings from local Chicano/a and Mexicano/a artists. Accordion notes from a Tejano song flit out of the speakers. Rosa Linda, the petite owner with short auburn hair, yells "Adios jóvenes!" to ten youth from the community organization, Padres Unidos.

The teenagers trickle out into the scorching summer heat and walk a few paces to a small building next door which houses the organization. They sit cramped around a long table, each one reading responses to survey questions that they developed and to which seven hundred students have responded. The surveys reveal concerns about lunch, college preparation, quality of instruction, discipline, student support, school culture, and security at their school, North High. Juan Evangelista, a stocky senior with glasses and a shaved head, reads one of the survey's comments: "Make North more like a school and less like a prison. They have us on lockdown." He laughs ironically, thinking how depressing it is.

Two of the adult allies, Jenny and Eduardo, step into the conversation and ask the youth to connect their conversation to the political education session on structural racism they held earlier that morning. Eva Bonilla, a senior with intense eyes and black curly hair pulled back in a ponytail, thinks it is an example of the intentional school-to-prison pipeline. Eduardo, holding up a sharpie to a blank sheet of butcher paper, asks the young people to brainstorm how to address the problem using the Padres approach.

Ten pairs of eyes look up at the paper. More than three decades ago, their predecessors—aunts, uncles, neighbors, parents—walked out of high schools in Denver to protest a dismal education. Now they will continue the work so that history will stop repeating itself, so that North's potential can be unearthed, and so that they can be secure in the knowledge that brown and black children, including their own little brothers and sisters, can attend a school where students are prepared for college and treated with respect. They are ready. And they will continue the struggle no matter how long it takes.

If you ask anyone familiar with Padres y Jóvenes Unidos how it got started, the answer will inevitably be in 1989 at Valverde Elementary, where a white principal punished Spanish-speaking children by making them eat their lunch while seated on the floor.[2] Within a year, Latino parents had organized themselves as Padres Unidos, or "Parents United" (the jóvenes, or youth component of the organization, would come later), and the principal was removed from the school. Members of Padres y Jóvenes Unidos (PJU) often harken back to the story of Valverde, which works as a narrative that succinctly informs outsiders about the racial and linguistic oppression faced by many of Denver's Spanish-speaking students. The narrative also speaks to the collective power of parents who banded together to fight for the rights of their children and other Latino children. Rosa Linda, a founding member of the group, explains:

> Yo digo una cosa, yo tengo cinco hijos pero realmente tengo más de cinco mil ¿Sí? Porque si tu hijo tiene problemas yo voy a ver qué problemas tiene. Entonces cuando Padres comenzó recuerdo que estábamos todos ahí, estábamos furiosos.

> Let me tell you something, I have five children, but the truth is that I have more than five thousand. Right? Because if your child has problems, I'm going to see to his problems. So, when Padres started I remember that we were all there, we were furious.

In order to understand the processes through which PJU has fought for and attained educational reforms in Denver in the two decades since the incident at

Valverde, this chapter will examine PJU's four-year campaign to redesign North High School, a historically low-performing school with a largely Latino immigrant population. This campaign, like all other PJU campaigns, is rooted in the tenets and history of the Chicano and Civil Rights movements, the educational landscape in Denver, and PJU's particular way of countering systemic oppression through a process that the members of the organization call *political education*. Political education serves as the driving force that enables youth and adult members to recognize that they are part of a larger and continuing struggle for human rights. By situating their work in that struggle, PJU equips its members with the knowledge to understand the hidden structural elements of current educational issues, provides the agitation they need to take action, and instills the hope and strength necessary to carry forward the struggle.

We will begin by outlining the particular context in which PJU operates—focusing on the organization's development as well as Denver's historical, political, and educational milieu—in order to provide a framework from which to understand how PJU became a major player in education reform. Then we will discuss the part political education has played in the successful development and expansion of PJU. Through the narrative of PJU's campaign to reform North High School, we will examine the role that political education, power, alliances, and framing play in PJU's organizing work overall. Finally, we will end with a discussion of the tensions PJU balances as it broadens its scope of organizing.

Historical Context: Forging Relationships, Building "strength and community"

It is a spring day as we drive on Denver's Interstate 80 to the current office of Padres y Jóvenes Unidos. Dry grass, spotty green trees, bushes, and brush border either side of the highway. When we exit, we see pick-up trucks, an SUV covered with a layer of dirt, horse-trailers in driveways, and Spanish storefronts crouched together on the same streets. Electric towers and power-lines stand exposed from the land. The numerous peaks of the Rocky Mountains loom expansively across the landscape. Juxtaposed to this natural beauty are strip malls, large highway arteries, and pristine golf courses.

Small brick houses with well-kept lawns, bright flowers, and leafy trees fill the neighborhood in which PJU is located. The office is on the second floor of a Presbyterian church with a large multiethnic collage on the front. We knock on the door, and Ricardo lets us in. He is a broad-shouldered man with a deadpan sense of humor. "You don't have to knock, just come right in," he says, his small eyes squinted in a smile. He is dressed casually in a collared short-sleeved shirt and jeans. His black hair, generously intermixed with gray, is pulled back in a bun, and he has a full goatee, equally mixed with black and gray. His wife Pam is dressed simply as well, in a long flowing skirt and a knit poncho. She has a round youthful face framed by bangs and shoulder length brown hair, and she gives each of us a hug. She tells us to sit down at the meeting table in the middle of the central, open space, which is surrounded by a small kitchen, three rooms with clear glass walls, and posters scrawled with campaign goals. Bookshelves line one wall and are filled artfully with photos of protests and titles such as *The Autobiography of Malcolm X, No One is Illegal, Los Aztecas, Aztec Times, Deacons for Defense,* and a "Rethinking Schools" issue. Above a fireplace on this same wall is a large framed picture of Malcolm X with the quote:

> Time is on the side of the oppressed today; it's against the oppressor.
> Truth is on the side of the oppressed today; it's against the oppressor.
> You don't need anything else.

Padres Unidos came from modest beginnings. In 1989, parents—including Sam Gallegos, Rosa Linda Aguirre, Dolores Obregon, Joel and Lucia Navarro, and Gilberto Gutierrez—met on a volunteer basis, after work or on the weekends, at Rosa Linda's restaurant. Pam and Ricardo Martinez, the current co-directors of PJU, moved to Denver in the 1980s with a wealth of organizing experience. They contacted Padres after hearing Gilberto Gutierrez put out a call to action on TV following the incident at Valverde.

Ricardo, a former farm worker himself, had organized farm workers in California, Texas, and Arizona. Pam's organizing began in the 1960s as a student at San Diego State University,[3] where she organized for the creation of Chicano studies and Black studies departments, and the first women's studies program in the country. Later she organized women in the garment and electronics industries. After meeting Ricardo in Texas, the couple worked on the landmark Supreme Court case *Plyler v. Doe* (1982), which ultimately defeated a Texas state law authorizing school districts to deny funding for the enrollment of undocumented students.

As Ricardo puts it, he and Pam were able to combine their knowledge of organizing practiced in the Chicano and Civil Rights movements with these parents' efforts to organize to build a solid foundation for the group:

> Padres evolved as a continuation of experiences of people who had been involved in the movement in the sixties. They were able to apply that experience here in Denver at that time. We're asked how do you evolve so quickly, how do you win so much? It was because there was a set of experiences here and expertise that helped it . . . We have

evolved from the experience of the Civil Rights movement, the Chicano movement, applied now to Denver.

The relationships that parents in Padres Unidos formed with one another would ultimately be crucial to education reform in Denver, as many of the organization's members and supporters would go on to become leaders in the community, including members of the city council and the school board. Because Denver is a relatively small city, it has been easier for these parents to build social networks and social capital through their participation in different struggles for social justice. When we asked allies and members how they knew PJU or other educational players in Denver, several stated that they moved in the same circles for decades. For example, parent activist Marty Roberts talked about living behind Lucia Guzman, who would go on to become a school board member. Marty knew Lucia was close to Pam Martinez and always heard Pam's name mentioned by many who frequented Rosa Linda's restaurant:

> See, we all are connected . . . Everything builds on something else. It's never one moment, one time, even though that one moment in time is usually documented and put in the newspapers. But it's all so many relationships and things that go on beforehand, and afterward. That builds strength and community, right. It's never just one moment.

PJU members consider themselves to be part of a larger struggle, one that goes back as far as the European colonization of the Americas. When PJU organizers discuss the group's wins and losses, they often do so with the perspective of comparing their campaigns to campaigns that took much longer periods of time—whether it was women fighting for the right to vote or labor activists fighting for an eight-hour work day. As a result, PJU looks to different campaigns as means, not ends, in the overall struggle for human rights. Pam says:

> In the early days, I'm talking our history of being involved in social justice, we always took years . . . if you're inside trying to democratize and build people's power up from within the union, you're in there for the long haul. It's not a three-month thing. You're in there for at least a couple years. Sometimes longer. Depending on how it goes. So we were used to that, the longevity of things.

Despite winning a victory at Valverde Elementary School, Latino parents continued to tell stories about how the educational system had let them down.

For example, founding member Dolores Obregon recalled that her daughter's counselor would not provide a transcript needed for a college application:

> Le dije, "Tú me vas a dar ese papel ó tú no te vas a ir, porque de ese papel depende que mi hija entre a la universidad." "Y no te lo doy, y no te lo doy." "Si me lo vas a dar y no me voy a mover." Y ella se enojó mucho porque mi hija iba a entrar a la universidad.

> I told [the counselor], "You're going to give me that paper or you're going to have to go, because whether my daughter goes to college or not depends on that paper." She said, "I'm not going to give it to you; I'm not going to give it to you." "Yes, you are, and I'm not moving." And she was very upset because my daughter was going to go to college.

As a result of hearing story after story similar to Dolores', parents decided to do more about the discriminatory treatment of Latino children in the Denver Public Schools (DPS). Under the leadership of parent Gilberto Gutierrez, who had been a force in the Valverde campaign, Padres Unidos was able to get eighty parents to file a petition with the Office of Civil Rights charging the district with racial bias against their children. The petition noted DPS' noncompliance with a 1997 federal court mandate that required schools to provide equal access to non-English speakers and students with special needs. Four years later, DPS was found guilty of discrimination, which meant that the district could stand to lose $30 million in federal funds. Padres Unidos had garnered a major victory all while being run and organized by volunteers.

The successful complaint with the Office of Civil Rights provided an unexpected catalyst for the organization's expansion. Raul Yzaguirre, the president of the National Council of La Raza, offered PJU $70,000 in funding for two years. Funding would allow the group to deepen and expand its work, but the organization had to first learn how to build an infrastructure. Pam was hired as the director of PJU; Ricardo eventually came on board as a full-time organizer. PJU moved out of its space adjacent to Rosa Linda's restaurant and to a new office just a few blocks from North High School in Denver's Northwest quadrant, within easy reach of the parents and youth of North. It is here that the North reform campaign begins.

North High School: A Microcosm of a System in Need of Repair

> This public school system has been bad, bad, bad for our kids for fifty years. We did better before integration; the schools were better. We don't have any more integration today than we did back before

busing . . . We walked out in the sixties for these same reasons. We're not educating our kids. Senator [Ken] Salazar said to me, "Lucia, I was with the group that walked in the streets against the public schools in the sixties. If we don't fix these public schools now in this twenty-first century, in this decade, then how can we continue to save public education as it is?" So that's why I say it's the last chance [for public education].

—Former Denver Public Schools School Board member and PJU ally, Reverend Lucia Guzman

As Reverend Guzman conveys, parents and leaders in the Latino community have been disturbed about the state of public school education in Denver, and North High School in particular, for several decades. Founded in 1872, North is one of the oldest high schools in Denver,[4] an imposing red brick building with rust red columns and multiple flights of stairs that lead to arched entryways. Specific concerns about North High School emerged again in 2002 when parents expressed concerns about the educational rigor of the school due to the low graduation rate of 60 percent[5] and the fact that they saw children hanging outside of the campus during the school day. Many felt that North had been an underperforming school for too long, and that it had been habitually ignored as well. As Johanna Leyba, a former North student, states,

I can't believe North has not changed yet. I graduated in 1990 and we are still hearing the same stories from students. We started with over five hundred students in my freshman class and only graduated two hundred forty! If teachers, parents, and students are still frustrated, we are still doing something wrong. It doesn't matter whose fault it is— what does matter is what we're going to do to prepare our students to succeed in college and beyond.[6]

Indeed, PJU collected data showing that only 15 percent of North High students scored advanced or proficient on standardized state tests for reading, while only 23 percent met those standards in writing and 2 percent in math.[7]

Most of the students in Denver Public Schools are students of color: 54 percent are Latino, while African American and white students each comprise about 16 and 25 percent of the population, respectively.[8] The failure of North to educate the children of PJU members was therefore indicative of a system that was failing poor students, immigrant students, and students of color throughout Denver.

Developing Parent Leaders: Political Education

The North High School campaign started in a Padres political education leadership course with parents of North students. Parents had concerns about high levels of depression among students at the school and also had questions about how to read their children's report cards, which were very different from what they were accustomed to in Mexico. One parent brought in her son's report card to analyze, which helped the group understand why they saw so many young people out of school during school hours. Parents started to see that their students were taking far too many electives and did not always have full schedules. Part of the purpose of political education was to help parents understand the school system, how this might happen, and why the school might be ignoring the needs of these particular students.

To PJU, political education is something more than a form of leadership development. Political education is organizer training; it is the work of teaching how systemic oppression works and what might be done about it. Political education occurs during an established meeting time, where a topic—such as *machismo*, racism, feudalism, colonialism, or immigration law—is introduced and people are then split into small groups to discuss the root causes of that particular topic. Diagrams and ideas are recorded on chart paper, and different groups reconvene to share and synthesize ideas about the topic. The staff or members in attendance then examine PJU's current organizing work as it relates to the political education topic, which helps them deepen their analysis and understand how their work is tied to the long-term struggle for human rights. Political education, then, is a way to both understand that struggle and become a part of the struggle. Former youth member and current PJU youth organizer LaLo Montoya is a passionate young man with short, spiky black hair, a light goatee, and black framed glasses. His demeanor is gentle and he speaks with urgency about how political education links the historical struggle with PJU's current campaigns:[9]

> I think it's a very important part of the organization, to always keep learning about past movements, to keep learning about the structure that we're fighting against because knowledge is power, and we have to keep analyzing ourselves, and I feel really lucky that we actually do that here.

There are many functions of political education for PJU, but as the story of the North High School redesign will reveal, political education plays an indispensable role in the Padres Approach. The "Padres Approach" is PJU's overarching organizing strategy that includes three steps: *understand the problem, analyze the impact, and identify concrete solutions.* Political education features in all of the steps, each of which might take several weeks or months to develop.

Understanding the problem is about identifying the issue, which nearly always comes from personal experience. Ricardo, who led a parent leadership class in 2002 with approximately fifteen parents, explains:

> It's that broader discussion that really provides people with the more critical analysis of the school system. So it's not just *that* school or *that* principal or *that* teacher. It's really looking at systemic changes, not just, we'll get that counselor out and bring someone else in. That's a solution, but not maybe the solution to the real problem. And there was a lot of discussion to better understand the school system.

When parents begin to understand the problem from multiple perspectives, they shift from blaming their own children, as in "my kid is ditching school," to the systemic factors that might lead students to make that choice. However, understanding the problem is only the first step. Pam and Ricardo felt that the parents also needed to understand what *impact* not having the correct classes would have on their students and, by extension, their community. Ricardo explains the connections they might make with parents in the following example:

> So why are black and brown kids being thrown in jail more? Why are they being pushed out and encouraged to drop out of high school? . . . If you are less educated, you're less likely to vote. If you are in a jail more than once, you're less likely to vote. If you're poor, you're less likely to vote. So do you or any of your family members fit that criteria? Well, yeah, we're poor. We're uneducated, and my uncle just came out of jail. So then what does that mean from a democratic point of view? If you're looking at democracy and electoral politics, what does that mean then for you and your family and other family members? That you're less likely to vote. And who's making all these laws that affect us? Politicians. And if you don't have a voice on how to get those things changed, then we're pretty much screwed again. So there's a reason why poor people are the least educated and the most likely to end up in jail . . . and it comes from a question of power.

The impact often has implications for power relations. For PJU, power is something that people have even if they do not realize it. Organizing is a way to tap into that unrealized power. Julie Gonzalez, former PJU youth and political organizer, talks about the differences between parent involvement and parent organizing in terms of their relationship to power:

> [You do the] volunteer thing 'cause it's nice to do—you help out your community . . . It's this very fuzzy kind of thing like, "Let's get parents involved." I was like no, we don't [organize] 'cause it's nice. We do it because there are structural inequities and because there's a power structure that exists, and we as people of color or as low-income people or as immigrants or as Chicanos, we come to this, and we're not powerless, but we come with our own strength, and our strength is not money. Our strength is the power of our community to come up and make these changes that we see as being in the best interest of our community. And so that's a very different kind of power, and it has very different qualities to it.

Political education, in other words, is the mechanism by which the members and staff get to examine what impacts structural inequities and power structures have on their day-to-day lives.

The solutions stage of the Padres Approach is where the action happens. Through taking action, more issues are often identified and impacts discovered. This seemingly linear process, therefore, is actually much more iterative. Part of the purpose of political education is to foster a sense of hope that change is possible. As office manager Elsa Oliva Rocha explains:

> [We are always] making sure we talk about the next steps or, "What are we going to do about it?" Pam and Ricardo always make sure not to end a political education on the downside—like, "Oh my God. I can't believe I went through this," or, "I can't believe my school is so messed up. They didn't prepare me." . . . If they see people down, they just immediately call people and say, "Hey, you know what? We didn't close this right. We need to talk about it." Because it does bring people down if you don't talk about the next steps, like, "These are examples of resistance, or movements. And we can actually do something about it."

The North Campaign

THE NORTH HIGH SCHOOL SURVEY: CONNECTING THE PERSONAL TO THE POLITICAL

Through the political education process, parents decided to take the issues facing their children's lives into their own hands. In 2002, they developed a survey to see what students thought of their school, and they began distributing it to students who gathered along the 32nd Street strip around the corner from North during the school's lunch time. While the survey was intended to gather information regarding students' level of preparation for college and the culture and climate of North, it also functioned as a tool that helped them recruit student members to PJU. Up to this point the survey had been primarily parent led. Eva Bonilla, a former North student and PJU youth member, highlights her experience of taking the survey as a stepping stone to becoming involved in the work. Ricardo handed her a survey that asked if she wanted to be contacted with further information. She said no, but later joined a friend who wanted to go: "And then, afterwards, I was learning more about being involved in issues that affected me. And so I wanted to keep going for that reason." Juan Evangelista, a former youth member and youth organizer with PJU, says he was "very shy and terrible at first . . . I was shy going up to people and saying, 'Hey, do you feel you're being prepared to go on to college? Do you want to go to college?'" Through practice and political education trainings, he became more confident as he approached students during lunchtime or out on 32nd Street.

Eventually, the young people took complete ownership over the process by designing their own survey and, from that point forward, the organization was referred to as Padres y Jóvenes Unidos, with youth as an integral component. PJU members came to see the power of an intergenerational model with leadership from both students and parents; moreover, they understood that they were developing leadership among young people who would grow up to be the future fighters for equality. While PJU operates from the belief that adults have a responsibility to share what they know, the group also believes that youth participation is particularly powerful because young people tend to be less fearful than adults and more willing to challenge people in power.

For many of the youth, the survey was the first time they had ever contemplated the quality of their schools or recognized that there might be a problem. Former youth member Monica Acosta, who graduated from the University of Denver in 2009, notes that she had never been asked what she thought about her education or whether she thought it was good enough for her. However, after receiving the survey and attending a few meetings and political education trainings, she realized that there were issues in her school and community that she had never previously considered:

> They started talking to us about the Dream Act[10] and what the parents were doing with the school reform at North, and it just seemed like they were educating us, and so it was appealing to me because that was stuff that we never learned in school. That's the reason that I kept going back.

Based on their new insight, PJU youth decided to recreate the survey from a student's perspective and began distributing it themselves. In their minds, they were the ones inside of the school with access to the entire student population, and they could therefore design a survey that was in touch with student concerns.

The youth began distributing the survey in the 2002–2003 academic year during the lunch period. When they found that students were not taking the surveys seriously enough, they gained permission from their teachers and Principal Hobbs, the newly hired administrator who was sympathetic to PJU's work, to distribute the surveys during class time. They attempted to survey a representative sample of students by taking into account the makeup of the student body and the percentage of students in advanced placement courses, general-track classes, and English-language acquisition classes. Youth organizer Julieta Quiñonez, a short young woman with round cheeks, light brown eyes, and passionate oratory skills, was a youth member at the time. According to Julieta, the teachers were relatively supportive of the work they were doing because they looked to the PJU youth as leaders in the school. After collecting approximately seven hundred surveys, a core group of ten youth members worked throughout the summer at PJU's summer institute under the guidance of organizers Jenny Santos, Eduardo Gabrieloff, Amy Beres, and Pam Martinez to read, tally, and document the results of the survey.

Reflecting on the tallying, Julieta said she was most surprised by the testimonials in the surveys. She did not expect to read comments from so many students who compared North to a prison. Julieta remembered doing political education sessions in the mornings, and tallying and analyzing survey responses in the evenings. Political education trainings allowed her to move beyond anger and to deepen her analysis by zooming in on the situation at North:

> In the morning we would do PEs [political educations], and then in the afternoons we would be doing the report, so by the time we got to the afternoon we were already all mad and agitated . . . which was really good, because it gave us a framework for what we were seeing, and so we were able to connect it to what we had learned.

Through political education, PJU youth realized that the causes of the current situation at North included institutional racism and discriminatory immigration policy. In this way, the political education trainings enabled the youth to better understand the root cause of the problems, the impact of those problems, and the potential solutions.

THE NORTH REPORT: FINDING VOICE, USING MEDIA, AND FACING BACKLASH

> Over 90 percent of the students that we surveyed wanted to go to college. But over 50 percent of them felt that they weren't prepared to go to college . . . And we had a lot of people who specifically said that their teachers had told them that, "You're just good enough to be working flipping burgers at a McDonald's or a Burger King." And so when those specific examples came up, it was surprising, because these are the people that are supposed to be encouraging you to rise up to your potential, to try your hardest, yet they're the people telling you, "Yeah, really, no. This is all that you can do."
>
> —Youth organizer, Jenny Santos

The surveys yielded information that provided a concrete basis from which to discuss intuitions that students had about North all along. After sorting through the surveys, PJU youth began brainstorming how they wanted to write up their findings. Youth organizer Amy Beres and PJU researcher Eduardo Gabrieloff worked with the students to draft their ideas. PJU office manager Elsa Oliva Rocha, who was a youth organizer at the time, recalled the months-long iterative process that took place while Amy Beres worked with students to draft the report:

> I can remember . . . just going through the whole report with students and saying, "Is this what you mean?" and just going page per page, just looking at that, and then giving it to Amy . . . So it was just a back-and-forth process. But she was really involved in that piece, and rewriting it, and getting it to where it is now, and the way it was published.

Amy involved the students in conducting research on other schools around the country that worked with similar low-income, Latino, and immigrant students. They found that schools like El Puente Academy in Brooklyn were able to provide an academic environment that led to higher rates of achievement and student attendance than at North. She says:

> Any time you're doing this kind of school reform, we just heard over and over and over from the teachers and administrators, "Well, we can't do anything, because it's the students. It's the quality of students that we get . . . How do you expect us to perform miracles with these students?" And so, we felt like it was really important to bring in all the facts that we could that would show, here are schools around the

country with the exact same kinds of students, exact same population of students of color, low-income students, students who come in reading below grade level, who aren't scoring well on tests, who are at high risk of dropping out, and because of what they're doing in these schools, they're turning things around.

Through this research, students were able to connect their experiences with those of students nationwide. According to Luis Rodriguez, a youth member at the time, being involved with the report writing helped him realize how "messed up" things were at school, and motivated him to stay in school rather than drop out:

> I gotta say, because of Jóvenes, I actually ended up staying in school . . . it was actually boring to be at school. Not because they weren't teaching you something, because it was boring, just plain boring. So after Jóvenes, I kind of figured it's better to stay in school and actually try to change it, and do something about it, than just wandering off like a lot of students did.

In fact, Amy believes that PJU's model of engaging youth in participatory action research and training them through political education is transformational:

> I think it's very personally transformational for people who are involved in it, and so, that's something that I saw with the youth for sure, it's just this kind of transformation . . . really having a deeper understanding of this is who I am within this and I have certain power and skills and rights to really be able to make a difference within the system and out-side of it. And so to me, that's why Padres' work is so powerful—it's not only about the end goal of "we're going to reform this school, we're going to get a new principal, we're going to have more AP classes," but it's the process.

PJU organizers worked with students to come up with recommendations and solutions to the issues they found at North, which became the basis for the report they helped the students draft. In the 2003–2004 school year, they began pre-senting their findings to the district administration. They met first with the newly placed principal Darlene LeDoux and then with members of the school board to express concern over the quality of instruction at North. Luis remembers holding up an outdated textbook that fell apart at the seams during the meeting:

> And when I was presenting all this and telling them about the books and everything, I actually grabbed one book from the cover, and it almost slipped out of my hand, and I was able to grab it by the cover, but

it just ripped, like totally ripped . . . so I was like, all right . . . what more proof do you guys want?

PJU asked LeDoux on several different occasions to form a reform committee where parents and students could discuss the recommendations they had for the school. Pam and LaLo remember LeDoux consistently responding to their multiple queries by saying, "I'll take it under advisement." The challenge of making demands on the principal became an opportunity for leadership development for the youth in PJU. The youth had to learn how to overcome their fears of public speaking and to make demands on authority figures. In a meeting with Superintendent Jerry Wartgow, Julieta remembered how others viewed her after she spoke up on behalf of other students:

> I just remember, because I'm always getting teased about it . . . He said something like, "You're going to the wrong sources, I'm not the right guy." And I think I told him, "Well, aren't you the superintendent?" And now, they're always making fun of me, because they couldn't believe that—I was like 17 or 16?—that I was speaking out to a white man with power and who was much older than me.

After repeatedly hearing "I'll take it under advisement," the students became agitated. Because PJU felt they were not being heard by the school or the district officials, they employed a new tactic: that of building urgency around the issue by taking it to the media. Eva says, "We were getting nowhere. And so, at that point we decided that we needed to do something else to get the word out about what we had done and try to reach people in a different way." The students sponsored a community night to explain their findings to parents and anyone who wanted to come. They then held a press conference to publicize the report.

Several school staff did not like the media attention. As tension with some of the staff members mounted, youth recounted several incidents of harassment and remembered feeling alienated from teachers with whom they had once been close. Luis said many of his teachers felt betrayed for having let the youth administer the survey in the first place. Many students were worried about being graded differently and not receiving letters of recommendation for college because of their involvement in writing the North High Report. According to LaLo, PJU responded by having students make copies of all their assignments in case any teacher tried to retaliate by changing students' grades. Students also had cell phones to contact PJU if they felt harassed while at school. LaLo himself felt pressured by some teachers and students:

> I would be put on the spot with the teachers. They would put me in front of class and explain to the class what we were doing. I would just

do it, and even though the teacher was against me, teachers that—
sometimes I had admired them . . . but then they started putting me on
the spot and telling me I was doing something wrong, but I really knew
what I was doing was right. So I would go and I would do it, and it was
a good experience because I was never outspoken or any anything like
that. I was always in the shadows over here, doing my own thing.

The backlash many youth experienced was a double burden to carry as they
attempted to address their school's problems and think about applying for college at the same time; unfortunately, the backlash would continue against some
of their siblings in future years. However, the youth were not working alone at
this point. Parent member Marty Roberts circulated a petition at Rosa Linda's
restaurant that was signed by over six hundred community members demanding
a reform committee. The media pressure induced by the youth action, in conjunction with the parent and community action, led LeDoux to finally concede
and establish a reform committee.

REFORM COMMITTEE: STRUGGLING FOR POWER, NOT JUST VOICE

At this point, it had been two years since PJU parents began distributing the
survey along 32nd Street. Although the youth had developed as leaders—a
success in and of itself—winning the reform committee was a huge accomplishment. It also signified that PJU had proven itself as a major contender
in school reform and had gained representation at the decision-making
table. Melissa Underwood-Verdeal was a North teacher at the time of the
report's release who would later become vice president of the Denver Classroom Teachers Association (DCTA), the teachers union. She talks about
the transition from the original teacher/administrator-led reform process to
a more inclusive reform committee amid what was a divisive environment
at North:

> So we got a group of teachers together, and we came up with a reform
> committee to look at things like scheduling and course offerings and
> how do we deal with things like our attendance rate and our achieve-
> ment . . . I think maybe Padres felt like we were trying to work around
> them when that was certainly never my intention . . . Eventually the two
> groups came together and expanded, and so we created the North High
> Reform Committee, which was where the teacher contingencies and
> the Padre contingency [came together] . . . It started out huge. In the
> first meeting, there was nowhere to sit. There were a hundred people in

our library, and of course it dwindled down, and we had a pretty good core of people who were working on this for a couple of years.

While Melissa describes the transition to those meetings as being relatively smooth, PJU explains it otherwise. PJU felt LeDoux only wanted certain people to be official members of the committee in order to keep attendance consistent and to ensure adherence to certain rules and responsibilities. PJU viewed these restrictions as one more way to shut the community out of the school reform process. In order for the reforms to reflect the concerns of the community, PJU insisted that the meetings remain open, arguing that the committee should be comprised of community members, students, administrators, teachers, and parents working *together* to reform the school. The fight for equal representation took place during the first meeting. According to LaLo, a North student at the time, even the way the room was organized situated the principal and her allies at the head of the table, communicating their attempt to retain authority over the process.

To ensure that their voices were heard in the first meeting, PJU organized members and staff to pack the meeting. LeDoux initially required that people write their questions on a piece of paper that would then be passed to the administration for an answer or comment. Because this approach would have enabled LeDoux to control the flow and the agenda of the meeting, PJU objected, demanding that everyone have an equal voice and equal decision-making power at the table. Throughout this stand-off, PJU held their ground because they believed the North Report had what the administration did not; namely, the voices of over seven hundred youth saying that North was not preparing them for college. Juan, a North student at the time, describes this sense of power:

> It was three hours of just putting down the guidelines of how we wanted those reform committee meetings to go. They saw towards the third hour that we were not budging at all. So, I remember the principal and her assistant at the time stepped aside in a caucus, and then the assistant came and said, "Oh, guys, I'm sorry. This was the form for another meeting." [Laughter] And Ricardo looks at me and grins—we had won. So, after that it was open to pretty much everybody who wanted to be involved in it.

For the next two years, PJU staff and members worked in collaboration with the administration and some teachers at North High School with the purpose of improving the learning conditions and opportunities for all students at North, particularly Latino youth. Early in the collaboration, a group of members from the reform committee, including PJU youth, staff, teachers, and administrators,

attended a conference convened by the Education Trust, a nonprofit organization dedicated to closing the "achievement gap." The Education Trust agreed to
work with North High School because its mission so closely aligned with the
reform committee efforts and, more importantly, because of the high quality of
the North Report that the PJU youth members had recently produced. As LaLo
Montoya recalls:

> Juan and I met Kati Haycock [of Education Trust]. She's the president.
> We gave her our report and she loved it. They typically reform whole
> districts, but they loved the report, and they wanted to work with just
> North, which is a big win.

Melissa Underwood-Verdeal concurred that the partnership engendered
much enthusiasm because "They [Education Trust] were talking about all the
things that we were trying to work on, the achievement gap, motivating our kids,
getting our scores up, no more excuses, how to get those kids into the higher
level classes and still give them all of those things."

After raising approximately $600,000 through PJU's grant writing and district
funds, the reform committee was able to bring Education Trust to Northwest
Denver to work on teacher training in North High School. Through what was
described by both PJU and teachers as a productive collaboration, Education
Trust evaluated teachers' curricula to ensure that they were teaching the appropriate grade-level standards and provided professional development to help
teachers make their curricula more rigorous. Melissa describes the energy that
the collaboration with Education Trust brought to North High School:

> The Ed Trust brought people out to work with the teachers, and the
> momentum was catching, teachers were catching the bug . . . There
> were initial grumblings, especially from veteran teachers. We've had
> lots of people coming in and out of our classrooms over the years telling
> us how to do things, and what was great about the Trust, they weren't
> telling us how to do things. They were just telling us here's a way to help
> you do what you do and really evaluate it at the level that the kids
> needed. So it was awesome.

Despite this partnership, after two years of reform committee meetings PJU
felt that the momentum for change was grinding to a halt. From its perspective,
improvements were too incremental, teachers were not on board, and systemic
change was not happening at the school-wide level. Ultimately, PJU concluded
that this process would never lead to large-scale culture change where children
of all racial and ethnic backgrounds were valued and respected. The situation

at North was well known around the district, and was closely watched by Superintendent Michael Bennet, who says, "I think it was clear to Padres that it [the reform] was stalling out. I think there was some question about whether there was enough universal commitment by the staff to do the work. It was very clear that there were issues far greater than the shared work on the reform that was creating huge issues for the adults in the building."

For many PJU members and staff, the division between PJU and the teachers/administrators at North was deep-seated and stemmed from a fundamental disagreement about the root cause of the problem. LaLo sensed that many teachers, some of whom had been at North for twenty years, were reluctant to accept the reality of North, which he defined as failing youth through low teacher expectations. While he acknowledged that there were enthusiastic and committed teachers at the school, in his experience, teachers would hold up the five or ten "stars of North" as proof that they were doing well and that the other students who were academically failing simply did not want to learn. Given this division of understanding and way of seeing the school, it is not surprising that some teachers were reluctant to push reform especially since they felt they were improving the school at a proper and realistic pace. PJU felt the reform was slow and plodding, with teachers only making small tweaks when PJU put forth proposals at the meetings.

Because the meetings began to feel unproductive, PJU youth gradually stopped going. Pam explains:

> It was a mockery ... people would do research for different programs and they'd come from Padres and Jóvenes or allies and they'd come back and report, and teachers would be sitting there snickering, laughing, going "Oh, they don't know what they're talking about" ... And our students would hear announcements on the intercom of the teachers' reform committee meeting, so she was doing dual stuff with the teachers ... you add all those things together and you're like, "What is the point?"

Although Ricardo continued to attend the reform meetings, the remaining PJU members began discussing alternative options, including the redesign of North High School. By state law, redesigning North High School would require that all current teachers reapply for their jobs and would enable the district administration to revise the school's curriculum to be college preparatory for all students. Juan describes why the redesign of North was the clear solution:

> We had always seen that in North High School, the teachers always had their special chosen few, and we didn't want that anymore. We wanted everybody to have the same education. We wanted everybody, if they

wanted, to go to advanced placement classes, to be enrolled in them . . . we wanted the whole school to be redesigned.

By calling for redesign, PJU declared that it would no longer allow North to be a second-rate high school; instead, members were demanding high-quality education for all students. Ultimately, the call for redesign reinforced the divide between North teachers and the Denver Classroom Teachers Association on the one hand, and PJU and its allies on the other, creating what would be a contentious relationship for the remainder of the campaign and beyond. Kim Ursetta, DCTA president, describes the push for redesign this way: "There's ways that you can bring people along and have everyone working together, or you can throw the bomb, and let it explode, and I think that they [PJU] chose to throw the grenade."

ORGANIZING FOR REDESIGN: BUILDING A COALITION AND A PARTNERSHIP

Although redesign may have been the obvious solution for PJU and its community supporters, the Denver Classroom Teachers Association and the vast majority of teachers at North felt that the call for redesign was a rash decision. Many felt that all of the blame was being placed on the teachers, making them the scapegoat for a larger community problem. Their jobs were on the line, and as DCTA president Kim Ursetta states, teachers felt they were making real progress amid what they saw as a collaborative relationship:

> I just know from what I would read in the newspapers that [Padres] claimed that things weren't fast enough. But like I said, how much movement do you need to see in a year when you have a school that is showing greater gains than almost any other high school in the city, when is enough enough? So, it's just what's realistic? Fifteen percent gains in one year on a standardized test, is that really reasonable? Of course you want to say yes, it is, and all of our kids will jump 20 percent, but is it realistic? And does it need to happen? Of course, but it's not going to happen overnight.

However, Superintendent Michael Bennet acknowledges that the failure of education was a system-wide problem:

> The inevitable complaint was, why do you blame the teachers? That is a huge problem in the conversation because it truly is not about blaming the teachers. I have worked in all these other jobs and professions and

I truly have never seen people work harder than the people that work in DPS, no question . . . I would say that the failure is too big for anybody to take the blame except for Denver, since this is Denver's biggest public good; it's us.

Whether North's failures were the result of an entire system's failure or the result of an entrenched teacher culture resistant to reform—or other factors as well—PJU felt that change was not happening fast enough and that North students could not wait any longer. In the end, the division between PJU and the teachers union was solidified, with both groups convinced that they were right.

Meanwhile, many community members who had built relationships with PJU over the years stepped forward to place their support behind the idea of redesign. This support, which coalesced as a broad-based group of community stakeholders, came to be known as the Coalition to Save North and included several city council members, Northwest Denver business owners, and many other long-standing PJU members and supporters. City council member Judy Montero explains her decision to join the call for redesign:

Instinctively, I just knew. Sometimes, in your life, haven't things just been so clear? Like you know that the sun's going to go down tonight, and it's going to come up tomorrow, it's so crystal clear that you need to make a decision and that's it. You make it regardless of how much pain it causes you, your family, your community, you just feel so strongly that it's the right thing to do. So that's all I can say. I mean because if I were to try to play it safe, I'd still be playing it safe. But my hope is that in the reform-redesign effort that my daughter can go there. And today, she can't, but maybe she's closer to being able to do that.

In a time that PJU needed a broad-based front that could help decide how to move forward in a stagnant situation, the organization pulled together an alliance of folks who they felt would understand the long struggle of Northwest Denver's Chicano/Mexicano community and North High School: people like Rosa Linda and Dolores, Marty Roberts, North teacher Susana De Leon, school board member Lucia Guzman, and politicians with ties to North like Judy Montero and Rick Garcia. Nita Gonzales, daughter of poet and Chicano rights leader, Rodolfo "Corky" Gonzales,[11] also participated in the campaign to improve North. For her, the experience was part of a longer struggle that she and others had been involved with for at least twenty years, since the founding of her Chicano/Mexicano freedom school, Escuela Tlatelolco, which had a mission of promoting and expanding Chicano pride.

Judy Montero explains that part of her relationship with PJU comes from a shared history and vision for the future of North specifically, and the Latino community generally:

> I would say that [my relationship with Pam and Ricardo is] very genuine, because I think that we all have experienced the same kind of marginalization or disenfranchisement, but it's when you come from the same neighborhood that you grew up in and work in, it's just a part of you and maybe that's the thread that keeps everybody going because some people just get it. And they just know each other and there's that connection. The other thing about Denver is that there's only one or two degrees of separation, and two is stretching it, because everybody's related to somebody, then it's just an amazing community that is very interwoven.

Students had walked out of Denver schools in the late 1960s in protest over the conditions for Latino students; it is this legacy on which the alliance was built. Though the political ideologies of the various allies differed, there is no doubt that race was an underpinning factor in their coming together. For PJU, race and class are at the heart of the matter at North and all over the country, as Pam explains:

> We came to the conclusion that in its heart and soul, it's what goes on in the classroom. And in it's heart and soul, it's do you believe in the intel-lectual capacity of all youth to be critical thinkers, to be high-level learners? The overwhelming majority can do it. It's just they're barred from it. We call it "educational apartheid." It's a system rooted in race and class. You can go to any inner-city high school and usually you'll know what class you're in by the color of the complexion of the kids.

The Coalition to Save North began to meet regularly to plot its strategy. Although the meetings were not explicitly closed, PJU wanted them to be a place where community members and allies who identified with the larger struggle surrounding the Chicano and Civil Rights movements could decide together what next steps they would take. Julie Gonzales, a youth organizer at the time, describes the power of the predominately Latino Coalition to keep certain people out, including Representative Jerry Frangas, who supported the Denver Classroom Teachers Association:

> Representative Jerry Frangas . . . he's got really good politics, but he's also really tight with labor, and he came in at one meeting, and it was

really weird because he had not been invited . . . It became very, very clear that he had been sent from the Denver Classroom Teachers Association. So Pam said, "I'm sorry, but you have to leave," and I just remember thinking, "Wow. He's a representative. He's a state representative, so he's even a different level of power [in our campaign] in terms of this whole hierarchy of city council and state."

Although some wanted the Coalition to consider pushing for North to become a charter school or even open a private school of its own, in the end the Coalition felt it was essential to keep North open as a traditional public school. Members were worried about contributing to the fast-moving trend toward privatization, which they feared would lead to the demise of public education. Ricardo and other PJU members saw the threat to public education as an intentional act that is meant to undermine the political power of marginalized people in this society, thereby threatening our democracy. For those reasons, PJU demanded North be redesigned as a premier public institution with a college preparatory curriculum for *all* kids, particularly for Latino youth.

Solidifying their vision for the redesign of North required many consensus-building meetings with the members of the Coalition to Save North, including fifteen students from the school itself. The youth were involved in a PJU Summer Institute at the time. Political education sessions at the institute were designed to help the young people place the call for redesign into historical context. Julie Gonzales explains:

All of these big Chicano community leaders were redesigning North . . . and Julieta and Juan would go to those meetings and raise the concerns that the Jóvenes brought. That's important to remember because it wasn't as if this group of Chicano leaders were making these plans. It was very much informed by the youth, and they would sit and stare and listen to Julieta . . . because it was what the students were saying.

In order to achieve their demands, PJU and the Coalition knew that they would need the support of Superintendent Michael Bennet, who, in conjunction with the school board, ultimately had the power to call for redesign. Bennet, a lawyer by training, came to be superintendent from his role as the mayor's chief of staff. He had never before worked in education, but from the beginning he impressed PJU leaders with his sense of the issues plaguing the system and his concrete plans to address them. Yet the politics of education reform were complicated, as Bennet would learn with the closing of Manual High School.

Manual High School, the first school in the area that had been open to black and Chicano students, was low performing and had experienced declining enrollment for several years. As such, Bennet and the school board made the decision to close the school. However, because they did not systematically seek out community input before making the decision, Bennet suffered a great deal of backlash from black community leaders, including being labeled a new version of the Ku Klux Klan. In order to avoid similar censure, Bennet proceeded carefully, taking steps to ensure that there was a formal process of eliciting input from PJU and the broader community. In that way, PJU was able to put the possibility of redesign on the table. As Bennet explains:

> Padres ultimately was the organizing force that called for the redesign of North . . . It would not have happened without them. It was critical that they organized the city council folks over there, they organized the other community folks over there to say, "This has to change, this can't stay the same."

The result was a partnership between Bennet and PJU that proved to be mutually beneficial and ultimately resulted in a call for redesign.

In July of 2006, PJU held a community meeting in its basement that was attended by over two hundred community members, teachers, and students. Bennet was asked to come so that he could hear different community members voice their opinions about what should happen at North. Each group of stakeholders got a chance to be heard, while PJU and the Coalition to Save North presented their demands for change. After considering the data and various perspectives, Bennet felt that his views more closely aligned with PJU's, marking a key turning point in the decision to redesign North High School. Still, PJU had more work to do to broaden the base of support for redesign.

"MY HIGH SCHOOL, MY PARK, MY NEIGHBORHOOD": ALLIANCES IN THE DEMAND FOR REDESIGN

The organizing work of the Coalition to Save North in the summer of 2006 culminated in a press conference at Viking Park, named for the North High mascot. Long time PJU parent member Marty Roberts describes the event as drawing key politicians from the north side who either "graduated from North High or were involved in it." PJU and their supporters called the press conference to publicly demand the redesign of North. They made five specific demands:

1. North High School will not be closed.
2. North will become a premier high school, a reflection of its global citizens, where all students are prepared to attend college and succeed.

3. North will have educational equity, i.e. students will have access to Advanced Placement and accelerated classes.
4. Superintendent Bennet will immediately commit district resources and expertise necessary to make North a premier high school.
5. In order to achieve all of the above, there will be a full redesign of North High School by the district.

PJU reached into its many networks and close relationships to mobilize its supporters to Viking Park. Ricardo explains that many of the long-term PJU members could not participate all the time, but could be called on at specific times like this. Because PJU has built long-standing relationships based on common struggles, mobilizations like Viking Park were often successful. The situation at North was also deeply personal for community members. Judy Montero had participated in actions for education reform before, but this one moved her the most:

> It was just that it was *my* high school, and it was *my* park, and it was *my* neighborhood, and some of the teachers there were teachers that I actually had. So it was my, my, my.

However, this was not a day the Coalition members had to themselves; teachers also showed up. According to Juan:

> We met at Viking Park, and people knew about it, because like I told you, we had the teachers who were working on reform . . . they came and counter-protested us. We were giving our press conference, and they were on the other side with their hard hats. Later on I heard that expression means that they're ready to fight.

While PJU students had experienced backlash in the school, this was the first organized teacher action outside of the school building. Former North teacher, Missy Underwood-Verdeal, regarded the press conference as a publicity stunt, a way for certain people to get in the paper. She says many teachers felt "blindsided" by the press conference and so that is why they mobilized. According to her, the teachers "played back just a little," passing out brochures that showed improvement in state standardized test scores.

PJU worried that if students spoke, teachers might retaliate against them in class. So Julieta called on Eva Bonilla to speak:

> Julieta called me to ask me if I would be willing to speak. And a large reason why I decided to do it and why Julieta asked me was because we didn't think it was a good idea for any current student to speak at the

rally, because of what we had experienced when we had the previous press conference, and then had to go back into the school. So we thought it'd be better if they were mad at me than for another student to have to deal with what we went through.

BUILDING YOUTH AND PARENT LEADERSHIP FOR REDESIGN

Despite their strategy to protect the youth, following Viking Park, Julieta Quiño-nez, who had come up through the organization first as a youth member and then hired as an organizer, saw the young people with whom she worked at North going through a lot of the same backlash she experienced after PJU's North High Report was released. Julieta emphasizes the importance of political education in helping young people understand the purpose of redesign and strengthen their resolve in the face of threats. She says her students "got a lot of heat" from teachers, and that it was training them through political education that bolstered their commitment to the work. Julieta's deep understanding was one of the advantages of this "grow your own" model of developing organizers, in which Jóvenes graduate and become youth organizers in PJU. Speaking about the three former youth members turned organizers—Juan, Julieta, and LaLo—Julie Gonzales says:

> They came out of the work, and Pam and Ricardo . . . made that invest-ment and said that we're not going to hire someone out of college to go lead the youth work. No, we're saying we believe in the power of youth. We're gonna hire these youth to be organizers and we're gonna train them, and they've done an excellent job in doing that. All three of them are fierce, fierce organizers, and they get respect from the rest of the social justice community here in Denver when they go and make pre-sentations.

Fierce was not an identity Julieta would have claimed when she started with the organization as a youth member. At the time, she did not have very strong knowledge of or opinions about gender, ethnicity, and leadership; she gives credit to the political education training and the support and encouragement of PJU staff for her personal transformation. The confidence and expectations PJU staff had in the youth members were particularly important for young people like Julieta to strengthen their own beliefs in themselves:

> It's just like I've never really had anyone tell me you're going to go to college, or you're a student, you're a leader. And just learning those

skills and standing up and presenting and seeing others, like Monica and like Eva do the same things, it just made me want to come back because I had never really gotten that opportunity anywhere.

Political education played a key role in challenging gender roles and her sense of self-worth:

I think a lot of it has come from this organization because I wouldn't have learned the way patriarchy works out, or how the oppression of women worked out. And I think eventually I would have just gotten married and not even went off to college. So I think a lot of it, I do owe it to what I've learned here.

Through the opportunities for leadership with the North campaign, Julieta came to realize her personal power. As described before, the formerly shy young woman challenged district Superintendent Wartgow, an older and powerful white man. According to Julieta, her life trajectory would have been far different without her experience with PJU. As an organizer, she began to work with other youth, providing them with political education and opportunities for leadership, all of which strengthened the North campaign.

Although the Viking Park event had been a great success, PJU knew there were still obstacles to face. Juan reported one particularly memorable incident that occurred the day the students formally presented their proposal for redesign to the school board:

We had teachers in the back of the room, and they were actually booing the students for demanding all of these things. It was actually pretty exciting. You had grown women and men booing on kids for demanding a better education. So, it was pretty intense.

The summer organizing work, including the Coalition to Save North, had also been an opportunity to re-engage parents in the work. One of the ways in which parents supported the youth was in drafting a letter of support and presenting the letter to Superintendent Michael Bennet in a meeting. Juan recalls, "The parents went to Michael Bennet. And it was pretty awesome, because that was one of the first times that the meeting was in Spanish, so Michael Bennet and Happy Hanes [a community partnerships administrator] had to wear the translation devices." Juan breaks into a smile, laughing at the flip in power relations.

Parents typically have to adjust in order to participate in school matters; this time the district's highest-ranking school official had to adjust to them. PJU uses this example to show that people have to approach authority with confidence and as equals. Ricardo believes that people in authority try to use fear, including the fear of embarrassment, to demobilize people. PJU knows that even when acting without fear people might still embarrass themselves; however, people can learn from that experience. At the end of the meeting, parents told the officials they would no longer wait, that they expected a decision on redesign before the semester was out. This interchange demonstrated the superintendent's commitment to engage this community and spoke to the importance of his role in the redesign. He also knew that PJU could help him think of ways to get community input, and thus was born the 19 Nights of North.

"COLLEGE PREP FOR ALL": YOUTH, PARENTS, AND COMMUNITY FRAME A PUBLIC CASE FOR REDESIGN

The "19 Nights of North" was a series of community meetings held in the northwest quadrant at various elementary and middle schools that fed into North High. According to Bennet it was symbolically important that the meetings were held at neutral venues. "Instead of having them in the usual sort of Padres venue or Northwest Mommies venue,[12] we would have them in the schools in the hope that it was sort of neutral ground."

PJU utilized those meetings to get their main message across—they wanted College Prep for All. For PJU, the phrase "College Prep for All" was a proxy for racial equity and was the kind of framing that could get broad support from the public. According to Julie, this framing was a major part of the work of the meetings:

> We had a joke running around with the organizers . . . it would be like, what's your name? College prep for all. How old are you? College prep for all. What's your favorite—college prep for all. No matter what, that was our message, and, man, we hit them over the head with it. By the end of it, that facilitator, the woman, she knew us, and she'd be [whispering] okay, college prep, I get it!

Using this framing, PJU was able to convey its values in a consistent and simple manner. The district hired an artist to facilitate and record the sentiments at those meetings. For each meeting the artist created a mural-like poster that reflected the discussion in the meeting. Every single one of those drawings has some reference to College Prep for All. Shortly after, Bennet adopted PJU's frame and placed it at the center of his emerging redesign plan.

The culminating community meeting was held at North High School. PJU presented a wealth of evidence that revealed the abysmal state of academics at the school. The group almost expected Bennet to call for redesign that night.

He did not. In fact, Bennet waited several weeks. Finally, just before winter break, word got out that Bennet was going to announce the redesign of North High School. The teachers had planned a protest at the school and PJU made plans to protect its youth from retaliation even as it prepared to celebrate. But Mother Nature had other plans: a major snowstorm hit, leading to school closures across the city. Bennet had to send word about redesign through an e-mail. The blizzard story was told by all participants; however, the meaning each side made about the blizzard was very different. For the teachers it was "getting fired over e-mail" which felt like "salt in the wound." For PJU, it was the dramatic marking of a victory.

The blizzard provides an endpoint to a multiyear campaign that saw upheaval and the start of healing for a school, personal transformation and the loss of personal relationships, a new sense of belonging and purpose for a group of young people, and bitterness and hurt for a group of teachers. PJU, however, focuses on the bigger picture as the struggle continues. According to Ricardo, "It is that political understanding that gives you the opportunity to sustain and build on the campaign, so it's not just about redesigning North High School."

THE FUTURE OF NORTH

> Now the biggest challenge is sort of like the World Series. The fight is getting there, but the biggest challenge is winning it . . . If you didn't win the World Series, does it matter that you are the National Pennant Winner? So, for Padres, if North High never becomes a great school, was it worth it? Did they do anything? If it doesn't take care of its goal, if this district doesn't reform, this is our last chance. Many of us are saying, "This is Denver's last chance to reform its public school system."
> —Reverend Lucia Guzman

This is where the North Campaign ends; however, because "the struggle continues," it is not where the story of North, its students, or the work of PJU ends. In February 2007, the teachers at North reapplied for their jobs and half were retained. And although North, now known as the Denver North Institute of World Learning, is not yet the high school its reformers aspire it to be, the accomplishments of the North campaign are many. Its impact can be seen at the district level as the district promoted the College Prep for All framework used by PJU during the 19 Nights of North for all its high schools. Youth involved in the campaign experienced personal transformation and developed leadership skills that allowed them to push for power and a place at the table to reform their school. PJU garnered a reputation from its work at North that has allowed it to approach broader, systemic campaigns such as rewriting the district's discipline code and working toward in-state tuition for undocumented students.

The Future of Education Organizing at PJU: Holding the Work in Tension

PJU faces a number of challenges as it tries to advance the struggle for educational justice. Many of these challenges relate to the tensions PJU experiences as it tries to balance its ever-expanding role in education reform with its focus on depth versus breadth. As Ricardo says, "breadth" does not lead to sustained systemic change; rather, it is the focus on depth and developing leaders that allows for true change:

> It's not just that you want to cover more area. It's that you really want to go in depth into an area. That's what gives you that sustained movements. Breadth doesn't do that. With breadth you can cover a lot of territory, but the more ground you cover, the less likely you're going to be able to develop leadership unless you have a whole bunch of people doing it.

NORTH HIGH SCHOOL REFORM VERSUS DISTRICT AND STATEWIDE REFORM

The point of the North High School campaign was not solely the redesign of North High School. Part of the work was about empowering students and community members to take ownership in the educational process and to struggle for the ability to act in meaningful ways with regard to their own lives. Another part was to begin dismantling the conditions that shackle brown children in Denver. Through the North campaign, PJU realized that while improving conditions at North was important in its own right, it was ultimately insufficient to address the broader systemic issues affecting Latino children. There are district issues like the discipline policy and statewide issues like in-state tuition for undocumented students that must be addressed. In addition PJU has come to understand the importance of working with the elementary and middle schools that feed into the high school.

In those ways, the particular outcomes at North are less pressing. Nevertheless, North *does* matter. The outcomes at North matter for the students who organized and for their sisters and brothers and cousins. All the students at North deserve a chance to become their full selves. North is also important symbolically. It is the principal high school of Northwest Denver. Generations of Chicano and Mexicano students have gone through North. As such, PJU must hold this tension—on the one hand, recognizing North is only one mechanism through which power differentials and structures need to be challenged, while at the same time caring deeply about the people inside and the institution itself.

Meanwhile, PJU staff members have limited time and resources. The organizers have to decide when to increase intensity in their local work at North or in their statewide work, even as both have to continue. For PJU members, the local work feels much more urgent, relevant, and personal; yet the statewide work may be just as or more important.

There are times, though, when the tension is temporarily resolved, when the connection between the local and the statewide becomes clear. North helped PJU understand that fighting for College Prep For All was the right vision, but that if college is inaccessible to undocumented students, then much of the work is lost. So political education and recognizing the interconnectedness of the local and statewide can help ease the tension, but it is a constant balancing act. Overall, historical movements are the inspiration for political education trainings; in turn, political education helps PJU members connect their work to statewide and nationwide issues and structures that impact educational issues at the local level.

ORGANIZERS VERSUS SCHOOL REFORMERS

PJU's work to reform North High School also lies in tension with their role as outside agitators. As PJU becomes more committed to trying to make sure the day-to-day work is being done, the group runs the risk of losing the outside perspective that served them so well in the original campaign. PJU staff members face the question: are they school reformers or organizers? PJU wants to work closely with the school to design structures and curricula that reflect their vision for education. In order to help develop those rubrics, PJU travels to schools that have been successful in raising test scores with Latino students. This kind of research and education work not only takes time that might be spent developing more traditional organizing processes, but in some ways positions the organization as insiders rather than representatives of the wider community. PJU is trying to build the capacity of students and community members to monitor implementation of reform at North, which is important organizing work itself. In PJU's view, the original "win" should be a catalyst to provide opportunities for community members to step into and demonstrate their power. However, this work takes time and energy, and PJU has learned that foundations want to fund campaigns and wins, not the long-term work to implement change.

EXPANSION VERSUS POLITICAL EDUCATION

Since its inception in 1989, PJU has earned many wins that have enabled them to secure more funding, hire more staff, and thus expand their efforts to include multiprong campaigns that extend beyond individual schools into district, state, and nationwide levels. One of the most important components of PJU's strategic approach that has enabled the organization to achieve these wins and expand its work is the political education in which the staff and members of PJU have engaged. Political education helps members see the problem, the impact, and the solutions beyond their immediate experience. Ultimately, political education helps PJU to be more systemic in its work, which attracts funders. Funds were used initially to hire full-time staff and later to hire more organizers and administrative staff. This expansion in personnel allowed PJU to organize more people and develop more campaigns, which in turn led to increased funding.

With additional funding PJU hired three former Service Employees International Union organizers in the year after winning the redesign of North. The organizers brought with them a wealth of experience and organizing strategies that pushed the PJU staff to focus more explicitly on base building and to escalate their efforts toward more strategic regional and national work. While PJU recognizes that political education has been instrumental to their organizing success, the staff has more recently focused on building other organizing skills (e.g., conducting house visits and one-on-one meetings) so that they can build their base and apply their political education knowledge to a broader constituency of people. While this shift has enabled PJU to expand their important work and to be effective at various sites, their focus on political education has diminished because time spent learning how to conduct house meetings is time away from political education trainings—a point not taken lightly by the staff. In the end, political education and its connection to the struggle are still at the heart of PJU; yet it remains in tension with skill building that will allow this knowledge to be applied more broadly, helping to make the movement more sustainable.

WORKING WITH TEACHERS RESISTANT TO REFORM

As PJU moves forward with its school reform work, the group continues to struggle with how to work with the DCTA and other teachers within the district. Moreover, the organization knows that, in the end, teachers are the people who have to carry out its reforms in the classroom. PJU had concerns that a large contingency of teachers were not serving students at North; yet several teachers who were not rehired there now work at other schools in Denver. How will these teachers be supported and developed at their new schools, and how will PJU collaborate with them in the future? The organization must hold in tension the fact that many teachers were alienated by the reapplication process, which they essentially viewed as a firing process. This may lead to collateral damage in the larger struggle to repair a broken system. Although there is a need to reform teacher practices at the classroom level, the move to fire teachers who ultimately will teach elsewhere must be analyzed in the broader context of district-wide reform, particularly as PJU expands its work in other schools.

PJU is aware of the hard work many teachers put in every day; but it is also aware that many teachers, though perhaps well intentioned, are trained in ways that do not see communities of color as communities with assets. To address this issue, they have has sent staff members to talk to pre-service teachers at the University of Denver, creating a dialogue that many of the teachers in training found useful. PJU also knows of many teachers of color in the community who have started their own charter schools as a result of being disgruntled with the district. The organization wrestles with the issue of whether to support the high-performing charters it has studied while at the same time trying to reform traditional public schools. PJU members are especially cautious because they believe that charters cannot "replace the right to a quality education."

PJU believes it has a new opportunity to create alliances with groups of teachers who believe in their reforms. The staff, however, is grappling with how to support these teachers who may suffer because of their alliances with the organization. After all, PJU did have teacher allies who were involved in the redesign of North High School until they felt it professionally risky to continue. Yet PJU is hopeful that new teacher allies will be able to work with the more resistant ones, thereby garnering additional support for its reform efforts.

YOUTH POWER VERSUS THE EMOTIONAL TOLL PLACED ON YOUTH

Almost all of the youth organizers who were youth members at the time of the survey release talk about the challenges they faced inside school during the reform campaign, suggesting that organizing work can oftentimes be stressful for youth who are on the frontlines of education reform. They also report the emotional toll taken as a result of severed relationships with once trusted teachers and administrators. The youth became targets because they were easily accessible to teachers who were opponents of the reform efforts. These problems were further exacerbated when the broken student-teacher relationships led to disagreements with fellow students. This is a tension that seems inevitable; as young people become more empowered, those who already have power may become threatened and attack.

All of the students deeply involved in the North campaign say that they would do the work again because it was so important and personally transformational;

however, they also have the scars to show from the struggle and remember the time with a hint of loss. Nevertheless, the youth seemed to persist in a hopeful way because they knew and understood what they were fighting for; and this purpose was gained through political education. Without a sense of the past and a positive view of the future, it seems less likely that the youth would have persevered. Further, although the backlash from teachers was severe, young people had the vital support of PJU staff, adult members, and parents. Through this kind of intergenerational organizing, youth can realize that they are a part of a larger struggle that is backed by determination and hope.

One can always say that a group like PJU could have tried harder to be collaborative during such a campaign. Yet PJU did try hard to engage teachers, the principal of North, and the superintendent about the findings in their report. They also tried to enter the reform efforts and bring in the assistance of Education Trust. In the end, however, this became a power struggle and as Frederick Douglass famously said, "power concedes nothing without demand." As PJU demanded a quality education at North, they found themselves in a struggle with the teachers and administrators with few concessions being made. The group believed they had to turn to media pressure to get the process moving in the school. From PJU's perspective, the teachers were ready to wait it out; yet for the students and parents who were most affected by the poor quality of their education, it was a matter of urgency. Conflict was not the group's first strategic choice, but in the end it became a necessary direction to take.

UNDERSTANDING PJU

> We face life together in sorrow,
> anger, joy, faith and wishful
> thoughts.
> I shed the tears of anguish
> as I see my children disappear
> behind the shroud of mediocrity,
> never to look back to remember me.
> I am Joaquín.
> I must fight
> and win this struggle
> for my sons, and they
> must know from me
> who I am.
>
> —Corky Gonzales[13]

The North story witnessed elements of political education, backlash, power, alliances, and framing, but ultimately it is a story about the long Chicano struggle for liberation and the broader struggle of people for human rights. Political education is particularly salient because it allows young people and adults to connect with this struggle in ways that illuminate their current situation. This kind of education is fundamentally different than what occurs in typical civics or social studies courses in school because the intention is to connect knowledge to young people's lives and inspire action. In PJU, young people (and parents as well) do not simply learn about how a bill becomes a law in order to become informed citizens; rather, they actually work to make bills, like college access for undocumented students, become law. Similarly, a student might read about a social movement in a history class; however, with political education, students recognize the social movement as a part of their history and their current struggle.

The power struggle over school reform is not a new story either. Many generations of Chicanos have fought for access to quality education because it is so central to the overall struggle. Having a say in school means having a say in both economic and political outcomes for the future. As Ricardo points out, students who are pushed out of school are more likely to end up in jail, and those in jail are less likely to find jobs and more likely to have their voting rights revoked. Viewed this way, the struggle for power at North is much bigger than simply gaining a student voice on a school committee. People in the Civil Rights and Chicano movements sought to both obtain rights and wrest control of their lives. The youth of PJU want a good education at North, but they want and need to have a say in what a good education will be.

The people that PJU called on who helped make Viking Park a reality were allies who understood their struggle. This is not to say that PJU does not have other kinds of allies. However, in order to anchor the campaign firmly in the community's interests and values, PJU felt it should turn to its roots and to its allies who understood that brown people were being systematically underserved. PJU might reach out to different kinds of allies to do some of its state-level work, for instance, but the North Campaign was about Northwest Denver, and their allies understood that this struggle was connected to Corky Gonzales's struggle and the historical struggle of Chicano people.

To understand how PJU operates, to understand its members' motivation, persistence, and drive, to understand their political education and leadership development, to understand their place in the community, one must understand the struggle within which PJU situates itself. For PJU, the tradition and mechanisms of the historical struggle for human rights are the heart of the work and the power that keeps them moving forward.

5

"Weaving a Tapestry That Won't Unravel"

The Transformation of Education in the Mississippi Delta

PRIMARY AUTHORS: KENNETH RUSSELL AND MARA CASEY TIEKEN

It's early November, and the air is still and quiet over the swamp, the few houses, and the train tracks in Glendora, Mississippi.[1] A low haze rings the tall cypresses, a ghostly haze that spills from the shadows. Fifty-five years ago, a black teen-ager, Emmett Till, was beaten and murdered here, a seventy-pound cotton-gin fan fastened around his neck with barbed wire, his young body dumped in the stagnant bayou waters. The town's mayor—a black man in his sixties, only a child at the time—tells us this as we stand gathered around him outside the old mill that remains as an eerie testament to the brutal crime. His words seem a plea, a plea to see this place, to witness what happened here, to learn.

The next day we are thirty miles from Glendora, squeezed into an auditorium on the campus of Mississippi Valley State University for the Dismantling the Achievement Gap Conference. Participants fill the 506 stadium seats and stand in the aisles, all focused on the small wiry man near the glass podium in the audi-torium's center. Civil rights veteran Hollis Watkins starts with a prayer, asking the Lord to bless this gathering; then he begins singing, slowly and softly at first, almost more statement than melody, but then louder, rhythmically, with dancing feet: "This little light of mine . . ."—soon everyone's standing, joining—"I'm going to let it shine . . ." we are clapping, swaying, to the familiar rhythm. The words are different—"Tell Governor Barbour, I'm going to let it shine. Tell Gov-ernor Barbour, I'm going to let it shine"—but the meaning is the same as it has always been—the promise, the power, to bring change.

Change doesn't come easily to the Mississippi Delta; here, history runs deep. Two hundred years of slavery cast a long shadow over the state's politics, economy, social structure, and educational system. Yet threaded through this legacy of oppression is also a legacy of hope and struggle to overcome oppression, work that began with slave rebellions and early twentieth-century protests, continued with the Civil Rights movement, and persists in various forms today. Southern Echo, a community organizing group founded in 1989, is a product of these legacies: a witness to the atrocities and the promise of history and an agent to foster change for the future. By cultivating awareness and building capacity in black Delta communities, supporting local communities and creating a larger state network, Echo is rewriting the future of schools and communities in the Mississippi Delta.

This chapter attempts to reveal how Southern Echo does its work, that is, how it fights to bring educational justice to a context fraught with inequality. We begin this analysis with a close look at this Delta context, followed by a discussion of Echo's theory of change. We then examine four themes—relationships, knowledge, community consciousness, and accountability—that appear central to the way Echo does its work. Though we consider these four processes separately, describing an event or campaign in Echo's history that illustrates the point, each builds on the other and together they create an integrated whole. The chapter concludes with a discussion of Echo's major achievements and some tensions it confronts as it continues to build a contemporary movement for justice in the South.

The Delta Context

Long drives on the rural highways of Mississippi reveal a land of cotton, catfish, and casinos. The state—which ratified the Thirteenth Amendment abolishing slavery only in 1995—lies deep in the heart of the old Confederacy. Today, African Americans make up about 37 percent of the state's population, while whites comprise 60 percent.[2] Racial dynamics are central to life in the Delta. As a state senator explains, "I think in Mississippi, just about every issue we face of social significance goes back to race—race or the undertone." Racism, defined by Echo as "a system of domination and control by whites over people of color," continues to shape the Delta's economy, its culture, its politics, and its communities. The Delta's geography, for example, is influenced by the racialized history of the state, as the small, isolated, mostly black communities that dot the Delta landscape reflect old plantation lines and divisions. The economic and political contexts have, in many ways, changed little from plantation times, with whites still controlling land and factories, employing blacks in low-wage jobs with strict uniform policies and monitored bathroom breaks, and also holding the primary positions of political power in the local and state government. Even in the casino-focused counties on the river, the jobs available to locals are, according to one Echo organizer, "still like the plantation jobs, they aren't meaningful careers." Cecil Brown, a state legislator and chair of the House

Education Committee, acknowledges, "We've got a lot of poor communities in the state, particularly in the Delta, that are majority black communities, and there's been no real commitment on the part of the state to help with the infrastructure in those communities." Thus, even for all the strides and successes of the Civil Rights movement—the policies changed, the culture of resistance fostered, and the leaders cultivated—the period of African American enslavement never seems like a closed chapter of history; in fact, Echo characterizes the current era as a period of "neocolonialism" written into today's politics, economics, and social structures.

This legacy of neocolonialism also shapes the state's educational context. Mississippi's refusal to provide black students an equitable education is as old as the history of education in the state: it began during slavery and was formalized during the era of segregation. Beyond simply separating black students into black schools, segregation also meant that these black schools were systematically underfunded and under-resourced, severely compromising the quality of education black students could receive. Following *Brown v. Board of Education,* the Mississippi legislature, in a desperate bid to avoid desegregation, came one vote short of abolishing its public education system. Instead, the eventual integration of schools in 1970 replaced the dual white and black educational systems with a new duality—a private-public system—that simply replicated the old divisions. White flight from public schools quickly followed the state-mandated desegregation, and a crop of private religious and secular schools rose up to replace the old white public schools. Most public schools remained staffed by white teachers—in the 2000–2001 school year, more than two-thirds of Mississippi's teachers were white[3]—and controlled by white superintendents or school board members. Public education never seemed to be the priority for the white-dominated power structure in the state. In fact, until quite recently the state only funded public education through the third grade. According to Echo director Leroy Johnson, many state legislators believed, "Anything beyond a third grade education would ruin a good field hand."[4]

The educational system appears to continue to function as a mechanism for white domination. Black Delta community members describe decrepit facilities, unaccountable school officials, undertrained teachers, outdated textbooks, and opaque school-level policies. Youth detention centers and county jails often have larger and more sophisticated facilities than public schools, with sprawling fenced campuses that rise from the cotton fields. In Echo's view these conditions are intentional. By continuing to underfund the public schools, by enforcing the subordination of students through draconian discipline systems and school uniform policies, by funneling drop outs to the extensive juvenile justice system, public officials ensure a second-class black citizenry—disengaged and disempowered youth without the skills required for meaningful employment or civic life.

Indeed, Mississippi's schools have some of the highest drop-out rates and lowest measures of educational attainment in the country. For the 2003–04 school year, for example, Mississippi's graduation rate was less than 63 percent, while the national rate was 75 percent; meanwhile, in 2005, the state had the largest proportion of fourth graders in the country scoring below basic in reading scores on the National Assessment of Educational Progress tests.[5] As Echo illustrates through its careful mapping of the state, these statistics are often most alarming in Delta communities with the highest concentrations of black students.

Others, though, view the source of the educational problem in Mississippi differently, blaming black communities for a failure to properly appreciate the worth of education and schooling. As Hank Bounds, the state's school superintendent, explains:

> In Mississippi, due to a number of issues, particularly poverty, education is not valued in the state ... If you've never seen beyond the end of the next block, if you've never seen beyond the end of the next cotton field or over the next catfish pond, you don't know what good education looks like, and so it's not that poor parents don't want the best for their children, they just don't know what it looks like, and what opportunity looks like.

Steve Williams, the state's former deputy superintendent, also describes a "poor perception of education" and the challenge that comes with it. "What is the value of education? How do you create the community will and the will of the state as a whole to understand the fundamental importance of that?" In the end, many educators and officials employed by the state believe that Mississippi's primary challenge is to cultivate a value for education in the black community.

Echo's Mission and Theory of Change

Echo leaders find that assumption to be misguided, racist, and—quite simply— wrong, as it places blame on the black victims of oppression rather than putting responsibility in the hands of white power-holders. "White people," Echo explains in one of its training reports, feared two things the most that could undermine their domination and control:

1. The development of *independent black political organization* that could not be run and controlled by whites.
2. An *effective public education system* accessible to all children and adults of color where they could develop critical thinking; master mathematics and

the humanities; understand the political process; and develop the working tools and skills needed to sustain the kind of personal, political, and economic independence that is at the core of genuine freedom.

In response to these conditions, Echo was created as "a leadership development, education and training organization working to develop effective accountable grassroots leadership in the African American communities in rural Mississippi and the surrounding region." A leader, in Echo's view, emerges through the work to bring justice to Delta communities. As Joyce Parker, the director of Echo affiliate Citizens for a Better Greenville, explains, leaders "are the ones that will take on the responsibility of taking a stand and . . . moving the work forward, whether it be through actions, whether it be through engagement in other activities, whether it be laying out the agenda." Leaders can be anyone from a public official accountable to the needs of the community, to a parent demanding services for the children of her community. Echo does not directly create leaders; instead, it provides training and technical assistance to local, black-based, black-led community organizations so that they may build leadership. These organizations develop community members who can identify the needs of their community, create and support local solutions, hold public officials and policymakers accountable, and even step into these roles themselves. Echo, moreover, links these local organizations into a statewide network that addresses the collective needs of these communities.

In Echo's view it is *community organizing* that will counter white domination and lead to systemic change. Echo lends its support primarily to community organizing groups, rather than advocacy organizations. Helen Johnson, a director of one of these local organizing groups, Citizens for Quality Education (CQE), explains:

> Community organizing is about empowerment. It's not about doing something for somebody else. It really is about sharing or giving people tools and skills that enable them to change their situation. And it's really about changing this whole culture of power and really speaking to power because we're talking about race issues, we're talking about class issues for people who are living in African American communities.

Echo helps communities to name the injustices they have suffered and hold officials accountable for creating and enforcing more equitable policies. Since its founding, Echo has increasingly focused on the injustices of Mississippi's educational system—a focus that stands in stark contrast to many state officials' perception of a community disregard for public education. Instead, Echo believes that addressing the flawed education system is a means to disrupt the "culture of power," as Robert Hall, president of local affiliate Concerned Citizens for a Better Tunica County, explains, for "education is the only equalizer of sort in America." Education has always been valued by black communities, and Echo sees its focus on education as a legacy of the Civil Rights movement. According to Echo, these dual goals—a quality statewide educational system and the development of an independent black-led political organization—can begin to rewrite Mississippi's racist policies and practices.

Relationships and the Origins of Echo

The whole idea of community organizing is really about relationship building.
—Helen Johnson, Director of Citizens for Quality Education

Southern Echo began in 1989 through dialogue and work facilitated by three people—Hollis Watkins, Leroy Johnson, and Mike Sayer. All three were products of the Civil Rights movement.[6] As a young activist, Hollis participated in one of Mississippi's first sit-ins:

We were supposed to have been going to the public library because black folks couldn't go to the public library. So, we hadn't done our research thoroughly to know that the library would not be open on that particular day . . . but we decided that we would not be defeated, that we were going to jail that day. We knew right down the street from the library was a Woolworth lunch counter; that's where we went in and had a sit-in demonstration.

After that first library-turned-Woolworth demonstration in 1961, Hollis became more and more involved in voter registration work, emerging as a key leader of the Student Nonviolent Coordinating Committee (SNCC). Leroy was a young child at the time, witnessing these initial challenges to white power-holders and attending organizing meetings with Hollis and his father, who was involved in the movement in Holmes County protecting black voters at the polls. Mike, a young, white New York native and recent college graduate, came down to Mississippi from the Northeast as an employee of SNCC and a co-chair of the 1963 Freedom Vote.

Over the next decades their paths continued to cross occasionally, and then, in 1989, they convened more purposefully—Hollis after a number of years working a variety of jobs that kept him tied to the community, Leroy after a career in business and then time with various Mississippi community organizations including Mississippi Action for Community Education and the Rural Organizing and Cultural Center, and Mike after a return to Mississippi as a lawyer for the Center for Constitutional Rights. With his reputation as a civil rights leader and his social work background, Hollis explains:

> People continuously began to request me to come and help them in their communities, to give them some workshops, on these things, on those things, and the more those requests began to come in . . . that said to me that I needed to start a training institute where I could teach and train others to do the same things that I could do.

The three organizers began talking among themselves and with others, realizing that the current "organizations were not going deep enough in terms of aid and assistance in working with the community." As Mike describes:

> These communities were not devoid of organizations . . . Every one of these communities had numerous, numerous churches, NAACP branches, voters' leagues, or a Concerned Citizens . . . sometimes more than one . . . So it wasn't an absence of organization. But they did not have a notion about how to organize to achieve the capacity to make things happen or not to happen.

By the late 1980s, many felt that the progress toward racial justice started by the Civil Rights movement had stagnated. The sheer number of organizations created divisions within the black community and, more importantly, their tactics did not often involve many community members or empower them to bring about change on their own behalf. Furthermore, public offices were rarely held by black leaders, and the few who became public leaders were often unresponsive to the communities they supposedly represented; thus, the white appropriation of all positions of real economic and political import created a "leadership vacuum." The sensation that the momentum of the Civil Rights movement could soon be lost—coupled with this leadership vacuum and the general lack of community capacity—caused Hollis, Leroy, and Mike to turn to community organizing as a mechanism for effecting change. Hollis explains that during the Civil Rights movement, "Our mobilizing and organizing in the community had been so effective, and now there's a void; this is still needed but there is no organization that is actively engaged in doing this kind of thing . . . In order to fill this void then something has to be created . . ." This "something" was Southern Echo.

Echo's founders realized that the last thing black communities needed was one more organization sweeping in to identify and neatly resolve the problems of the Mississippi Delta. Instead, they began with a series of listening tours, traveling across black Delta communities from Tunica down through Madison, talking with community members and hearing their concerns. Mike remembers:

> In this six-week tour, where we went to fifteen counties, during the day we talked individually to a cross-section of community people. We talked to activists. We talked to school principals—all in the black community. We weren't talking to folks in the white community. But all of these were majority black counties at the time. And so we talked to different kinds of public officials who were black, who had been elected, who had obviously been activists if they'd been elected to public office. And we talked to local black businessmen and so forth.

They identified individuals to speak with based on the recommendations of locals they knew from their own work. These individuals then named others, Mike explains, revealing the "existing networks of people who are already doing the work." Some were older citizens long involved in community issues. Others, though, were younger. In Tunica County, Mike waited all day to meet Marilyn Young, "this little kid about nineteen-years-old," the person, he'd been told, he just had to meet "because there's no person who works harder, no person's busier." Through these meetings, more conversations ensued. And then, Mike continues:

> We would bring this same group of folks together at night to talk about the same questions in a group setting. And the purpose of that was to compare how people talked when they were alone and how they talked in group, because you could see where the hedges would come when somebody could hear them and they didn't feel as safe as they felt when they were talking alone, or where people would gain courage to talk stuff in a group setting where there was support.

In this space, Hollis, Leroy, and Mike began to hear common concerns, often about substandard housing and little job availability. Some community members, Mike explains, also expressed a

> great and universal distress that for all of the work that they had done, all of the lives that had been lost and all of the heartache that had been experienced . . . and all of the black elected officials that had been elected . . . they felt they had some serious questions about whether it was worth it, because the black public officials were treating them every bit as badly as the white public officials.

Thus, the leadership vacuum was a matter of both representation and accountability.

Addressing these issues would be difficult. Echo's organizers learned that these communities thought of themselves as isolated and distinct, "like the Free State of Tallahatchie." Fear often divided the communities. "The plantation line was the initial Berlin Wall," Leroy explains, and it brought a "fear of what that meant if you got caught on the other side of the line after dark." Plantation owners had cultivated distrust among blacks toward those from other plantations, and this fear, isolation, and distrust still lingered. "What was remarkable," Mike describes, was that "in each of these counties, people thought they were unique, that their situation was absolutely the worst of the worst, and that any work that was done should focus on their county, because there can't be any place worse than they are." Consequently, Hollis, Leroy, and Mike began to conceive of a two-pronged strategy: working to develop local leadership and capacity while, at the same time, creating a larger statewide network linking these local communities.

Since they couldn't rely upon a strong, cohesive group of existing community organizations, they decided to draw upon a rich network of personal connections to foster the organization, development, and growth of responsive local organizations. These relationships would provide Echo's foundation. Co-director of Citizens for Quality Education Helen Johnson, for example, came to organize in Mississippi after marrying Leroy, soon pulling in her sister, Ellen Reddy, to serve as the other co-director. Relationships also led to the growth of Concerned Citizens for a Better Tunica County. Robert Hall, the group's president, explains, "Being from the community we called on personal relationships that we have with individuals in the community, and then once we meet with these individuals we talk about concerns of interest." Indianola Parent Student Group (now Sunflower County Parents and Students Organization) began similarly, relying upon existing relationships to gather a core group of stakeholders— a strategy it continues today. Betty Petty, the director of the group, explains:

> Take, for instance, Gwendolyn Parnell that works here with the Indianola Parent Student Group. Gwendolyn Parnell may have a relationship with some parents in Moorhead because her husband is from Moorhead . . . I may not have that relationship, but if we want those parents involved in our work, it wouldn't be good for me to go and ask them because they don't know me. They know Gwen, so Gwen would actually do that.

In each community, with each local organization, Mike notes, "You're dealing with a community that already exists." Echo capitalizes on this local community:

We tended not to work from what you might call a mass call sort of a meeting process . . . For the most part what you would do is you'd start out with one or two people and engage in conversation . . . sometimes you'd go through ten people before you found two people who were solid. And then you would use that to enlarge, to get them to bring in a couple of people each, two to three. The next thing you know, you've got a group of five, six, seven, eight and . . . that then becomes the core in each meeting of people who already understand what's going on and why this needs to happen.

Hollis describes a "sense of family and sense of community" that gets more people involved in the work, as one community members pulls in another. Community organizing itself is a matter of relationships, Robert Hall explains, in which there "is one individual talking to another one to help him or her to understand issues involved and the way that the solution can be derived at that's beneficial for those concerned." Hollis, Mike, and Leroy looked to engage new people, hiring, for example, Brenda Hyde as a college intern and then as an assistant director, but they also sought out established leaders with the influence and authority to provoke the buy-in and involvement of others. In addition, they engaged those considered gatekeepers, Leroy explains, "So we'd understand how we had to address the barriers they were throwing up to people about getting involved."

This diverse array of community relationships was necessary to begin building local capacity. However, because Mississippi has a strong and centralized state government with considerable policymaking power, an organized, statewide force would be necessary to enact any sort of meaningful change. So as they worked to build on personal relationships and cultivate networks within communities, Hollis, Leroy, and Mike also began to tackle the isolation dividing these distant, rural locales; in other words, they began to build relationships across communities. In order to counter the fear and distrust among them, Mike explains:

We had to win over a whole other concept, which was the idea that people could work together across county lines . . . It took a lot of work to get people to see that the things that they wanted to achieve, they couldn't achieve in their county alone . . . because so much of the policy that they were concerned about was controlled at the state level, especially around education . . . And that they needed to create a larger capacity than any one county had if they were going to win this fight.

To create this larger capacity and foster the understanding it depended upon, Echo's organizers needed to build relationships that went beyond mere contact to actual trust and respect. When they pulled together groups of individuals from different towns, they began defining and using a set of common terms across communities, a "common language," Leroy says, "so when we talk to each other, we will be talking about the same things." This emphasis on commonality included a focus on accountability, that is, the "need to put the interest of the community above your own individual organization's interest, and your own personal interest." According to Mike:

> Out of that came the phrase, "accountability means putting community interest above self-interest" . . . We had to talk about how you can't do it as an individual. You don't have enough capacity as an individual to hold them accountable or to make things happen or not happen. You have to do it as a community.

With a common vocabulary, Echo could then build new relationships, relationships that were fostered through the work, relationships that carried across communities and not just within them, relationships that established a new, statewide community. These local and state relationships would allow the organization to take on its first major campaign—redistricting.

Knowledge and the Redistricting Campaigns

> That's how you empower people, by imparting the knowledge to them.
> —Robert Hall, president of Concerned Citizens for a Better Tunica

During the listening tours, Hollis, Leroy, and Mike heard a number of concerns articulated, but one issue was conspicuously absent. Community members rarely talked about the problem of the state's voting districts—specifically, that their shape limited the number of black elected officials. Perhaps this silence was unsurprising because, given the lack of accountable leadership, community members oftentimes saw little connection between their vote and subsequent policymaking. Mike notes:

> There was a complete disconnect between what they saw as the electoral work, which is preceded by the redistricting work, and the substantive policy issues about which they were most concerned. Disconnect. Fascinating. Did not see the relationship between them, and very logical, because historically there was no reason, no basis for seeing the connection between being in public office and being able to impact substantive policy . . . This is 1990 in the fall, and we

are twenty-five years into the Voting Rights Act, and they did not see
the connection.

In Echo's view, however, the only way to make progress on any of the concerns
community members named required increasing the number of black elected
officials; only through political redistricting would the legislature's black caucus
grow large enough to change state policy. The redistricting issue would also
build upon the new cross-community relationships established in Mississippi
through the listening tours.

Indeed, with the court system becoming increasingly conservative, the early
1990s seemed to offer the last opportunity to finally give Delta communities a
voice. Before the work could begin, however, the community also needed to
understand the importance of the redistricting issue, to become aware of the
current reality and its effects. According to Hollis, the redistricting work was
first a matter of grasping the means by which, even in the 1980s, district lines
perpetuated the disenfranchisement of black Delta communities, "the method
that white people in Mississippi used to nullify the Voting Rights Act of 1965."
He continues:

> After the passage of the Voting Rights Act in 1965, they divided the
> Delta area of Mississippi into four different congressional districts,
> which means even though all of these black folks up here in this district
> became registered to vote they couldn't elect anybody . . . They basically
> used three different methods of diluting the black voting strength. That
> process they used with the Delta area of Mississippi was called cracking.
> That's where rather than leaving them you divide them up into different
> areas to reduce their effectiveness if they were all in one.

A campaign to create a meaningful black vote would require knowledge,
which, in Echo's view, involved building an understanding that goes beyond
textbook definitions or simple facts to a deeper awareness of systemic inequity,
to a usable base of skills, and to a fundamental confidence in one's own abilities.
Consequently, Mike, Leroy, and Hollis decided to organize a series of trainings
that covered the historical context of districting in Mississippi, the process of
redistricting, and the legal ramifications of the process. Inviting two long-time
civil rights workers, demographer and Senator Henry Kirskey and attorney Car-
ole Rhodes, to explain these processes, they traveled across the state, using local
elders to share the history of the community and their own voting rights struggles. They put young people to work coloring maps of voting districts, from
Tunica County, where Marilyn Young, now a part of Concerned Citizens, created detailed maps with the help of her five-year-old daughter Ashley, down to

Holmes County, where Helen and Ellen worked with community members on these same maps. "What we saw on those maps," Helen explains, was "the skills, the knowledge, the tools that we are also learning and passing on." These inter-generational trainings helped community members understand the effects of current district lines and taught them how to draw new district lines and con-sider the impact of different plans. Echo wanted communities "not only to understand the process of redistricting but how to actually draw a redistricting plan," according to Hollis. Thus, trainings went beyond providing information to cultivating skills and empowering people to use those skills. With knowledge comes power, as Robert Hall, the president of Concerned Citizens, explains: "We share the knowledge to empower people."

Echo also tries to build as broad a group of knowledgeable people as pos-sible. Robert continues, "We found out that if one person has the knowledge then he or she normally is identified, isolated, and destroyed, and that's the method that the power structure has always used, but when we all have the knowledge, we all have the information, then it doesn't matter who's not there, the work goes on." The fundamental goal of these trainings, according to Mike, is for "as many people as possible to develop the tools and skills of crit-ical thinking, strategic planning, organizational development of the substan-tive knowledge of a particular area, whether it's redistricting or issues around public education, or around housing, or around health . . . so that they have a democratized body of knowledge." For Echo, knowledge involves an awareness of inequity, a deep understanding of its causes and ideas for possible solutions, and a confidence in one's own expert skills and information, and that kind of knowledge brings empowerment. Empowerment is both personal, as individ-uals learn to advocate for themselves or their children, and collective, as a com-munity becomes able to draw upon its own expert resources to hold those in power accountable.

Echo could have contracted an outside agency to complete much of the redistricting work and then mobilized people to fight for the plans proposed by these outsiders. But Echo's leaders made a deliberate decision to equip commu-nity members with the skills and understanding needed to do the work them-selves. This knowledge, Hollis explains, gives you a voice. "When I come and present you with this plan, you're going to say, 'Oh no Hollis, that won't work, see that dilutes our vote.'" By giving people the tools with which to understand the process of redistricting and to redraw the lines themselves, they are no longer dependent on officials or data experts to interpret the situation, to distin-guish a good plan from a bad one, or to determine fairness. This knowledge, coupled with their familiarity with the local context—their own information about who lived where—made the community members the actual experts. In short, Leroy notes:

> We sold them on their expertness . . . because a lot of folk come in and beat community down and talk about what's wrong with you and . . . "you don't have this, you don't have that." And our argument was, with the degree of expert that's in this room, how can you not do it? How can you not do it? And they says, "What do you mean, we're expert?" And then we defined what expert means. And in the glossary of terms, we said that an expert was somebody that knows just a little bit more than you do.

The process established community members as experts; that is, people who know more than anyone else about the locales, the redistricting processes, and the communities' interests. While the demographers that had been hired by state officials had abstract computer models, Leroy explains, they knew little "when it came to knowing who lived where, who would vote and would not vote, who would work together to support a candidate and who would not . . . Our folks became the experts upon whom the demographers relied." Being an expert—having the skills *and* the confidence to use them—is the power that brings change. Expert skills enable accountability, and these skills are lasting, according to Helen, "because no matter where you are, you can employ those skills, so it's a sense of empowerment, changing your own condition." The combination of relationships and knowledge creates a collective capacity out of which leaders can be held accountable to their communities.

In the end, working together across the state, these community experts created a redistricting plan that was eventually passed, leading to a doubling of the state's Legislative Black Caucus from twenty-one to forty-two. Eventually the caucus grew to fifty, or 28 percent of the total seats. According to Leroy, the black community's power grew and led to an historic victory: "In 1995, really the Black Caucus flexing its muscles for the first time, Mississippi was forced to ratify the 13th Amendment abolishing slavery." Equipped with the awareness, information, and confidence to affect the redistricting process, communities reconciled a part of Mississippi's shameful history and established a legislative voice—a voice they would need if they truly wanted to change public schools in Mississippi.

Though Echo still continues to work on voting rights, Mississippi's public education system is now the primary focus of the group's work. The knowledge Echo currently provides and develops typically centers on issues related to the school system, cultivating among communities the power to hold school officials accountable, to ensure that state or district policies are implemented, to find solutions to school-based issues, and, in the end, to transform the public education system. The attention to the public education system is crucial, as Brenda Hyde, Echo's assistant director, explains, because "the type and quality of education you get also dictates the type of quality of life that you want to live, whether it's being able to have affordable health care, whether it's being able to live in a decent affordable housing." Because education is so important, Mike cautions, the public education system is "the real battleground."

Building knowledge is at the center of Echo's work in education. A member's first experience with a local organization is a process of becoming aware—seeing anew the inequity underlying district lines or school experiences. Awareness may come through a meeting that one community member persuades another to attend, meetings focused on special education practices or understanding state test scores. As Rachel, a parent working with Sunflower County Parents and Students Organization, explains, "It's a lot that you learn, even with the new state rules of the school, like when the No Child Left Behind law came about. We didn't know anything about that." Like many others, she first got involved—and then stayed involved—for the awareness of issues that the organization provided. This awareness is also important to youth participating in Echo's work. Through their involvement, they gain access to information that changes their perceptions. Echo's youth leaders often used to accept the conditions of their schools or institutions, thinking the conditions were normal or just necessary. However, as they come to learn their rights, they are more likely to defend these rights. A member of Youth as Public Speakers explains, "I think this group has power, because we become knowledgeable of the things that we were once not knowledgeable of—and I believe that when you have that knowledge, then you have power."

Often this awareness is proffered on an individual level. A parent or caregiver approaches an Echo organizer with a particular issue facing his or her child; a child, for example, is falling further and further behind in school. Then these leaders provide counsel, perhaps explaining what special education services their child should receive. As Gwendolyn Parnell, a community organizer with the Sunflower County Parents and Students Organization, explains:

> If they are having problems, if the child is failing or whatever the issue is that's keeping them from learning, we prepare them to be able to go into the school and talk to the teacher, talk to the principal, and ask these different questions on what's going on with the child, and if they tell you what's going on you ask them, "Why hasn't this been implemented because I know this is in place and mandated and why haven't you taken advantage of this?"

After building awareness of a school-related issue, Echo and the local organizations it works with then provide communities with related information and skills through local trainings. Oftentimes, these trainings center on particular issues or topics that are named as important by community members. Joyce

Parker, the director of Citizens for a Better Greenville, explains how she relies upon Echo to give her information that she then passes on to the community through trainings. "Our work is research-based; we make sure that there is data to support the work that we're doing because we know where it is that we're trying to go with improving our educational system. So, when I go to meetings and I get information and bring it back, we can do trainings and try to inform the parents in the community of the information that we have."

But awareness and information alone are insufficient to bring change; community members must "feel the ability to do work," to see, Leroy explains, the "worth of the community." Consequently, just as they once cultivated redistricting expertise rooted in a community's own knowledge and abilities, Echo now cultivates this kind of expert knowledge around issues related to the public education system. The empowerment that comes with expertise is even noted by some of Echo's key allies. As Steve Williams, former deputy superintendent of the Mississippi Department of Education, reports:

> What the leaders of Echo have done in my opinion, at least, has shown community members, "You're not helpless." That doesn't mean the district is going to change overnight or you're going to get everything you want by any means—but . . . "I know what the school's responsibilities are, and I know as a customer of yours the service you're supposed to provide to me."

With this knowledge—awareness, information, and expertise—community members are empowered to act and hold education officials accountable. Such knowledge and empowerment, coupled with a growing concern for a collective well-being, allowed Echo and its local affiliates to take on one of its biggest and most public campaigns—the fight against the Robinsonville school.

Community Consciousness and the Robinsonville School Fight

> It's not about "I" but it's about what it is that we can do together in order to make our communities the communities we want to see, and in doing that it would take all of us working together having that same vision that we can see it together.
> —Betty Petty, Sunflower County Parents and Students Organization

Ashley McKay vividly remembers her participation in the campaign against the Robinsonville school. "I'm remembering myself and other young people actually going through and labeling the streets and neighborhoods, and saying, 'And this house there are no children. They've got no kids in elementary school. In this house there are two. In this house . . .'" As the school buses shuttled children across the county, she and her friends would count the number of children riding the buses, note where the buses stopped, and report this information to their parents. They mapped the neighborhood with a simple mission: find the five hundred children for whom the new school was being built. It was the 1996–1997 school year; Ashley was in the second grade.[7]

Word of the intention to build a new elementary school in Robinsonville was first received well by the community. The planned school promised new facilities for five hundred students. But then the details emerged. With no provisions for busing, plans indicated that children who did not live in Robinsonville would not attend the new school. Robinsonville, meanwhile, was the predominantly white area in the northern end of Tunica County, housing the county's casinos and the very rich. The plan also diverted to this new school money allocated for repairing existing public schools, some of which had no running water and poorly maintained sanitary facilities.

Tunica-native Marilyn Young—the nineteen-year-old that Hollis, Mike, and Leroy encountered during their 1989 listening tours, now an Echo organizer and a director of Concerned Citizens for a Better Tunica County—recalls that these details made Echo-affiliated Concerned Citizens immediately suspicious:

> They wanted the school district to borrow the money, build the school in Robinsonville, and if it was any money left over, do the badly needed renovations here in Tunica at the existing schools that we had. So, we knew that in itself there was another plan somewhere, but we didn't know all of the details.

Concerned Citizens' investigation suggested that the white members of the community wanted to replace their financially strapped, private academy with a publicly funded school. Concerned Citizens' skepticism was based on their research, including information from insiders like their current Executive Director Melvin Young, who came to Tunica County as a supermarket manager and served on the boards of a number of white-dominated county organizations. Melvin describes himself as a "token black" at the time, "the one that they could put on the board that wasn't going to raise too much Cain, just say 'Yes ma'am, yes sir'" and who, therefore, "got to hear the plans from the beginning." Information provided by insiders like Melvin and comments by some of the prominent landowners made it clear that whites wanted their own public schools. According to Melvin, they felt, "We want back in. We're tired of paying for private school and . . . we're not coming back unless we can have an all-white public school." An additional motivation was a desire to increase the attractiveness of the Robinsonville area to prospective investors with a high-end housing development, built by the landowners who proposed the school. Homes were priced in excess of $100,000, which was far beyond what the vast majority of black residents could afford; the new school, Concerned Citizens believed, was an effort to attract white residents. Consequently, Concerned Citizens decided to expose this move toward publicly funded racial segregation, putting the issue at the heart of the campaign and arguing that it threatened the resources available to the larger black community and progress toward racial justice.

Concerned Citizens went into action to stop the school. It began to educate its members and other citizens about the motives behind the school, providing them information about the issue and possible responses through meetings and trainings. Concerned Citizens created a communal awareness of the issue through a range of strategies—public meetings, flyers, petitions, surveys, door knocking, and workshops—that shifted the black community's view of the proposed new school. For example, Karen Bonds, a former teacher and deputy superintendent of Tunica schools, said at first community members saw the campaign against the school as "a big to-do over nothing," thinking the building of a new school would be good for the community. She shared this view until, through the work of Concerned Citizens, she "heard all the ins and outs." She soon signed a Concerned Citizens petition against the building of the school. Like Karen, when other members of the local community became aware of the real intentions behind the proposed new school, they joined in the efforts to prevent its construction.

Concerned Citizens also mobilized the larger Echo network, linking with state and regional community organizations that could then serve as resources. They found that the surrounding communities were concerned about the potential impact on their own school systems if a ruling that favored the white landowners was passed. As a result, they saw their own interest tied into the fight and quickly joined to support Concerned Citizens' efforts. One critical form of support from these communities came through legal aid. Echo and the Mississippi Education Working Group (MEWG), a statewide coalition of organizations from communities of color working together to influence changes in Mississippi's educational policies, joined Concerned Citizens in filing a complaint with the Mississippi Department of Education, the Mississippi Attorney General, and the United States Justice Department.[8] The complaint argued that the new school was intended to be racially segregated (a violation of the 14th Amendment) and that the housing development violated fair-housing laws. A report by a Memphis firm counter-argued that the school was necessary and found that the demographics of the area warranted the new school. In rebuttal,

Concerned Citizens set about conducting their own study of the situation—with Ashley and her friends counting the children on the school buses and groups of parents meeting the buses at the schools every morning for another counting. Concerned Citizens created a block-by-block map with this information, showing where the area's children actually lived, directly countering the data from the Memphis firm. After investigating, the U.S. Justice Department ruled that, *inter alia*, the demographics of the county did not support building a new school and that the planned use of the school to attract whites to the county raised concerns under federal desegregation orders. This ruling confirmed Concerned Citizens' position and validated the communal efforts that led to this success.

But still the fight dragged on. After the Justice Department's ruling, the Tunica County School Board, supported by the state department of education, returned to federal court to have the school desegregation order terminated on the grounds that the current racial makeup of the county no longer warranted its continuation. Concerned Citizens was not allowed to intervene in the proceedings.[9] The 5th Circuit Court, described by Echo as ultra-conservative at the time, ruled that the Justice Department could represent Concerned Citizens and all other plaintiffs. At the same time, the state decided to place the district under conservatorship in response to years of poor performance. Many community members believed this move was part of a conspiracy to further the plans for the new school because, in years past—when the district's academic performance was weaker and it struggled financially—the state had refused to take over the district. The state-appointed conservator, Dr. Ronald Love, came to the district promising that he would improve reading scores within nine months and would not involve himself with political decisions regarding the Robinsonville school. However, his relationship with some community members soon soured. He refused requests for information about the district's plans for the Robinsonville school and, according to Echo, described Concerned Citizens as a "small band of malcontents" bent on disrupting the education system. Marilyn suggests the conservator was a failure, with reading scores actually declining.

A tremendous strength of Concerned Citizens' organizing was the capacity to tap into varied ways of involving local, state, and national communities. Small, local, black communities like Tunica's require allies to win a fight of this magnitude; they build power when linked together as a large whole. In this fight, statewide support was evident in the over 350 people that Concerned Citizens and partners mobilized to attend a 1997 public hearing with twelve members of the Legislative Black Caucus and another 200 to attend a State Board of Education public hearing in Jackson later that year. Meanwhile, Echo helped Concerned Citizens form a partnership with the Washington-based Advancement Project to bring national resources and attention to its effort.

Concerned Citizens combined this highly visible public campaign with small, more private house meetings. Indeed, the group paid careful attention to the need for security in a context of fear and intimidation. It shied away from maintaining membership lists to protect those who did not want to be publicly identified with the fight, and it reached out to include others who wanted to remain anonymous but who would leave information in planned locations or other accessible manners. Some offered their homes for meetings and their office equipment for preparing informational materials. Marilyn explains:

> We knew they would identify them, isolate them, and destroy them;
> that was a tactic they use. So, if they didn't know who the "we" were . . .
> they cannot pick off certain people. We took the initiative that we would
> be the front-runners, and if someone would be attacked it would be us.

As the Robinsonville school fight intensified, fear mongering was used to silence the organizers and the community more broadly. Not only were the leaders verbally attacked, persons involved in the campaign reported being blacklisted in the community. According to Eddie Hawkins, a member of Concerned Citizens, the supporters had to contend with the power structure that wanted the school: "That meant no jobs for Melvin; it meant if they went to the banks to try to get loans, they were not gonna get 'em." It was even reported that one of the plantation owners boasted, had it been ten years earlier, he would have "taken care of the insiders." On occasion during the fight, the sheriff had to provide security escorts for Echo members while they were leaving Tunica due to safety concerns.

Echo encourages the acknowledgement of individual fears and the mobilization of *community* action as a strategy to allay these fears. As Leroy explains, fear was to be expected because, historically, individuals who opposed the power structure were targeted. However, there must be a collective willingness to move beyond the fear:

> And so we weren't asking people to deny, but rather to lift up the fear
> and then to talk about what the basis was on which you could proceed.
> And that's why the collective work was critical. Extremely difficult to
> ask an individual who has reason to be afraid to do something all by
> themselves and make themselves a singular target. When people moved
> collectively, they diffuse the risk.

While the case was before the courts, Concerned Citizens continued its work to build community knowledge of the case, the possible outcomes, and their consequences—both for Tunica and for other areas of Mississippi where similar "re-segregation" tactics were being tried. In 1999, working with Echo and the MEWG, Concerned Citizens initiated negotiations with the Tunica school board, the state department of education, the Justice Department, and the representatives of the white plaintiffs to reach an out-of-court settlement. Concerned Citizens proposed three alternate locations for the school, all closer to predominantly black communities and further from the original site. In each of the sites, according to Echo, at least one black community was the closest neighborhood to the new elementary school, making it impossible for these students to be denied access. In 2000, an agreement was reached to build the school two miles south of the original site and about a mile from a black community. This settlement was accepted by the judge in the federal court case; the judge also ruled that the district had to continue abiding by the desegregation orders. Although they got the least preferred of the three sites proposed for the school, Concerned Citizens and its allies hailed the overall agreement as a historic victory and immediately began pushing for its implementation.

Almost ten years after the fight, Marilyn and Melvin still describe the experience with the Robinsonville school fight as monumental. Concerned Citizens' role in the campaign built their credibility with the black community and strengthened the group's belief that, by building relationships and providing relevant knowledge, they could make things happen. Furthermore, Concerned Citizens became synonymous with the black community's fight against oppression more broadly. Yolanda Kemp, director of youth programs at the Tunica YMCA and one of Concerned Citizens' partners, thinks this role of champion against oppression is reflected in the community's perception of Concerned Citizens as a source of support in situations of injustice. "I have heard people say, 'Don't make me call Concerned Citizens,'" she explains. Such respect is earned through the group's ability to hold public officials accountable to the community and to act on behalf of a shared interest. It comes from the cultivation of a community consciousness, that is, people's awareness of who they are as a community and the shared factors that give rise to their experiences.

The process of coming to understand one's responsibility to self and the community is at the core of community organizing and central to the awakening required for community consciousness to occur. The experience of Melvin Young, the current executive director of Concerned Citizens, exemplifies this process. Melvin admits that, as an outsider, he unwittingly sided with the white community and was unable to acknowledge the ingrained racism that structured life in Tunica. As he developed a romantic relationship with Marilyn, he was introduced to black residents who taught him about the town's history. He began to see his role differently, realizing how he was part of a historic practice of using some blacks against others:

I was a problem when I first came to Tunica County as far as being the outside black person who comes into a community and then the white community puts that outside black person over the other black people. That's a common method used to disenfranchise the current blacks in the community.

Eventually, Melvin became publicly involved with Concerned Citizens, a decision that culminated in him leaving his job, abandoning his board positions, and ending his "token black" relationship with the white community. This kind of individual development toward understanding one's relationship and responsibility to the black community lies at the heart of the community consciousness Echo tries to foster.

Also critical to an organizing approach aimed at individual growth and systemic change is the involvement of youth, from counting bus-riders to speaking out about the conditions of their schools. Youth represent a critical part of the power of the collective; they contribute to its sustainability by linking the past, present, and future. The Civil Rights movement's more successful aspects, Hollis explains, were those that had younger and older people working together, and, consequently, Echo adopted an intergenerational model. While the implementation of the model varies across localities, all of Echo's community partners include youth in their work, often encompassing multiple generations of the same family, especially those of the organizers. According to Greg Johnson, Leroy's nephew and someone involved in organizing at a young age, the input of youth is valued as much as that of adults—an important statement in the Mississippi context where "children are to be seen and not heard." Youth involvement seems particularly important to an issue like education, as he explains:

> With a lot of issues like public education, which directly affect and involve youth, the history is that the people who are making all the decisions, the people who are having all the discussion, are not the people who are directly affected by what's going to happen as a result of the policies that are produced out of these conversations . . . That is what the history and what the culture has been, and in many instances still is. Inside of the Echo structure, which believes strongly in an intergenerational model, we get rid of all of that, because, again, everyone is brought to the table as an expert.

The intergenerational model undoubtedly adds other layers of complexity to the organization, including different interests, motivations, and ways of understanding. However, these differences can also be viewed as strengths, bringing more resources, new ideas, and long-term continuity into the network.

Echo builds community consciousness beyond the local level as it creates shared understandings across the state. Historically, according to Mike, the white community of Mississippi worked to "keep black communities separated from each other and keep their consciousness separated from each other." A locally rooted yet statewide network forms the basis from which Echo and its partners can hold state-level leaders accountable for making and implementing policies that challenge, and even reverse, centuries of domination and control.

Accountability and Funding Public Education in Mississippi

Accountability is community interest over self-interest.
—Southern Echo

In 1997, while the Robinsonville school fight was continuing in Tunica, Echo decided to take on a bold campaign that would put the condition of black education squarely at the center of policy debate in Jackson—a campaign for full funding of the Mississippi Adequate Education Program (MAEP), the state's primary policy for the provision of public education.[10] At the time, funding levels in rural black counties were abysmally low. Holmes County, for example, spent only $3,942 per pupil for the 1996–97 school year.[11] Although the legislature passed MAEP in 1997, it never fully funded its provisions, so public school children, especially black students in the Delta, continued to be confined to a second-class education. If MAEP were fully funded, an additional $650 million dollars would be directed into the public education system, potentially an enormous boon to cash-poor Delta districts.

MAEP was already the subject of some controversy. Earlier in the year the Legislative Black Caucus led efforts to override Mississippi Governor Kirk Fordice's veto of the MAEP legislation—an override that passed by one vote in the Senate and three in the House of Representatives. However, even with the override and the passage of the program into law, everyone was skeptical about whether the estimated $650 million annual cost would be funded. Echo's leaders, too, doubted the probability of funding, given the state's reputation on public education—after all, this was Mississippi, a state where, in 1955, the legislature fell one vote shy of killing the public education system; where 1954's Minimum Education Funding Act limiting the education of blacks to the third grade remained in force until 1996; and where myriad policies and legislation created to improve public education were simply never funded. "We didn't think we were going to get there," Leroy reports. "But somebody had to say that was the vision, and then we also had to say that was our aim, and it was our goal."

After Echo publicly declared its intention to push for full funding of the MAEP formula, it began pulling together its base of black-led, community-based organizations, committees, and individuals. White policymakers and advocates who had their own interest in full funding took notice and invited Echo to work with them. This was a notable move, as it was the first time major white-based groups, like the teachers union, sought to work with Echo. To date, Echo was still perceived as a "radical" group and a less-than-ideal partner; they were uncompromising, it was thought, relied heavily on protest to convey their message, and would not hesitate to publicly name and shame leaders they saw as unaccountable. With this perception, however, also came a reputation as a genuine representative of marginalized communities and one that created a space for communities to be heard.

Echo had its doubts about the sincerity of these white-led groups and worried that Echo's agenda might get hijacked. According to Leroy, "The moment folks found out we were really serious about it, white-led educational organizations said we'll work with you, and what they meant was, they wanted us to work for them, and they wanted to control the agenda, what our aim was, what our vision was, and what was victory." When Echo rebuffed these overtures, a number of messengers were sent to Echo to get them to cooperate—one of them, according to Echo, was speaker pro tempore of the House, Robert Clark, the first black elected to the legislature since Reconstruction. Leroy reports that Representative Clark lauded Echo's achievements and then, trying to be helpful, told them they needed to "listen to other folks." Echo thanked Representative Clark for his compliment and then told him they knew who listen to—not him or anyone he identified. Echo wanted to make clear its intent to maintain control of its agenda and resist any attempts to be dictated to by others.

Meanwhile, to strengthen its capacity to lead on this issue, Echo also worked to develop expertise on education funding at all levels within the organization. This strategy entailed building awareness of the links between funding and children's educational experiences, like dropping out, excessive use of suspension and expulsion, and poor teaching practices. Echo and its local organizing partners held meetings and workshops in communities to build organizational capacity and define what a quality education entails. They conducted trainings about state and local budgets and funding apparatuses, and they worked with local partners to deliver similar trainings. Once educated and informed, members were then mobilized to attend meetings at the legislature during deliberations as a way to show the "faces of the community." Echo also worked with members so that they could make presentations to the legislative committees and state board hearings on budget issues.

In 2000 Echo further increased its advocacy for full MAEP funding by proposing the concept of "justice funding." Justice funding, according to Leroy, requires really looking at systemic disparities in the way in which education is delivered and the biases that are built into the curriculum, that are built into the teaching force, the way people are prepared to be teachers, their inability to understand the culture in which they're teaching or their hostility to it.

Although Echo pushed for full funding of MAEP, the group never believed that an "adequate education" was enough. According to Echo, the MAEP funding formula was developed to provide resources based on what a "moderately successful Mississippi school appears to need when certain specific criteria are met." In the justice-funding framework, by contrast, the funds have to be distributed in a way that addresses the impact of the historical failure to fulfill responsibilities to children. Leroy explains, "The question was, how do we make up or repair deprivations? So if you were eighteen miles behind, what was the money that was going to catch you back up that eighteen-mile stretch?"

As part of their effort to answer this question, Echo partnered with Mississippi Valley State University in 2000 to bring in a team of experts to prepare a costing of quality education and a justice-funding proposal. They developed a formula that called for an additional 144 percent of base funding for children at risk, a designation applied to 65 percent of the student body in the Mississippi Delta.[12] This amount substantially exceeded those provided in the funding formulas used by MAEP and recommended by consultants Augenblich and Myer. Echo used this justice-funding formula and its attendant Brown Paper to build awareness of the extent of funding really necessary to provide a quality education and to press the issue with members of the legislature.

The election year 2003 saw increased funding for MAEP, and the MAEP formula was used for the first time to decide funding amounts. However, funding continued to fall below the full amount required by the MAEP formula. And then, in 2004, funding for all forms of public education was drastically reduced under the Education Reform Act, the first official act by newly elected Governor Haley Barbour. Ironically, this reduction provided a window of opportunity for Echo; the network used mapping to show visually, county by county, how each school district would be affected by the cuts. The maps revealed that some majority white areas with considerable support for the governor would also experience severe funding cuts, creating leverage that helped Echo to build what it called "unusual alliances" with predominantly white districts and organizations. This relationship was formalized in 2006 as the Education Stakeholders Alliance, a group that started as a forum for education interest groups—including the Parents' Campaign, the Mississippi Association of Educators, and Parents for Public Schools—to find common ground in the push for MAEP funding.

Echo also continued to build strategic alliances with black-led Delta organizations to strengthen the base for its campaign. In 2005 it formed the Mississippi Delta Catalyst Roundtable, a coalition of ten black-led organizations focused on boosting education in the Delta. The Roundtable formed a partnership with Mississippi Valley State University and the Mississippi Department of Education to host the Dismantling the Achievement Gap Conference, an annual event that pulls together hundreds of local group members, allies, partners from other organizations, key officials working for school districts and the Mississippi Department of Education, and students from across the Delta for presentations and workshops on key educational issues. Education funding was the focus of the 2006 conference, during which attendees discussed MAEP funding and agreed on strategies to prompt the state to act.

As Echo considered what action to take to mark the opening of the 2007 legislative session, the youth of Echo decided to implement one of the strategies suggested during the conference; they circulated a petition to pressure the governor and the legislature to act on the issue of MAEP funding with urgency. Over a two-week period during the 2006 winter break, youth from local partnering groups collected ten thousand signatures in communities across sixty-eight counties. Armed with binders of petitions, Echo and its allies publicly presented the signatures at a news conference held in the rotunda of the state capitol. According to Betty Petty, "Bringing community to the capitol at that short of a period of time was our way to then involve all . . . and then having a community person actually speaking on it, and then delivering those signatures to the chairs of the [House and Senate] education committees, to the governor, lieutenant governor, it was a very, very powerful piece for community."

But Echo met with challenges during this period, too. The media and political attention this event attracted masked Echo's struggles with members of the Education Stakeholders Alliance who opposed the petition campaign and public presentation of the signatures. The leadership of the Alliance argued that the petition campaign could be counter-productive to ongoing negotiations and even embarrassing to the Alliance; it decided that Echo could not continue as a member if it used protests and petitions and pushed the DOE on issues beyond MAEP funding. Echo leaders took seriously the loss of this new-found partnership with white groups, yet Echo chose to continue its multi-pronged agenda supported by a range of strategies, including those the leadership team discouraged. Echo was removed from the Alliance's leadership team, but, according to Leroy, they were not deterred: "We were able to play in their field and still hold and control our own agenda." In refusing to cede to the leadership team's demands, Echo could also keep applying the public pressure it felt necessary to secure full funding.

Echo also continued to pay attention to developing and supporting leaders who would be accountable representatives in state and local political offices. The nature of education policymaking in Mississippi makes attention at the state level very important, as Mike explains:

> Seventy percent of local school district revenue is provided by the state . . . Most regulations about what goes on—curriculum, discipline, everything else—is or can be controlled at the state level . . . Our legislators at the state level could not be effective without a strong community base to hold their backs, to protect them, but also to push them.

Beyond "protecting" and "pushing" elected leaders to ensure they are accountable to the community, there were additional benefits to community involvement for both the leaders and the communities, Joyce Parker notes, like

> seeing us in the room, and that's just something that didn't happen for our communities, until we got a part of this process, where . . . we could look in the face of people that were actually from our community that really were supporting it . . . I watched one of my legislators really grow and evolve in this process, because we were down here holding him accountable, but I think at the same time they needed that, because some of the things they were up against.

This combination of pressure and support may have been the key to MAEP's eventual funding. In February 2007, Governor Barbour, who, according to Echo, had fought "tooth and nail up 'til then," declared his support for full funding of the MAEP formula, calling the law the crowning achievement of the legislative session and thanking everyone for their support for fully funding public education. Though Echo was pleased, they were surprised by the governor's about-face, as were others outside the organization. Yet this long-term commitment seems to be holding; even in the harsh economic conditions of 2009 the MAEP formula was fully funded.

Echo's partners and legislators readily point out Echo's important contribution to the result, even as they celebrate their own roles in the win. Representative Cecil Brown believes "Southern Echo played a large role" in the process, highlighting their advocacy and mobilization of communities to influence their representatives. Marvin Haire, interim director of the Delta Research and Cultural Institute, describes Echo's work around MAEP funding as historic and calls Echo's relationship with DOE extraordinary: "For a grassroots *community* organization dealing with these kinds of issues, it's unheard of to have the state open up its doors to statistical resources, to do analysis and reporting, to have inroads into specific programmatic offices."

However, while Echo describes as "transformational" the legislature's renewal of full funding in 2008 without debate,[13] its leaders also suggest that vigilance is required so that this policy is not used to further domination and control, a role that, historically, public policy has often played. Echo argues that requiring the approval of MAEP funds each year creates the possibility that critical education needs will not be met and the long-standing practice of providing substandard public education will persist. As a result, Echo believes it must continue to work to hold public officials accountable to an organized community.

This sort of accountability also extends to the work of local partnering organizations. Citizens for a Better Greenville, for example, is working to create opportunities for community conversations with local representatives, a type of public check-in during which elected and appointed officials can report directly to and hear from those they represent. In nearby Indianola, the Sunflower County Parents and Students Organization has facilitated community involvement in selecting the new superintendent for the district. In Holmes County, Citizens for Quality Education advocated for and won a change in board meeting times, moving them to evenings so members of the community can attend. These groups have used different approaches to increase accountability, but all involve a dialogue, a continual conversation between public officials and community members. Echo works on both sides of this conversation; it helps to build leaders—elected or otherwise—that remain "checked-in" with the community and also creates citizens and members who are aware and informed, experts able to articulate their needs. In this way, the community is empowered to keep tabs on the actions of its representatives and act if they stray from protecting community interests.

At the state level, Echo continues to work to build what it calls "power relationships" or "accountability relationships" with state legislators so that issues that Echo brings to the legislative table receive support. These relationships influence the policy process and also bolster Echo's ties to the Mississippi Department of Education, the state board of education, and other organizations. According to Dr. Haire, the benefits of these relationships transfer across policy issues and give Echo a special relationship with the Mississippi Department of Education. He suggests that when critical legislation or issues around state budget and educational financing are discussed, Echo's presence at the table ensures that "things that might normally have slipped through the cracks or get overlooked" no longer do. However, Echo believes that accountability must be coupled with power. According to Leroy, "Accountability without power really means that you're just accounting. You ain't making 'em do anything; you just document, you just accountant." Echo's power to sanction comes from organized and knowledgeable communities, and in that way it is powered by community.

The role of accountable, elected political representatives is especially important given the significant policy and legislation focus of Echo's work. It is Echo's goal to help build local communities that have the capacity to develop leaders and then hold them accountable for making responsive policies and repealing those policies that have, for too long, furthered the racist and inequitable practices of what it sees as neocolonialism.

The Evolution of Echo's Work

> They're the only group that comes to me and says, "These are the people I represent. This is who we are, and this is what we do." And, when . . . you talk to the people that work with Southern Echo and listen to their backgrounds . . . they're not people that have done this for other groups. They're activists, but they're not paid lobbyists. They're not representing the power company; they're representing poor people and people that need help.
>
> —Mississippi State Representative Cecil Brown

FROM PROTEST TO POLICY . . . TO GOVERNANCE?

Over the years, Echo has employed a variety of strategies to realize its policy goals and increase accountability. Indeed, the network continues to strategically choose actions that most appropriately suit a given situation. Nevertheless, there has been a gradual shift in strategy from a more protest-oriented approach to a policymaking one, a level of political engagement that Echo, as a more established and experienced organization, can now meaningfully support.

The shift in Echo's approach is reflected in its collaboration with the Mississippi Department of Education and other state and local agencies. "Part of what we got out of collaboration," Leroy explains, "is that we got entrée—an opportunity to be inside the processes and get value from stuff and learn stuff that we wouldn't have learned any other way." With this entrée, Echo was "right inside of the official committee meetings, and we kept being folks who were asked to be making presentations to education committees at the state level . . . and so we were expert witnesses on basically everything that was education." Through this new policymaking model, Echo can use "accountability relationships" to not only provide community members with a voice in the policy process, but to participate directly in shaping policies.

This shift in strategy has also required a new model of leadership training. As Mike explains:

> When you're banging on the door and the window to get inside, the wish is fairly simple. We're being excluded. We have a right to be inside. We demand to be inside. We're comin' inside. But when you're at the table, it gets much more complicated because there's no point in being at the table unless you come with policy remedies for the problems you're describing because the endless repetition—what I would call the complaint framework in the protest model—doesn't go anywhere when the other side says, "I'll listen all day long," and then not do anything. That's why the organizing is necessary. It's why the analysis is necessary. It's why you have to ratchet up the sophistication of your work because you're now in system building and system correction.

To accommodate the demands of its new policymaking role, Echo has broadened its expertise on educational issues at all levels of the organization, providing a deeper understanding of race and class and their relationship to educational and other contextual factors and creating a community consciousness that incorporates a systemic analysis of problems and solutions.

Different stakeholders conceptualize Echo's "protest-to-policy" shift in different ways. Echo's allies often describe it as a shift from a "radical" to a more "collaborative" style. According to Steve Williams, former state deputy superintendent:

> When they first came to the state many, many years ago their style initially was more of a "we're going to make you do this," more of the confrontational style, which is not uncommon when you go in and you see wrong and people are angry, and they have transformed that completely into this "we're going to show you where you're making mistakes and where you're implementing policies and procedures that are nonproductive to you and your community and your students and show you a better way to do it."

Despite the shift in approach, Echo has not abandoned the use of protest. In early 2007, for example, Echo organized large rallies on the Capitol lawn to reveal broad public support for full funding of the Mississippi Adequate Education Program, even as it negotiated with lawmakers inside the state house. This kind of strategic sensitivity to both situation and resources—knowing when to mobilize numbers and when to push policy—allows Echo and its local affiliates to become central players in educational policy in Mississippi.

As a central player, Echo is forward-looking in its perspective. Today's accomplishments are seen in the context of a long struggle for equity. Big wins lay the foundation for the next level of work. Indeed, all of the leaders we spoke with in Echo and its local organizations appear constantly focused on the work ahead. In Indianola, for example, the Sunflower County Parents and Students Organization provided information to community members about the 2010 census, explaining that getting counted as a part of the census ensures that more federal money comes to the county. Citizens for a Better Greenville is working with thirty-five parents to develop a parent handbook that supports the district's recently enacted parent involvement policy. Concerned Citizens for a Better Tunica County continues to support the implementation of a comprehensive five-year education plan, while Holmes County's Citizens for Quality Education focuses on drop out prevention and juvenile justice. While issues change, however, the core organizing strategies remain. As Betty Petty notes, overcoming community fear to name inequity and advocate for rights is one continual challenge; another continues to be increasing the participation of community members in the political system, as either local leaders or simply aware citizens.

There are signs that Echo is now looking ahead to yet a new strategic direction as a new governance model seems to be coming to the fore. An increasing number of Echo's organizers and members of its local partnering groups have been elected to formal leadership positions, like membership on local school boards. As a result, Echo is not just invited to the policymaking table as a source of community information or voice; now, more and more, their members actually have a full seat at the table. These elected members have a responsibility to represent a community perspective, providing a new vehicle for community agency. With this new governance model comes the possibility, according to Mike, that "black schools, black children, would have the same opportunity as white children . . . We're still fighting that fight. The whole playing field has changed as a result of this organizing work. But we're not out of those woods." Shaping governance, then, is emerging as one more tool for Echo to use in its efforts to create that opportunity.

FUTURE TENSIONS AND QUESTIONS

As Echo moves forward, though, there are a number of challenges and tensions it will confront, dilemmas that will ultimately impact its organizational sustainability. These *questions* do not come with "right" or "wrong" answers. Instead, we see them as dilemmas that Echo must navigate in order to sustain and expand its effectiveness, coherence, and impact.

One tension may draw from Echo's organizing strategy—that it uses protest to draw attention to issues while also engaging in policymaking and, increasingly, governance itself. It seems that the protesting—and the accompanying appearance of radicalism these protests may feed—could undermine Echo's policymaking roles, especially if other stakeholders are reluctant to fund, collaborate with, or even associate with a "radical" organization. Yet, interestingly, those within Echo do not view protest and policymaking as contradictory. Melvin Young, the director of Concerned Citizens, explains, "Protest is a valuable influence on the policy." In Echo's view, engaging in public protests and working with education officials to make policy are two strategic tools of organizing; good organizing is a matter of knowing which tool is most appropriate in a given situation.

Another particularly salient tension, one that those within Echo readily acknowledge, stems from the insider-outsider perspective that Echo has cultivated. Echo now enjoys increased presence of its leaders on district and state decision-making bodies: three of the four local sites we studied, for example, have an organization leader or organizer, paid by Echo, sitting on the local school board. The advantages of such a position are clear—the opportunity to influence district policy, to change the minds and hearts of other board members, and to make the voices of the community heard. But these opportunities are accompanied by some clear tensions in the dual responsibility of organizer and policymaker. Betty Petty, who is executive director of the Sunflower County Parents and Students Organization and an Echo organizer, is also a school board member. Betty suggests that she has had to redefine the boundaries of her role within the organization by allowing other members of the organization to work with parents when the issues involve direct school action, such as confronting school administrators or organizing for specific school policy changes. Moreover, beyond simply changing the scope of a leader's organizational role, the dual responsibilities can often conflict, forcing the leader-board member to make hard choices. Ellen Reddy, co-director of Citizens for Quality Education, describes the difficult position of her sister Helen Johnson, CQE's other director and Holmes County School Board member:

> Her work becomes even greater, I think, because she's a community person; she represents the community; she's trying to build consensus and build relationships with the governing body, but at the same time she's got community folk like me and a husband and a son and the rest of us in the room saying, "Step on it, Helen, why are you moving that direction?"

This tension also does not go unnoticed by other school leaders and officials; at least one superintendent suggested that, with an organization's leader serving as a member of the school board, the organization is no longer in a position to organize against decisions of the board since its leader was involved in making them. Thus far, elected representatives from Echo-affiliated groups have managed these tensions on a decision-by-decision basis. Echo, meanwhile, recognizes that these individuals need increased training and support to negotiate their two roles. If Echo continues to pursue additional governance roles, however, this tension may only increase, putting others in this often challenging position.

Another tension lies in the relationship between state and local work. Echo made a strategic decision long ago to keep leaders in their local communities. Yet the group increasingly works at the state level and requires leaders focused on that arena. As state policymaking and even governance responsibilities grow, Echo may be hard pressed to continue working as deeply as is necessary at both the local and state levels.

A related issue involves accountability within Echo itself, given that the majority of Echo's organizers are also the leaders of local organizations. These dual responsibilities are by design; Echo believes that when staff members share roles, local work can better inform state work and ensure community support for state-level initiatives. However, these individuals may occasionally find themselves in situations where the needs of the local community conflict with the interests of Echo or its state work. This particular tension may be especially resonant now, as the state is considering legislation to boost the quality of school superintendents by adopting a statewide model of appointed, rather than elected, superintendents. Most of Echo's leaders support this change. However, in many of the counties in which superintendents are currently elected, this proposition has been met with significant resistance from black residents who feel that a move to appointed positions brings disenfranchisement, a belief with which at least one leader of a local organization agrees. Managing both local demands and Echo's organizational well-being is always a balancing act, Echo's organizers note. "It's not a mathematical equation," Mike argues. "There are many super-facets of the diamond, so to speak, as you turn to try to understand what the choices are and how different organizations will feel differently. So you negotiate, and then you try to find the right place, the right approach at each turn." Melvin Young agrees: "Everybody in all of the local organizations are always negotiating with Echo around their participation," concluding that it's ultimately a matter of finding a balance between the local and state work and showing local communities that their interest is bound up in statewide issues. The issue of superintendent appointment may prove to be a particularly tough test of the ability of Echo's leaders to reach a balance, but it will not likely be the last.

Conclusion

Echo works to influence the development of social policies to prevent their continued use as instruments of racial domination and control. It views a quality education as the right of every citizen and a fundamental social justice issue; its education work aims to influence the policies that govern education systems in order to improve access, quality, and equity. Echo strives to achieve this goal by using an intergenerational model of organizing that builds community capacity to hold policymakers accountable.

Beneath these strategies lay some deeper processes. Echo builds on existing networks of relationships to access community voices to determine shared interests and concerns; it systemically gathers, cultivates, and shares knowledge about the issues identified; it develops a sense of community consciousness about these common concerns; and it works to hold elected officials accountable to their communities. This process is conducted on two levels—both state and local. Local organizations pursue issues based on local needs, and they then band together across the state in pursuit of broadly shared concerns.

Context shapes not only why Echo does community organizing but the issues it addresses and the approaches it uses. Rooted in the tradition emerging from the Civil Rights movement, Echo draws upon Mississippi's historical, political, cultural and economic context, and the experiences of African Americans within it, to bring people together around shared experiences and help them work together toward a shared vision of the future. Due to Mississippi's history, especially the way in which education has been used as a tool to disempower African Americans and the high value black communities put on education, Echo centers its organizing around the struggle for equity and justice in education in the Mississippi Delta.

It is difficult to fully capture the ways in which community organizing for education reform as practiced by Echo affects the people, communities, and education systems where it is done. It is perhaps easier to identify the big public wins, like full funding of MAEP. Through campaigns like this, Echo has transformed the relationship between the institutions of public education and organized black communities. However, the deeper effects lie within local communities and individuals themselves—the African American parents across the Delta who, by banding with other residents, realize their rights as American citizens to make demands of schools: demands to hold school board meetings at the end of a work day, demands to stop the aerial spraying of fields close to schools and residential neighborhoods, demands to resist the use of public funds to build a school that would serve only white students, and demands to make policymakers accountable to the families they serve and for the decisions they make.

From listening tours in fifteen Delta counties to a long battle for equitable educational funding, Echo has spent the last two decades working to build communities that resist and reshape policies that further domination and control. This is work based on relationships that endure, knowledge that empowers, a community consciousness that unites, and an accountability that brings real change. This work creates empowered communities that are beginning to transform the educational landscape of Mississippi.

PACT parent leaders Junior Muñoz and Art Meza co-chair the action "Saving Our Children with Excellent Schools" at St. John Vianney Church. Spring 2009. (Photo by Jacqueline Ramseyer).

Founding L.U.C.H.A. principal Preston Smith speaks with a parent about the PACT-initiated small schools at a St. John Vianney parish event. 2006. (Photo by PACT)

PACT makes the ACE charter middle school a reality for students Jennifer Portillo, Anastacia Bravo, and Yessica Ramirez. (Photo by Gabriela Rico)

Principal Robert Cordova, a One LA leader, surveys the Harmony Elementary School auditorium in preparation for the community-wide Gang Reduction and Youth Development (GRYD) meeting with the Los Angeles Mayor's office. (Photo by Soojin Oh)

Parents and teachers of Harmony Elementary School students attend a One LA house meeting about neighbor-hood safety and gang violence prevention. (Photo by Soojin Oh)

After a One LA parent leadership training session, Luz Benitez (left) and a fellow Harmony parent leader plan their response to the School Board members' morning addresses at the Los Angeles Unified School District Parent Summit. (Photo by Soojin Oh)

Padres y Jovenes Unidos members collect petitions at Lincoln High School in support of in-state tuition. Winter 2008. (Photo by PJU)

Padres y Jovenes Unidos leader Amber Mendoza calls for College Prep for All at a press conference launching the Campaign for Accountable Public Schools. August 18, 2009. (Photo by PJU)

Padres y Jovenes Unidos organizes and leads a march calling for passage of the DREAM Act. Spring 2006. (Photo by PJU)

Joyce Parker presents data on school districts after a mapping exercise. (Photo by Southern Echo)

Southern Echo delegates participate in a march at the United States Social Forum. (Photo by Southern Echo)

Hollis Watkins leads the Southern Echo team in a presentation. (Photo by Southern Echo)

Teacher Clarinda Luckett shares a book with families during a Literacy Ambassador house visit in Logan Square, as fellow ambassador LSNA Parent Mentor Juanita Pedroza looks on (lower right). (Photo by Jeff Brown)

LSNA Parent Mentors prepare for a meeting with the Police Commander. (Photo by LSNA)

LSNA members march for a just state budget. 2010. (Photo by LSNA)

Teresa Andersen and Jatnna Ramirez co-MC the Northwest Bronx Community and Clergy Coalition Shared Fate Action Forum. May 2008. (Photo by Dan Perez)

Youth from Sistas and Brothas United and the Northwest Bronx Coalition join a rally to support education funding with Crystal Reyes (center) and Jatnna Ramirez (far right).

Hundreds gather at St. Nicholas of Tolentine Church for the Northwest Bronx Coalition's Shared Fate Action Forum. (Photo by Dan Perez)

6

"Acts of Leadership"

Building Powerful Forms of Parent Participation in Chicago

PRIMARY AUTHOR: SOO HONG

On a cold February day in Chicago, crowds of parents, young people, community members, and local residents gather together, generating movement and momentum on a relatively quiet day.[1] Children and adults wave bright signs that read, "LSNA supports bilingual students!" The crowd is abuzz with conversation, and there is excitement in the air. Parent leaders welcome families who are just joining as the crowd grows larger. Students start waving signs higher, mimicking the words and actions of their parents. Slowly, murmurs escalate to more assertive voices, and parents begin to take center stage in front of news cameras that have arrived for the event. The families are gathered for a press conference arranged by fellow parent leaders and community organizers to challenge the use of the Illinois Standards Achievement Test (ISAT) with bilingual students. Previously, parents explain, bilingual students who were not fully proficient in English were given the IMAGE test, for its ease of use with English-language learners. Early in 2008, as the federal government pressured Chicago Public Schools to use the ISAT test, parents organized an effort to challenge that decision, insisting that the new test would set their children up to fail. During the press conference, a group of parents who had studied the issue spoke to the crowd about what they knew to be an injustice for bilingual students. Erica Soto, a parent leader at McAuliffe Elementary School whose child is in the bilingual program, argued:

> The English in the ISAT test is too hard for third-grade bilingual students, and the children will just feel stupid if they are forced to take it ... We want to make sure that students and parents don't feel it's their fault when the children do badly. It's not their fault or the teacher's fault.[2]

As gathered parents and students listened intently, they cheered Erica and the other parents who spoke against the recent proposition. They argued that teachers and students were not prepared for the change, scheduled just weeks away, and the results would only discourage teachers, students, and their families. As parents like Erica spoke out, they expressed a clear knowledge and understanding of the educational environments of schools and classrooms. One parent leader, Patricia Lopez, studying to become a bilingual education teacher herself after years of involvement in her children's schools, held up an ISAT testing booklet to show the crowd how challenging the test would prove for students still gaining proficiency in English. She argued, "It takes five to seven years for a bilingual student to be academically proficient in her second language."[3]

These parents have built a base of knowledge about schools and developed the confidence to lead public rallies like this one through their involvement with the Logan Square Neighborhood Association (LSNA). Involved in LSNA's parent organizing projects, they have worked alongside teachers to support students in classrooms, become intimately aware of the educational issues schools face, and emerged as forceful leaders and role models in schools. This campaign was driven by the passion and expertise of parents like Erica and Patricia who have taken the matters of school reform into their own hands. Upon reflecting on this parent-inspired campaign, Ofelia Sanchez and Leticia Barrera, two parent leaders and LSNA organizers discuss their own motivations in getting involved:

> We are not afraid to speak up if it will benefit our children. We are the ones who have their best interests in mind.

> Before, I didn't have the information to really push back on initiatives or policies or anything like that, but this is different now. I have knowledge and that gives me power.

Rather than accepting the directives and initiatives passed along to schools from the city or state, parents like Ofelia, Leticia, Patricia, and Erica have learned to be critical and challenge policies when necessary. They have also worked closely with educators to initiate new programs to benefit their children and mobilize support among parents and families in the community. With their knowledge and experience, they have generated collective power to promote necessary change.

This chapter examines LSNA's education organizing efforts and describes the experiences of parents as they become active participants and leaders within school settings. The chapter begins with a discussion of LSNA's origins and the group's entry into education organizing in Chicago. It then discusses the group's efforts to develop campaigns and programs to build parent leadership— first bringing parents into the often unfamiliar environment of schools, then integrating them into the life and culture of schools, and finally developing them as leaders within the school and broader community. The chapter concludes with a discussion of the implications of LSNA's education organizing in building a model of school reform centered on meaningful forms of parent leadership and forged connections between school and community.

Charting a Path for Education Organizing

LSNA was founded in the Logan Square neighborhood on the Northwest Side of Chicago in the early 1960s in response to the increasing deindustrialization and ensuing suburbanization of the greater Chicago metropolitan area. During those years, the working-class European immigrant families who made up the neighborhood fought to curb the community deterioration that resulted from the exodus of long-term residents and businesses. In the seventies and eighties, though, the neighborhood experienced a dramatic demographic shift toward the predominantly Latino community it is today. The incoming Latino families—primarily of Cuban and Puerto Rican descent—viewed their move to Logan Square, despite its challenges, as a step up. With Latinos approaching two-thirds of the population, Logan Square also experienced a subsequent influx of Latino businesses that developed the neighborhood's main streets into a commercial destination for many Latino families.[4] By the early nineties, 90 percent of the children in the schools in Logan Square were Latino (including many of Mexican descent), while 95 percent qualified for free or reduced-price lunch.

Working with Latino families in the group's early organizing campaigns for affordable housing, neighborhood safety, and immigration reform, LSNA organizers soon found that education was a central issue and concern for these newcomers. However, many found schools to be distant places where they felt unwelcome. Yet LSNA organizers saw strong schools as fundamentally interconnected with community well-being. According to education organizer Leticia Barrera:

> To address the housing and the rental problem, you have to see it is connected to the school, because if families are moving because they are not paying the rent, then schools will be facing too many changes in students and that is a problem for the school.

In response, LSNA charted a path of education organizing that sought to change the nature of school involvement and community involvement by connecting the two. With a growing awareness that improving schools would be central to improving communities, LSNA began to set their sights on organizing within schools, with the assistance of a sweeping change in Chicago school politics.[5]

Building a Collective Voice within the Context of Chicago School Reform

School reform in Chicago took a distinct turn in 1988 when lawmakers created local school councils (LSCs) that would serve as administrative bodies to individual schools. Passed one year after then U.S. Secretary of Education William Bennett referred to the Chicago school system as the worst in the nation, this law opened up school governance to elected parents and community members and created institutional mechanisms for community organizations to become involved in the city's schools.[6] According to some experts, this policy change was a direct result of the growing civic capacity of a well-organized and tightly knit Chicago business community and a strong network of community-based organizations—both with a vested interest in local schools. Chicago Public Schools had been notorious for resisting change. The long-term efforts of community groups calling for openness, transparency, and community involvement finally culminated in a mounting public outcry over the school system's persistent failure. The LSCs created by the new law were to have a majority of parents and community members, as well as the school principal and teachers, and they were given real power—the authority to hire principals and approve the school's improvement plans and discretionary budget.[7]

For LSNA's Executive Director, Nancy Aardema, this was an exciting time for community organizing groups that were interested in education. "Across the city, you have these very actively engaged and powerful organizing groups, and suddenly, we are given an opportunity to encourage our community members— these parents and families—to become critical voices in schools." As was the case for many community groups, the goal for LSNA's early work in schools, according to Nancy, "was to get strong LSCs that would function smoothly and encourage broad participation in the community." However, many schools were profoundly disconnected from families and the community experiences of their students. According to lead education organizer Joanna Brown who helped to pioneer LSNA's early work in schools:

> There was this significant separation between families and schools, and then all of a sudden, you have this school reform law that says parents and community need to be part of school decision-making, but how? We knew we needed to lay the groundwork for this collaboration in a way that would be relational and that would help to build trust and eliminate some of the barriers.

LSC involvement became an entry point for LSNA into schools, and as organizers began building relationships with parents and schools, they discovered that schools could become significant sites for community building and organizing. As LSNA organizers began working in schools and connecting them to families, they also began to identify common issues and concerns that could potentially serve as a catalyst for collaboration. Through these conversations, school overcrowding emerged as a shared concern among school staff and parents. Principals were worried about swelling enrollments that placed added stress on schools already strapped for classroom space; parents were displeased with the prospect that their children would be bused to schools outside of the neighborhood as a result of over-enrollment.

Under the direction of LSNA's Education Committee, LSCs, school principals, and community members joined together in a campaign to address school overcrowding. Through this campaign, Nancy recalls, LSNA "began to create trust with the parents, with the administrators, with some of the teachers and some of the students." By combining forces, the campaign was able to win an outcome that principals had failed to attain on their own. According to Joanna, "The principals had been struggling with the overcrowding issue for years and had been trying to get something done and couldn't get it done." With LSNA leading in the public confrontation with the Board of Education, principals were protected from having to take an openly antagonistic role. Amanda Rivera, a current Chicago assistant principal who worked with LSNA as a teacher and principal during this time, recalls that until schools began working collaboratively with LSNA, they did not realize that each was often struggling with the same issues of bureaucratic unresponsiveness as the other. School leaders realized that in smaller, isolated efforts, they failed to generate the power and momentum that was necessary to win significant change. Through the collective effort initiated by LSNA, however, local educators began to be heard. Amanda explains:

> We became a collective voice, a more unified and powerful voice . . . we were getting answers; we were getting meetings; we got a response . . . And it was, we were told, because we were the squeaky wheel, which was good for us, but unfortunate for other schools who didn't have the backing of an organizing group.

By working alongside rather than in opposition to school leaders, Nancy believes LSNA was able to build relationships and trust with schools that would later prove to be instrumental:

> The smart thing we did was that we brought the administrators to the table. We weren't confronting the principal. We were bringing the

principal in to be part of the process, to say, "I need more space." It was far better for all of us to be at the table. Right then and there, we began building those relationships.

Through these campaigns and the development of new relationships, LSNA strived toward collaborative interactions with schools—a significant departure from previous arrangements that were tense and divisive. These collaborative efforts produced the development of five new annexes and two new middle schools over several years along with acknowledgement from school leaders that community groups had valuable resources to offer in school reform efforts.

Consequently, education became a key issue in LSNA's first Holistic Plan, a mission statement adopted in 1995 that charted a vision for the group's work. In the plan, LSNA resolved to:[8]

1. Develop schools as community centers because "the health of any community is dependent on the availability of common space for interaction, education, service provision, recreation, culture and arts."
2. Train parents to work in the classrooms of LSNA schools because "children learn better when their parents are actively involved in their education."
3. Support community controlled education because the "health of any community is dependent on the quality of education provided to its residents."

With this plan, Nancy explains, LSNA made a strong statement that "schools shape communities and communities shape schools." Upon adoption of the Holistic Plan, LSNA began to chart a course that would bring parents into schools and classrooms in meaningful ways. It was a plan shaped by conversations with parents and also with school principals who saw a need to engage families without a clear understanding of how this could be done. From these conversations emerged the Parent Mentor program and a continuous effort to bring the previously isolated worlds of school and community together in new, dynamic, and interactive ways.

Building Relationships between Schools and Communities: The Evolution of Parent Mentors

One cold winter evening, as Karla Mack discussed with her children what they would have for dinner that night, they heard an abrupt and loud knock on their apartment door. As she opened the door to an anxious and upset neighbor, Karla quickly learned that the building was on fire. Rushing out of the house with her children, she recalls, "Before our eyes, these four families that were there, everything burned ... one minute, we're sitting there about to figure out what we want to eat, and we lost everything." While her neighbors instantly turned to family members for assistance, Karla recalls feeling alone that night on the street as she watched flames engulf her apartment building. She did not have immediate family members to help her.

As this tragic event unfolded, Karla lost everything and suddenly faced a frightening future for her children. Without renter's insurance to replace their belongings and without a long-term place to stay, she recalls, "I had no home, and I had nothing for my children. Nothing." But the following day, Karla was received by an outpouring of support from fellow parent mentors and LSNA organizers. As news of her loss moved through the school community, Silvia Gonzalez, the Parent Mentor program coordinator at McAuliffe Elementary School, reached out to Karla on behalf of an organized effort by the LSNA community to temporarily house and provide for her family. Karla describes the outpouring of support:

> And within two weeks—it was a rough two weeks, But I guarantee you, every day, we ate. Every day, we slept somewhere clean and safe. I had friends that helped, but that was, like, a place here or there . . . Everyday, LSNA would have something for us to eat, a gift card ... I don't even know these people ... but everyone came and gave us so much love and support.

Karla soon realized that she would also have to face the possibility of leaving the very neighborhood and school community that had reached out to her:

> LSNA and McAuliffe were my family, because I really don't have any family. It's just me and my children, and I was like, 'What am I going to do?' I don't want to leave McAuliffe. I don't want to leave this community. My daughter goes to high school in this neighborhood. I'm starting to like what I do here and kind of see what my options are.

With the community's support, Karla and her children found a new apartment in the neighborhood after just two weeks of temporary housing. As a result, her children remained at McAuliffe, and Karla developed a renewed sense of community and hope:

> This community saved me and put me on my feet again. My children cried not once. We lost everything ... What sustained me was this community, the love and support . . . so anything I can do to pass on that type of love, that type of support, that's what I'm here to do, because someone did that for me. This is someplace I know I want to stay.

Karla describes an environment where the lines between school and community are blurred. Through her participation in the Parent Mentor program, she became connected to school staff and families in ways that were profoundly meaningful and important to her.

According to Joanna Brown, the isolation Karla used to feel within her own community is not uncommon for the many working and immigrant families who struggle to create a life for themselves and their children in Logan Square. Parents "struggle to make ends meet, they spend little time connecting to folks in the community, and the school is probably the most unfamiliar environment of all. Even for schools that want to involve parents, it's hard, because parents are not even there in the first place." Combating this isolation—from schools and the broader community—was precisely one of LSNA's original goals in creating the Parent Mentor program.

Some local school principals had their own reasons for being interested in developing a program for parents. Sally Acker, principal of Funston Elementary School at the time of the program's creation, noticed that Latino parents, many of whom were Spanish speaking, rarely came into the school building beyond the quick, daily responsibilities of dropping off and picking up their children. How could the school encourage more widespread parent involvement? Nancy recalls the principal's dilemma:

> [Sally Acker] felt like the issue was that parents only came to the school when there was a problem, or if they were the "good parents of the good kids." . . . She felt like we had to figure out a way as a community to get just the average parents, or the parents of the kids who were struggling into the school—not in a way that they felt like they were there to be told what was wrong, not in a way that put them at a disadvantage, or put them down—but she felt they should be in the school in a very real, continuous way.

At the same time, another group, Community Organizing and Family Issues (COFI), began working on a project to train parents to become more involved in Chicago schools. With the goal of making parent involvement more continuous and meaningful, LSNA and COFI worked with Amanda Rivera at Funston to create training that would become the basis for the emerging program.

The Parent Mentor program was launched at Funston Elementary School in 1995. It was designed to bring parents out of their homes and into classrooms where they would work alongside teachers as classroom assistants. For four days a week, two hours each morning, over the duration of an entire school year, parent mentors work in a classroom—reading to children in small groups, working with individual students, and supporting classroom activities. Each

Friday morning, parent mentors come together for training sessions as a cohort within the school; once a month they meet as a group across all of the participating schools in Logan Square. Parents are paid a small stipend to facilitate and encourage consistent participation, as well as to respect and recognize the value of their work. By bringing parents into schools in this way, LSNA sought to build a sense of familiarity with schools and the broader community among immigrant parents. Meanwhile, the program also strived to encourage a more open attitude toward families among neighborhood schools.

To make parents essential to the life of a school environment would require institutional change—a paradigm shift. Teachers were not accustomed to having parents in the school, particularly in their classrooms working with students. Amanda Rivera remembers navigating the delicate relationships with both teachers and parents at Funston school:

> For me it was very difficult, because I had to then meet with the teachers, and let them know that we were going to have parents, but they're going to be placed in classrooms to assist them. And because this was so new, there was no prior practice of parents being engaged in the classroom a significant way. So, I had to figure out how do we change this paradigm where there's this mistrust of parents in the school, in the classroom, and people feeling that I'm going to be spied upon, and critiqued, or feeling threatened by the parents in the classroom?

Interactions between parents and teachers were infrequent but were often hostile and antagonistic, centered on disagreements concerning a child. The predominance of negative interchanges between parents and teachers only escalated feelings of mistrust, fear, and resentment, and Amanda was worried that teachers would simply not volunteer to have parent mentors in their classrooms. Sensing that fear—among parents and teachers—was the overriding barrier to building these new relationships, she designed a training program that would seek to dispel the myths, break down the sense of mistrust, and develop some common ground. She recalls the goals of the first training sessions:

> Little did the teachers realize that the parents felt just as fearful about going in the classroom, so we always did some team building at the beginning with the teachers and the parents, where we actually put them together, and did activities—teachers and parents—to help them talk about their commonalities as human beings first, and they realized, "Oh, I'm a mother, and you're a mother, and these are some of my hobbies, or some of my interests, and these are some of my challenges," so just team-building activities like that.

These team-building activities created a sense of common purpose and shared experience among parents and teachers. That foundation was essential to the successful start of the Parent Mentor program. By developing these relationships intentionally, Amanda says, "We began to build rapport and began to break down barriers before parent mentors actually were placed in the classroom."

The primary focus of the parent mentor trainings, however, was on parents, especially on the personal goals and leadership development of parents. Treating parents as leaders and role models to children, organizers encouraged parents to identify personal goals they would commit to meeting over the course of the year. For many parents, personal goals are centered on education—such as obtaining a GED or taking English classes—or employment. Throughout the year, parents chart their progress in accomplishing their goals, supporting each other in their parent mentor cohort.

Parent Mentor training sessions are also designed to foster parent leadership. LSNA teaches parents about issues of power and inequality and builds the skills they need to work together to improve school and community life. Indeed, the program introduces parents to broader community issues beyond the school, issues like affordable housing and public health. By working with a focus on leadership development and the explicit recognition of power and inequality, LSNA encouraged parents to view themselves as active agents for personal and community transformation.

From its beginning in 1995, the program grew quickly to include eight elementary and middle schools across Logan Square. Each year the program trains over 150 parents; since its inception more than 1,200 parents have graduated as parent mentors. Meanwhile, the Parent Mentor program has become a springboard for new programs and initiatives that have provided added opportunities for parent and community engagement in schools. As parents become immersed in a training program that connects them to the school community and fosters a sense of leadership, they begin to alter the environment and encourage schools to view families in a different light. Despite the program's evolution and the host of initiatives that have since developed from its existence, the Parent Mentor program remains as a foundation to LSNA's work in schools and the community. As one education organizer explains:

> And then it's [the Parent Mentor program] a steppingstone for everything else. These parents go on to find full-time jobs outside, or they start working in the schools as tutors or paraprofessionals, serve on school committees, lead one of our programs, or become elected on the local school council. It's a little seed that gets planted that grows into a whole bunch of other things. As parent mentors, they build new skills of leadership and activism and this becomes the base for their work as

leaders in many of our other programs or in the school and community more broadly.

From Parent Involvement to Parent Engagement

For many parents and teachers who come to know the Parent Mentor program, it is not, as one parent leader explains, "your typical parent involvement program." In contrast to other programs "where schools decide who comes and goes and who gets to be involved in what way and how, this program is really about meeting parents where they are and trying to figure out what they need from schools." While parents might typically support teachers in classrooms, the program encourages parent mentors and teachers to view themselves as partners. From an organizing perspective, LSNA believes these relationships and the power that is created through them are critical to changing the nature of school-family interactions.

To LSNA organizers, the Parent Mentor program's strength lies in its attempt to break traditional notions of parent involvement. LSNA moves schools beyond a practice of transferring or depositing knowledge to parents through brochures, flyers, formal events, and meetings to a system of engagement where parents are invited and incorporated into the life of schools and learn about schools through their own interactions within the environment. By inviting parents to participate in the real work of schools and classrooms, the Parent Mentor program builds parents' understanding of school culture—the people, the interactions, the expectations, and the practice.

In addition to deepening parent participation in schools to become more powerful and meaningful, the Parent Mentor program also seeks to broaden parent participation by bringing previously uninvolved parents into schools and classrooms. The program develops an approach that addresses the barriers that may typically impede parent participation. For example, parents with limited English fluency are still encouraged to participate, and organizers place these parent mentors in bilingual classrooms or with younger children. One parent mentor describes her experience in the classroom as a newly involved parent with limited English fluency:

> I did not think the school would be a place for me. I knew some English, but I was always too nervous to speak it. I was in the classroom with these children, learning new things and understanding the way of the teacher, and it was wonderful. It did not matter if my English was not perfect, and in that time, my English became much better.

For parents like her, LSNA's Parent Mentor program becomes "a new chance, a new beginning, it is a new opportunity for me to be a different kind of parent for my children."

Branching Out: Changing the Nature of Relationships between Schools and Families

Six children are gathered on the floor around a teacher who reads from the book *Love You Forever*. Those who are not right in front of the teacher sit on their knees to get a good look at the pictures. The teacher, Susana Rojas, is animated in her reading of the story, inviting participation by encouraging students to repeat the story's refrain with her. Her reading is peppered with questions to elicit discussion—about baby brothers, mothers and children, and about growing up. With each question, children raise their hands and sit up to respond. Susana then reads the book a second time, this time in Spanish, and the children chant the refrain with her at the end:

> Para siempre te amare,
> Para siempre te querre,
> Mientras en mi haya vida,
> Siempre seras mi bebe.

Susana is a classroom teacher at Mozart Elementary School, but on this occasion, she reads this book in the living room of the home of one of the students. She is there one late afternoon after school, with the hosting family and three other families who were invited to attend with their children. This is part of LSNA's Literacy Ambassadors program, created to encourage mutual learning and stronger partnerships between parents and teachers in the education of children.

A couple years into the Parent Mentor program, organizers and parents began to realize that parents alone could not shoulder the burden of transforming parent-teacher relationships. As Nancy Aardema recalls:

> From the beginning we always had this concept of parent-teacher mentoring—the teacher was mentoring the parent but the parent was also helping the teacher understand more about the culture of the community. That's the unusual part, because teachers teach, but teachers aren't looking to learn the culture of the community necessarily.

While the Parent Mentor program was successful in helping parents understand the classroom environment, "having teachers learn from parents" was a more challenging endeavor. Through focus group conversations with parent mentors, LSNA found that in order for teachers to truly understand the experiences of families, they had to experience children in their homes.

LSNA designed the Literacy Ambassadors program based on the vision of parent mentors who wanted, according to Joanna Brown, "to build a bridge between the school and home." Teachers visit a student's home to talk with parents and children, who are invited by the hosting family, about reading together at home. A classroom parent mentor accompanies the teacher on the home visit and serves as a bridge between the teacher and the family. Together, the teacher and parent mentor plan activities for parents and children that support the goal of literacy and give parents ideas on how to support their child's reading at home. In this way, the Literacy Ambassadors program builds stronger parent-teacher relationships while also reaching out to families that had little previous connection to schools and little exposure to classroom expectations.

Families embrace the opportunity to meet teachers in a familiar home environment. In doing so, they not only learn about the ways they can support their child's literacy development, they also establish connections with fellow parents. According to Lisa Contreras, a former Literacy Ambassadors program coordinator at Funston Elementary School, "Students are so excited to see teachers at their home, and families often feel less intimidated by teachers and the school environment because of this experience." The informal environment allows families to feel more comfortable when connecting with teachers. Lisa adds, "These parents don't have to feel intimidated, because now they know the teacher . . . they have been actually having a conversation."

Lisa believes, however, that the benefits for teachers are just as compelling. While she has often heard from teachers who are "nervous to be out of their comfort zone and into a family's home" for the first time, "that nervousness just goes away, and they leave excited to do this again," after an evening of shared experiences. Melva Patock, a Funston teacher who has often participated in the Literacy Ambassadors program agrees:

> It's hard to build that connection with parents when you don't know them. And when you only meet them in school, you don't really have to think about it. But when you come a student's house and you sit down together for dinner with his parents and you can see where they live, then you can really focus on the family and the community that they are a part of. You start to see everything in a different light, but especially from that student's perspective.

Because schools typically reflect the values and perspectives of white middle-class families, programs such as this work to challenge those traditional power dynamics. By bringing teachers into the community and directly into a student's home, LSNA encourages parents and teachers to examine their own assumptions and move toward practices that bring families and school staff together on more equal footing and into more meaningful relationships.

Changing schools requires, according to Nancy, "a constant reassessment of the situation, a continuous evaluation of what we're doing, and plenty of opportunities for parents themselves to be part of this assessment and evaluation process." Indeed, the creation of the Literacy Ambassadors program is a good example of LSNA's ability to listen closely to parents and engage them in new and innovative initiatives. According to City Clerk Miguel Del Valle, who has worked with LSNA in the past as a community organizer and Illinois state senator, LSNA's ability "to move with the times and to intimately involve themselves in what's going on in the community and intelligently know what the next step needs to be," is critical in pushing for change in schools.

Meanwhile, during the first year of the Parent Mentor program, parents and organizers quickly began to understand that while the program worked to build a core of visible and engaged parents within the school, there were still many parents who could not be involved. For working parents, who often did not have time during the school day to commit to working in classrooms, their only interactions with schools occurred in those brief moments while picking up or dropping off their children. Ada Ayala was among that first group of parent mentors who strove to find a way to open the school to the broader community. She recalls:

> And when we first started the community center, we wanted the school to be a place more for the families—and for more than just the families that can be here during the day. This is their school too, and we want the school to be a place where they feel safe and comfortable and welcome. I see the families in the evening, and it makes me feel good, because they know that this is their place too.

Ada, along with fellow parent mentors, went from door to door in the community, combing neighborhood streets to talk with families about the possibility of starting a community learning center at the school. The center would offer classes for adults and children in the evenings, and they wanted to know from families what kinds of classes they wanted in the center. Ada recalls:

> We wanted to know what was important for the families and what would bring them into the school. For many of them, it was the first time, and if we wanted them to come, we knew that we would have to find out what they wanted.

As parents knocked on doors, organizing support for the community learning center, they became more connected, according to Ada, "to the lives of the families—that many were struggling, that they had things they wanted to achieve but did not have the time or the money or the connections. When we talked to them about bringing these programs into the schools, we also heard that they did not spend any time in the school." This organizing effort confirmed to parents like Ada that schools could be powerful points of connection into community life for many of these families. Leaving schools open only during the relatively short school day was, according to Joanna, a "disservice to the community and a waste of their public space."

Ada became the coordinator for Funston Elementary School's Community Learning Center (CLC). Over the course of her journey from parent mentor to parent leader to CLC coordinator, she has watched the school become more open and accessible to a broad range of families—from those who don't yet speak English and take an ESL class in the center, to those who attend with their children for enrichment and cultural classes, as well as those whose busy work schedules and commitments to family life would make an evening GED class nearly impossible without the childcare provided in the center. After Funston, LSNA quickly launched five CLCs across their partner schools. The CLCs open their doors to children and their families after each school day, offering classes for children such as Mexican folkloric dance, after-school homework support, guitar lessons, and choir. For adults, the center provides GED and ESL classes to support their education, as well as a host of opportunities to meet other parents and families through book clubs, dance classes, and interest-based activities. The centers also provide childcare services for parents with young children. Not only do these programs offer educational resources to neighborhood families, they offer a place for parents to connect with other families and to build a sense of belonging and familiarity with the school. According to parent leader Lisa Contreras, CLCs provide "an opportunity to meet other families, get to know parents, and really get a sense of the school." Lisa adds:

> For these parents, they are busy during the day, so they can't be parent mentors, but this way, the school still offers them something valuable. And when they spend all that time coming to the school and walking around the building to take these classes, they start to feel a lot more comfortable in the school like, "Hey, I know this place, this place that my kids are in all day." Just by being in the school, they meet other parents and start getting connected to the other families, and schools are no longer this strange place to them.

CLCs were started through the organizing efforts of parents, and they continue to grow through such organizing. Parents lead regular efforts to go door-knocking, surveying families in the neighborhood about what they would like to see offered in the center. These organizing efforts are often spearheaded by parent mentors who view these experiences as leadership-development opportunities. During her work as a parent mentor, Karla Mack was involved in a door-knocking campaign to raise awareness and generate community input for a newly formed community center at McAuliffe. She argues that the experience both raised her awareness of the surrounding community and encouraged her to tap into those leadership skills LSNA nurtures:

> If you would have told me a year ago that I would be knocking on the door of strangers—people I don't know—to strike up conversation with you, I would never have believed you. This experience gets us in contact with all these families around the neighborhood. We start to feel connected as a group and as a community, and we start to understand what our neighbors care about . . . and then for me, this is just raising my own level of confidence that I can oversee this project and get out there and start doing things for my community.

Leadership Development

That Karla sees herself as an emerging leader is part of an intentional leadership development strategy that LSNA places at the center of its education organizing work. Organizers view leadership development as occurring through stages, particularly for the immigrant women who make up the base of their parent mentors. For many of these mothers, this is their first foray into community life, and they often find themselves without the language and cultural and institutional knowledge they need to feel confident and self-assured. For this reason, the Parent Mentor program is seen as a foundational first-step to encourage parents to participate in school-community life. Organizers use a training curriculum throughout the program that focuses on providing parents with knowledge about schools, connects them to each other to create a supportive network, and serves as a foundation for building leaders. Through the training, parents are taught about school practices and expectations; they are given opportunities to develop confidence in a new environment and set personal goals that will shape their development as mentors and role models. By working in the public space of classrooms, parent mentors engage in a host of activities that build their skills. Parent mentors learn to bring students together to work in a classroom, they converse with parents who inquire about their children, they work collaboratively with teachers to support students in classrooms, and they become public figures in a public institution. These are, according to Joanna, "acts of leadership," in and of themselves.

This initial phase of leadership development, according to LSNA organizer Leticia Barrera, "is critical, because before you can become a leader, you have to understand a lot about the environment—who is there, what is going on, and how things work." Through a training program that is focused on the development of personal goals and confidence in the public sphere of schools, parent mentors are encouraged to think about their experiences and contemplate their potential contributions, their potential "acts of leadership" within schools and classrooms. Through constant connections with past and present parent mentors—who lead training sessions, become LSNA organizers, or coordinate a Community Learning Center—new parent mentors gain a clearer sense of what those possible contributions might be. According to Parent Mentor coordinator Silvia Gonzalez:

> It pushes you to be a leader and to reflect on your experience—at home, at school, in your community—and to think about what you can do to contribute, what you can do to build yourself up, and what are those personal things like the goals in your life and the dreams that you have that you can work on? . . . We believe that it takes that to get to action. And action will change the community.

Indeed, the fact that parent mentor graduates take on a variety of leadership responsibilities, with some becoming full-time, paid organizers, is part of LSNA's intentional strategy. LSNA organizers are constantly looking to identify parent mentors who could be suited for greater leadership responsibilities. During the school year they spend with each cohort, LSNA organizers seek out potential leaders who show an interest in added responsibilities and have an outlook and disposition toward leadership.

As they worked with these emerging parent leaders, LSNA organizers found the need for a more advanced leadership-development strategy that takes parents beyond an introduction to leadership opportunities. LSNA created a week-long training session that, each year, gives forty potential leaders further grounding in the tenets and praxis of community organizing as well as an understanding of power and accountability within the community context. Participants analyze community power dynamics, examine forms of accountability, explore the nature of publicly accountable and private relationships, and analyze their own strengths and weaknesses in the public sphere. For a culminating training project, leaders design an action plan that would push an elected official toward a vote change. The training is designed to be interactive, and the action plans are presented in a simulated learning environment. Leticia, who got her start as a parent mentor herself, arranged and facilitated the first leadership training session along with another education organizer. She explains some of the intentions behind the training:

> There is some information that we as organizers and leaders have to know—about how decisions are made, who our leaders are, how we can push for changes. We have to educate our leaders about account-ability and how we can use the power we have to push our elected offi-cials to act in ways that are good for our people. And this cannot happen by just waiting and hoping that people will act.

With growing knowledge of community institutions as well as the develop-ment of explicit leadership skills, LSNA organizers make sure to provide poten-tial leaders with the opportunities to lead, in effect, testing their leadership knowledge and abilities. Whether parents are talking with funders, speaking at a rally, sharing testimony in front of the state legislature, working on a door-knocking campaign, or reading with a first grader, Joanna describes the wealth of opportunities that are available for developing leadership. Part of LSNA's vision is to "bring people into the leadership of actions and campaigns that fundamen-tally matter to our work in the community." Learning by doing is key. Joanna calls this an apprenticeship model, where individuals are given opportunities to lead and are supported by other organizers and leaders in ways that will ensure their success.

Maria Marquez, an LSNA organizer and parent leader, recalls some of her early experiences where she testified in front of legislators or spoke at commu-nity meetings. While she learned by doing, she felt well-prepared for the task because LSNA organizers briefed her on the plan for the meeting, helped her think through responses to potential questions, and listened as she practiced her speeches. In effect, organizers prepared her for success, and Maria reports the sense of self-empowerment that comes through this kind of experience. "After an event or accomplishment like that—whether it's leading our annual congress or testifying to state legislators, you leave that event feeling like you have changed, that your voice is important, and that you have an ability to make a difference and can lead others to action."

By providing a range of opportunities to lead, LSNA creates a ladder for lead-ership within schools. With each experience and the support that comes from LSNA organizers, parent mentors gain experience and confidence to move up the ladder and take on larger and more challenging leadership responsibilities. In reflecting on the early goals of the Parent Mentor program, Amanda Rivera describes how LSNA's leadership-development strategies with parent mentors created a "pool for school leadership" that led to greater voice and decision making within the school:

> Once parents completed the [Parent Mentor] program, then they were recruited to be members of the local school council, for which they needed to be elected . . . which is really great, because they were learning and making the major decisions of hiring a principal, and/or evaluating how we would develop the school-improvement plan, or the rollback of the school, learning about budgets and approving budgets that are connected to the school-improvement plan. So, they were getting more involved in the greater life of the school, and the community . . . So the Parent Mentor program became a venue to not only attract parents, but to train them and better prepare them to serve in a leadership capacity.

Opportunities to lead can have a profound effect on parents as they change their perceptions of the role they can play in schools and the influence they can have within the broader community. LSNA organizer Ofelia Sanchez describes her personal transformation as she became committed to her work in schools and her subsequent involvement in the community. Ofelia recalls becoming involved as a parent mentor to support her child's education; as she met and encountered other parent leaders who played an active role in school committees and the LSC, she began to think about the possibilities of leadership herself. Faced with her own shyness and intimidation, she recalls being challenged and supported by Maria Alviso, her Parent Mentor coordinator, who encouraged her to open up in public meetings and practice the skills of leadership:

> But Maria Alviso would take me to these meetings, she wouldn't even ask. But once I was at the meeting, she would tell me that I would have to talk. I was put on the spot and I would have to talk. I would come for the education committee meetings—I would listen to what everyone had to say, and Maria would encourage me to talk, telling me to say something. She would say, "You were telling me on the way over here so now say it."

Since these early days as a parent mentor, Ofelia has become an LSC member, an active parent at the Monroe school, an LSNA organizer who coordinates parent tutors across partner schools, and a community member who has testified in front of state legislators to argue in support for passage of a statewide initiative for a Grow Your Own Teachers (GYO) program. Amid these multiple commitments, Ofelia is also studying to be a bilingual teacher through Maestros

Sin Fronteras, an LSNA-sponsored GYO program that, in conjunction with Chicago State University, will award Sanchez with a college degree in education as well as certification to teach in the very Logan Square schools where she began her community involvement. Looking back on this personal transformation, Ofelia reflects that leadership was something she "learned as a parent mentor—and not something that came naturally."

Transforming Communities

On a weekday evening in the Logan Square YMCA, Ofelia sits in a meeting room, taking notes on algebraic methods. She is enrolled in a math class taught by a Chicago State University professor that is part of the course sequence for Maestros Sin Fronteras. The students in this class do not represent the typical teacher candidate. In fact, they are older, many are mothers, often working full time and taking care of families even as they return to school to complete their college degrees in education. Some have completed their high school education in the United States, while others have degrees from other countries. Some have just acquired a GED for the sole purpose of joining the GYO program. While they bring a rich array of experiences to the program as parents, community members, and school leaders, many are anxious about returning to school after many years away. Ofelia admits it is a radical adjustment for her and many of her colleagues. In the second year of a program that is time intensive and intellectually demanding, she has often felt overwhelmed and questioned her own ability to complete the program:

> There is always something—my kids, their school, the work at home, the work here [at LSNA], being there for everyone—it is harder than you can imagine. There have been moments, I won't lie to you, where I'm not sure if I can do it all. My family has been so patient and so supportive throughout the whole process, and that keeps me going, but also the fact that I will be teaching in this community one day. That is important to me—feeling like I am preparing myself to make a difference in my community.

Math represents a subject that is particularly challenging and sometimes overwhelming for these students. For this reason, according to her professor, Dr. Timothy Harrington, they are often fearful of his class, citing previous experiences of failure and struggles during school. Dr. Harrington considers math a language, and in order for students to be fluent in math, they must be taught the language—the processes, the symbols, and the codes. In teaching this language, he explicitly addresses the students' anxieties and fears about math, and he makes an intentional effort to design his class in ways that make learning more comfortable and achievable.

This evening, students are working on problem sets in small groups while tutors walk around, assisting those who need some extra support. One tutor, a graduate student in education, walks around with a portable dry-erase board, working through math problems with students in the class. Maria, a teacher candidate in the first GYO cohort who took this class years ago with Dr. Harrington, now works as a tutor as well. In speaking of Maria's presence and support, one student says, "She saves us. She is a constant reminder that we can get through this class and succeed in the program. There are already so many difficulties when you are coming back to school after such a long time, so it helps to have someone who understands your situation and can support you and encourage you to succeed."

GYO candidates enter this program because they want to provide the same kind of motivation and encouragement to schoolchildren that they receive in Dr. Harrington's class. As a parent mentor, Ofelia found that schools needed parents like her; that is, adults who knew the experiences of families in the communities and could relate to them, but who also had a sense of familiarity with schools as institutions. Like the organizers who worked with parents to create the first GYO program, she felt that teachers could have a powerful impact if they had firsthand knowledge of the community. She describes how her experiences growing up in Logan Square and attending schools in the neighborhood shape her desire to be a teacher who cares about all aspects of the lives of her students:

> I want to be a teacher in this community because I know this community. I grew up here and I know what problems that are coming up every year. I know what's going on during the summer. But a lot of these teachers, they just pack up and go home. They don't know what's going on. I had a teacher for example—she used to live way out far, and she would come in and just do what she had to do, and basically she didn't care and then once I remember telling her that I couldn't do my homework, because there were shootings and I was scared. And she said that's not an excuse and she just decided to give me a big old F, and she packed up and went home. And I thought, she just doesn't care, no one cares what's happening.

As a mother who sends her children to schools in the neighborhood, Ofelia understands how community life continues to shape the experience children have in schools. Armed with her knowledge of both schools and communities, she feels committed to making the necessary changes in schools that will create a better understanding between families and schools:

> I grew up in this community and I know every summer, there are certain gangs that come around and everything gets started. And a lot of

times at home, a lot of the Latino children have to live with other family members, and they don't have the space or the room or the time because mom and dad are working and there's no one there to help. That motivated me to do something, to change things. If other teachers are just coming in and leaving and they don't care where these children are going to end up or don't think about their lives and future, then I have to do something . . . I want to be the type of person who's in the community and watching out for these kids and make a difference.

Ofelia found her ability to not only relate to students' experiences, but as a bilingual parent to freely communicate with them and their families was a valuable and needed skill.

Former parent mentor Leticia Barrera, who is a LSNA education organizer overseeing the Parent Mentor programs, also found the connection between what schools need and what parents have to offer a compelling one:

> In the schools, we could see there is a great need for good bilingual teachers. Maybe they come and go, or they are not that effective or they do not understand the families. And many of the schools struggle to get the bilingual teachers they need. But here we also have these parents who find out they are enjoying the time in the classroom and are successful in working with the children. They are from the community, so they can make the connection between the family and the school.

This connection—between what schools needed and what parents had to offer—became the basis for LSNA's campaign to develop the first GYO initiative. In collaboration with Chicago State University, LSNA created a program, Nueva Generación, that would allow individuals like Ofelia and Leticia to enroll in a teacher education program and prepare to become certified bilingual education teachers committed to teaching in the local community upon graduation. Developing a cohort of teachers committed to the community was also thought to be a powerful way to address the pressing issue of teacher retention. According to Anne Hallett, director of Grow Your Own Illinois:

> It creates a pipeline of teachers who are really very connected to the kids, to communities, to their cultures, who want to be there, who passed the zip code test. They already live there. Now, it isn't like they're parachuting in from Kenilworth; they are already home. And if 85 percent of teachers go home to teach—85 percent of teachers end up teaching within forty miles of where they grew up—then an underlying

strategy of Grow Your Own is let's invest in the people who are already home.

Based on LSNA's success with Nueva Generación, community organizations and higher education institutions came together with Anne and others to launch a statewide campaign to develop GYO consortia across the state of Illinois. This organizing campaign led to the 2004 passage of the Grow Your Own Teachers Act by the Illinois state legislature. With the assistance of state funding, sixteen consortia have formed, each consortium consisting of a community organization, a higher education partner, and a school district. The consortia have graduated the first eleven teacher candidates, placing them in classrooms as fully accredited teachers and are currently training five hundred candidates—mostly women of color. By 2016, GYO Illinois hopes to place one thousand teachers in the state's low-income, often hard-to-staff schools.[9] As part of this statewide initiative, LSNA has initiated a second GYO cohort, the Maestros Sin Fronteras program mentioned earlier, of which parent mentors like Ofelia are a part. Meanwhile, GYO programs have been building across the country, ushering in a nontraditional teaching force that is usually older, more mature, and committed to those communities that struggle to recruit and retain teachers. The program provides opportunities for both teacher candidates and schools. According to Anne Hallett:

> It not only is creating academic and educational opportunities for wonderful people who've never been able to afford to go to college, of course, it's tapping all their maturity and their assets and their strengths, and all—and their culture, and their language.

Through initiatives like GYO, LSNA works to transform the individual parents who participate in organizing as well as the community in which they become embedded. Like Ofelia and Leticia, parents are seen as leaders with the potential to drive change in schools and communities. Campaigns and initiatives often originate from the concerns and wishes of parents. Meanwhile, as parents like Ofelia and Leticia study to become teachers within the community, schools begin to view the possibilities and potential of parents differently. Ascension Juarez, former chief human resources officer of the Chicago Public Schools and a GYO partner, describes the potential changes among children when they begin to see their parents and community members become teachers in their schools:

> The children know, particularly when these teachers come back to the school in which they started as parents or come back to the community in which they live to teach, and I think they will. The children in the

community know them. The children in those schools know them as teacher assistants. It shows the children that if you go to school and you, of course, not just go but you study and learn, that there is a future for you.

From Schools to the Community

While parent mentors begin their organizing journeys in schools and classrooms and pursue more substantial leadership roles in schools, schools also become a launching pad for work in the broader community. In this way, LSNA connects schools to communities. Indeed, it places schools at the center of community life as institutional sites around which to build leadership for the community.

As a multi-issue organization, LSNA introduces parents to a broad array of community issues and campaigns—on immigration reform, health, safety, and housing. It does this through weekly training sessions at each school, neighborhood-wide parent mentor workshops across the schools, and one-on-one conversations between organizers and parents. During one such neighborhood-wide training session for parent mentors, LSNA organizers kicked off the session with a series of campaign announcements. The most pressing issue was related to a longstanding balanced development campaign. Gentrification was threatening Logan Square and LSNA was fighting hard to preserve affordable housing stock for its community. LSNA and other community groups were concerned with the most recent news that City Councilman Ray Suarez, head of the Housing Committee, along with then Chicago Mayor Richard Daley decided to call an extra meeting immediately before the new city council would be sworn in. The meeting was designed to push through the Affordable Requirements Ordinance that would call for 10 percent of new developments in the city to be sold at affordable prices, which the ordinance set at $220,000. By setting the "affordable" benchmark using incomes across six counties and not solely within Chicago, LSNA organizers argued that units with that "affordable" price tag would simply be unaffordable to 75 percent of Chicago families. When organizers asked parent mentors whether they or many families they knew could afford a condo for $220,000, they were met with a resounding "No!" Organizers explained that parents could take one or more of three actions: they could call the alderman and ask him to cancel the meeting, distribute campaign flyers in the 31st Ward and talk to residents about the ordinance, or attend the City Hall meeting and show their presence.

Given the urgency of the matter, parent mentors decided to use the time during the meeting to call the alderman's office. As cell phones across the room dialed into the alderman's office, the lines became busy and calls went straight to voice mail. Due to this temporary setback, several parents suggested that they stage a rally at the alderman's office. With the enthusiastic support of parents and organizers in the room, thirty parent mentors decided to go immediately to the 31st Ward neighborhood while the remaining group stayed on site to complete the agenda for the meeting. For the next two hours, parent mentors led a protest at the alderman's office after a failed attempt to meet with him; they also distributed flyers in the 31st Ward and informed neighborhood residents and business owners about the alderman's meeting and the scheduled vote on the ordinance.

Parent mentors were engaged in making decisions and leading the action through every stage. They chose representatives to request a meeting with the alderman. They decided the next course of action when his office refused to grant entry to representatives, and they planned the style and manner of the public protest. To the chants of "Sí, se puede!" (Yes, we can!), the group used their presence to express dissent against the alderman and inform residents about the community issue. Ultimately, the scheduled city council meeting went ahead as planned, and the ordinance was passed by the departing city council with the contested affordability terms. However, as one parent mentor explained during the protest at the alderman's office, "What matters most is that we are here and we are showing that we know what's going on and we feel something about it. Even if the ordinance passes on Monday, we will feel good knowing that we tried." For many parents like this parent mentor, who are usually not involved in public life and community activism, the opportunity "to come out of your house and be involved in something bigger" can make them feel more invested in their neighborhood, leaving them with a renewed sense of power and possibility:

> I feel I have some power—power that I can make a difference. And even though myself, I am not a leader or not someone who can change a lot of things in the community myself, when I am part of a group like this, we all feel different. We feel that together, we can do this, and that is what we were saying in the circle—we can do this together.

Every year, about 150 parents—parent mentors, leaders, and community members—make up the core of LSNA's education organizing efforts. These efforts are consistently linked to the broader social issues in the community. John McDermott, a housing organizer for LSNA, describes the power in numbers that comes from school organizing. In his view, the sheer mass of support from parent mentors accelerates and accentuates LSNA's work in the area of housing:

> If it weren't for the parents, a lot of these campaigns—some of them would not happen and most of them would not have the kind of power

and impact that they have. On the balanced development campaign, LSNA has been one of the key members of the coalition, and when there are citywide actions or some major hearings at the City Council Housing and Real Estate Committee, the education leaders, parent mentors, and, to some extent, the community center students, are really the lion's share of the turnout of the force.

Knowing the importance of parent leaders, John comes to schools regularly to build relationships with parents and spark their interest in issues beyond schools; so does Elena Hernandez, another LSNA staff person who also works on housing. Elena attends neighborhood-wide workshops, facilitates discussions at schools during the Friday workshops, and attends education events to meet and maintain relationships with parents. She explains, "It's really important for me to try and build relationships with the parents, because ultimately, when there are big public meetings, when we have to do an action, whatever it is we have to do, we're going to go to them first and ask them for their support."

This ability to mobilize parents is fundamental to LSNA's overall success in the neighborhood, according to Alderman Rey Colon. Before his position as an elected city official, Colon worked with LSNA as a community activist in Logan Square. In his continued work with the organization as alderman, he finds that LSNA has the unique ability to develop a broad base of parent support through their work in schools and use this base to make an impact on diverse community issues. Through its regular relationships with parents, LSNA can tap into the issues that concern them the most. He explains, "LSNA can mobilize its parents—they've got people working in the schools who can get other people together and if they need to send people to the alderman's office, then it's a lot easier, because you have people in all these different schools."

As illustrated in the action to stop the city council meeting, parents can organize themselves quickly in school teams or across the partner schools, and it is this ability to organize rapidly and effectively that is fundamental to LSNA's strength in the community. Parents who are involved in John's housing campaigns come in with a sense of power, compared to the other individuals and groups he may organize. He explains:

> We have people who walk in off the street. And we have some relationships that we build through other member groups like churches and block clubs. But the schools are these intense hubs, these intense webs of relationships. There is such a huge level of trust and relationship between the educational organizers and the parent mentors, among the parent mentors, that the parent mentors at a given school are like this already formed team. They have a common base, they

have a lot of common in terms of life issues. They are moms, they have a school in common, they tend to have a neighborhood in common because they live around the school. So they are like a team that's already somewhat powerful.

Conclusion

By organizing parent mentors at each school, LSNA develops both an intimate base of parent participation that seeks to change the nature of relationships between schools and families as well as a larger, more powerful base of members across the community. This strategy reflects an awareness that schools are unique sites for community organizing. Unlike organizing within the broader community, where LSNA believes campaigns are often aggressive and tactics sometimes confrontational, school-based organizing requires a fundamentally collaborative approach. Indeed, it requires a delicate balance between working with schools in support of common goals and pushing schools to make necessary changes. According to Nancy Aardema:

> In our work outside of schools, as is often the case with traditional community organizing groups, there is usually an external enemy, an institution or individual that you have identified and associated with a concrete problem. And if you are a strong, powerful organizing group, you are going to push up against that external enemy until you win. It's you versus them. But in schools, it's not that clear—is there a clear external enemy? In most cases, no. We have to share space with principals; in some ways, you would say we need their blessing to do the work in schools. So our strategy for working with them has to be different, more collaborative.

To create desired changes in schools, LSNA organizes parents by giving them access to classrooms, providing them with the institutional knowledge of schools, and developing them as leaders. To improve the interactions between families and school staff, LSNA designs a relational approach to parent engagement that seeks to build trust and communication between parents and teachers.

This approach has worked to transform Logan Square schools from disconnected and isolated institutions into parent-friendly places. Indeed, parents are everywhere now—in classrooms, hallways, lending libraries, community learning centers, and on school site councils. Parents are not just welcome in schools; they have gained a legitimate and important role in the real work of education. As a result, LSNA has begun to transform the culture of schooling across its neighborhood.

Nevertheless, LSNA faces some important challenges in continuing to deepen its work. While participation in the Parent Mentor program may encourage dialogue between parents and teachers, building the trust and relationships necessary for positive change, it does not guarantee a change in teachers' beliefs nor does it promise sustained change in classroom practices. As one organizer explains, "Teachers will do what they want to do at the end of the day. They will be involved in the program or they will choose not to do it. And parents are essentially in there following the structure and guidelines of that teacher's classroom." As a result, while parents have access to classrooms, they are not always in a position of power to change the practices within those classrooms.

While this may be the case, through their sustained participation in classrooms, parent mentors nevertheless become intimately connected to the inner world of classrooms. As one newly involved parent mentor explains, "I have this insider view now. Even though I was in the school before, I didn't really understand what was going on before. Now, I do." As parents like Isabel develop opportunities to understand the culture of schools, they become what LSNA education organizer Bridget Murphy describes as "critical observers of school culture." In essence, through their immersion in classrooms, they become keyed into the beliefs, practices, and expectations of schools. Through these interactions, they are armed with knowledge that allows them to be critical and actively engaged in school decision making—in Isabel's words, "ready to act, not react." In that sense, they provide a force for long-term change in teaching practice.

LSNA may not be well-positioned to directly address teaching and learning, nor is the group necessarily interested in directly affecting these issues. Joanna explains that the purpose that drives LSNA's education organizing is not to "change classroom curriculum or radically alter classroom practices." Rather, the organization strives to change the nature of relationships between schools and families, opening lines of communication and areas of mutual interest, all through a process that nurtures trust and dialogue. It is then up to teachers to act differently based on these relationships, and Joanna believes that, over time, many do.

Nevertheless, LSNA believes that parents do have a critical role in education reform, contributing their own authority in educational matters to the authority of professional educators. Many educators see the potential value of this contribution, yet it is a challenge to change deep-seated school cultures. According to Arne Duncan, then chief executive officer of the Chicago Public Schools, the kind of parent engagement that LSNA promises requires a change in school culture and a restructuring of the educational environment traditionally conceived:

> I would argue that historically we created an environment where not only weren't parents welcome, they were sort of actively told not to come, and so again, we're talking about now trying to change that culture so that our schools are welcoming, that they're inviting parents in and that schools are places where parents feel they want to come.

According to Duncan, who developed a community schools initiative in Chicago, community organizations like LSNA with a rich tradition and experience in local communities offer viable solutions for school districts, that often need success stories to drive school reform and practice:

> When you're trying to push the kind of culture change I'm pushing, you need success stories. You need to be able to point at something, and they came to me early on to say this not only can work, but is working, and to have something that's concrete, and to have something that's real I think is so important at changing people's beliefs and aspirations about what's possible.

Within school environments that are so separated from the life of families, organizations like LSNA do the intense work necessary to break traditions and to alter the attitudes and beliefs of school staff.

LSNA has been gradually making progress in this endeavor, offering powerful success stories for meaningful parent engagement and new kinds of relationships in schools. Indeed, when school staff, families, and communities work together in support of school environments that open up lines of communication between parents and teachers and develop models of engagement that invite and integrate families into schools, students ultimately benefit. Parents and teachers work together for the healthy development of children. Students, meanwhile, receive powerful messages about the role models and educators in their lives.

LSNA, with its Parent Mentor program at the center, has found a potent way to work with schools and families to develop parent participation that moves beyond the distant, deficit-oriented patterns that often exist in schools. Instead, through LSNA organizing, parents emerge as powerful actors both in school and community life. In the process, schools begin to re-create themselves as community institutions that integrate families and build communities.

7

"Cement between the Bricks"

Building Schools and Communities in New York City

PRIMARY AUTHORS: PAUL KUTTNER, AMANDA

TAYLOR, AND HELEN WESTMORELAND

Ronn Jordan and Teresa Andersen remember well the meeting in 2006 when they, along with other members of the Northwest Bronx Community and Clergy Coalition, discovered startling new evidence that the New York City public school system was failing the city's youth.[1] Ronn, a father of Native American heritage, had been with the organization for years. With his white hair and resonant deep voice, Ronn describes how, through his work with the Coalition, he first realized that his kindergarten son was not the only one being affected by overcrowded schools, and that he wasn't the only parent concerned enough to take some action:

> I started going to education meetings and meeting parents from schools
> all over the community and all of them were saying the same kind of
> stuff about how overcrowded it was and the conditions that the kids
> were going to school in—that they were in renovated bathrooms and
> closets and storage spaces, sitting out in the hallways.

Since that time in the late 1990s, Ronn has continually deepened his engagement in the Coalition and has become a steadfast core leader. He eventually served a term as president of the Coalition's governing board, all the while never losing sight of the school overcrowding issue.

Teresa, a tall, mocha-skinned mother and union organizer with roots in Cuba, first came to the Coalition through an environmental campaign. A dynamic personality, she was quickly encouraged to join the Education Committee—a group of community leaders that includes both youth and adults and that oversees all the Coalition's education-related campaigns. She, too, has become a committed community leader and is currently serving as Coalition board president. These two leaders and friends knew firsthand, and from talking with others in the community, that overcrowding in Bronx public schools was a widespread and urgent problem.

Planning for Failure

At that 2006 meeting, Ronn, Teresa, and other members of the Education Committee worked diligently to understand why the New York City Department of Education (DoE) had failed to build the new schools that were so desperately needed in their neighborhoods. For years, the DoE had based their school construction plans—and thus, their determinations of which neighborhoods, if any, required additional school space—on the public school enrollment projections of a private Maryland-based consulting firm, the Grier Partnership. The more the committee members looked at the most recent Grier report, the more problematic and unrealistic the numbers became. According to Teresa, "To really look at the discrepancies, if you really sit there and start playing with the numbers and adding and subtracting and moving things around, you realize that none of it makes sense. It's not based on reality."

Ronn and Teresa also uncovered some deeply troubling assumptions in the report, which guided the DoE's decision-making about how many seats to allocate for students in the Bronx. It turned out that all of the future school enrollment predictions for the Bronx were based on a four-year "survival rate"—the percentage of students who will enroll in twelfth grade in their fourth year of high school—of a dismal 36 percent. The DoE, they realized, was making plans for school construction based on the assumption that the vast majority of high school students would not even make it to senior year in four years, even though the DoE's stated goal was to raise the citywide four-year graduation rate to 70 percent.[2]

Such low expectations for Bronx high school students angered not only Ronn and Teresa, but infuriated other Coalition leaders and parents like Desiree Pilgrim-Hunter. An immigrant, born in England to Guyanese parents, Desiree had spent years working in New York's corporate sector and knew the importance of a high-quality education. Desiree was outraged at this irresponsible attitude on the part of the DoE when it came to the city's youth:

> When you've made a determination that only 36 percent of Bronx students are even going to reach the twelfth grade, so we're only going to build enough schools for the 36 percent, and you drop out the other 60-whatever percent, what are you saying? Where are these other 64 percent going? Where? If you're not being responsible for doing something about that bunch, the failure is built in.

Ronn was the first to say it: the department of education was "planning for failure." This new information would form the basis for the revitalization of a decade-old Coalition effort. "Planning for failure" would become a new call to action on an old and pressing issue, that is, ending school overcrowding in the Bronx and across New York City.

Chapter Overview

The Coalition's effort to combat school overcrowding has a long and dynamic history spanning more than a decade, with a large cast of characters from both inside and outside the Coalition. Over time, this work has shifted and regrouped to adapt to internal and external contexts—from organizational turnover in its own staff to changing school reform agendas and political regimes in New York City. The exact focus of the overcrowding campaign has moved through several phases. It is partially because of their ability to learn and adapt as needs and contexts change that the Coalition and its youth-led affiliate, Sistas and Brothas United (SBU), have become major actors in the world of New York City education reform. Over the past decade, the Coalition and SBU have successfully won thousands of additional school seats, and generated political and public support to help ease overcrowding in Bronx public schools.

In this chapter, we will focus on a recent phase of the Coalition's efforts to end school overcrowding in the Bronx and citywide, starting with the "planning for failure" discovery in 2006 and continuing through the 2009 school construction campaign called NY SEATS—Schools Exploding At The Seams. Through this story we will uncover two major processes that we found threaded throughout the Coalition's education organizing.[3] The first of these is *building leaders,* which takes place through formal and informal leadership development activities and informs how all meetings, alliances, actions, and other activities are carried out. The second is *building connections* between individuals, institutions, issues, generations, and campaigns, often crossing potential barriers of race, ethnicity, religion, and language.

Along the way we will highlight a number of organizing methods the Coalition employs. These methods are each related to the dual goals of building leaders and building connections. We will highlight the way that a shared issue—school overcrowding—arises from community concerns and develops into a Coalition campaign. We will look at how the Coalition utilizes research and knowledge-building to design, frame and implement organizing campaigns. We will see how the group strategically draws on diverse allies, and how they build coalitions with both powerful individuals and key organizations in order to take concerted action on a citywide scale. We will witness some of the ways they engage both youth and adults, separately and together, drawing on the particular strengths and experiences of each to build deep community power. Finally, we will reveal how these targeted efforts result in successfully engaging key political leaders. Taken together, these processes helped build the Coalition's reputation as an organization that can unite diverse constituencies and issues. The Coalition, as dynamic youth leader Jason Monegro says, serves as "the cement between the bricks."

The Northwest Bronx

Severe school overcrowding is not a new problem for public schools in the Bronx. Nor is it their only problem. A cursory glance at enrollment and performance data on Northwest Bronx schools reveals an overcrowded and chronically underperforming school system. Within Community School District 10, the main catchment area of the Coalition in the Bronx and one of the largest subdistricts in the city school system, the department of education reports that between twenty-eight and thirty-eight of a total of fifty-five elementary and middle schools are over 100 percent capacity. Five to six of twenty-seven Northwest Bronx high schools are also reported as over 100 percent capacity. Dewitt Clinton High School, one of the largest in the area, has an excess of 956 students over the 3,432 seats it is allocated.[4] These figures are the official numbers, which, as we will see below, significantly underplay the extent of the problem. But numbers do not tell the full story of what overcrowding looks like in school buildings, as one description of the daily life of a Northwest Bronx high school by Celina Su shows:

> Students showed up to school only to wait in long lines to get through metal detectors, thus arriving late to classes. There were windows missing glass panes and safety bars in upper-floor classrooms, and in these classrooms, students froze through the winters. Others rooms felt hot and stuffy because there were too many classmates crammed in them and the windows could not be opened. At John F. Kennedy High School there were so many students that five lunch sessions were held each day so that the cafeteria could accommodate them all; the first lunch period began at 9:21 in the morning.[5]

It is not surprising, then, that many community members, including students, feel that overcrowding has created an inhospitable learning environment and has contributed to high drop-out/push-out rates. According to Coalition leader Nancy Maldonado, "When the class size is at forty, the teacher cannot focus on any one particular child—it's more like babysitting than teaching—you just can't teach forty kids at the same time. Overcrowding can lead to conflict in the schools—students and staff are frustrated, and students are forced to learn in hallways, closets, and storage spaces."[6] In fact, public schools within the Northwest Bronx, and high schools in particular, are notorious for the poor quality of education they provide. For example, John F. Kennedy High School, where a number of Coalition youth leaders are enrolled, has a four-year graduation rate of only 43 percent.[7]

This lack of school resources is one symptom of a broader neighborhood context of concentrated poverty, racial segregation and government neglect. The Bronx is the poorest urban county in America, with 27 percent of the population living below the poverty level.[8] Among the neighborhoods where the almost 450,000 Northwest Bronx residents live, poverty rates range from 18 percent to 42 percent, with approximately 53 percent of the overall population receiving some form of public assistance.[9] At the same time, Bronx history holds a long tradition of activism, organizing, and resistance, from the transit workers strike of 1916 to the founding of a Bronx branch of the NAACP in the 1940s, and from the civil rights work of groups like CORE starting in the 1960s to the rise of hip-hop in the 1970s. Today the Bronx boasts many organizations working for social change, including a number of thriving community organizing groups like the Northwest Bronx Community and Clergy Coalition.

The borough itself is massive, and the Northwest Bronx neighborhoods cover about a fourth of the borough's forty-four square miles, spanning the Hudson and Harlem Rivers on the west, Southern Boulevard on the east, the Cross Bronx Expressway on the south, and city limits on the north. According to the Coalition, half of the residents of the Northwest Bronx were born outside of the United States, and the borough has experienced ongoing immigration from the Dominican Republic and the Caribbean as well as sharp growth in its West African, Mexican and Central American, and Eastern European communities. All told, approximately 65 percent of the Northwest Bronx community is Latino, with 20 percent African American, 10 percent white, and 5 percent Asian and other.[10]

This dynamic mix of ethnicities, languages, religions, and countries of origin helps to shape the work of the Coalition, presenting both opportunities and challenges for an organization seeking to build connections among individuals and institutions. In education, the Coalition has found a set of concerns that resonates in the hearts of almost all Northwest Bronx residents, no matter their background. Miguel Gomez, an immigrant parent and new Coalition leader, describes the power of education to unite:

> When you go to these meetings [of the Coalition's Education Committee], you have this rainbow of communities coming along, from

Africa, South America, even some Asians. You realize, "Wow, I'm absolutely part of something big." You see all of these people from all over
the community and recognize how things are affecting all of us at the
same time even though we have different backgrounds.

Through its education work, the Coalition brings together community residents
from various linguistic, ethnic, religious, racial, and economic backgrounds to
help them see that they face common problems and to help them build the
power necessary to address them.

The Coalition's Beginnings

The Coalition was founded in the early 1970s, when the Bronx was burning.
Through the treachery of absentee and negligent landlords, there was widespread abandonment and arson across a wide swath of Bronx apartment buildings. A group of Catholic priests pulled together a coalition of sixteen local
parishes to hold a conference and develop a strategy to combat the destruction
of their neighborhoods. Officially founded in 1974, the Northwest Bronx Community and Clergy Coalition emerged with a mission to empower "everyday,
ordinary people to take ownership of the community campaigns that have
renewed life in the Bronx." The Coalition's members recruited organizers trained
in Saul Alinksy's tradition of community organizing to help work with Bronx
tenants to combat arson and other types of landlord malevolence. They were
committed to the idea that the change agents in a community must be the community members themselves.[11]

Over the next decade, Coalition clergy and community leaders helped win
the creation and renovation of thousands of affordable housing units in the
Northwest Bronx and successfully spun off a number of development and nonprofit organizations. The Coalition continued to focus on neighborhood organizing and expanded to work on issues other than housing, including economic
development, environmental protection, and immigration.

An Education Campaign Emerges

In the mid 1990s, Lois Harr, a longtime community resident and volunteer
leader with the Coalition, provided the spark that ignited a new focus on education reform.[12] Concerns about education had arisen from a number of community members over the years and sporadic school-specific campaigns had been
organized in response to these concerns; but momentum had not gathered

around any shared educational issue. After running a series of one-on-ones with community members, Lois and Coalition organizer Clay Smith called a house meeting to offer community members an opportunity to share and possibly build momentum around their concerns about education. The Coalition uses the tools of one-on-ones and house meetings, common among many organizing groups, to allow shared concerns to "bubble up" from the community, while at the same time building relationships among community members and discovering potential leaders. Clay, who eventually became the Coalition's first education organizer, had originally expected that the house meeting, which took place in the Norwood neighborhood, would be a local meeting in which a group of parents from one or two schools would advocate for specific changes at their schools. A soft-spoken white man with a generous manner and a deep commitment to community power, Clay said that both he and Lois were surprised to find a huge turnout at that meeting, drawing from across neighborhoods. During the meeting, parents and community members expressed a deep and urgent concern about the poor quality of education in Northwest Bronx public schools. As the meeting went on, the gathered parents came to an emerging consensus on the biggest challenge facing the schools—overcrowding. As Clay remembered:

> The parents said, "Our schools are so overcrowded that until that issue is addressed it's not going to be possible for anything else to have a really positive impact in our schools. Whether it's the quality of teaching or something else, it is not going to help unless we have more space."

After identifying overcrowding as their target issue, Coalition leaders began pushing the city to finish two half-completed school buildings in the neighborhood. The construction of these schools, which were promised by central New York City education officials as a means to reduce overcrowding, had been long delayed. The Coalition organized a series of Bronx-based actions to push the department of education to complete these projects quickly. In one notable action, Coalition parents bearing construction check-sheets and timelines joined with local politicians in school site visits to keep the construction company accountable. According to Clay, "It was powerful to see that these big political leaders were there with the parents saying, 'Why is that wall missing and why are you behind schedule on this?'" Through these efforts the Coalition and its allies demanded and won rapid completion of the projects.

Ronn Jordan got involved with the Coalition during this campaign. Like the parents who had gathered at that initial house meeting, Ronn had a very personal issue directly affecting his children, that is, the closing of his son's kindergarten classroom. Seeing his frustration, a local reporter suggested he and another parent go speak with Coalition organizer Clay Smith:

We went over to the main office and sat down with Clay and he helped us write a petition. He said, "Take this petition, get some signatures, and come back and we'll talk." So this woman and I went out and got fifteen hundred signatures in three days and when we came back to the office, Clay was like, "Fifteen hundred signatures? That's incredible!" I asked, "Well, do we need more? We can get more." And neither one of us had a clue what community organizing was. We had never done it before. In our first meeting at the Mosholu-Woodlawn office we had sixty-nine parents show up.

By asking Ronn to collect signatures, Clay was enacting a leadership development technique commonly used by Coalition organizers. He was not only encouraging Ronn to begin organizing fellow parents; he was also "testing" Ronn's commitment and leadership potential. Ronn passed the test with flying colors and Clay became eager to help Ronn grow and develop as a leader.

Though a large number of fellow parents had signed his petition, Ronn found that many still felt there was "nothing we can do" when it came to decreasing school overcrowding. Ronn disagreed and was agitated to take action:

That really is what lit the fire in me. I didn't want to believe that you can't fight City Hall. So that's when I started going to education meetings, where we had on average about twenty to twenty-five parents at every meeting representing about thirteen or fourteen different schools in the community. All of them were saying the same kind of stuff about how overcrowded it was.

Ronn's story offers a window into how organizers at the Coalition build connections between individuals by discovering and activating their shared concerns. Through one-on-ones and group meetings like those lead by Lois Harr, and through organizer-community member relationships like that between Clay and Ronn, emerging leaders listen to the concerns of their neighbors. Like Ronn, they can discover that the people around them are worrying about "the same kind of stuff" that they are. Tied together by this web of shared interests, these community leaders are the bricks on which the Coalition seeks to build a strong campaign and a strong community.

Ronn's move from concern about his children's kindergarten class to involvement in organizing a broader effort among parents from many schools to fight borough-wide overcrowding is no accident. The Coalition works systematically to build pathways that connect individual leaders to each other and individual campaigns to broader, more overarching efforts to create systemic change. Amanda Devecka-Rinear, the Coalition's education organizer during this research, has created terms for this process. This talented white organizer, who succeeded Clay Smith after he left the Coalition, distinguishes between "on-our-own" and "all-together" campaigns.

The kindergarten campaign that initially engaged Ronn is an example of what Amanda calls an "on-our-own" campaign, which generally organizes parents, students, and/or educators around specific issues at an individual school. On-our-own campaigns tend to address community members' immediate concerns and are often resolved quickly. These campaigns, while important in their own right, also serve to engage new community members in organizing work and help the Coalition target potential new leaders who can be brought into "all-together" campaigns. Like the school overcrowding campaign, "all-together" campaigns are what Amanda calls the next level of organizing work. These campaigns are larger scale initiatives that can engage community members from across the Northwest Bronx, or even, as we will see later in this chapter, across the city. On-our-own and all-together campaigns mutually support one another, and are both necessary for successful education organizing work. Laura Vazquez, current co-executive director of the Coalition, explains how these two kinds of campaigns operate to support both the Coalition's short- and long-term goals:

> We have this school construction campaign going on, so we want this long-term goal. But what can we win in the meantime to show parents that organizing works right now and keep them involved? Because, if not, the campaign just starts to get too long and people get less interested.

The dynamic tension between responding to the immediate interests of individual leaders and building broad consensus around larger issues is one that the Coalition constantly navigates in both their education campaign and in regards to other community issues. Moreover, as campaigns continue over time, the context within which they are waged is constantly shifting, requiring Coalition leaders to design new strategies and responses. The school overcrowding campaign, in particular, weathered several major shifts in the structural organization, leadership, and governance of New York City's Department of Education.

Early Campaigns and a Big Victory

Throughout the late 1990s, Ronn, Clay, Lois, and the rest of the Education Committee worked to get more school seats added to the city's capital plan—the plan for where and when to build and renovate schools. This work is largely outside the scope of this chapter, but has been documented in other places, for example by a 2009 case study on the impacts of education organizing.[13] This period of time was marked both by local work, seeking out potential sites for schools, as well as by a number of coalitions through which the Coalition addressed overcrowding and other vital education concerns across New York City. The Coalition's efforts paid off, getting an additional three thousand seats included in the 1999 amendment to the capital plan. Meanwhile, the changes the group helped initiate to the processes for creating new schools and the potential school sites discovered by Coalition leaders would lead indirectly to another estimated eleven thousand new seats over the next seven years.

By 2005, the Coalition's education organizing had gone in a number of different directions. Local school-specific campaigns had led to reforms around bilingual programs, neighborhood safety, and parent-teacher communication. The Coalition meanwhile continued to work in larger alliances on such issues as financial equity and teacher quality. But the issue of overcrowding remained. Parents and students in the community continued to tell stories like this one, from two students at a local high school:

> Student 1: When I was a freshman I was so excited to go to such a big school. Then as soon as sophomore year came, it was as if every junior high school combined came to our school. And then junior year they started putting in more schools . . . As soon as the bell rang the hallway was crowded. You had to walk like this and hold your book bag like this [she holds her arms tight around her bag, pulled in close to her body].

> Student 2: There was a time that we couldn't pass through the halls to the other side of the school, but we had to pass, and there was so much fighting.

> Student 1: You could ask my mom. I was crying not to go to that school.

In response to these concerns, the Coalition had continued to hold political leaders accountable for past promises, and had developed a campaign to have four schools built in or around the Kingsbridge Armory, an enormous former military establishment down the street from its office. The Coalition and its allies wanted the Armory to be used to meet a variety of community needs, and central to this plan was classroom space.[14]

Research Leads to Revitalized Campaign

It was against this backdrop that Ronn, Teresa, and the rest of the Education Committee discovered that the DoE was planning for failure by anticipating low graduation rates among Bronx high school students. These leaders also learned that

the School Construction Authority (SCA)—an agency created in 1988 to over-
see school construction and maintenance—was using flawed methods to calcu-
late school facility needs. Ronn remembers trying to figure out why the New York
City Department of Education was claiming that many Bronx schools were under
capacity, when students' experience of crowded hallways and bathrooms con-
verted to classrooms told them that these same schools were highly overcrowded.
"I was sure," Ronn explains, "that the numbers that the Board of Ed were putting
out were false and I just didn't know the details. I have this thing about numbers,
and numbers stick out in my head, and it just didn't make sense, and there was
something in my gut that said, 'this is bullshit.'" For assistance in deconstructing
the dense and convoluted school capacity data in 2006, they turned to a friend
and ally, Sarah Morgridge, in the office of City Councilman Robert Jackson.

Sarah had become an expert on the SCA's report on school usage and capacity known as the Blue Book. Along with Sarah, Ronn and Teresa pored over
this 700-page behemoth of a report until they could understand it well enough
to teach it to others. What it showed was disturbing, if unsurprising, to the two
leaders. At the time, the Blue Book only considered the current use of school
space and did not take into account whether this space had previously been used
for other purposes. Consequently, if a school was forced to use a science lab,
storage room, or art studio as regular classroom space one year to ease overcrowding, in the following year the Blue Book would designate that storage
room or science lab as legitimate classroom space. As a result, that school would
no longer be considered overcrowded. As Sarah explains, "I'm looking at schools
that I know guidance counselors work in bathrooms and the DoE is telling me
that they're 93 percent utilized, not overcrowded at all."

The type of tenacity, curiosity, and hands-on knowledge-building approach
that prompted Ronn and Teresa to pursue the meaning behind the Grier and
Blue Book numbers appears both necessary to make progress in the complex
world of New York City bureaucracies and typical of Coalition leaders. The Coalition strives to develop leaders who adopt a similar approach to any of the issues that confront them in their lives. Mary Corsey, a parent leader who is
constantly armed with relevant community stories and data, as well as a warm
smile, explained the value of learning to examine evidence firsthand:

> Like my mother would always say, just because someone says something
> doesn't mean it's true. That's why you have to investigate it yourself. You
> might find out that what they said is true. You might find out it's nothing
> like that, okay? And that will make you a leader versus a follower.

Once Coalition leaders learned how to access and interpret Blue Book
numbers, they moved to spread this understanding throughout the community.

Rather than simply announcing their findings through a press release or other event, they sat down face to face with community members to help them learn how to read and interpret the Blue Book and the Grier report for themselves. Teresa explained in 2008:

> What we're doing right now is making sure that we teach as many people as possible how to read the Blue Book report. So once they understand how to read it and the light goes on, then the community members start looking through the document and finding other things on their own and then they all of a sudden call back and say, "Did you know this?" and "Did you see this!" So it's exciting for us . . . And it really creates a sense of unity because it's like, "Wait a minute, the Coalition leaders are not lying. I'm seeing it for myself, I'm reading it."

In this way, the Coalition builds both individual and group capacity. Community members are not only better equipped to engage in education reform, but they are developing research skills and an increased sense that they too can be experts. This type of active leadership development and capacity building through a campaign is a hallmark of the Coalition's approach to education organizing.

Re-Framing Overcrowding by Connecting Issues

With the Education Committee's discovery of the 36 percent "survival rate" assumption in the Grier report, and the data on how the department of education and the School Construction Authority were undercounting school capacity, the Coalition had a new way of understanding and framing the debate around overcrowding. They began to tie together the two issues of overcrowding and graduation rates. Drawing on Ronn's suggestion, the Coalition began to publicly charge the DoE with "planning for failure." One of their longstanding allies, New York City Public Advocate Betsy Gotbaum, describes how the Coalition's framing of the issue was unique:

> The whole premise of that argument is that if you really want all these kids to graduate, and you're improving graduation rates, you don't cut back on the number of seats that are available. That premise is a very clever premise, and that's the only one I know of its kind in the city. Nobody else is looking at it from that perspective as far as I know.

The Coalition typically pays great attention to how it frames issues so that they resonate with the community and highlight what it sees as the core problems to be addressed. In the Coalition's hands, framing is a tool used to strategically describe an issue in a clear, compelling, and thoughtful way that focuses attention on a particular aspect of the issue or illuminates a particular perspective. The process of refining a frame is ongoing, with constant reflection and adjustment in conversations among organizers and leaders. According to former education organizer Amanda Devecka-Rinear, the Coalition judges the success of a frame in part by how it "sticks" in the minds of community members, potential allies, and the broader public. "You know an issue framing is effective," she says, "when you can communicate it clearly to anyone in the media and to people who you're meeting on the street that you want to get involved, when the leaders feel like it represents what we're fighting for, and when you hear other people repeating it." The Coalition's "planning for failure" charge was picked up by media outlets, public officials, and local high school students, making it successful on all fronts.

Getting the Message Out

Though "planning for failure" was easily understood and resonated with the local Bronx community, the Coalition knew that the impact of the campaign would be limited unless the message reached a broader audience. So the group turned to their longstanding friends Kavitha Mediratta and Dana Lockwood, researchers at the Annenberg Institute for School Reform, who study and support community organizing efforts in New York and across the country. The Coalition has had an ongoing relationship with this group of researchers (formerly located at New York University), and has often looked to the group for their support and assistance with analyzing local and national data. Kavitha describes the way her organization worked to support the Coalition's research efforts around the school overcrowding campaign:

> We created graphs and tables showing the high levels of overcrowding and how, because schools had no space, they were not able to access important resources such as universal pre-kindergarten funds. We also looked into how districts around the country were responding to overcrowding through year-round school schedules and other strategies and shared that information with them. The Northwest Bronx was doing its own research to understand why there were delays in the school construction and who was the target to go after to get schools built on time . . . And our role, in relationship to that, was to provide education-related knowledge to their leaders and organizers that would help them shape effective facilities campaigns.

Kavitha, Dana, and the Annenberg Institute produced a detailed PowerPoint presentation to graphically represent the enormous gap between the DoE's stated goals for the high school graduation rate and its assumptions underlying school construction decisions.

Meanwhile, with concern about overcrowding arising in multiple boroughs, the Coalition decided to expand the analysis to look at overcrowding citywide. This task required more staff than Annenberg could provide. The Coalition approached another longstanding ally, Betsy Gotbaum, the New York City Public Advocate, for help replicating Annenberg's methodology in a citywide analysis. The Coalition had nurtured an ongoing relationship with Gotbaum's office and her education advisor Tomas Hunt through personal communication and by supporting each other at events. The resulting analysis, a citywide Planning for Failure report, was presented in a joint press conference sponsored by Gotbaum's office and the Coalition in early 2007.

This process of research, framing, and dissemination highlights how the Coalition functions in the large and complex context of New York City. The group has built numerous connections over time with politicians, researchers, universities, nonprofits, and other organizing groups. These connections are based upon shared interests and values, fostered through reciprocity, and also strengthened by the kind of individual relationship building that is at the core of much of the Coalition's work. Sometimes these alliances build on the trust created from previously formed relationships between individuals. For instance, the partnership between Annenberg and the Coalition was strengthened in part by the fact that Kavitha Mediratta is married to Clay Smith, the Coalition's first education organizer, and the relationship with Betsy Gotbaum's office may have been helped along by a prior acquaintance between Tomas Hunt and Coalition organizer Ava Farkas. These webs of connections are powerful sources of social capital for the organization and allow the Coalition to gain expertise, financial support, political connections, and other resources when necessary.

SEATS: Taking Overcrowding Citywide

As the planning for failure work heated up, the school construction situation in the Bronx faced continuing challenges. In the fall of 2006, the department of education actually announced that it would be *decreasing* the number of new school seats allocated to the Bronx by 1,700. Fortunately, however, the issue of overcrowding was gaining political traction in areas outside the Bronx, including Manhattan. A window for potential political action to rectify this situation was about to open, as the five-year capital plan was up for revision in November. It was in this climate that the Coalition's Education Committee launched a new initiative, called NY SEATS: Schools Exploding At the Seams. The SEATS campaign drew on the planning for failure frame, calling for an end to overcrowding and an increase in the graduation rate in the New York City public school system.[15] Before announcing the campaign, the Coalition sought and received a large number of public endorsements for the SEATS campaign from city council members, nonprofit and advocacy groups, principals, schools, and the teacher's union.

The campaign was formally announced at a press conference on a hot June day in 2007. Parents, students, organizers, and allies on the city council stood on the steps of New York's City Hall, holding signs and chanting, "What do we want? More schools! When do we want them? Now!" Gina Ortiz, a student at the event, spoke passionately, as did Coalition President Teresa Andersen. Teresa was quoted in the local *Norwood News* as describing NY SEATS as an attempt to ignite a citywide effort to end overcrowding—illustrated by the fact that the city council members who spoke at the event represented neighborhoods in the Bronx, Queens, Brooklyn, and Manhattan. The central demand of SEATS was to get the department of education and the School Construction Authority to increase the number of seats allocated in the capital plan.[16]

Coalition Building

The SEATS initiative became a chance to build new connections across boroughs and to enhance the Coalition's existing relationships with groups like the United Federation of Teachers (UFT). The Education Committee invited the union to join SEATS, asking that it provide some of its considerable resources and political power to the campaign. Teresa explains the shared interests between the Coalition and the UFT around school construction:

> More seats mean more buildings, more teachers, more dues, more money, more power. That's their self-interest. They're not doing it 'cause they like us. We know that but that's fine. Everybody works for their self-interest. And they really like the campaign 'cause the union struggles as much as any other organization pushing the DoE or the city government on funding and so forth. At that level it's like we all have that same level of frustration.

By bringing together the UFT and other partners, the Coalition was continuing its long tradition of coalition building. During the late 1990s and early 2000s, the group became known for its capacity to "build a table" around educational issues by creating mechanisms through which community voices could be united and demand a say in decisions affecting their lives. Such alliances have been vital to the Coalition's ability to work at multiple levels to effect school change—whether at the borough, city, state, or national level. In 1996, the Coalition joined a cross-borough coalition called the Parent Organizing Consortium that worked on issues related to class size, textbook allocation, and overcrowding. In 1998, the Coalition formed the School Construction Working Group, whose members pressured the School Construction Authority and the department of education to develop an innovative nonprofit leasing program to create new school space faster and at lower cost. In 2006 the Coalition was a founding member of the Statewide Alliance for Quality Education, which worked to restore billions of dollars in cuts to the New York City capital budget. Meanwhile, the Coalition has taken an active role as a member of National People's Action, helping to make education a top priority for this nationwide organizing network.

The Coalition has amassed a unique combination of allies—from trade unions to political offices and from businesses to tenant organizations—to turn the Kingsbridge Armory into a community-led development offering recreational space, union jobs, living wages, and brand new schools. Coalition building around education became especially important after 2002, when the city implemented a policy of mayoral control under Michael Bloomberg. This decision centralized control of the public school system, which, according to Coalition organizers and leaders, functionally disempowered principals around key aspects of reform and made school-by-school organizing efforts increasingly challenging.

Though they can be powerful tools for creating change, working with coalitions is not without its difficulties. Clay Smith explains how important it is to strike a balance between working in large coalitions and maintaining focus on local organizing:

> Always in coalition work there's the challenge of having time to do your local work, so that the coalition work can be strong, and not having all your energy pulled into the coalition . . . [until there's] no leadership and disconnection from the base that you are trying to organize . . . If you don't have that balance, I don't think it works: you have coalitions that are detached from the local work. But if you just do local work, you have something that's small and not going to have a big impact.

The Coalition has been purposeful about entering and exiting alliances in such a way as to stay true to its long-term goals and values. These include the central goal of leadership development and the core principle that those most affected by an issue should lead the effort to change it. In one case, the Coalition decided to leave a coalition (and forego the funds that came with membership) because it did not feel that its participation was supporting local work or providing enough avenues for local leaders to speak for themselves and directly participate in the campaign. As James Mumm, executive director during this research, passionately proclaims, "If there is the best education organizing campaign in the country, and our parents and students cannot be at the leadership table, then we're not participating. I don't care if it's going to win."

SEATS at the Local Level: The Leadership Institute

While the Coalition was strategizing with partners across the city about the best ways to move forward on amending the DoE's capital plan, its leaders did not take their eyes off of their local educational priorities. After all, the Coalition had its own overcrowded school to attend to. The Leadership Institute high school, located in the Bronx neighborhood of East Tremont, is an organizing- and social-justice-themed small school founded through the efforts of the Coalition's youth-led affiliate, Sistas and Brothas United. Sited in an annex originally built for elementary and middle school students, the Leadership Institute had to share space with a K-8 school and had become increasingly crowded since it opened in 2005. By 2009, having graduated its first cohort of seniors, the school was completely full and a clear example of a school that was truly "exploding at the seams."

Laura Vazquez, who in 2009 became one of the co-executive directors of the Coalition, had been closely involved in all stages of the development of the Leadership Institute. A New York native of Puerto Rican descent, Laura emphasizes the dual academic and organizing missions of the school. Wearing her characteristic dark-rimmed glasses and speaking in rapid-fire low tones, she explains how the lack of space has become an obstacle:

> You've got to just try to make things work. So, for next year we came up with a new schedule. Our school is going to be overcrowded this year, so we're going to have students coming in three different sessions with students coming in at 7:40, students coming in at 8:25, and then other students coming at 9:25. It's going to be kind of hard to do the organizing piece . . . so I don't know what's going to really happen with that.

Because of this overcrowding, SBU and the Coalition began to look for a new building to house the school. In fact, during our first visit to the Coalition we found fourteen young people gathered around a large, central table in the SBU offices working on this project. They represented a number of schools, but the majority came from the Leadership Institute. The meeting began with introductions led by SBU leader Angel Gonzales, followed by space for the youth to discuss their opinions and feelings surrounding the effort to find a new building for the Leadership Institute. The group expressed almost unanimous agreement that they had to move forward actively on the campaign. As one student said, "Even if I graduate, I want the next generation to have a new building."

Former education organizer Amanda Devecka-Rinear asked the youth to create a timeline for the campaign by forming two groups and arranging a series of paper cut-outs labeled with aspects of organizing campaigns—"mobilization," "allies," "media," etc.—with descriptions on the back. Each group debated and rearranged the pieces, adding some of their own. When should they contact the media? Will some sort of mobilization be necessary if they want a meeting with one of their elected officials? Once they were done, representatives from the two groups presented their plans. Amanda asked for a volunteer to facilitate the approval of a combined version of the timeline, stressing to the youth that it was their plan, not hers, so one of them should facilitate. One youth leader Sheyla stood up and in very little time helped the group reach consensus on a plan.

Amanda spent much of her time working with high school aged youth. Though originally hired to organize parents, she began to connect with young people, like those around the table, because they were so central to the issues being addressed. As Jason Monegro, a youth leader, explains, "It's like trying to fight the struggle without really being in the struggle. If you don't have the taste of [overcrowded schools], then how can you fight against it?" The Coalition's close work with youth leaders, especially on education issues, has become particularly salient, as the SEATS campaign and the needs of the Leadership Institute have led to an increasing focus on high schools. As Amanda explains:

> High school students are big enough to fight for themselves. So there's
> an overlap . . . I work with the parents, the staff and the students . . . You
> can't have a campaign that has high school students being expected to
> fail as one of the main messages without having high school students as
> leadership on the campaign.

Youth have long been involved in the Coalition's work, mostly through the vehicle of Sistas and Brothas United, although now the Leadership Institute and other campaigns have begun to offer different avenues for participation. In the late 1990s, Laura Vazquez, then still a very new addition to the organization, began to work with a group of middle school aged youth who hung out at one of the Coalition's offices during the afternoons. As they began to raise issues like inadequate guidance counseling services, Laura pushed them to do something about their concerns. This led to the founding of SBU as a youth-led entity, which has its own governing board but remains under the umbrella of the Coalition. SBU runs its own campaigns, which adults from the Coalition are asked to support, and in turn SBU works to support adult-led initiatives.[17]

The experiences and opinions of young people have been instrumental in continuing the fight for new schools. Including more youth voice, and bringing youth and adults together on generally equal footing, has, according to many, enhanced the effectiveness of the organization. It has allowed the Coalition to be flexible yet purposeful about using the most effective leaders—who may be youth or adults, parents, teachers, or students—for each job of public speaking, negotiating, or outreach. Almost every adult that we spoke with commented on the energy and passion that youth bring to meetings and events. On the way to a major rally for education funding in Manhattan, for example, youth were the ones who used cheers and poems to educate and agitate everyone who stepped in the subway car. They recited, "Schools are overcrowded like this train . . . this is what it feels like in the hood." Elected officials also often comment on how moved they are by the young people from SBU. In fact, sometimes young people can be the most effective at getting meetings with elected officials. Jesse Mojica, from the office of former Bronx Borough President Adolfo Carrion, explains:

> [The Coalition and SBU] are preparing the next generation of leaders—their students—to be advocates. These students are not a backdrop; they're front and center advocating on issues, and the Coalition is constantly educating them on effective advocacy . . .
>
> The students are very eloquent. I have seen them advocate in educational policy meetings and come up to public forums and speak, and they're always very much on message, and very passionate about what they have to say. But they also give room to agree to disagree, and I think it's important that they engage those that they don't agree with. They don't exclude those individuals. They invite them to the table to have a constructive conversation. I've always admired that.

In this way, the Coalition builds student leaders today and creates a pool of future adult leaders for the community. It also builds connections between the generations. Youth and adults sit beside each other on the Coalition's board; young people run leadership development trainings for both students and parents; and they speak side-by-side in public actions. But this process has not been without challenges. Especially in the beginning, some adult Coalition leaders have resisted including SBU leaders on the Coalition's governing board. But through relational and advocacy work on the part of SBU and its adult allies on the board, the resisting adults gradually realized that despite the tensions that sometimes arose, these intergenerational networks were vital to the group's power. As Jason Monegro explained:

> We are trying to build that relationship with everyone, especially between youth and adults. Everyone together—students, staff, parents, teachers, principals. That's what we do. We bring them together. So, basically, we're like the cement between all these bricks.

Taking Action on School Construction

In 2008, SBU leaders were moving forward with their plans to secure a new building for the Leadership Institute in the upcoming capital plan. Meanwhile, two new youth leaders, Jatnna Ramirez and Julia Ramirez (no relation) had been working with Amanda and other students to identify potential targets and allies in the broader SEATS campaign. Amanda suggested that Jatnna and Julia give a presentation to SBU, sharing the knowledge they had gained about school over-crowding through their work and research with Amanda. After they shared ideas, the young leaders decided to take action. They had learned, with Amanda's help, how to identify the key education players in the city's political scene. They chose Dennis Walcott, the deputy mayor of Education and Community Development, as their target for action.

They first contacted Deputy Mayor Walcott to try to set up a meeting. In their subsequent conversations with his staffers, the young leaders highlighted how each of them attended an overcrowded Bronx high school. They also made clear, as Jatnna explains, that this was a citywide problem that demanded a systemic response: "We can't fix just a few schools because that won't end the problem of overcrowding." Deputy Mayor Walcott's staffers insisted that they had limited ability to help and resisted scheduling a meeting with the youth, arguing that not only was the school seats allocation out of their hands, but they had already recently met with some members of the Coalition. The youth leaders persisted, and—although it was rescheduled several times—they finally secured a meeting.

In preparation for this meeting, the youth leaders worked closely with Amanda to outline a strategy. They gathered concrete data to help support their arguments, drawing on the flawed school seats allocation formula highlighted in the Planning for Failure report, and put together a video to represent what over-crowding looked like in their hallways and classrooms. They debated about who was going to take on what role in the conversation. Jatnna offered to be the facil-itator as this was going to be her first "real negotiation." Standing a proud 5'3", Jatnna, like a number of the youth leaders in the Coalition and SBU, immigrated at a young age from the Dominican Republic. She joined the Coalition in September after Amanda met her during a visit to her high school. Coalition leaders and organizers identified Jatnna as a potential leader when she stood side-by-side with the youth leaders at her first rally, initiating chants and cheers in support of the Kingsbridge Armory redevelopment. Since then, she had worked to overcome her discomfort with public speaking, delivering a few speeches on overcrowding, and, coaxed by Amanda, had led conversations at the monthly education committee meetings. The personal development plan that she had created with Amanda's help required that she take on this additional challenge in order to grow as a leader. But she was still not comfortable committing to being the lead negotiator in the meeting with the deputy mayor.

During the course of the meeting, however, Jatnna found herself getting so angry that she began challenging Deputy Mayor Walcott. Walcott told the Coalition representatives that there would be no new schools in the capital plan. He suggested that he had to do his own research before he could determine if the schools were in fact overcrowded. Jatnna and the other youth leaders explained that they had already done the research, citing statistics in support of their argument. One of the youth, Nikki Hamilton, stepped up in the meeting as well. A quiet powerhouse with short-cropped hair, Nikki originally joined SBU in middle school. Nikki became deeply involved in the Coalition as a Leadership Institute student and a member of the Coalition's Education Committee, although she sees herself as an SBU member first. Nikki invited the deputy mayor to visit the Leadership Institute to experience its overcrowded conditions for himself. Jatnna followed up by telling Deputy Mayor Walcott that if he was going to do his own research, it was his job to report his findings back to them in no less than three weeks. "I get motivated by seeing how these politicians respond to us," Jatnna explains. "They think we are asking a favor but what we are really doing is asking them to do their jobs right."

Leadership Development through Action

The Coalition uses ongoing campaigns and individual actions as vehicles by which to identify and test new leaders and also to engage in purposeful, ongoing mentorship and training with their current core leaders. Coalition organizers like Amanda are charged with directing the ongoing development of the leaders they recruit to the organization. Organizers both respond to leaders as they identify their own needs and actively push leaders to grow in ways they do not necessarily feel ready for, encouraging them to speak publicly, communicate clearly, and negotiate in increasingly difficult contexts. This support-challenge leadership development strategy allows for personal empowerment as well as the building of organizational power. Leaders themselves become authentically and personally empowered because they set their own agenda for action and inform the Coalition's strategy on various campaigns. Meanwhile, as the Coalition helps these leaders achieve their goals, they simultaneously build the organization's overall capacity and power to effect change.

When "tested" as Jatnna was in this negotiation, many leaders discover that they really are capable of meeting new challenges, as they find themselves taking risks, moving outside of their comfort zones, and holding public officials accountable for doing their jobs. For individual leaders, the effects stretch far beyond specific organizing-related skills, as Jatnna points out:

> It always happens that you need to do something. Like you say, you need to get out of your comfort zone, but it actually helps us. It actually helps you to develop as a leader, as a human being. I'm always telling my mom that if it wasn't because of the Coalition, I don't know what would become of me in college, because in college you need to do everything by yourself, you need to go to this building, to that building, and you need to do all the process by yourself. And, I used to be very easily intimidated.

Coalition leaders gain skills and confidence both through organizer-led mentorship, as well as through their participation in more formal leadership development trainings. Most trainings are done in-house, but the Coalition occasionally sends its leaders to formal trainings with external national affiliate organizations like National People's Action or the Gamaliel Foundation. Sometimes the Coalition brings these external trainers to the Bronx where they serve to agitate their leaders and organizers as a group.

In the past several years, the Coalition has also developed a robust array of internal leadership development trainings, including a Community Leadership Academy and the Training Institute for Careers in Organizing, with offerings tiered for leaders with different levels of experience and commitment. These tiers range from general members who are new to the organization and/or minimally participate; to Level 1 active members who show commitment and participate in local work; to Level 2 leaders who work beyond the local and address more Coalition-wide issues; to Level 3 core leaders who take on responsibility even beyond the Coalition and work to build citywide, statewide, and national networks and coalitions. The Coalition has defined specific but varied skills and capacities expected of each type of leader across their strategic areas, and they offer formal trainings to help develop leaders at each level.

The Coalition has an excellent reputation for the quality of its leaders, who actively direct negotiations with politicians and policymakers, make all major decisions for the group, and engage with the media. Indeed, the Coalition firmly believes in and studiously enacts the "iron rule" of organizing: organizers should never do for others what they can do for themselves. This can at times be difficult. Staff members, who, after all, are there all day and are paid for their work, are sometimes tempted to do the work themselves rather than put it on a leader who is a volunteer and spends the whole day at a job. At one Coalition leadership training session we attended, organizers were pushed to remember that as staff they were only there to "train, agitate, and strategize;" all the rest is to be done by leaders. In this way, the Coalition maintains focus on long-term goals of leadership development and community empowerment, and does not risk those goals in the rush to get things done in the heat of a campaign. So Coalition leaders, like Ronn, Teresa, Nikki, and Jatnna are the public faces and voices of the SEATS campaign, whether behind closed doors in negotiations or in well-publicized newspaper articles and television news segments. As Amanda explains, this commitment to empowerment pays off:

> I think that the leaders at the Coalition are off the chain. They're unbelievably sophisticated, brave, daring, dedicated people. There are other groups that are working on school construction, but in the meeting with Deputy Mayor Dennis Walcott . . . I had that feeling that we have to be the community group that has the most sophisticated community members who can sit across from the deputy mayor and know exactly what they are talking about. They totally understand the School Construction Authority, the Blue Book, capacity and utilization, the Capital Plan, the message, what the battle of ideas is. These people are leading this charge.

One way developing such leaders builds organizational power is that the leaders are prepared and empowered to create opportunities and to take strategic advantage of them when they arise spontaneously. One such moment occurred following the Coalition leaders' initial meeting with Deputy Mayor Walcott.

Since Nikki had invited Walcott to "do his own research" and see just how crowded the Leadership Institute was, Amanda prompted her to prepare the school community to be ready in case he actually visited. Nikki updated the School Leadership Team at the Leadership Institute the next day, highlighting how important it was that they all be "on message" if and when Walcott arrived. As Nikki was talking, Ms. Katz, a teacher at the Institute who had been working with the Coalition, looked up a picture of the deputy mayor online and passed it around to everyone at the meeting. As it turned out, Deputy Mayor Walcott came to the school the following day. Nikki, Ms. Katz, and other leaders were prepared. They were able to recognize Walcott immediately and offer him a personal tour of the school, which highlighted the most compelling evidence of overcrowding, and presented him with their assessment of the most economically sound solutions to the problem.

As a result, Ms. Katz says, "I think we surprised him more than he surprised us." Following the tour, Deputy Mayor Walcott passed along the youth leaders' report of their overcrowded schools to the School Construction Authority and started a conversation about potential sites with the office of portfolio development. This event also helped Nikki get further energized about the power of organizing and challenged her to further develop as a leader. "I'd call that success," Ms. Katz declares.

The Shared Fate Action Forum

Just as the effort to find a school for the Leadership Institute became part of a broader school construction effort, the school construction campaign was embedded in a larger context of community action on multiple issues. This was clearly on display when, in May 2008, close to eight hundred community members from across the Northwest Bronx gathered at St. Nicholas of Tolentine Catholic Church for the Coalition's annual meeting, one of the largest in recent years. Dubbed the "Shared Fate Action Forum," the Coalition hoped that the meeting would serve to remind the gathered community members and politicians about the importance and urgency of their continued fight against school overcrowding.

Just before the meeting was scheduled to begin, the corner of University Avenue and Fordham Road was alive with the sounds of a marching band and the commotion of arriving community residents. A few Coalition leaders carried clipboards and had cell phones glued to their ears as they confirmed the attendance of media contacts and elected officials. As invited policymakers arrived, Coalition leaders and staff greeted them at the door, escorting them down the aisles to their seats at the front of the church and reminding them of their role in the day's events. Inside the church lobby, Coalition staff and leaders wearing bright yellow t-shirts welcomed community members, asking them to sign in and offering translation equipment and childcare.

Jatnna Ramirez and Teresa Andersen stood together at the front of the church, co-emcee's for the evening. After opening prayers by a Muslim imam and a Jewish rabbi, Jatnna stepped to the microphone, telling the assembled crowd:

> Even though this is a very diverse community with many different issues, many of which we'll be addressing today, we are here because we care about each other and because we care about our community and

because we know that only if we come together like we have today, we'll be able to make that change we want to see in our community. Like many of you, I am an immigrant who just came to this country five years ago. I am also a student who attends an overcrowded school. I am a teenager looking for a job to help my parents because they pay so much rent. Thank you very much for being here.

Teresa asked each person in the room to turn to the person next to them and explain why they were there. This exercise symbolized the kind of sharing and relationship building that the Coalition encourages and set a tone for the meeting that would carry through the diverse array of issues presented. Leader Kwasi Akyeampong asked the collected group to sign a "Fair Immigration Reform Movement Pledge." Crystal Reyes, an SBU leader, elicited commitments from a city council member and a state senator to support SBU's creation of a "student success center" at an old library building in the neighborhood. Leader Ramona Santana spoke passionately in Spanish about the need to pass pro-tenant legislation. Between each of these sections of the meeting, Teresa or Jatnna made connections between the issues. For example, after the housing section and before moving to health care, Teresa said, "I just want to reiterate that we're in this together. We fight for our rights in our homes, and we have to fight for our rights in the workplace also where often healthcare bureaucracy dictates how healthy or how sick we are. Workers' rights are also a human right."

The school construction campaign came up near the end of the night. Mirquia Capellán, a Coalition leader and mother of three, stepped up to the microphone with Jatnna, who translated in English while Mirquia spoke in Spanish. Jatnna's English version was as follows:

> There is a common problem in all the schools. What is the problem? Overcrowding. The schools don't have the facilities they need. They are missing computer labs, science labs and libraries, and that's not all, because they have to take lessons in hallways, offices, and trailers like I have . . . We believe all of the elected officials and communities should work together to make sure that we get the schools we are missing in the Bronx. Now, I would like to ask a question to our Borough President Carrion. What are you planning to do to relieve the problem of overcrowding?

This event was more than an opportunity to get a public commitment from the borough president to work with the Coalition to end overcrowding. By placing the SEATS campaign alongside the Coalition's work on housing, immigration, religion and labor under the call of "Shared Fate," the Coalition leaders were making it clear that they do not see the issues as separable. In fact, the Coalition had recently joined with the Center for Community Change (CCC) in adopting a language of "community values" to serve as an umbrella for all the issues on which they work. Coalition leader Desiree Pilgrim-Hunter had become interested in this approach, attended CCC trainings and brought back ideas so the Coalition could try them on for size. The CCC's Campaign for Community Values promotes the idea that "we are all connected to each other and interdependent, that the American community includes everyone and leaves no one behind, that we care for each other and believe in shared responsibility and shared sacrifice, that we know everyone has inherent value and worth in the American story."[18] An increasing number of leaders have found this frame to be an excellent way to think and talk about the way they work with the diverse Northwest Bronx community. Shared values help the Coalition to connect individuals across race, ethnicity, religion and neighborhood, thereby increasing the group's overall capacity to build power.

As the eight hundred or so attendees headed home, it was clear that momentum had been built behind the fight against overcrowding as an integral part of a broader community vision. Adolfo Carrion, the then Bronx borough president, had announced a meeting of Bronx political leaders to develop a set of school construction needs with which to approach the city—a concept the Coalition brought to Carrion. Even more important for the Coalition, leaders like Jatnna had gained valuable new leadership development opportunities. The community had stood united—mothers and politicians, students and teachers, immigrants and nonimmigrants, Christians and Muslims—under the banner of a shared fate.

Conclusion: Building Connections and Leadership

This story of the Coalition's school construction work represents an important part of the group's long history of education organizing and illustrates many of the core processes that make up how the Coalition does its work. We saw how leaders and organizers use relational meetings—both one-on-one and in groups—to bring out individual stories, listen for common areas of concern, and help community members realize that there are many others like them, who care about "the same kind of stuff." This process brings out both the issues and the potential leaders that make up an organizing campaign.

We also saw a number of the ways that the Coalition develops and utilizes diverse allies. Built on shared interests, and individual, trusting relationships, allies are sources of knowledge, expertise, resources, and power. The Coalition often finds it necessary to call upon these webs of alliances to form more cohesive coalitions—like SEATS or the School Construction Working Group—so that they can address issues on a larger scale. However, the Coalition strives to balance alliances with attention to local work; it makes sure that the activities of such coalitions flow from local priorities, help to promote the group's core goal of leadership development, and place community members at the head of every campaign.

This chapter also highlighted how the Coalition uses data as it develops the ability of leaders to access, collect, understand, and utilize such information. We saw how the knowledge built from this process can help the organization in its efforts to frame issues in such a way that they resonate with their membership and address some of the root causes of the problems. Working with allies the Coalition spreads knowledge and education throughout their membership and disseminates their perspectives through the use of the media and academia.

Meanwhile, youth have taken center-stage right beside parents in the Coalition's efforts in school reform, largely through the development of a youth-led organization in which students' voices, concerns, and goals are at the forefront of organizing. This, in turn, has created space for adults and young people to work together on an equal footing, benefiting both groups and increasing their overall power.

We have seen throughout how building leaders is truly the core vehicle for, motivation behind, and outcome of the Coalition's efforts. Leaders and organizers repeatedly stress that leadership development is the central goal for the Coalition's work, in education and beyond; campaign wins, though important, are in this sense secondary. This is not always easy to keep in mind in the midst of a heated campaign. Ava Farkas remembers struggling with the concept when she first became lead organizer for the Kingsbridge Armory campaign.

> The Armory campaign is in part about developing leaders, so even if we lose, people will learn something . . . That's not how I thought of it when I first started. I remember when [SBU Executive Director] Mustafa told me, "This is not about winning campaigns. It is about developing leaders." And I was like, "What?" . . . In a union, you don't think about it like that. You think about trying to win . . . So, when I heard that I was confused.

Ava has since then gained a reputation as an organizer who is excellent at building local leaders. Her focus on leadership development highlights how each Coalition action, meeting, or decision can be understood as a vehicle by which to promote leadership development. The research and number-crunching done by Ronn Jordan and Teresa Andersen were opportunities for them to build their capacities to analyze and understand data, and then to turn around and teach others. The meeting with Walcott became an opportunity for Jatnna to step up and test herself in a challenging leadership role. Even the Shared Fate Action Forum was rife with leaders playing small or large roles that pushed them in their knowledge, commitment, and self-confidence. As a result, the Coalition's smart, flexible, confident leaders represent themselves, the issues, the Coalition, and the community powerfully at rallies, press conferences, and negotiations with politicians.

Just as leadership development is a thread tying all of the Coalition's work together, we also see a constant attention to building connections. Because of the diverse nature of the Northwest Bronx, connections between individuals bridge real and perceived social barriers based on race, ethnicity, language, religion, and country of origin. The Coalition also builds connections between institutions—whether schools, unions, political organizations or other community-based groups—that cross boroughs, cities and states. The group fosters intergenerational connections in multiple ways, by creating a space for young people to lead on their own issues and through opportunities to stand side-by-side with adults. Finally, the Coalition builds connections between the multiple issues facing the community, under concepts like "community values" and "shared fate."

Each of these types of connection, in the end, promotes stronger ties among people, increasing community capacity and power. Education, many have told us, is central to this process, because it is particularly compelling to a diverse array of community members new and old, and from various racial, cultural, linguistic, and ethnic backgrounds. Some in the Coalition call education their "bread and butter" issue, something that in the past may have been said about the housing work on which the organization was founded. Ava Farkas explains:

> I think everybody is really motivated right now to fight for the schools. That is the number one concern of the community, from what I can tell. I think it's schools, and recreation space for youth. Yeah, who wouldn't love a great job? But I feel like that doesn't motivate people as much getting involved with schools.

The building of leaders and the building of connections are central to the Coalition's methods because they directly address the organization's overarching, long-term visions for the Northwest Bronx. Immediate campaigns are important; it is vital to residents that they have ample and equal access to the opportunity to learn today. But the Coalition is also seeking to increase the community's ability to address the next issue, the next concern, and gain greater control over its own future. A region that is highly interconnected and which boasts a plethora of committed, confident, and adept leaders is a more powerful community and is better prepared to shape the future. Former executive director James Mumm explains it this way:

> While we address immediate issues, we are also trying to get a community that is stable enough and healthy enough to be able to make even more ambitious decisions about how it would like to live . . . to build what Christians will call the "Kingdom of God," and what others would call a "beloved community." The community is actually better, and better organized to respond to things that erupt. If something like a fire occurs on a block that Fordham Bedford has buildings in, they can respond. If a building becomes abandoned, they can buy it. And if a shooting happens on a block, a priest will respond and a march will occur. And it's not us as the Coalition organizing it. It could be our members. It could be other folks. This neighborhood is just better organized.

The Coalition has done impressive work to build power for the Northwest Bronx community to address the profound failures of public education in the Bronx. It has proven adept at responding to new developments. Yet it is continually challenged by several factors. First of all, the political terrain of New York City is incredibly complex with the education system run by a notoriously unresponsive bureaucracy. In this context, the SEATS campaign has continued to grow and develop, but it has faced its ups and downs. On the city level, the Coalition has been working with allied elected officials to gather more accurate data on overcrowding. Councilman Oliver Koppell's office has created a survey for school principals that asks detailed questions about how space is being used, and it is coming back with very unsettling stories of schools far over capacity. The Coalition and its allies hope to use this data to create a "True Book" to counterbalance the city's Blue Book. On the local level, efforts have begun to bear fruit, although the worldwide economic recession created new barriers to increasing school construction. The School Construction Authority has conceded the need for some new seats in the Coalition's own District 10, so there are plans to build a new school on Webster Avenue. The Coalition considers this an important step forward, yet since the school only adds 640 seats, it falls far short of the tremendous need. Meanwhile, a new potential site was offered to the Leadership Institute. Youth leaders, however, determined that it was not an improvement over the current site, so they will continue looking for an appropriate location.

The Coalition also faces turnover in staffing. At the beginning of our data collection, the group had recently hired James Mumm, a long-time organizer from Chicago, as the new executive director; he put the group through a strategic planning process that had led to plans for a series of significant shifts in the way the organization functioned. By the end of data collection, however, James had left to work for the National Training and Information Center (NTIC). He was succeeded by co-directors Laura Vazquez and Aleciah Anthony who brought renewed energy and talent, as well as years of experience in the organization, to the role. Former education organizer Amanda Devecka-Rinear also recently moved on to work on national-level issues with NTIC.

Finally, the Coalition continues to look for new ways to bring the diverse residents of the Bronx together and engage those they have not yet reached. When we began this study, the Coalition was in a period of reflection and change. It looked to a renewed focus on increasing the religious membership of the Coalition as a way to ground its organizing. The Coalition created a new sub-committee of the governing board composed of leaders from religious institutions and made an overture to joining the national faith-based Gamaliel organizing network.

Though these changes have required periods of reorganization, the Coalition long ago demonstrated its ability to adapt and regroup as its internal and external contexts changed. Indeed, the group's flexibility may be one of its greatest assets. The Coalition has proved able to build a strong base of organized and powerful leaders who represent deeply held community values. At the same time, Coalition leaders have the ability to analyze and respond quickly to new opportunities. To the extent that the Coalition continues to build these two capacities, it will only increase its ability to play a leading role in demanding equity and justice in education in New York City and beyond.

8

Building Power and Relationships to Transform Communities and Schools

We set out to analyze how community organizing groups work to improve quality and advance equity and social justice in public education.[1] In the case chapters of this book we identify and describe the important processes through which each organizing group does their education work. There appears to be tremendous diversity in organizing strategies and in the kinds of education reform goals groups pursue—opening small schools, increasing resources and the number of classroom seats, and building relational cultures. Indeed, one of our important findings is that community organizing is not a monolithic approach. Rather, drawing from diverse organizing traditions and responding to local communities and contexts, organizing efforts take shape differently across the country. To understand community organizing we need to look closely at how organizing has developed in any particular place, just as we have done in the previous chapters of this book.

At the same time, we find that groups in our study do share a number of core processes. In this chapter, we look across the six cases to identify key features we find present in the organizing groups. We draw a composite picture of how strong forms of community organizing work to effect education reform. While we mainly emphasize commonalities in this chapter, we also describe some of the variation we found across the groups.[2]

Our synthetic approach is different from other analysts who have compared organizing groups and traditions and highlighted the differences between them. We argue, in contrast, that despite the variation we found, strong forms of organizing share deeper processes in common, as we show in this chapter. We acknowledge variation across the groups, but believe that analysts who focus on difference miss the larger underlying similarities in core processes that build the capacity of organizing groups to make significant and sustained contributions to school reform.[3]

All of the groups in our study have sustained their education organizing over a long period of time and have brought about important reforms. However, as we will discuss in this chapter, education reforms are not the only goals of organizing groups. Their success cannot be measured entirely by the achievement of reform goals, but rather through the effect of the processes by which they do their work, which we define as being transformative. We use the term transformational change in contrast to transactional change. Transactional change refers to the achievement of specific goals or objectives, like the opening of new small autonomous schools or increasing state spending to low-income schools. Transformational change involves an internal change in how people or institutions act. Community organizing groups do attempt to create transactional change in their campaigns. But without transformational change, they have to keep pursuing "win" after "win." The more profound and sustainable change occurs as organizing creates new ways for people as individuals and people in communities and institutions to think and act.[4]

Transformation through Power and Relationships

Community organizing groups in our study pursue education organizing as part of a broader effort to transform power relations. In other words, they believe school reform will only occur if embedded in a long-term process of building capacity and power for low-income communities. Through this process, they seek to change the way power-holders think and act so that they come to recognize the value of organized communities and agree to work with them. Organizing groups do pursue school reform initiatives that specifically contribute to the improvement of education for children in their communities. But we heard organizers and leaders repeatedly emphasize that discrete reform "wins" are not enough. Organizing groups do not see any particular reform making a significant difference unless their communities build the power to be taken seriously in reform discussions and decision-making processes in education and other arenas. This requires the cultivation of broad participation and leadership that is accountable to community concerns. Organizing groups pursue education reform in order to build this capacity and leadership for long-term systemic change as well as for desperately needed, immediate improvements in the quality of education children receive.

Groups in our study have somewhat different ways of conceptualizing the relationship between education reform and political change. Organizers and leaders connected to Southern Echo believe that education and liberation for African Americans in Mississippi are inextricably bound together. The poor quality of education provided to black children has historically kept them impoverished and disenfranchised. The struggle to transform education can only come through the building of political power in black communities even as better education lays the basis for the full development of African Americans in the Delta. In One LA's "power before program" approach, the group seeks to build a political constituency for quality education in a city torn by deep divisions. One LA works in and through institutions, like churches and schools, to cultivate leadership and bring institutional leaders together for concerted action to improve communities and schools. In One LA's approach, improving education and building a strong and inclusive democratic culture proceed in tandem. Each of the other four groups has their own specific understanding of the relationship between educational and political change—yet all approach education reform as part of a broader process of building power and transforming power relations.

Organizing groups help communities develop their own reform initiatives as well as the political will to pursue them. They place demands upon the institutions of public education and work to hold those institutions accountable. Building this kind of unilateral power in communities, however, is not a sufficient strategy to transform public schooling; that is, "banging on the doors" of the schoolhouse from the outside proves inadequate. Organizing groups find they also need to build new kinds of relationships between the institutions of public education and empowered communities. One LA has placed a central focus on creating what it calls a relational culture in schools by bringing all adults in the school community together to pursue meaningful dialogue and action. Southern Echo organizes community leaders for election to local school boards, engages with officials in the state department of education in order to dismantle the achievement gap, and collaborates with a range of educators and other parent groups on special education reform in the state. The other groups in our study also combine placing demands on the institutions of public education with collaborative strategies that seek to create new kinds of relationships. Indeed, the concept of relational power discussed in chapter 1 helps us understand the kinds of transformation that can occur through new relationships.

In the end, organizing groups build relationships and power for transformational change in communities and schools. The way they pursue their educational work, however, is highly context specific. Communities have different histories, traditions, and circumstances that affect how they enter the educational arena. In addition, the opportunities and constraints they face in the field of education reform—like the willingness of educators to collaborate with them—vary widely across our sites. We find that successful organizing groups prove adept at responding to local conditions at the interface of communities and schools.

In chapter 1 of this book, we provided a framework for understanding how organizing groups root themselves in the deeply held traditions and salient identities of communities while building relationships and power. We used the metaphor of a tree as a heuristic diagram (see figure 8.1). In this chapter we focus on the branches of the tree. We argue that strong forms of organizing work at transformation at three levels: the individual, community, and institutional levels. We first treat each of these separately. We then consider how transformation at any one level requires work at the other two. We start with the community because that level constitutes the central focus of organizing efforts. In the end, however, we find that building power and relationships to transform communities and schools requires a comprehensive strategy that links all three levels.

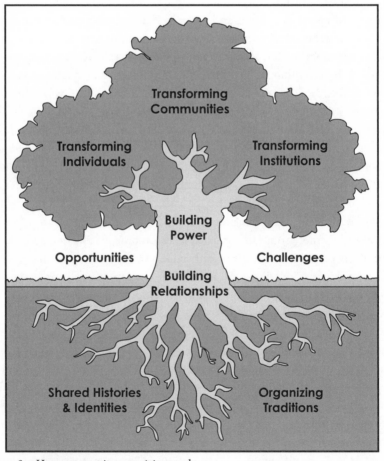

Figure 8.1 How community organizing works.

Transforming Communities

Organizing is often misunderstood as simply representing a set of techniques that can be employed to bring individuals together for quick action. There certainly are techniques to organizing, and we have detailed many of them in the case chapters. But we found that strong organizing groups do not approach individuals as disconnected or isolated from one another. They root themselves in and build themselves out of the sometimes latent connections between people that already exist; they find an organic way to bring people together, based upon people's shared history, identity, and traditions.

Organizers, however, do not simply tap extant ties. Strong forms of organizing weave new connections within and across communities, sometimes connecting people who were once distrustful of each other. This kind of bridging social capital provides a broader base of power for the organizing group. When done well, it creates a dynamic mix of people, ideas, and talents that energizes the organizing process. Such an approach constitutes organizing a community rather than simply mobilizing individuals for a specific purpose.[5]

The transformational work of organizing lies in the creation of a broader sense of shared fate through the engagement of connected people into action for equity and justice. Indeed, it is through working together that community ties are strengthened and broadened. Organizing groups build independent organizations as key vehicles for communities to act and create change according to their values and interests. These organizations construct a space where issues of justice, collective action, and community building are valued, discussed, and pursued. No community organization is coterminous with an entire community, but these groups do work to connect their leaders with broader networks and in that way hold themselves accountable to the larger community.

All groups emphasize listening and conversation as core processes to build relationships and community. Southern Echo conducted listening tours at the beginning of its organizing. One LA and PACT in San Jose have institutionalized the one-on-one relational meeting. Parent mentors from the Logan Square Neighborhood Association (LSNA) in Chicago meet in a group every Friday to share their experiences.

Through these processes, people come to see that many of their concerns are shared by others. By discussing their values and interests together, people develop a sense of "we." Indeed, organizing groups tap deeply held values as they help communities identify common interests for urgent action. In this way they shape a story about who they are but also about what they are trying to achieve. As people come together, they begin to develop a vision of what can be accomplished.[6]

How groups work to engage and transform communities—how groups define the "we"—varies in important ways. Some groups in our study define community primarily along racial lines. Southern Echo grows directly out of the experience of African Americans in the Mississippi Delta and draws explicitly upon the Civil Rights movement tradition in its organizing. African Americans in the Delta share a deeply rooted, black Christian tradition and that culture and its symbols can be found at every step of the group's organizing—singing gospel songs, using call-and-response at meetings, and beginning shared meals with a blessing. Echo works to strengthen rural communities and re-energize them into action. To combat the fear and isolation felt in small rural communities, the network connects African American leaders across the Delta to support each other and build a broader base of power. Echo builds new ties across counties and works to create a sense of a larger and more powerful black community, a stronger and more inclusive "we." In Echo's view, the state has played the primary role in keeping education underfunded and maintaining racial inequality. In response, Echo works to build power to deliver greater resources from the state to Delta communities and ensure that these resources are used in ways that are accountable to empowered communities. In this way Southern Echo expands people's experience of community as African Americans struggling against historic racism and in pursuit of educational justice and liberation.

Padres y Jóvenes Unidos (PJU) in Denver, for its part, grows directly out of the Chicano movement experience. It engages both a shared history of racial oppression as well as a history of struggle. Indeed, PJU is quite intentional about using political education processes to teach parent and youth leaders about this history as a foundation for them to write a new chapter in their struggle. PJU draws upon long-established relationships in Denver's Latino community. Rosa Linda's restaurant has provided both a physical and symbolic center for organizing efforts. But PJU also works to create new kinds of ties among older activists, parents and young people in the community. PJU taps the anger many young Latinos feel about the racism they experience at places like North High School. But, through political education, PJU helps young people understand their personal and immediate experience from a larger historical standpoint— the long struggle of people for human rights. Meanwhile, it directs their anger toward strategies for meaningful change, like the redesign of North High School. PJU works to create a new "we" that is critically minded and action-oriented with deep historical roots and a vision for a more just future.

LSNA roots itself in the experiences and shared identity of new Latina immigrants in Chicago. LSNA found that many Latina mothers felt isolated in their community. Coming together for weekly meetings in the parent mentor program, these women had a chance to share their experiences and struggles with others who understood them. They moved beyond thinking about "my child" to develop a sense of caring for "our children" as a community. Parent mentors went on to establish community learning centers that taught Latino dance, arts and culture, among other things. As parents took action around their concerns, they reached out to other parents and their sense of community and its power expanded even further. From this base in Latina experience, LSNA brings hundreds of parents (mainly mothers) into neighborhood schools where they build new relationships with teachers and principals. Through its organizing, LSNA establishes schools as vital centers for community building. In the end, LSNA creates an expansive and inclusive notion of community, rooted in and focused on the Latina immigrant experience but reaching out to include residents and educators of diverse backgrounds.

Other organizing groups in our study do not focus so exclusively on one racially or ethnically defined community. PACT, drawing more directly from the Alinsky organizing tradition, seeks to organize "regular folks" across lines of race. PACT engages members of congregations around their deeply held faith values. PACT builds local organizing committees around congregations where people share a specific faith tradition. But PACT also brings people from different faith traditions together. The group works hard to create new ties, a sense of shared fate and vision for great schools across the organization. PACT brought Latino parents in Alum Rock into relationship and action with its diverse group of leaders and with a group of educators as they established new small schools. For PACT, community emerges out of the efforts of people of faith to act together with others in the public world in pursuit of their shared interests and social justice values.

One LA also draws upon faith traditions to build broad-based organizations. Yet it seeks to include schools and other institutions as members as well. In the Fernangeles school, the ties to neighborhood Catholic parishes reflect the important role these churches play in the lives of families and reveal the foundation of faith tradition that anchors One LA's work in the school. Yet its work in the Harmony school shows the group's effort to engage with the country's democratic traditions in public education as well. Within each of these institutions, One LA draws upon extant ties and shared traditions out of which the group helps develop leaders. One LA then weaves these leaders together to create a sense of shared fate and a broader base of power. Nevertheless, One LA and the IAF network of which it is a part, primarily work with faith traditions that call people to public action for social justice values. These faith values, as with PACT, do not determine the public agenda, but rather motivate, sustain, and frame people's participation in such work. Indeed, it is really through working together and taking action that ties form and strengthen. In the end, One LA envisions a broad and diverse constituency of many traditions that comes together for collective action for social justice in public education and in the public realm more broadly.

The Northwest Bronx Community and Clergy Coalition follows a hybrid approach, appealing to people's multiple identities and connections: as residents of Northwest Bronx neighborhoods, as immigrants, and as members of faith traditions. To this end the Coalition makes space for both institutional and individual membership in the organization. This multipronged approach presents challenges, but may be well suited to this geographically large and ethnically diverse area with large numbers of new immigrants. The Coalition has found that action on public education, as a shared concern and a deeply held value, is particularly potent for bringing together its widely varied population and institutional base. The group creates the "cement" between individuals and institutions and across generations, often crossing potential barriers of race, ethnicity, religion, and language. In the end, the Coalition uses organizing to weave together the diverse strands that its leaders and institutions bring to create a new tradition, a new sense of a shared fate as members of a Northwest Bronx community.

In these many ways, strong forms of organizing all find an authentic means to engage communities around a sense of shared history, tradition, and narrative. Meanwhile, they work to reshape and expand those ties to create a broader understanding of shared fate and a new history through concerted action. We conceptualized this process as the building of bridging social capital in chapter 1 of this book. But notions of ties and capital, while important, do not fully capture the deep cultural work of organizing; that is, the effort to engage and reshape values, traditions, cultural practices, and collective identities. Building broader ties is necessary to transformation. But transformation occurs more fully when people change the way they think about their community—as more broadly inclusive as committed to social justice, and as more powerful.

Transforming Individuals

A community is not a "thing" that acts. Organizing groups bring together the people who make up a community and build their capacity for action. The groups in our study conceptualize this capacity-building process as leadership development, and they place a high priority on this objective. In fact, many organizers told us that the development of leaders is *the* central goal of organizing, more important than any particular campaign victory. Many organizing groups call all participants in their efforts leaders, whether they hold a formal leadership position in the organization or not. This approach is meant to recognize the potential of any participant to become a leader and to signal the group's expectation of their role. It is also the first step in beginning to reshape the way individuals think about themselves.

We began this study with some expectation that leadership development would be important to organizing. But we left with a much more profound appreciation for how processes of personal transformation lay at the heart of organizing efforts. Indeed, we might say that personal transformation represents the heart and soul of community organizing. It provides the spark that ignites community transformation.[7]

Organizing groups build the leadership of individual participants in the context of community ties. Organizing groups look for parents, youth, and community residents who are connected to others, coming out of schools, congregations and neighborhoods. Leaders are not expected to solve problems on their own or to direct others in a unilateral fashion. Indeed, a key part of becoming a leader in these groups involves building one's capacity to connect with others and engage them in action.

School reformers and others who care about parent or citizen participation often focus on the development of skills and knowledge. If parents and community residents are to become powerful actors in education reform, they need to gain knowledge about educational issues. They also need to develop such civic skills as how to chair a meeting or speak in public. The groups in our study certainly pay great attention to building these kinds of skills and knowledge. But they do more: they take a holistic approach that often creates a profound transformation in the lives of participants. They provide opportunities for people to think differently about themselves as they move from private citizens to public leaders.[8]

In the chapter on LSNA in Chicago, we heard Ofelia Sanchez talk about being a shy and reserved Latina mother at home with her children and intimidated by schools. Starting as a parent mentor in LSNA, she began to take a more and more active role in schools and education work. At present, she has a job as an organizer for LSNA where she coordinates parent tutors; she is also studying for a bilingual education degree and plans to teach in Logan Square schools. The formerly shy parent now speaks eloquently and passionately in front of the state legislator as part of the Grow Your Own Teacher campaign.

In Denver we saw young people like Julieta Quiñonez who felt bored and alienated in school come alive in political education sessions sponsored by PJU. No one had ever asked for her opinion on the quality of the education she received at North High School. Through PJU she learned how to design surveys, organize her fellow students, and participate in planning the redesign of the school with district officials. Now a college graduate and paid organizer for the group, Julieta leads other youth in political education sessions, passing on the research and public speaking skills she acquired to the next generation of *jóvenes*.

In San Jose teachers like Kristin Henny never thought they could impact the larger educational system. But they became energized as they built new kinds of relationships with each other and with parents through PACT's organizing processes. Kristin shared "blood, sweat, and tears" with parents as they worked together to design the new small autonomous schools. Kristin took the opportunity to become principal of one of these new schools, L.U.C.H.A. With PACT's support, she proceeded to build a relational culture at the school. PACT initiated the design team process, supported her development as a teacher leader, provided coaching from education experts, and helped her build relationships with parents in L.U.C.H.A. Kristin is now a public figure in the community, a dynamic principal who fosters shared leadership with active parents and collaborative teachers.

In these and other examples, we have seen people's lives transformed through their participation in organizing efforts. At its core, this transformation involves the movement from being a private person to a public actor as a community leader. In other words, organizing groups provide people the opportunity to develop themselves to become leaders working with others to make change. At the same time, organizing groups do not entirely separate the public from the private. Taking a holistic approach, organizers support leaders in achieving their personal goals as well, like pursuing education or career enhancement.

Looking across our cases, we can identify a set of common practices strong organizing groups follow to foster this kind of leadership development. First, organizing groups start out by listening carefully to people. They ask people about their concerns and also why they care about these issues. They seek to identify their talents and where they want to devote their energies. Organizing groups listen closely to what parents, young people, community residents, and educators have to say, engaging their values, interests, and passions. In this way, organizing grounds itself in the context of people's lives as they experience it. Organizing provides people with the opportunity to pursue their values and passions and, through connection and action with others, it is a venue for discovering new facets of themselves.

Beyond listening, this kind of engagement occurs through two-way conversation and group connection with others. As potential leaders engage with organizers and other leaders, they can come to see that their individual problems represent a collective concern. For example, if a child is not doing well in school, her parents may find the child at fault. But, through conversations with other parents, participants can begin to locate the source of the problem in the inequities and failures of public institutions. In this way, organizing groups help people move from blaming themselves to seeing the systemic nature of educational failure while also recognizing the potential of their role—both individually and collectively—in making change.

At the heart of leadership development, then, lies a combination of attention to personal growth and relationship building. LSNA in Chicago, for example, places a particular emphasis on the link between the personal and political, paying special attention to the personal lives of emerging leaders. The mostly Latina mothers who join the Parent Mentor program are required to set personal goals that may include learning English, earning a GED, or even obtaining a driver's license. LSNA also focuses intentionally on confidence building, scaffolding new leaders through various stages of development from participation in the classroom to school-wide leadership and to action around broader community issues. Meanwhile, parent leaders devised a range of programs to meet their needs, including a Grow Your Own Teacher program that offers opportunities for a college education. In this way LSNA encourages parents to see themselves as active agents for personal and community transformation.

Leadership development in organizing occurs through taking action. Leaders acquire new skills as they practice them. They learn how to research an issue as part of a campaign and gain knowledge of educational issues through research and engagement with educators. Leaders learn how to speak in public or chair a meeting by doing so. They develop a greater understanding of how public institutions operate—both positively and negatively—as they work to change policy and practice. Indeed, as community leaders build knowledge, they develop the capacity to act and are transformed in the process.

Organizers scaffold and support emerging leaders as they try out these new skills. We often witnessed an organizer carefully going over a new leader's prepared speech in advance of a meeting or rally and then debriefing with them afterwards. This kind of personal mentoring plays a critical role in the development of leaders.

While organizers build on people's talents and provide careful support, they are not shy to challenge them. One LA calls this "agitation." The Northwest Bronx Coalition and PACT both talk about the "push." People are encouraged to take risks and try out new roles. Organizers challenge people to face their fears and overcome the obstacles in their paths to leadership; they push people to see themselves in a new light and as a public leader. Organizers often work one-on-one with leaders to evaluate how well they did in these new roles and help prepare them for the next action or the next step in their personal development.

The Northwest Bronx Coalition, for example, places great emphasis on the organizer-leader relationship. Like many groups, the Coalition makes a clear distinction between the roles of organizer and leader. Indeed, the Coalition follows Saul Alinsky's "iron rule," that is, never do for others what they can do for themselves. Leaders make the formal decisions in the organization and always speak for the group in public. Organizers play an essential role behind the scenes, preparing leaders, challenging them, and strategizing with them. Perhaps because Coalition organizers stress challenging leaders, they are careful to develop strong relationships with them. Always reciprocal, at least in part, over time, these relationships develop into what can better be understood as bi-directional partnerships in which leaders also challenge organizers and help to develop their capacity. Indeed, some groups like PJU blur the distinction between organizer and leader with both types of participants speaking publicly for the group; PJU, in particular, has high expectations that many youth leaders will become organizers.[9]

Formal trainings and workshops play important roles in all of the groups we studied. Sometimes these trainings provide the knowledge of educational issues necessary for community leaders to become meaningful participants in complex school reform debates. But knowledge building also includes broader educational work that helps participants set current struggles in the context of historic efforts at social justice. Indeed, trainings are primarily designed as venues to learn the art and skill of political organizing. This includes how to build relationships geared to action and how to analyze and navigate power arrangements. One LA's training sessions, as we saw, ground leaders in the principles of community organizing. Participants learn to analyze power dynamics, examine forms of accountability, explore the nature of publicly accountable and private relationships, and analyze their own strengths and weaknesses as actors in the public sphere.

Organizing groups tailor their trainings to their specific organizing approach. Padres y Jóvenes Unidos centers all of its work in political education. The group emphasizes formal teaching contexts where they help parents and young people see the connection between the injustices they face in their personal lives and the larger systems that create these conditions. This kind of understanding is important to moving people from passive acceptance into action to change these systems. As individuals develop as leaders, they see themselves as part of an historic struggle for Chicano liberation and human rights more broadly, and this understanding works to embolden and sustain their participation.

Southern Echo shares this emphasis on locating oneself in the historic struggle against racism and on developing leaders' understanding of institutional racism in the educational system. It seeks to cultivate this kind of systemic analysis as well as to build knowledge about a wide range of educational issues at all levels of the organization. But Echo also has a particular analysis of the requirements of leadership in rural, Delta communities. In Echo's view, many African Americans elected or appointed to official public positions have abandoned community needs in favor of pursuing personal gain. Consequently, Echo places a special focus on accountability in the development of leaders. Leaders grow personally through their participation in Echo even as the group works to instill a sense of responsibility to community needs beyond the self.

The educational terrain is particularly complex for organizing groups, compared to other issues. As a result, groups have to provide ways to increase the knowledge of leaders so they can participate meaningfully in reform processes—through research and formal trainings. Northwest Bronx Coalition leaders, for example, studied the district's 700- page Blue Book on school usage and capacity and explained it to other participants as the Coalition developed its campaign for more classroom space. Southern Echo sponsors an annual Dismantling the Achievement Gap Conference that brings together youth and adult community members, educators, researchers, and officials from the state department of education. PACT leaders studied school autonomies and took parents, teachers, and congregational leaders on tours of successful small schools in Oakland and New York so they could campaign for and then help design new small schools.

Many organizing groups believe that leaders grow and develop through working with a diverse set of other leaders. Groups like One LA are particularly interested in leaders who are curious about working with people from different backgrounds than their own, and the group focuses on how to build those kinds of bridging relationships. In one-on-one relational meetings, people talk about their personal experiences—not just to become friends but rather to build a foundation of shared understandings for public relationships and action.

The Northwest Bronx Coalition has found that creating an intergenerational leadership group creates powerful effects on adult and youth leaders. Through its education organizing work, the Coalition has brought youth leadership to the center of its organizing, in close relationship to parents. Adult-youth dynamics have proved challenging but also transformative, as each group has had to learn how to think differently about the other and find ways to integrate the strengths of the two.

In the end, the personal and relational approach practiced by strong organizing groups creates transformative experiences for leaders while it builds organizational capacity. Organizing groups increase the number of people with the capacity to be leaders in their community. But they do more: they help create new kinds of leaders, ones who think and act differently in their personal and public lives. Leaders become authentically and personally empowered through organizing. Meanwhile, they develop the capacity to work with others to provide leadership to their community for educational change and social justice.

Transforming Institutions

Within the diversity of specific goals and reform strategies used by organizing groups in their education work, we found a central common approach. All the groups in our study seek to change the relationship between the institutions of public education and the low-income communities they serve. We consider this to be transformative work. Organizing groups are not satisfied to achieve discrete policy goals, though they often do undertake campaigns related to changing particular policies. More fundamentally, however, they want to transform the way institutions operate. They seek to make public institutions responsive to community concerns, inclusive of community participation, and accountable to community members for improving the quality and equity of public education.

We found that organizing groups seek to transform institutions by following a dual strategy that includes both demand and engagement. Many educators see only the value of collaboration and fear confrontation. Yet we have argued that the failure of public education to serve children in low-income communities and communities of color is rooted in fundamental power imbalances in our society. Organizing groups need to assert power to alter that balance and to push institutions to change. In other words, they build the capacity for an independent assertion of unilateral power so that they can leverage the capacity of communities to demand change.

Transformation, however, requires more than an "outside" demand; it entails what we have called relational power. In other words, it requires an effort to engage with institutional actors and build new relationships capable of changing their hearts and minds. At some point, educators have to come to embrace the changes if they are going to be truly responsive, inclusive, and accountable. Quite simply, you cannot force someone to teach well. Transformative change comes when multiple actors—district officials, principals, teachers, parents, young people, and community residents—find ways to work together in pursuit of a common vision through concrete strategies. In the end, then, we find that organizing groups build and utilize unilateral power even while they pursue deeply collaborative work to create relational power.

This dual strategy lies in contrast to stereotypical understandings of community organizing as protest activity. Many people see the public rallies or protests of organizing groups, that is, their assertion of unilateral power. The quieter and patient efforts of groups to find avenues for engagement and collaboration often occur behind the scenes or beneath the surface. This kind of action, however, is no less important as it creates the long-term conditions for transformation in the practice of public institutions.

Context plays a critical role in shaping collaboration and, more broadly, a group's strategy for school reform. Groups carefully analyze power arrangements to identify openings for engagement as they respond to opportunities and constraints. They look for potential allies within institutions and may adjust their tactics to follow new openings, even if their core values and goals remain unchanged. They attempt to form broader alliances to expand the base of power that can be brought to bear. No doubt powerful forces in the larger policy environment, like foundations willing to fund certain kinds of initiatives, have some influence on the choices groups make. For the most part, though, we have seen groups protect their independence even as they seek openings and resources from others.

Indeed, it is from this independent base of power that groups can decide when and how to engage with educators. The balance between demand and engagement varies across our groups and within our groups over time. But we found that all groups both assert their demands and seek to engage institutions. They attempt to maintain this dual strategy through the ups and downs of campaigns and alliances.

In Mississippi, Southern Echo found itself responding to a context where the denial of education to African Americans served as a central pillar of oppression dating back to slavery. After the Supreme Court's *Brown v. Board of Education* decision in 1954, the state legislature came within one vote of abolishing public education in the state. According to Echo, these legislators believed that "anything beyond a third grade education ruins a field hand." As the federal courts imposed racial integration, many whites fled the public system to private schools, and the state continued to underfund education for African Americans. When Southern Echo began working to increase funding for Delta schools in 1996, Holmes County's per pupil expenditure was a dismal $3,942. Rural black communities remained largely unorganized and excluded from decision making in Jackson, the state capital, where funding for rural schools was controlled.

Responding to the context of rural isolation, Southern Echo organized across rural counties to begin to change the balance of power in the state. Through redistricting work, Echo helped double the size of the Legislative Black Caucus and many of these legislators became important allies for advancing black education. When Echo launched its campaign to fully fund the Mississippi Adequate Education Program, the group worked hard to engage teachers unions and parent groups; eventually these groups formed the Education Stakeholders Alliance. Echo also began to work with officials in the state's department of education and board of education. Tension emerged in the alliance as Echo insisted on its right to gather petitions and hold rallies at the statehouse. In 2007, Echo and other funding advocates finally convinced the legislature to fully fund the Mississippi Adequate Education Program to the tune of $650 million, and funding in rural counties increased dramatically. Echo continues to push for a much greater level of "justice funding" and works to hold the state's department of education accountable for further progress; its work has been transformational. African Americans from Delta communities, long excluded from the halls of power, now regularly participate in educational policy discussions in Jackson and officials often invite Echo leaders to the policymaking table.

Padres y Jóvenes Unidos also sees the denial of quality education to Latino children as part of a racist system that has kept the Latino community poor and disempowered. The 38 percent drop-out rate at North High School, located in the heart of Denver's Latino community, served as a potent symbol of the historic failure of public education for Latinos. Dominant groups in Denver pushed to ban bilingual education, while Latinos remained largely excluded from decision making in educational policy and practice.

PJU organized first parents and then young people at North High School to bring their own voices to bear on the situation at North. Using the results of their student survey, PJU pushed the school's principal to establish a reform committee where the group tried to collaborate with teachers and administrators on needed changes. After two years, PJU felt motion stalling on the committee and began to call for a complete redesign of the school. Consequently, the principal, many teachers and their union officials came to oppose the process. Reaching out to community allies, PJU built the Coalition to Save North and they found a new and powerful ally in the district superintendent Michael Bennet. Bennet endorsed the redesign of North and looked to PJU to organize the community support necessary to overcome teacher opposition. In 2006, PJU achieved its objective and North was completely redesigned. From a symbol of low expectations and failure, North now offers college preparation classes to all students. PJU continues to struggle with its role in implementing this curriculum and making sure that North lives up to its new promise. What has changed in Denver is not simply that Latino students receive a better education. PJU has ensured that young people and their parents now have an organized voice in educational decisions while district officials invite them to participate in creating and implementing policies like the district's new restorative justice discipline code.

Some groups in our study take a deeply relational and especially collaborative approach to education reform. LSNA took advantage of the context of Chicago school reform which gave parents an important measure of power in local school councils. LSNA worked closely with neighborhood school principals to launch its parent mentor program. As parent leaders emerged, they partnered with educators to develop new initiatives like the Literacy Ambassadors program and the Grow Your Own Teacher preparation program. Nevertheless, LSNA maintains its capacity for independent action in communities and schools. For example, parents at Monroe school organized to stop the district from closing the school's seventh- and eighth-grade classrooms. Parent leaders have also emerged from schools to organize for affordable development in the neighborhood.

LSNA's deep and sustained work in a set of neighborhood schools also helps reveal the transformative potential of new relationships between educators and parents. Before LSNA began its educational organizing, parents were almost entirely absent from their children's schools and many of their encounters with teachers were laced with mistrust, misunderstanding, and fear.

LSNA organizers felt the school operated out of white middle-class norms that were not completely appropriate for educating the children of Latino immigrants. Now parents are everywhere, working in classrooms as parent mentors and tutors, gathered in the library running literacy programs, and taking classes in the after-hours community learning centers. Parents are not confined to auxiliary support roles; they participate in the real work of schools. By bringing parents into classrooms and sending teachers out to children's homes, parents and teachers are building collaborative relationships. Through these relationships, teachers begin to understand parents' strengths and the culture of the Latino community. Although not all teachers change their attitudes and practice, the steady expansion of parent participation and collaboration is gradually transforming the culture of neighborhood schools from disconnection to engagement. Meanwhile, LSNA's Grow Your Own Teacher program promises to take a further step in culture change by bring parents directly into the schools as community-based teachers.

One LA's educational strategy is entirely premised on changing the culture of the institutions of public education to focus on relationships. IAF organizers honed a deeply collaborative approach to education reform in Texas. When a new set of IAF organizers arrived in Los Angeles, they faced a massive school system notorious for its disconnection from families and communities. One LA originally set out to build a district-wide organization bringing congregations and schools together across a huge and divided region.

Although the group has struggled to unite institutions at this scale, One LA has proved able to sink deep roots in particular institutions and communities, collaborating with congregational pastors and school principals. Parent and teacher collaboration at Trinity school led to a campaign where One LA congregations and schools worked together to compel the district to change a budgeting schedule that disadvantaged the quarter of district students who attended the summer track of schools. At Fernangeles school, building collaborative relationships between the school, local congregations, and other community organizations closed a local dump whose pollution created severe health problems for students. At Harmony school, the building of a relational culture created collaborative relationships among teachers and between teachers and parents. In the end, One LA's organizing shows the potential to transform school-family-community relationships from profound disconnection to close collaboration through developing relational cultures.

PACT in San Jose built local organizing committees around its member congregations located on the east side of the city, a poor neighborhood so notorious that locals call it "Sal si puedes," i.e., "Get out if you can." In this context, PACT leaders developed a campaign to create new small schools with the autonomy to develop community-oriented and collaborative cultures. Although at times PACT faced intense opposition to these plans at the district level, the group proved able to win the establishment of three schools. A number of teachers came forward, excited and interested in working together to design these schools.

The group built close relationships between teachers, parents, and congregational leaders in the design of these schools, setting in motion a deep culture of family and community engagement. At the L.U.C.H.A. school, empowered parents reversed the traditional deferential role of immigrant parents in relationship to teachers. Meanwhile, principals and teachers came to see the value of collaborative cultures and shared decision making with parents. Teachers brought this approach into their teaching as well, addressing their students as "L.U.C.H.A. leaders." Despite the initial success of the new schools, opposition to PACT's organizing persisted at the district level. In pursuit of achieving their goal of providing great schools for San Jose's children, PACT leaders decided to support the creation of some charter schools as well. In the end, local contexts have led PACT to place demands at the district level while it engages educators at the school level. At the school level, PACT has proved able to institutionalize a relational culture that persists after the group's active involvement ceases. Meanwhile, continual pressure seems to have made the district more open to collaborating in the recent period.

The Northwest Bronx Coalition has struggled to improve schooling in the context of the massive New York City public education system. The Coalition charged the department of education with "planning for failure" when it discovered that the department creates its classroom space plans assuming only a third of Bronx students will make it to twelfth grade. With mayoral control, the system became even more centralized and disconnected from communities, leaving few avenues for input from organized parents and young people. Since the Coalition operates in just one area of the city, albeit a large one, it has worked hard to create allies within the Bronx as well as across the city to build the power necessary to influence a system widely seen as unresponsive.

Flexible and creative in response to openings for influence, the Coalition has made some important progress. The Coalition's youth-led affiliate, Sistas and Brothas United, worked closely with a set of educators to set up a new high school called the Leadership Institute; the school now works to help foster the development of a new generation of youth leaders for the community. Youth participate in the Coalition's broader educational alliance, which includes religious congregations, labor unions, nonprofit organizations, and advocacy groups. The alliance has begun to win increases in desperately needed classroom space as it works on the conversion of the massive Kingsbridge Armory building into a multipurpose community space that would include new schools. In the face of an unresponsive educational bureaucracy, the Coalition has organized parent and youth voice, expanded its range through alliances, and brought grass-roots participation to bear at multiple levels within the educational system.

In all these cases, organizing groups build processes that work to transform the institutions of public education. The independent assertion of community voice and demand opens up processes of change while engagement draws various institutional actors into collaboration. The balance between confrontation and collaboration varies somewhat across the groups and, over time, within the groups. Yet the dynamic between demand and engagement is a powerful one in all cases. As a result, the transformation of relationships between organized communities and the institutions of public education has made these institutions become more responsive, inclusive, and accountable.

Organizing at Multiple Levels

We have argued that organizing groups build community capacity and develop leaders in order to transform public education. But we have also emphasized that education reform is not their only goal. Rather, pursuing institutional change also represents a means to build communities and develop leaders. It is by working at all three levels—the community, individual, and institutional—that groups create transformational processes.

Indeed, change at one level often advances as change proceeds at the other levels. For example, personal transformation of parent and youth leaders comes in part as they feel the power of community. When a group achieves a victory, that success emboldens the group to move forward and reinforces the confidence and determination of individual leaders. At the same time, as leaders grow, they become more committed to building community and helping to transform others. Meanwhile, the efforts of organizing groups to change how power-holders act via new relationships are also transformational to community leaders. Community leaders grow not just through relationships with each other. They are challenged in new ways and develop an increased sense of their own capacities as they engage with educators and public officials.

Ronn Jordan, for example, first approached the Northwest Bronx Coalition when a school eliminated his son's kindergarten class due to lack of space. Through conversations with other parents in the Coalition, Ronn realized that his son's experience was shared by many and that overcrowding was a systemic problem in Bronx schools. Ronn worked with leaders like Teresa Anderson and organizers like Clay Smith and became emboldened to tackle the department of education's capital plan and 700-page Blue Book. Ronn and other leaders built new relationships with staffers in their local councilperson's office and the city's Office of the Public Advocate, researchers at the Annenberg Institute for School

Reform, and representatives of the United Federation of Teachers. The Coalition proceeded to build a "shared fate" campaign that linked its work on housing and immigration to education, placing Ronn, Teresa, and other leaders like Jatnna Ramirez in front of large action forums and in relationship to diverse institutions. The strong leader that Ronn is today comes, in part, as a result of all of these processes—building individual relationships across generations and institutions, working at the community level to develop common issues and a sense of shared fate, engaging with city officials and other allies, and shaping citywide campaigns for education reform.

We can also see how the capacities of communities can grow as leaders develop and as they gain experience working with educators. When new Latino immigrants arrived in Logan Square, they brought rich cultures and traditions but lacked the connections and knowledge necessary to address the challenges of urban institutions in Chicago. As LSNA built a new generation of Latina leaders through its education organizing, Logan Square has become a leader-filled neighborhood. Parent leaders are now working on a variety of community issues from public health to immigration. LSNA's latest campaign for affordable development shows the important difference that leadership and capacity building make. As pressure from gentrification mounted in Logan Square, housing values rose dramatically threatening to make the neighborhood unaffordable to most current residents. Prior to LSNA's education organizing, families would face rent increases by themselves. Now 150 parent mentors and many other parent and community leaders are working together to mount a campaign for affordable housing and balanced development.

Recognizing the multilevel work of community organizing reveals that these groups are not the entirely "bottom-up" organizations that simple stereotypes might have us believe. Organizing groups do bring people together for conversation and help them develop their voice. Issue campaigns grow out of these conversations but they are also influenced by other factors. Groups come out of organizing traditions; they have broader goals developed over time; they may have policy ideas developed earlier in their group or elsewhere in their network; and they are influenced by dialogue and relationships with policy and education experts.[10]

PACT's small schools campaign shows how organizing initiatives take root in community concerns and local knowledge but reach beyond them as well. PACT's organizing cycle, which it takes from the larger PICO network, begins with listening. Through listening in one-on-ones, house meetings, and local organizing committees, PACT learned about the frustration parents experienced with distant and unresponsive Alum Rock schools. Their stories and narratives formed the foundation for an approach that emphasized smaller, more caring environments for children in schools where families would be welcome and have a voice. But a new organizer, Matt Hammer, brought the specific strategy for new small autonomous schools with him from PACT's sister PICO organization in Oakland. The strategy resonated with local leaders in San Jose who built their own version of the initiative to suit their needs. PACT leaders also connected with policy advocates regionally and across the country as they mounted the campaign; meanwhile, the group assembled key alliances with elected officials in the city, county, and state government. After the school board approved three schools, PACT did another round of listening to parents and placed them at the table in the design process of each school. The L.U.C.H.A. school, moreover, institutionalized listening as teachers conducted home visits during its first month, an approach pioneered by another PICO affiliate in Sacramento. In this way, L.U.C.H.A. teachers were drawn into the organizing process, bringing the hopes and dreams of parents into their classroom practice as they built schools infused with collaborative relationships with parents.

As the example from PACT shows, strong organizing groups are grounded in community context and rooted in authentic listening, but they work through multiple levels. Indeed they set individuals, community, and broader institutional actors in relationship to each other. It is through this multilevel process that power relations begin to shift.

For this reason we describe organizing as a dynamic, process-oriented approach to education reform. In other words, organizing sets off and shapes a process of change without a predetermined education reform goal. Education reformers typically focus on achieving specific reform objectives, like the implementation of programs designed to increase student achievement. However, we have seen that organizing groups link each particular reform "win" to their broader goals in terms of individual and community transformation. In our view, the power of organizing itself comes from the dynamic tension between these interdependent processes and goals.

Diversity and Context in the Education Goals of Community Organizing

Although we have spent the bulk of this chapter drawing a composite picture of strong forms of community organizing for education reform, we want to return to our beginning point, that is, the diversity of organizing approaches. Indeed, the groups in our study work to improve education in a mix of ways, including increasing resources, promoting more equitable policies, and changing the culture of schooling. Some groups, like One LA and LSNA, see changing school culture as key, and that requires a focus on individual schools at the core of their work. Conversely, other groups, like Southern Echo, emphasize change in larger political structures so they focus more on resource and policy issues. Nevertheless, all groups know that school change cannot be dictated through district- and/or state-level work and so have some focus at the very local or school level. Conversely, all groups know individual schools cannot change in a vacuum, so they aspire to address district and state levels where possible.[11]

We found that there is no simple model to explain why organizing groups pursue education reform in the ways they do. This is because the focus of organizing efforts is not simply on winning particular reforms. We understand organizing as a process, one that is rooted in diverse traditions and local communities, and one that responds to a variety of opportunities and constraints in institutional contexts and policy environments. As a result, groups pursue educational change in ways that cannot be entirely predicted. Indeed, we find this diversity to be one of the field's great strengths as it grounds change efforts in particular local realities and interests.[12]

We have emphasized that community organizing is not defined by a set of techniques to bring disconnected individuals together for immediate action. Rather, strong organizing draws upon one or more traditions. It starts from a place. It has a theory behind it, an analysis, and a set of interconnected parts. Rooted in history and tradition, strong groups also grow and develop as they engage with communities and institutions over time. Organizing groups adapt to new circumstances and respond to changing contexts. But tradition gives meaning to the organizing and provides an anchor that sustains groups over the long and hard road of transforming communities and schools.

Organizing groups care about improving the quality of and increasing equity in public education because the economic future of children in low-income communities depends so heavily on school success. But education also matters because it provides the foundation for full participation in society, for the liberation of people subjugated by racism and poverty, and for the expansion of our democracy. In that sense, community organizing does not just bring new human and social resources to school reform. It brings rich traditions that ground change in community values while it connects education reform to a larger project of advancing democracy and social justice.

Conclusion

Lessons for School Reform and Democracy Building

Questions of educational equity and social justice will increasingly move to the center of debates over education reform. Nearly half of all public school students in the United States come from low-income families and that proportion is growing. Meanwhile, students of color are expected to become the majority of all students in public schools across the country within the next ten years.[1]

These children represent our country's future. If we cannot find a way for public schools to educate these children well, our society will face a profound crisis. We will not have the workforce we need to compete in an increasingly globalized economy nor the kind of citizenry prepared to address the challenges of an increasingly diverse society. Meanwhile, a new generation of adults will not have the education necessary to support a family and participate as full citizens in our democracy. American public education has traditionally been seen as the great equalizer in our society. Currently, it serves as an engine producing inequality in socio-economic and democratic life.[2]

Many school reformers and other activists have been working hard to reclaim the promise of American public education. They do not have to do this work alone. Indeed, they cannot fully address the deep problems in public education solely through school-improvement strategies. We have argued throughout this book that the problems of educational failure reside in systemic inequality in power and resources in American society. This is not to excuse school systems for their failures. Rather it is a hardheaded realization that we must address the poverty and racism that undermine family and community life, and that contribute to violence, poor health, and the myriad factors that prevent the healthy development of children in low-income communities.[3]

It is also a frank recognition that institutions change when the people with the most at stake build the power to demand change. The chapters in this book describe a number of important ways that low-income communities organize to demand higher quality and greater equity from our public education system. However, we have also stressed that organizing groups do not simply push for change. They also contribute directly to education reform efforts. Organizing groups increase resources to public schools serving low-income communities. They build strong participation by parents and sometimes young people in school change efforts, broadening and deepening the social resources available for school improvement. They go deeply into schools to change the culture and practice of teaching toward a more relational and culturally responsive approach. They create integrative strategies that tie school improvement to the revitalization of the communities in which students live and grow. In all these ways, they address education reform as part of a broader strategy to build the power necessary to address structural inequality in American society.

In this chapter we draw out the lessons from our study for educators and for all Americans who care about the future of public education and of our democracy. Community organizing itself does not provide the complete answer to failure in our public education system. But it provides important contributions to the search for new strategies and, we believe, makes an essential contribution to school-improvement efforts in low-income communities. In this chapter, we first highlight the distinctive contributions of organizing to school reform. We then discuss the prospects for increasing collaboration between educators and community organizing groups and consider the challenges that the field of community organizing faces in its attempt to become a more central player in school reform efforts. We end by highlighting the broader contributions that community organizing makes to democracy building and social justice.

The Contributions of Community Organizing to School Reform

A MULTIDIMENSIONAL, PROCESS-ORIENTED APPROACH

Organizing connects school reform to social justice. Social justice, however, is not primarily an outcome but a process where people who have been marginalized build the capacity to exert a measure of control over the institutions that shape their lives. Community organizing, in that sense, is not a program to be implemented. It is a process to be undertaken whose direction cannot be entirely foreseen or predicted—hence, the variety of strategies and outcomes in education reform reported in this book.[4]

As such, community organizing represents a different paradigm than the approach normally taken by school reformers. By school reform in this context we mean professional activity focused on improving schools in low-income communities. Education reform is typically undertaken as an expert-driven and technical enterprise. Researchers analyze the causes of school failure and develop appropriate strategies to address them. Indeed, federal policy has more and more prioritized evidence-based models and practices based on scientific research. These reforms are piloted, revised, and then "scaled-up." In other words, they are spread to other localities where they are adopted by districts and often imposed on schools and their teachers. The search is for universal programs, that is, reforms that will work everywhere, or at least that will work for large population groups.[5]

In many ways, this approach has led to disappointing results. Education reform initiatives often remain at the surface level, seldom penetrating deeply into educational practice in our most dysfunctional schools. Universalistic programs are not very sensitive to local cultural differences in schools and communities. The traditional top-down, programmatic emphasis of school reform initiatives fails to appreciate that institutional change is always a collective process. This approach lacks a strategy for engaging the hearts and minds of educators at the school level, for valuing their experience and understanding as part of the change process, and for bringing them together as a group committed to improvement. Meanwhile, it ignores the important role parents and young people themselves can play in school change initiatives.[6]

Community organizing brings a powerful bottom-up thrust to education reform efforts. The process approach of organizing starts with listening and conversation at the ground level. Organizing seldom starts with a preset agenda but rather responds to local context. It appreciates the local knowledge held by all actors and works to engage their passions and interests. These actors include parents, young people, and community residents, but also teachers who often feel powerless in typical school reform initiatives. Organizing builds broad participation and offers people a chance to become public leaders in change processes; participation often proves transformational and powerful for them. Indeed, organizers push people to grow and develop and take on new challenges. As people build relationships through action, they come to craft and refine reform initiatives. In these ways, people take ownership of the processes of change.

Yet community organizing is not an entirely bottom-up approach and, alone, does not provide all the answers needed to improve schools. Rather, organizing groups work on multiple levels. They engage people in analyzing the problems facing schools and communities and try to develop programs that can meet their needs. In doing so, they seek technical, expert knowledge and they build the capacity themselves to develop some of that analysis. Indeed, contrary to sometimes stereotypical views of community groups, many organizing groups are quite sophisticated in their use of the latest research and in learning from model initiatives around the country. If they find or help develop a good program that they think might work in other places, they promote the spread of the initiative.

Nevertheless, strong organizing efforts always anchor reform strategies in the relational processes they develop. In this way, reform agendas are rooted in the specific conditions faced in local schools and communities and the specific values, interests, and passions of actors on the ground. As a result, all actors in the school community, including teachers, parents, young people, and community residents, have the opportunity to develop strong ownership of the processes of change, and that promises to make reform initiatives deep and lasting. Organizing is a dynamic, multidimensional process that requires balancing different needs and goals but can create a powerful change process in the end.

We do not want to stereotype all educator-driven school reform as "top-down." There are many new currents in school improvement that are interested in creating authentic processes of change at the school level and in building relationships and collaboration across the school community. In the following sections, we discuss some of these new directions while highlighting the distinctive contributions community organizing can make to them.

BUILDING THE SOCIAL FOUNDATIONS FOR SCHOOL CHANGE

A growing number of scholars and researchers are beginning to recognize the importance of creating a change process within schools that engages the participation and leadership of the entire school community. Indeed, an important new development in school reform is the appreciation of the importance of building a social foundation for school-improvement efforts, that is, relationships and trust among all actors in the school community. Anthony Bryk and his colleagues have done the most to argue for the need to build social trust as the basis for any real improvement in education in distressed schools. In careful studies of the different kinds of progress public schools have made in Chicago, Bryk has shown that schools with strong and trusting relationships have greater capacity to genuinely embrace and effectively implement reform initiatives. Trusting relations among educators at the school feature prominently, but Bryk also demonstrates the importance of building trust and forging cooperation across all actors in the school community, including parents and community leaders.[7]

Indeed, in their most recent work Bryk and his colleagues identify parent and community engagement as one of the five essential supports to improving public schools. The researchers measured gains in student test scores in Chicago public schools from 1990 to 1996, comparing the top-quartile improving schools and the bottom-quartile stagnating schools. Analyzing this data, Bryk and his colleagues identified five supports necessary for improvement, including school leadership, professional capacity, student-centered learning climate, instructional guidance, and family and community engagement. The authors conclude, "We found that a sustained, material weakness in any one of these subsystems [including family and community engagement] undermined virtually all attempts at improving student learning."[8] Bryk and his colleagues also found that a school's level of relational trust was a strong predictor of parent and community engagement and that there was a reciprocal relationship between trust and engagement. Other studies also reinforce the importance of social capital, including family and community engagement, to school improvement. For example, a study by Designs for Change found that the low-performing schools that improved the most in Chicago between 1990 and 2005 were ones characterized by a collaborative culture within the school and across educators, parents, and community leaders.[9]

Community organizing approaches also align with new thinking on educational leadership like those that emphasize the value of distributed and adaptive approaches. Rather than seeing the principal as a heroic leader, this new paradigm stresses collaboration. The role of the principal is no longer to lead in a top-down manner but rather to help build the leadership of others, that is, teachers and staff at the school. Rather than emphasizing managerial and technical competencies, the new school leader is one who can adapt to new circumstances and lead others in change processes. In adaptive situations, people learn the solutions to their problems and develop the skills to solve them in the act of working together.[10]

These new conceptions of leadership connect to efforts to build what are called communities of practice in schools. This is an approach that emphasizes creating connections between teachers focused on discussion of their practice. Through developing communities of practice, educators can build trust over time as well as develop a shared sense of purpose and commitment to change processes. A recent contribution to this field draws upon the instructional rounds developed in the medical profession and recommends that teachers observe each other's teaching, analyze their practice together, and work collaboratively to improve teaching and learning in their classrooms. In this approach, educators draw from research and evidence about effective instruction, but, as in organizing approaches, they focus on practice at the local level and have some real control over the implementation of policy or programs.[11]

With its emphasis on relationship building and collective leadership, community organizing represents a powerful way to build social capital and engage educators, families and community leaders in collaborative efforts to improve schools. Rather than starting with improvement plans, organizing suggests the power of building deeply relational cultures in schools. In chapter 3, we saw how One LA helped create new kinds of relationships among teachers and staff at Harmony Elementary School in Los Angeles. Rather than focus first or narrowly on practice, Harmony principal Robert Cordova had staff take the time to build relationships that were deep and meaningful. Cordova and his administrative team used organizing strategies like one-on-one relational meetings. Trust built through these relationships encouraged teachers to be open and honest about the struggles they were having in classrooms. In the end, the combination of relationships and leadership led to authentic collaborative approaches to improve classroom instruction.

However, organizing approaches reach beyond educators to connect to parents as well. PACT in San Jose built design teams for new small autonomous schools that combined educators and parents from the congregations in which the group worked. Parents pushed strongly for a school that would fully incorporate their participation, where parents and teachers would see themselves in an active partnership, and where teaching would be responsive to the culture of their children. Out of this process emerged schools like L.U.C.H.A., where Principal Kristin Henny sees her role as building community not just among teachers but across the entire school community. Parents remain present throughout the school as teachers and families work together for the education of children.

Community organizing, with its expertise on relationship building, can affect what educators have come to call "the instructional core" of schools. A growing number of researchers and educators have emphasized that school change processes, if they are to significantly increase student achievement, must focus on instructional practice in the classroom. Teacher content knowledge matters to the core, but emphasis is also placed on the practice of the teacher in relationship to the student; in other words, teaching is understood as an inherently relational enterprise. In our view, when teachers are disconnected from the families and communities of their students, their ability to engage students and connect learning to their experience is fundamentally limited. When teachers can build rich and meaningful relationships with families and communities, as we have seen in the chapters in this book, they can better understand the culture of their students and incorporate their knowledge about the lives of children into classroom practice. They can also form partnerships with families to work together for the education of children.[12]

BUILDING STRONG PARENT PARTICIPATION IN SCHOOLS

Research on family and community engagement, like that by Anthony Bryk cited earlier, has shown how important parent participation is to school improvement and to children's educational success. More and more educators are becoming interested in finding ways to involve parents in the education of their children. The No Child Left Behind Act mandated parent outreach efforts in schools that receive Title I funding. Traditionally, schools have reached out to involve families as supporters of the school's agenda. A more recent emphasis has been placed on developing meaningful partnerships with parents and other community actors.

Some districts now even say they want to create "demand parents" who will both support their children's learning and demand that schools provide the quality education to which their children have a right.[13]

If mounting research demonstrates the essential role of family and community engagement in school improvement, few educators know how to do this work well. Our research on community organizing identifies effective ways to build broad and powerful forms of participation. Too often school-based educators focus on the dysfunction of families in low-income communities. Many blame parents for the problems of their children and expect little of them. Few educators inquire about, let alone admire, the strengths of parents who work long hours in low-wage jobs or struggle to survive on unemployment, who raise families in crowded and substandard housing conditions, who sacrifice to put food on the table for their children, and who counsel them daily about how to navigate dangerous streets. Many parents, it turns out, play active roles in faith communities, sports teams, and neighborhood organizations while others provide informal, day-to-day support for their friends and neighbors. Perhaps it is not surprising that many parents resist when teachers look down on them and treat them with paternalistic condescension.[14]

Organizing groups, by contrast, approach parents with dignity and as full citizens. They listen to their ideas. They engage their passions and interests, while they support their development. The Logan Square Neighborhood Association (LSNA) in Chicago, for example, shows how this approach can foster widespread and powerful forms of parent participation in schools. LSNA has trained over twelve hundred parents across eight schools through its model Parent Mentor program and offered them a variety of opportunities to participate and exert leadership. Parents have gone on to work with school staff to open community centers, create Literacy Ambassadors programs where teachers and parents pair up to make home visits to families, and start a Grow Your Own Teacher program offering pathways for parents to become bilingual teachers in neighborhood schools.

The organizing approach also shows the value of building ties among parents as part of the engagement process. Schools typically reach out to parents as individuals. Through community organizing, groups in our study have built a collective parent base that advocates for all children in a school or community and takes ownership for the school's practice in this regard. By working together, parents in some schools started by PACT in San Jose, for example, take so much ownership over their schools that they object to language that says the schools involve them in activities. Rather, they assert that parents helped design the school and create its activities in the first place.[15]

Some organizing groups add an entirely new dimension to engagement. They seek to organize young people as part of change efforts at the high school level. Typically, educators focus on the disengagement of students in low-income communities. By contrast, young people at North High School in Denver organized to demand a better education for themselves. Working through Padres y Jóvenes Unidos, they surveyed their fellow students and worked with parents and other community leaders to create a school reform plan. In other examples, young people in the Bronx campaigned to open a social justice high school and young people in the Southern Echo network organized to dramatically increase state funds available to their schools in the Mississippi Delta.

ADDRESSING INEQUALITY AND POWER
IN FAMILY-SCHOOL RELATIONS

As parents and young people become powerful actors in schools, they need to create meaningful partnerships with educators and that often means crossing the racial and class divides that separate them. A new group of reformers are challenging educators to address issues of race and power and pay explicit attention to historic mistrust when building school-family partnerships. A growing body of research shows that trust can be built when the two groups take the opportunity to have meaningful conversations. These conversations can be particularly successful when conducted in the context of working together for shared goals, like the healthy development of children. A recent survey by Curt Adams and his associates, for example, compared schools with different socio-economic compositions and found that trust was less dependent on context and more dependent on social norms and collaborative processes that brought parents from the periphery into the operating core of the schools.[16]

Organizing offers an intentional strategy that takes power seriously in forming these collaborations. Organizing groups are willing to assert their unilateral power if necessary, but their ultimate goal is to build the relational power that leads to collaboration. Rather than ignore issues of race and power, organizers help teachers and parents work through the inevitable tensions and conflicts that exist to find a common ground to move forward.[17]

Indeed, part of what makes organizing a dynamic process is that it intentionally creates a mix of people with diverse backgrounds and interests. For example, LSNA brings parents of different backgrounds together through neighborhood-wide training sessions for the purpose of supporting the education of their children in local schools. Although teachers were initially fearful of having parent mentors in their classrooms, over time LSNA helped them work to develop more collaborative relationships and strong partnerships with parent leaders, shifting the balance of power in schools.

As many schools and school districts become increasingly interested in fostering stronger forms of parent participation, community groups may come to play an essential role. First of all, community organizations are often better placed to engage families than schools. Many are rooted in communities and experts in social capital building while most teachers are not. Furthermore, their independent status outside of schools allows them to play a role as bridge-builders. They can help facilitate a process for parents, teachers and principals to deal with the inequalities and power imbalances that often mar the building of strong relationships.[18]

BUILDING SCHOOL-COMMUNITY COLLABORATIONS

Improving the education of children in low-income communities certainly involves greater family participation and improvements in teaching and learning in schools, but it entails something beyond that. It requires addressing the multiple effects of poverty and racism on families and their children so that students attend school safe, healthy, and ready to learn. Indeed, a growing body of research shows that the conditions children face at home and in the community have as much or even more of an effect on academic achievement than schooling practices.[19]

New research by Anthony Bryk and his colleagues shows that the level of a neighborhood's social capital and social needs have an important influence on the ability of public schools located there to improve. Using data from the Project on Human Development in Chicago Neighborhoods, Bryk demonstrates that schools in communities with higher levels of trust and civic engagement, all other things being equal, were best able to develop the essential supports necessary for school improvement and make effective use of those supports. Indeed, schools in communities without much social capital and with high levels of social needs proved resistant to change, leading the authors to conclude that in such neighborhoods, "A much more powerful model of school development is needed—one that melds a comprehensive community schools initiative."[20]

As understanding of these connections grow, an increasing number of educators are becoming interested in partnering with community-based organizations in order to take a more integrated strategy to children's healthy development and learning. We now have thousands of community or full-service schools that offer health and family support services in the school building. Initiatives like the Harlem Children's Zone (HCZ) take an even more extensive approach to linking family, community, and school. HCZ works to provide a comprehensive set of social supports for children from birth to college and explicitly coordinates this work with attempts to create high-quality education in local schools. Impressed with its early results, the federal government is now attempting to support the development of Promise Neighborhoods, modeled upon HCZ, in other communities across the country.[21]

Although HCZ concentrates on program provision, it does hire community organizers to engage parents and family members. HCZ and its supporters know that deep and lasting change requires the active engagement of parents and a range of other community actors, that is, the building of social capital. Organizing groups place this work at the center and not the periphery of their efforts. Since they focus centrally on building participation of people directly in change efforts, they have some important contributions to make to strengthen initiatives like HCZ and push this emerging field toward deeper forms of school-community collaboration.

Community organizing offers a political strategy to address neighborhood poverty and community development issues. Most school-community partnerships accept the unequal conditions faced by low-income communities and attempt to provide services to support families. Organizing groups sometimes lobby for additional services. But they also try to address the root causes of community decline, and this requires an approach that builds the social capacity and political power of neighborhood residents.

One LA, for example, brought congregations and schools together in the San Fernando Valley to close a dump that was contributing to serious health problems among children at Fernangeles school. By working with Principal Karen Jaye to organize teachers and school staff, and by linking those efforts with pastors at local churches as well as leaders in other neighborhood organizations, One LA created a powerful alliance. This neighborhood alliance, meanwhile, had the support of One LA's full membership of over one hundred institutions, which created a broad-based force capable of stopping the dump's expansion.

Meanwhile, other organizing groups continue to address a wide range of issues affecting children's development. PACT in San Jose led the effort to create the nation's first county-wide healthcare reform which guaranteed high-quality health care to all children in Santa Clara County. The Northwest Bronx Coalition built its reputation on stemming housing decline in the Bronx and has created thousands of units of affordable housing as well as small-business development opportunities for residents. Parents trained through LSNA's Parent Mentor program are now leading campaigns for public health and affordable housing in Logan Square. In other words, organizing groups bring together a diverse array of actors who together address a range of issues in schools and communities. They work to build social capital and take a more holistic approach to addressing the needs of children and their families.

INCREASING EQUITY IN RESOURCES AND POLICY

In the end, working for equity and social justice in education, and deeply reforming public education, requires something more than a change strategy within individual schools and neighborhoods. It ultimately requires building a political constituency that both supports public education and is committed to addressing inequitable resources and policies within it. Many school reformers understand that race and poverty are deeply implicated in the inequities in our public education system. Yet few perceive viable strategies for building a political base capable of addressing these issues.[22]

Community organizing groups constitute powerful efforts to build a political constituency both to link school reform to community revitalization as well as to address inequities in public education. Southern Echo, for example, provided the grassroots base for an effort to dramatically increase funding to public education across the state. Spending in rural Mississippi was abysmally low; at the start of Echo's campaign, for example, Holmes County was spending less than $4,000 per pupil. To address this profound inequity, Southern Echo allied with a number of advocacy groups and state education officials. Southern Echo collected ten thousand signatures across sixty-eight counties and repeatedly brought hundreds of community members to the state capital to press the case for funding. Ultimately, the state legislature passed the measure to fully fund the Mississippi Adequate Education Program and increase funding by $650 million across the state.

The Northwest Bronx Coalition has worked to build a very broad base of support in an effort to expand classroom space in overcrowded schools. The Coalition built an alliance that included religious congregations, labor unions, nonprofit organizations and advocacy groups, and collaborated with the city's Office of the Public Advocate. Working through alliances, the Coalition has won the building of thousands of additional classroom seats. Meanwhile, Padres y Jóvenes Unidos has worked to defend bilingual education and to provide in-state tuition for undocumented students to attend Colorado colleges and universities.

Educators are not in a position to build this kind of political constituency alone. Advocacy groups play an important role but typically lack a broad and deep citizen base. Organizing groups work precisely to build a political constituency for a high-quality and equitable public education system, cultivating the participation and leadership of low-income people themselves in efforts to increase resources for public education and to redress the profound inequities faced by children in low-income communities.

EFFECTS ON STUDENT ACHIEVEMENT

Community organizing impacts education reform and contributes to the improvement of schooling in low-income communities through a variety of pathways. We have not sought, however, to measure this impact directly on student achievement. In a couple of cases, we do report increases in student achievement as measured by test scores. For example, within a few years of its opening, L.U.C.H.A. had the second-highest scores in the Alum Rock district on California's standardized tests, which PACT believed was one important indication of the high-quality education children were beginning to receive. We do not rest our case, however, on such examples, and we have not attempted to precisely measure the impact of community organizing on student achievement in all the cases we discussed for several reasons. First of all, a variety of factors influence school-improvement processes and their impact on student achievement. Community organizing contributes to school improvement, but not in isolation from issues of school leadership, curriculum reform, and financial resources, among others; community organizing efforts can influence these other factors but not entirely control them. Second, the goals of community organizing are not limited to increases in student achievement, as important as they are, so we do not evaluate organizing solely on that criteria. Finally, we believe increases in test scores are a narrow and limited measure of school-improvement efforts, as many analysts are coming to realize.[23]

Nevertheless, test scores remain important as one measure of school improvement. An increasing number of studies show that family and community engagement are essential to school improvement efforts as measured by test scores. These studies measure family and community engagement and test score changes across a large number of schools and so they are more properly designed to measure effects than qualitative studies like ours. With our small number of cases, our study is not designed to test effects on student achievement. Rather, we build upon these other studies that show the vital importance of family and community engagement; the purpose of our study is to demonstrate *how* strong forms of this engagement can be created.[24]

LOCAL ORGANIZING AND NATIONAL POLICY DISCOURSE

We have emphasized that community organizing brings a process-oriented approach to school reform, not the advocacy of a specific reform agenda to be applied everywhere. Nevertheless, all organizing groups do, at times, advocate specific reforms for particular schools or localities. Our purpose was not to judge the merits of the specific reform agendas that groups advocated, but rather to show how they take shape out of community concerns and actions. PACT, for example, has organized for the creation of small, semi-autonomous schools. We recognize that research is mixed on the effectiveness of the small-schools movement. What we stress, however, is the way that PACT leaders were frustrated with the slow pace of change in a large, impersonal district and believed that this strategy responded well to local conditions and values. Indeed, using this strategy PACT has helped create schools with strong relationships between educators, parents and the communities they serve. PACT-supported small schools were not imposed on schools and communities in the way that the larger reform movement often was.[25]

Community organizing groups also operate in larger systems of policy discourse where resourceful networks are advocating specific reform plans. Indeed, we stressed above that organizing is not an entirely grassroots phenomenon and that organizing groups receive input from multiple levels as they respond to opportunities in the institutional or policy context. Some readers may be concerned about the alignment of certain initiatives with neoliberal reform agendas. PACT has supported the creation of some charter schools, and Padres y Jóvenes Unidos advanced a reform agenda at North High School that required teachers to reapply for their jobs. Community organizers are sophisticated reformers; they are aware of larger alignments even as they attempt to remain focused on campaigns that they believe respond to local conditions. Some organizers and leaders may worry that the charter school movement might ultimately undermine public education. However, parents and the community members are concerned with creating high-quality education in a timeframe that will actually make a difference for their children. Organizers and parents may not care so much that the research on charter schools shows that, in general, they perform no better than traditional district schools; they are frustrated with the slow pace of district change and are using that strategy to create specific schools of a type they believe will deliver a high-quality education. Some organizing groups may make use of resources that come from policy networks even as they do not wish to contribute to the larger success of a particular network's agenda. In the end, community organizing groups have to navigate problematic policy contexts and they sometimes defy easy categorization into liberal, neoliberal, or conservative reform camps.[26]

Building Collaborations between School Reformers and Community Organizing Groups

What can school reformers do if they appreciate the value of community organizing to education reform? Perhaps the most important thing is to look for and help create collaborations with organizing groups. As organizing groups build new kinds of relationships between organized communities and the institutions of public education, they set a course where change processes in schools and communities can inform and stimulate each other. Indeed, school reformers and organizing groups can each bring their special expertise to a combined approach.

Collaboration, however, requires a different approach by educators than is typical. Reformers often want to "get the job done," and do not want to spend the time to engage communities and build authentic collaborations. Indeed, sometimes educators think about engaging families and communities only when they are looking for backing for their own reform agendas. Serious collaboration, however, involves something different. It requires educators and organized communities to have honest conversations and work together to develop and implement change strategies. School reformers will have to become more responsive to community concerns and be willing to be held accountable in a more direct face-to-face way by their constituents. That makes the idea of serious collaboration with community organizing groups quite a novel approach and perhaps challenging for educators.[27]

Despite the risk and uncertainty associated with organizing approaches, collaboration with organizing groups has much to offer educators. In the end, what sense does it make to reform schools without addressing the broader issues that lead to community decline and affect children's ability to grow and learn? Community organizing groups can help build the social resources and will for change within schools. Through these alliances, educators and community organizing groups can work together to improve schools and address issues in the community, and they can work to build a political constituency committed to greater resources for and equity in our educational system.

We need a new model for how educators, parents, and community leaders can work together to tap research-based expertise as well as their own knowledge and capacity to create deep and lasting change. An older model of top-down program implementation seems spent. New initiatives, like communities of practice, turn our attention to relationships, local knowledge, and collaboration around practice in local schools. Organizing can connect to these new approaches while bringing fresh perspectives to addressing issues of power, to reaching beyond the four walls of the school, and to engaging actors through transformational processes.[28]

Meeting the Challenges Ahead

The contributions that organizing groups are beginning to make to education reform are significant and promising. Community organizing is poised to move from the margins toward the center of the field of education reform. We are optimistic about the possibilities for continued growth in size, scale, and sophistication of organizing work around public education. But our assessment is nevertheless a sober one. The field of organizing faces a number of important challenges, both in internal capacity and external environment, which will need to be addressed if it is to fulfill its promise.

FINANCIAL RESOURCES

First of all, the resources available to community organizing need to be significantly increased if these groups are going to expand their work. Organizing groups have accomplished quite a lot with modest levels of funding. But these resources remain small, meager really, compared to the undertaking at hand.

One survey of faith-based organizing groups in the late nineties found that the median annual budget of these groups was about $150,000. Another survey put the average amount for organizing groups working on education closer to $250,000. Because organizing groups are multi-issue organizations, these funds have to cover work on education as well as on a range of other pressing concerns. Indeed, organizing groups typically spend only a portion of their budgets on education work. Most groups have only one or two organizers devoted to education organizing, or their staff members share their time between education and other issues.[29]

Organizing groups have limited sources for their income. They typically raise their funds from a mix of member dues, private foundations and local fundraising. Groups may draw upon public funding for the programs they help develop. But most groups refuse to seek government funds for their operating budgets in order to protect political independence. Meanwhile, the funds that can be raised from membership dues in low-income communities are limited. Institutionally based groups like One LA and PACT do tap their congregational members for dues; but even here the amount that can be raised, while significant, is rather limited.

The role of private philanthropy is therefore critical. More than half of the organizing groups covered in one study received 80 percent of their funding from private foundations. Yet private foundations continue to devote a small proportion of their funding to organizing. We have no precise figures on overall funding of organizing per se. One study, however, found that private foundations devote only 11 percent of their grants to social justice efforts, and this is mostly project funding rather than support for organizing or advocacy. Meanwhile, another study reported that only 7 percent of all foundation giving went to projects targeted in communities of color.[30]

Many funders are more inclined to fund programs and projects rather than the sometimes politically controversial and unpredictable campaigns of community organizing. Moreover, since organizing is about process, organizing groups cannot always define the outcomes or deliverables ahead of time; the specifics of issue campaigns develop from the particular needs, interests, and passions of the individuals they organize. To the extent that organizing groups have to shape their objectives to meet the interests of funders, they are detracting from the authentic internal processes that create the power of organizing in the first place.[31]

Private foundations have increasingly understood this dynamic and have shown renewed interest in supporting community organizing. Foundations concerned with education reform, community development, and democratic participation have all begun to devote resources to organizing groups. There are now several funder collaboratives that work to increase funding to organizing. In doing so, these collaboratives have stressed the importance of supporting the core organizing work of groups rather than program and project support. They have also emphasized the need to honor the integrity of organizing groups' internal processes.[32]

PROFESSIONAL DEVELOPMENT OF ORGANIZERS

There is growing interest in the profession of community organizing on the part of many Americans, especially among young people. Barack Obama attracted a large number of young people as volunteers in his presidential election campaign, and they got a taste of organizing there. Those who find value in community organizing will need to build on these new developments to increase the opportunities for young people to enter the field and remain. Despite the low pay and long hours, many people devote their lives to careers in organizing. Organizers typically find this work exciting and meaningful, a chance to live out their social justice and community values. Yet, if organizing is going to be established as a professional field like others, ways will need to be found to increase the pay and status of community organizers.[33]

Meanwhile, there is a need for greater access to professional training for community organizer. Groups in our study consistently mentioned the small number of skilled organizers available, even if the groups had the funds to hire them. Currently, most organizing groups conduct in-house training for their organizers. This consists of on-the-job training which typically includes strong mentoring by senior staff. The four or five national organizing networks, like the Industrial Areas Foundation and the PICO National Network, offer support structures for this kind of training. A couple of other centers, like the Midwest Academy and the Applied Research Center, offer training opportunities for organizers who may go on to work for independent groups. Unions also train organizers who increasingly find their way into community organizing groups.[34]

Institutions of higher education are just beginning to offer training in community organizing, and this is a promising direction. Some schools of social work have long offered tracks in community organizing. Although their graduates typically gravitate to social service organizations, some join organizing groups. Over the past decade or so, a wide variety of graduate schools of education and other institutions in higher education have begun offering courses in community organizing, which can at least serve as an initial route into the field for young people. There are now some important experiments in offering online courses in community organizing as well.[35]

Through offering courses on organizing, graduate schools of education can introduce emerging teachers, school leaders, and district officials to community organizing. Rather than focus solely on preparation in curriculum and pedagogy within the classroom, these schools can help teachers think about their work within the framework of social change, school transformation, and community organizing. Teachers can begin to learn the skills and orientations to help them connect with parents and build strong partnerships, while principals develop the capacity to collaborate with community organizations as an integral part of their training. To accomplish this, schools of education will have to teach more than technical and managerial skills; they will need to teach relationship building and collaborative leadership.

OPPORTUNITIES TO COLLABORATE

Growth in the influence of community organizing on education reform also depends on increasing the ranks of existing educators who are willing to collaborate with organizing groups. Obstacles exist here too. High-stakes testing regimes often push educators to narrow their focus to raising standardized test scores immediately, crowding out the room for experimentation necessary to build collaborations with community organizing groups. Mayoral control of school districts may limit opportunities for organizing groups to exert influence. Privatization of schooling pulls education out of the public domain, again potentially limiting the influence of organizing groups.[36]

Meanwhile, some educators may want community involvement but resist a real decision-making role for organized parents and young people. They may be skeptical about the value of organizing or feel threatened by independent organizations. Moreover, deep collaborations take time to develop and the often rapid turnover of district or school leadership disrupts relationship building. Teacher's unions often seek to protect existing arrangements at the expense of the experimentation and flexibility necessary in collaborations.

Despite these obstacles, educators increasingly recognize the importance of parent and community engagement, and more and more are willing to search for ways to collaborate with organizing groups. We have seen how serious organizing groups are about finding ways to collaborate, take seriously the concerns of educators, and work to create a common vision and agenda for action. There have even been some notable partnerships between teachers unions and organizing groups as well.[37] Meanwhile, as more districts establish family and community engagement offices, they can provide greater encouragement and support for educators to take the risks involved in collaborative experiments.

Despite these internal and external challenges, community organizing continues to grow and increase its role in equity-oriented education reform. All things considered, what organizing groups have accomplished with limited resources and unfamiliar strategies is quite impressive. We would encourage school reformers, funders, educators, and other stakeholders in public education to support these organizing experiments, test them out, push them forward, and critically engage with this new and promising field.

The Promise of Education and Democracy

Community organizing groups bring organizing into schools and schools out into organizing. In other words, organizing increases civic participation within schools, but it also helps overcome the isolation public schools face by connecting them to a range of community institutions. In this way, community organizing works to revive the democratic purposes of schooling. Organizing creates a powerful dynamic as it forges an interactive connection between education and other institutions of democracy.[38]

American public education contains rich democratic traditions going back to Horace Mann and the Common School ideal. Education is meant to provide a common ground for Americans across the social spectrum, however incompletely that vision is fulfilled in practice. In the Progressive Era, John Dewey reworked the common school tradition for the urban twentieth century. He envisioned public schools as a vital community institution, where schools prepare children to contribute to their communities and to participate as democratic citizens in an increasingly diverse and technocratic society. Adults from the community would regularly visit such schools to teach children skills while also creating a sense of democratic community life. Dewey and his progressive associates believed that educators had to get involved in the big social issues of the day, to work toward a vision of a better society with social welfare at its core. They envisioned the school at the center of the community and as an integral part of the effort to build a new social order.[39]

If the common school ideal represented the democratic tradition of American public education for the nineteenth century, and John Dewey's progressive vision reinvented that tradition for the twentieth century, we might understand community organizing as working toward developing a twenty-first century model for democratic education. When educators are brought out of the confines of school through organizing and as they build new relationships with youth, families, and communities, then schools can emerge as centers of community and democratic life. In Los Angeles, San Jose, Chicago, and other localities, organizing groups find schools to be important places to reach families and bring them into public life. In many ways, organizing is just beginning to demonstrate the promise of this approach, but this vision nevertheless inspires and sustains organizing.[40]

As much as American public education has aspired to be inclusive, however, it is also profoundly implicated in exclusion. African Americans, Latinos, and other excluded groups have historically had to fight their way into public education. Today, African Americans in Mississippi and Latinos in Denver continue to struggle against racial exclusion, placing education at the heart of their struggle for social justice.[41]

For this reason, we see community organizing rooted both in the Deweyan tradition and also in the Freirean popular education tradition. Paolo Freire was a Brazilian educator who developed his core ideas during the period of the anti-colonial struggles of the sixties. Freire envisioned education as a democratic process critical to the liberation of the oppressed. Freire advocated an educational approach that engaged people around their own knowledge of their lived experience while teaching people tools for critical social inquiry of the systems that oppress them. As people develop an understanding of their oppression, they acquire the critical consciousness necessary to act collectively for their own liberation. Reflection upon such action would provide the main mode of democratic learning, culminating in praxis. Praxis allows for a radical democracy where students and teachers become capable of transforming the world.[42]

Freire is best known among American educators for his influence on the practice of critical pedagogy, which has been mainly taken up by classroom teachers working with young people. Yet Freire's ideas have also profoundly enriched a deep, if somewhat submerged, tradition of popular education. Labor organizers in the thirties and later civil rights workers trained at the Highlander Center worked to educate people as a central part of the struggle for social justice.[43]

Community organizing today draws from Freire's stress on the direct participation of those most excluded to transform systems into ones that serve their needs. Organizers work with parents and young people, teaching critical thinking and research skills tied directly to action campaigns. Organizing groups focus on reflection after every action as a way for leaders to grow and develop. Indeed, this kind of praxis lies at the heart of leadership development and is a distinctive feature of the entire field of community organizing.

We find that the dynamism of community organizing lies in the fruitful interaction between Deweyan and Freirean traditions. Organizing reaches out to educators and the broader American public, promoting an inclusive and collaborative effort in the Deweyan spirit. At the same time, its radical features shake up the complacency that consigns so many young people who live in low-income communities of color to educational failure and destines them to lives of poverty. The transformative power of the Freirean spirit provides the energy and spark that pushes change forward.

In the end, Americans continue to invest their faith in public education as what Horace Mann termed the "great equalizer," that is, the means to provide opportunity and upward mobility to all children. In that sense, public education is perhaps our premier instrument for advancing social justice. Education promises individuals the means to participate fully in American society while it also provides the foundation for renewed efforts to strengthen and expand democratic life. In a country that remains deeply unequal, community organizing is committed to finding new ways to make the promise of American education a reality in our lives.

A Collaborative Research Process

In the introduction to this book, we provided a brief overview of our research design and methods. We also discussed the collaborative process we created within our project and reported on the criteria for the selection of our cases. In this appendix, we provide further details about our research design and methods. This discussion is meant to supplement the treatment presented in the introduction and will not repeat the points made there. We hope it will help researchers and other readers better understand and evaluate the findings and conclusions we present in the book.

Building Knowledge for a New Field

The study of community organizing for education reform is relatively new. We wanted to understand how strong forms of community organizing work to effect reform in public education. Consequently, we chose to conduct qualitative case studies because that is an appropriate strategy for building new knowledge and theory in a field that lacks a long tradition of research and testable hypotheses. Moreover, case studies allow researchers to develop contextually grounded and richly detailed analyses. It is a particularly good method for identifying processes—for examining the "how" of organizing—which was our goal. We chose a multiple case study design because this strategy allows us to compare across the groups to identify similarities and differences in the ways strong forms of organizing operate.[1]

We took a strongly inductive approach to our research. We wanted to build new knowledge for the field through close ethnographic methods. Moreover, we wanted the case studies to respond authentically to each particular organizing group and to its local context. Nevertheless, we believed it important to develop a conceptual framework to guide the field research. Previous research on community organizing identified several processes through which organizing was understood to work. We wanted to make sure to examine these processes even while we looked for new mechanisms and factors in our fieldwork. In the end, we believed that having a common framework for the investigation of the six cases would be important to our ability to compare across these cases.

In order to develop the conceptual framework, we reviewed the research on community organizing efforts at education reform as well as several other bodies of literature we thought relevant. From this literature, we identified five core processes we wanted to investigate across all our cases. First, previous research identifies relationship building, or the building of social capital, as a crucial process through which community organizing groups develop capacity.[2] Second, much research on community organizing stresses the importance of leadership development.[3] Third, a newer body of research examines how groups build alliances, and we also knew from the literature on social movements that alliances are particularly important to the ability of marginalized groups to assert power.[4] Fourth, the development and utilization of new forms of power appears central to organizing strategies, and we wanted to examine these processes.[5] Finally, newer research on the cultural aspects of community organizing and social movements directed our attention to how community organizing groups engage with a community's sense of identity and develop a public narrative of their efforts.[6] Moreover, some research suggests that context influences organizing and we decided to examine contextual factors closely across the six cases.[7] In the end, we designed a data-collection strategy that would investigate these processes as well as be open enough to identify new and unexpected processes and factors.[8]

Building a Team Research Process

We built a collaborative research project where teams of two or three students took responsibility for each case study. Each of these teams took four weeklong fieldwork trips to each site over the course of the 2007–2008 academic year. Some teams took additional trips to complete data collection or to attend special meetings. Most teams had three members, and they were engaged intensely with the research during full, long days. During these field research trips, we collected several kinds of data about each organizing group. We interviewed participants, observed meetings and activities, and reviewed relevant documents.[9]

We interviewed the executive director(s) and organizers from each group; local leaders (parents, young people, and others); educators with whom they work; allies and sometimes opponents; and independent observers or actors in the local area. These interviews were designed to understand organizing processes from multiple perspectives. We used our conceptual framework to design our interview questions in order to obtain a certain degree of consistency across the six groups. At the same time, we tailored individual interviews to the particulars of each team's research as well as the particular knowledge or role of the interviewee. On average, each team conducted about fifty formal, in-depth interviews of one-hour duration. Teams also spoke informally with a wide variety of participants, and these informal conversations also enriched our understanding of organizing processes. Many of the teams conducted a small number of focus groups to help gather a broader range of views and experiences than could be captured in individual interviews.

We observed a variety of organizational activities in community and school settings. We observed internal organizational meetings, training and political education sessions, house meetings, direct action events and public meetings; we also visited schools and other institutions where the groups worked. These observations were designed to see organizing in action, to better understand the role of various kinds of participants, and to detect dynamics in the relationships between various stakeholders (volunteer leaders, paid organizers, allies, and educators). Each team took detailed field notes on about twenty of these observational activities. However, we were making informal observations all the time that we were in the field. We spent many hours walking through neighborhoods and schools, eating lunch with participants in local restaurants, and watching people interact in a variety of settings. We summarized our impressions of these observations in notes. In the end, our analyses draw on our formal field notes and interviews, but also from all of the various gatherings, chance encounters, and side conversations that fill in the rich texture of ethnographic work.

Finally, each team collected and reviewed a variety of documents. These included organizational leaflets and annual reports. We also collected relevant data on the education systems and schools in which the organizing occurred. When available, we examined newspaper articles and other publications about organizational activities. These documents helped us understand the history of each group, its internal dynamics, and its public activities. In the chapters of the book, we have not cited the data sources (interviews, observations) for all of the specifics and details in our findings. These sources are available from the authors upon request.

At the end of each fieldwork trip, teams wrote a detailed report that was discussed in the project as a whole. These reports documented research activities and identified significant observations and emerging findings. Using these reports, teams updated and sometimes refocused their research plan as they prepared to return to the field. Meanwhile, we developed a rigorous method of dialogue across the teams. Teams questioned and critiqued each other's work, and drew upon emerging findings and analytical lines from one case to reflect on research on the others. We continually highlighted points of similarity and contrast across the cases. We also shared research experiences, helping teams with challenges and problems while learning from effective practices. With guidance from the project leaders, and with feedback from other members of the project, each team interrogated the data they were collecting, developed initial themes and refined datacollection strategies.

After the period of formal data collection ended, we proceeded to systematically analyze the data collected in each case. Each team examined the processes identified in our conceptual framework and identified themes that emerged from the case itself. We used MAXQDA, a qualitative data analysis software system, to help us in this effort. Teams systematically coded the interview transcripts, analyzed their observational field notes, and examined documents. In order to increase the accuracy of the analysis, data sources were triangulated by checking wherever possible what people said in interviews against what we observed and what was stated in published accounts. At various stages in this process, each team reported out to the entire project to encourage cross-fertilization of ideas and analysis. Teams continued to refine their analysis as they wrote up the cases as chapter drafts. We read each other's outlines and drafts multiple times and provided feedback and critique that pushed each team's thinking and deepened our analysis. In this way we identified themes that appeared across the cases as well as ones that were particular to each case. We believe that this repeated, iterative approach increased the rigor of our analysis.

Since we chose groups we thought were strong, and because we relied often on information provided by participants, we knew our bias would be toward seeing the positive side of the groups. Consequently, we intentionally looked for tensions, problems, and unmet challenges during data collection. We also sought to interview people who would be independent and sometimes critical of the groups. During data analysis, we searched for discrepant data and alternative interpretations of emerging patterns in the analysis. We weighed all these data and alternatives in an effort to produce balanced and nuanced accounts of our organizing groups.

In writing the case chapters of the book, we sought to produce a compelling narrative that would identify and analyze the key processes through which each organizing group did its work. We chose to focus each case around one campaign or one set of initiatives in order to present the narrative within the space limitations of a chapter. In our data collection and analysis, we made sure that these processes were typical of the group's work and not unusual to the campaign we chose to discuss. We also took care to reveal the historical origins of each group and to set the group's work in its local context. Although we do not present a causal model, we do make an effort to link organizing processes with outcomes in each case, explaining how organizing efforts produce results.[10]

After the case chapters were drafted, we proceeded to compare and contrast processes across the groups. We had originally expected to find important variation in how groups organize for education reform. We even thought we might see a typology of organizing emerge. Instead, however, our analysis revealed a set of common themes—ways of organizing—which were largely shared across the cases. That led us to take a more integrative approach in our analysis. Nevertheless, we systematically reviewed the data for each case to make sure these emerging themes were present. Through this approach we found important variation across the cases *within* these common processes. We tied this variation to differences in local contexts and the organizing traditions out of which groups emerged. We presented our synthetic analysis in chapter 8 as the transformational work of community organizing at three levels.[11]

Building Collaborative Research Relationships

We believed it was important to build a collaborative relationship with the organizing groups we studied. Just as organizing gives voice to the normally voiceless, we wanted to ensure that in some real way our groups spoke through our research. This is, of course, one of the strengths of ethnographic research. We visited each organizing group and discussed our project with its key leaders. We promised that we would first endeavor to understand their organizing work from their point of view, to reveal why they pursued education organizing, and what they were trying to accomplish as they understood it. We did not want to impose an outside framework on the groups, but rather to make sure the research produced an authentic account. We agreed that their voices would hold a prominent place in our case studies.

At the same time, we are independent researchers responsible to a larger research and policy community and to a broader public. We are not just telling their stories; we are crafting our own analysis that includes each case but goes beyond them as well. We promised to share our analysis and writing with each group, to respond to their concerns, and to endeavor to be fair and balanced. In the end, however, we would be responsible for the arguments and analysis presented in the book.[12]

Consequently, we shared drafts of each case chapter with the community organizing group concerned. To various extents across the cases, community organizers, parents, educators, and young people read the drafts carefully. This process allowed for the correction of errors and a discussion of our analysis. Groups often confirmed that our account appeared true to their self-understanding and sometimes disagreed with our interpretation of certain issues. We listened closely to this feedback and discussed the issues thoroughly. In some situations, we revised our drafts based upon the feedback. In places where we largely held to our interpretation, feedback from the groups often pushed us to deepen our analysis or make it more nuanced.

This approach required constant dialogue and discussion. Community organizers are nothing if not strong advocates for their point of view. In some cases, we had to work through disagreement and tension. We had lengthy face-to-face meetings and in some cases produced several revised sections of the drafts. We believe that our commitment to this process resulted in a deeper and more complex analysis. At the same time, it is not for the faint of heart.

A Diverse Research Team

We began the research process with an understanding of the importance of researchers interrogating their own experiences and personal standpoints for how these might affect the research process. This is important in any kind of research, but is particularly important in qualitative research where the researcher *is* the research instrument. We all wrote researcher identity memos where we examined our past experiences, our personal goals, and the standpoints we brought to the project because of our particular identities shaped by race and other relevant factors. We wanted to be prepared for how our experiences and viewpoints might help us understand certain issues more deeply while they might also limit our understanding of others. Our backgrounds and predispositions might also influence us to see things one way versus another. We were not interested in trying to eliminate these perspectives. Rather, we wanted to bring them to light so that we could be conscious about the strengths and weaknesses we brought to our research and, if necessary, make intentional efforts to see things from other points of view.[13]

We also believed this self-examination was particularly important for our project because we sought to create collaborative relationships with the organizing groups we studied. We had to learn how to build authentic relationships with organizers and leaders who came from different places than we did. We were Harvard-based researchers studying folks working in low-income communities of color. We found that the ability of each of us to tell our story, that is, to explain why we cared about educational and social justice in terms of the concrete experiences of our lives, provided an essential foundation for trust and relationship building.

We confronted new challenges as we entered the field. For example, in Mississippi, we found ourselves in communities deeply polarized by race. Our research team consisted of a white woman and a black (Jamaican) man, while the faculty supervisor was a white man. We had to consider how our own racial and gendered identities influenced how we were variously perceived by African American leaders. We also had to take into account how our experiences and viewpoints shaped our ability to comprehend the perspectives of the people we studied. Explicit discussion among the team members and reflection across the entire project proved important to building our capacity to comprehend local contexts and the experiences of organizing groups on the ground.

In Denver, we heard about deep divisions between high school teachers on the one hand and parent and youth leaders on the other. We had to address how our own experiences as former teachers and organizers or as current parents shaped our sympathies for each side. Our diversity helped us develop a complex and balanced analysis, but not without our share of tension. Early discussions were sometimes heated as many of us had to move beyond the narrowness of our personal perspective to grasp the wider whole.

An additional issue was language. Few of us spoke Spanish well, and in some localities that limited our ability to engage in a sophisticated way with monolingual Spanish leaders. We employed translators for interviews, but learned how difficult it was to build a relationship and create a rich and responsive interview through translation.

We tried to take the time to reflect on these issues as they arose. Many of the students were new to this kind of fieldwork. However, the more experienced project leaders also learned important lessons from new situations and challenges.[14]

We intentionally set out to create a diverse research team. Our overall project group was, in fact, quite diverse by race and gender and in other ways as well. Of the fifteen students who participated throughout the entire project, nine were students of color and six were white. We also included a mix of men and women from a variety of backgrounds and experiences. Several had been public school teachers. Some had been community organizers. A few were parents. The faculty leadership brought diverse experience as well. Karen Mapp, an African American woman, had been a deputy superintendent for family and community engagement for Boston Public Schools. Mark Warren, a white man, had studied community organizing for many years. Moreover, we were intentional about creating case teams to maximize diversity as well, particularly by race. Most of the teams were racially diverse, but one was comprised of students who were all Asian American and another was all white; we had no Latino researchers in the project.

We believe the diversity of the seventeen researchers in our project proved particularly important to achieving our goals. Indeed, when planning our research and when responding to issues as they arose, we tried to take advantage of the diversity of experiences and perspectives that we had. These discussions were not always easy, as we noted. But we sought to weigh the evidence carefully as we considered all points of view. In the end, we feel the result was a much more rigorous and balanced account than could have been developed by any one person or by a homogeneous group.

We sought to build a research community as we studied how communities organize. We had different roles within this process. Mark Warren and Karen Mapp were faculty members who led the effort. They supervised the teams and helped provide apprenticeship training in research methods to doctoral students. Indeed, one of the purposes of this project was to help build a new generation of researchers interested in studying and working with community organizing groups.

We tried, as much as possible, to develop a collaborative process. We empowered graduate students to take responsibility and ownership for their case studies. Project-wide, we sought to make decisions by consensus, to address power dynamics within the group, to fully value all voices and perspectives, and to engage in constant learning and reflection on our research process. Overall, we worked hard to implement our shared vision for research that aims for high academic rigor while respecting our participants and their efforts. This approach made our research project a unique and powerful experience for all of us. We hope that our research will encourage more efforts to study community organizing and school reform in a variety of ways. We also hope that it will inspire others to experiment with new and rewarding kinds of relationships with community-based organizations and to pursue new models of collaborative research among faculty and students.

Notes

Introduction

1. Although we recognize that the practice varies, we have decided to use lowercase for racial identifications like black, white and brown, and reserve capitalization for ethnicity and nationality groups like African American and Latino.

2. Charles Payne (2008) identifies the complex reasons that school reform has largely failed in the aptly titled book, *So Much Reform, So Little Change*. Daniel Koretz (2008) examines whether increases in test scores on standardized tests reflect real increases in learning. On high school drop-out rates, see Orfield et al. (2004). For a recent study of the negative consequences of dropping out, see Sum, Khatiwada, and McLaughlin (2009).

3. For a discussion of inequality in education and its consequences, see Kozol (1991) and Darling-Hammond (2010). On the lack of political power by low-income parents, see Henig, Hula, Orr, and Pedelescleaux (1999). For a more detailed examination of school funding inequality, see Biddle and Berliner (2003).

4. See Noguera (2001, 298); for a further discussion of the need for a political constituency for school reform, see Warren (2011). For treatments of the superficial nature of school reform processes in urban districts, see Payne (2008) and Elmore (2004).

5. See Kozol (1991). For a sample of the extensive research and writing that ties school failure to social and political inequality, see Anyon (1997; 2005), Rothstein (2004), Neckerman (2007), Lipman (2004), and Oakes and Rogers (2005).

6. The link between educational improvement and efforts to change broader social structures can be made at the local or national level. For a discussion of the ways to connect schools to community revitalization at the local level, which is the focus of most community organizing, see Warren (2005); for a discussion of the need for political mobilization that links school reform to government policy at the federal level, see Anyon (2005).

7. A team at New York University (Mediratta and Fruchter, 2001) and at Research for Action (Gold, Simon, and Brown, 2002b) combined the results of their independent efforts to identify education organizing groups and estimated that there were somewhat more than two hundred community organizing groups actively working on public education in 1999. Of the sixty-six organizing groups surveyed by the NYU team, only six had been doing education work prior to 1990. Mark Warren (2010a) made the recent estimate. For a more thorough discussion of the turn of community organizing groups to education work in the nineties, see Warren (2005).

8. For an introduction to community organizing and its history, see Warren (2001), Fisher (1994) and Orr (2007).

9. For a further discussion of the differences between community organizing groups and other types of community organizations, see Warren (2005). For a broader discussion of the decline of civic organizations that claimed active membership and the rise of advocacy politics, see Skocpol (2003).

10. See Shirley (1997, 73); for other discussions of parent engagement, see Barton et al. (2004) and Warren et al. (2009); see also Olivos (2006). For a comprehensive discussion of the value of family involvement in education, see Henderson et al. (2007).

11. The findings from the Annenberg Institute study can be found in Mediratta, Shah, and McAlister (2009). For examples of new research on community organizing efforts at school reform, see Shirley (1997; 2002), Gold et al. (2002b), Beam and Irani (2003), Warren (2005), Oakes and Rogers (2005), Su (2009), McLaughlin et al. (2009), and Fabricant (2010).

12. On the Alliance Schools, see, for example, Shirley (1997; 2002); on the PICO-affiliated efforts, see Gold, Simon and Brown (2002a) and McLaughlin et al. (2009). Some research has identified the influence of the civil rights tradition in contemporary organizing (e.g. Oakes and Rogers, 2005) but it has not been systematically studied.

13. We use the term strong rather than successful or effective because, as we will explain later, we see organizing more as an ongoing process rather than a program that has a discrete effect. In that sense, our assessment of whether groups meet these criteria is qualitative. We consulted with knowledgeable experts in order to help us identify these groups. The groups we selected are strong, then, both by our qualitative assessment and by reputation.

14. There are some important limitations to our selection of cases. The majority of the work of the groups we studied focuses on Latinos, although one group works exclusively with African Americans. We were not able to identify a group that works primarily with Asian Americans or Native Americans that met our criteria. Also, we do not include any organizing group from the ACORN network, which collapsed in 2010 after a concerted attack by conservatives. For a discussion of ACORN organizing, see Fisher (2009) and Atlas (2010); for a discussion of ACORN's education work, see Beam and Irani (2003).

15. In general, we tried to use a similar style in writing the case chapters. However, we did allow for some variation to better capture the particularities of different group's style of operating. As a result, for example, most teams use first names when referring to participants while one team uses last names.

16. For a discussion of neoliberal reform in education, see Ross and Gibson (2007), see also Ravitch (2010).

Chapter 1

1. On nineteenth-century America as a nation of organizers, see Skocpol, Ganz, and Munson (2000). On African American fraternal associations, see Skocpol, Liazos, and Ganz (2006). On women's organizing, see Skocpol (1992). On the influences of settlement houses and the labor movement on organizing, as well as the influence of the Communist Party, see Fisher (1994).

2. Alinsky explained his organizing philosophy in two widely read books, *Rules for Radicals* (1971) and *Reveille for Radicals* (1969 [1946]). For a treatment of Alinsky's organizing practice, see Horwitt (1989).

3. Warren (2001) discusses the developments in Alinsky's organizing approach in the IAF after his death, concentrating on the role of faith institutions and values; see also Wood (2002). For further discussion of the Alinsky tradition and its influence, see Reitzes and Reitzes (1987), and Fisher (1994). On mediating institutions, see Berger and Neuhaus (1977).

4. On the local organizing tradition and the role of women in the Civil Rights movement, see Payne (1995) and Robnett (1997), see also Moses and Cobb (2001). On the relationship between Highlander and Freire, see Horton and Freire (1990). For a further discussion of

these issues, and of the role of critical social inquiry in organizing, see Oakes and Rogers (2005).

5. For a discussion of the link between education and liberation, see Perry (2003) and Payne and Strickland (2008). On the role of black churches, see Morris (1984). On the Chicano movement, see Munoz (2007).

6. For a discussion of feminist organizing, see Morgen and Bookman (1988), Naples (1998a; 1998b), Stall and Stoecker (1998) and McCourt (1977); on black feminism, see Collins (2000) and also Pardo (1998) and Thompson (2001).

7. For a discussion of immigrant and union organizing, see Milkman (2000), Fine (2006), Jayaraman and Ness (2005), and Brodkin (2007). On farm worker organizing in the sixties and beyond, see Ganz (2009).

8. For one discussion that stresses differences, see Smock (2004).

9. George Hillery (1955) found ninety-four definitions. For a discussion of definitions of and theories of community, see Keller (2003) and Day (2006).

10. See Putnam (2000), see also the work of Robert Sampson and his collaborators (Sampson et al.2005; Sampson, Morenoff, and Earls, 1999) on collective efficacy and the structure of neighborhood life as it pertains to collective civic action.

11. Fowler (1991) offers an extensive examination of different approaches to community in American political thought. See Anthony Cohen (1985) for a close examination of cultural processes in communities. Charles Taylor (1989) treats issues of meaning and identity extensively in *Sources of the Self*. Taylor has shown how community becomes the place where people come to some shared sense of how to live the moral life. Morris and Braine (2001) discuss social justice orientations in terms of oppositional consciousness. On the importance of tradition, see Wolin (1989).

12. Scholars of institutional organizing of the type pursued by the IAF and PICO have been somewhat more attuned to issues of shared religious culture, see, for example, Wood (2002). Robert Fisher (1994) is one of the few scholars to be explicit in his use of the term neighborhood organizing. For a critique of place-based approaches to organizing, see Delgado (1997). DeFilippis, Fisher, and Shragge (2010) offer a more recent assessment of local organizing.

13. For a discussion of the decline of local place as determining community and the increasing ability of people to be members of multiple communities, see Delanty (2010).

14. See Flaherty and Wood (2004). Warren (2001) calls the active interplay between organizing philosophy and faith beliefs in the IAF "a theology of organizing." For a broader discussion of the fractured state of American community, see Putnam (2000).

15. For an insightful treatment of how the HIV/AIDS epidemic challenged the boundaries of inclusion in the African American community, see Cathy Cohen (1999).

16. The inattention to context may come partly because most research has featured single case studies. With that methodology, researchers can describe the context but have less ability to analyze its impact. In one important exception, Warren (2009) analyzed the attempt to apply the American-based IAF organizing strategy in Britain, showing the effects created by the differing context of British social and political institutions. John Gaventa (1980) has also stressed the importance of local context for understanding the processes of building power in communities.

17. On white flight in Mississippi, see Munford (1973); on violence and repression in response to African American organizing, see Payne (1995).

18. On organizing in Oakland, see Mediratta, Shah and McAlister (2009).

19. For a useful overview of alliance work in social movements, see Rucht (2004). On the coalitional work of community organizing groups, including the Grow Your Own campaign in Illinois, see Mediratta, Shah and McAlister (2009), and McAlister, Mediratta, and Shah (2010). On education organizing coalitions in New York, see Fabricant (2010).

20. See Mediratta, Shah, and McAlister (2009) on Oakland small schools and McAlister, Mediratta, and Shah (2010) on the Illinois GYO program.

21. For discussions of ways organizing groups interacted with No Child Left Behind, for example, see Rogers (2006), and Shirley and Evans (2007). For an overview of organizational theory on open systems, see Scott and Davis (2007).

22. We follow Robert Putnam's (1993; 2000) general approach to social capital but are more attuned to issues of inequality and power as treated in Saegert, Thompson, and Warren (2001). Social capital can also serve as a resource for individuals, including children in schools. Since we are concerned with collective action in this study, we treat social capital as a collective asset and a public good. In one of the earliest studies to use the concept of social capital, Coleman and Hoffer (1987) argued that Catholic schools do a better job than public schools in educating inner-city children because of the tight connections and shared norms that exist among and between parents, teachers, and students in the Catholic school community. Any child in such a school-community benefits from the collective's social capital, even if his or her own parent is not particularly involved; see also Coleman (1988).

23. For treatments of the work of community organizing groups in building social capital, see Warren (2001) and Shirley (1997). For a discussion of the one-on-one relational meeting by the executive director of the IAF network, see Chambers (2003). For a discussion of the social connections among working-class parents compared to those among middle-class parents, see Horvat, Weininger, and Lareau (2003).

24. On bonding and bridging forms of social capital, see Putnam (2000), Briggs (1998) and Warren, Thompson, and Saegert (2001). Although she does not use the term bonding social capital, Delgado-Gaitan (2001) offers an extensive discussion of the processes of mutual support and coming together that occurs within a Latino community as it organizes to influence public schools. At a more general level, Warren, Thompson, and Saegert (2001) treat the importance of and limitations to bonding social capital in collective action in anti-poverty strategies.

25. Wood and Warren (2002) provide details on cross-racial participation in the field of faith-based community organizing. Wilson (1999) highlights the work of the IAF as a model for "bridging the racial divide"; for a critique of Alinsky's work in this area, and place-based strategies more generally, see Santow (2007). Warren (2001) presents a detailed examination of the Texas IAF efforts to cross racial lines; for another treatment of bridging in community organizing, see Rusch (2009). For a discussion of building cross-racial alliances outside of the faith-based context, see Guinier and Torres (2002).

26. For a review of community development efforts, see Briggs, Mueller and Sullivan (1997). On the weaknesses in the internal capacities of school systems, see Bryk and Schneider (2002), Kozol (1991), and Payne (2008). On the importance of creating social trust and collaboration in the school community as a foundation for school-improvement efforts, see Bryk and Schneider (2002), Bryk, Sebring, Allensworth, Luppescu, and Easton (2010), and Designs for Change (2005). On trust and parent participation, see Mapp (2003).

27. See Oakes and Rogers (2005); on culture, see Moll et al. (1992), and Valenzuela (1999). For a discussion of the transformation of teacher attitudes through new relationships, see Warren et al. (2009).

28. This understanding of power reflects Max Weber's (1946) classic treatment which defined power as the ability of an actor to realize his or her will in a social action, even against the will of other actors. There has been a long debate in political science and sociology about the nature of community power (e.g., Dahl, 1961; Gaventa, 1980; Polsby, 1963), but none of these scholars have considered the relational approach discussed here. However, Clarence Stone and his associates (Stone et al., 1999) do develop a similar concept. They call this kind of collaborative approach to power a social reproduction model and argue that it is critical to establishing the civic capacity necessary to effect district-level education reform. For a recent review of theories of power related to urban development, see Gendron (2006).

29. Seth Kreisberg (1992) provides an extended discussion of the relational form of power, which he calls "power with," tracing its multiple roots in feminism (e.g., Miller, 1982) and

other sources. According to Kreisberg, Mary Parker Follett (1924; 1942) offered the earliest treatment of this kind of power. Theologians have also developed the concept of relational power; for a seminal treatment, see Loomer (1976).

30. On the absence of talk about power in schools, see Nyberg (1981).
31. For an organizer's perspective on the positive nature of power, see Cortes (1993); see also Nyberg (1981).
32. On the power of educators vis a vis parents, see Fine (1993).
33. See Horvat, Weininger, and Lareau (2003). For a discussion of the historical struggle between parents and educators, see Cutler (2000). For a discussion of deficit views, see Valenzuela and Black (2002).
34. For a further treatment of knowledge building in organizing, see Oakes and Rogers (2005); on popular education, see Freire (2000 [1970]).
35. On community organizing groups as intermediaries, see Warren et al. (2009) and Lopez, Kreider, and Coffman (2005). For a broader discussion of African American parents' perceptions of their children's schools, see Diamond and Gomez (2004). On the relationship of Latino parents and schools, see Olivos (2006).
36. There are some groups that have abandoned confrontation entirely, calling their work "consensus organizing;" but these are a small minority. For a discussion, see Gittell and Vidal (1998).
37. For a further discussion of how new relationships created by community organizing affect accountability in public education, see Mediratta and Fruchter (2003).
38. Paul Speer and Joseph Hughey (1995) offer a related discussion of the empowerment work of community organizing at three levels: individual, community and organizational. By organizational, however, they refer to community-based organizations. They do not focus as we do on transformation at the level of public institutions.
39. For Alinsky's views on organizers and leaders, see *Rules for Radicals* (1971). Charles Payne (1995) and Belinda Robnett (1997) stress the contrast between Baker and King.
40. Our discussion of individual transformation is related to psychological approaches to individual empowerment (Zimmerman, 2000). We avoid the term empowerment because organizing emphasizes the building of power as a social process. On reflection and empowerment in organizing, see Speer and Hughey (1995).
41. On latent versus active social capital, see Krishna (2002). For a related discussion of social capital that helps people "to get by" versus the kind that helps people "to get ahead," see Briggs (1998).
42. For the classic work on framing, see Snow, Rochford, Worden, and Benford (1986). For a related discussion of story and strategic choice in social movements, see Polletta (2006). For a discussion of public narrative in social change, see Ganz (2010).
43. As noted in the introduction chapter, we are not primarily concerned with evaluating these initiatives or assessing them in relationship to larger education policy agendas. Rather, we focus on how organizing works and develops school reform agendas at the local level.

Chapter 2

1. Unless otherwise noted, data from this chapter come from the primary authors' original fieldwork; specific citations for interview and observational material are available upon request.
2. For further information on PACT, see Swarts (2008, chapter 7) and the organization's Web site at www.pactsj.org. PICO stands for People Improving Communities through Organizing. For more information on PICO, see Wood (2002) and the network's Web site at www.piconetwork.org.
3. On OCO's small schools campaign, see Mediratta, Shah, and McAlister (2009) and Gold, Simon, and Brown (2002a).

4. Student information is from an October 2007 presentation published on the district's Web site at www.arusd.org.
5. Test results are reported on the California Department of Education Web site at www.cde. ca.gov.
6. See Meier (1995).
7. See Shear et al. (2008).
8. ACE was originally called the New Schools Center of Silicon Valley.

Chapter 3

1. Unless otherwise noted, data from this chapter come from the primary authors' original fieldwork; specific citations for interview and observational material are available upon request. Further information on One LA can be found on the organization's Web site at www. onela-iaf.org.
2. In IAF terms, a leader is anyone who participates as a volunteer in organizing efforts, whether they hold a formal position in the group or not. Organizers are paid staff whose job is to recruit and train leaders.
3. Demographic information on Los Angeles drawn from the 2000 U.S. Census, available at www.census.gov.
4. See Shirley (1997, 220). Kavitha Mediratta and her colleagues (Mediratta, Shah, and McAlister, 2009) also found that teachers in these schools reported that organizing efforts had a high degree of influence on generating school climate and culture improvements. For further information on the Texas IAF, see Warren (2001), and Osterman (2002); and on the Alliance Schools in Texas, see also Shirley (2002) and Simon and Gold (2002).
5. Quoted from "One LA Education Plank," an unpublished 2008 document.
6. For demographic information on Sun Valley residents, see "City asked to order EIR in Spanish," Kerry Cavanaugh, *Daily News*, February 12, 2005, 3.
7. For newspaper coverage of the event, see "Bradley landfill provides opportunity for mayoral candidates Alarcon and Villaraigosa," Silvio J. Panta, *Weekly San Fernando Valley Sun*, February 17, 2005, 3, 7.
8. See Loomer (1976).

Chapter 4

1. Unless otherwise noted, all data from this chapter come from the primary authors' original fieldwork; specific citations for interview and observational material are available upon request.
2. "Padres y Jóvenes Unidos" is Spanish for Parents and Youth United. For more on the events at Valverde, see "Storming Denver: Padres Unidos Battles for Better Education," Patrisia Macias Rojas, *Color Lines* 2000 (summer), available at http://www.onenation.org/0006/summer2000.html. More information on Padres y Jóvenes Unidos can also be found on the organization's Web site at www.padresunidos.org.
3. Then known as San Diego State College.
4. For more information about North High School, see its Web site at http://www.denver-north.org/about/history.
5. Figure taken from the Colorado Department of Education Web site, available at http://www.cde.state.co.us/cdereval/2002GradsbySchoolLink.htm.
6. Quoted from the "North High School Report: The Voices of over 700 Students," available at www.padresunidos.org.
7. Ibid.
8. Figures taken from the district's Web site, available at http://communications.dpsk12.org/newsroom/73/55/.

9. In PJU, a "youth organizer" is a paid staff member, not a youth member of the group. The youth organizers in PJU are typically young adults, often in their early 20s, with experience in organizing, and include former youth members of PJU who are then hired as staff.

10. Monica is referring to proposed federal legislation, which in 2003 was officially called the Development, Relief and Education for Alien Minors Act. This legislation would provide undocumented students who attend college a path to residency; for more information see http://dreamact.info/.

11. Corky Gonzales is considered one of the founders of the Chicano movement. Among his many achievements, he organized the first youth Chicano conference in the country and authored the poem *Yo Soy Joaquin* (I am Joaquin), which offered a new vision of Chicanos. For more information, see the school's Web site at http://www.escuelatlatelolco.org/website/corky_bio.html.

12. The Northwest Mommies was a group of mostly white, middle-class mothers who also supported the redesign.

13. This is an excerpt from the 1967 poem "I am Joaquin" by Corky Gonzales.

Chapter 5

1. Unless otherwise noted, data from this chapter come from the primary authors' original fieldwork; specific citations for interview and observational material are available upon request.

2. Data on the demographic composition of Mississippi is taken from the U.S. Census, available at http://quickfacts.census.gov/qfd/states/28000.html.

3. Data on Mississippi's teaching force come from http://www.monarchcenter.org/pdfs/teacher_recruitment.pdf.

4. For a further discussion of the educational experience of African Americans in Mississippi, see Anderson (1988). On the establishment of a dual school system after 1970, see Bolton (2009).

5. For data on educational attainment in Mississippi, see Laird, DeBell, and Chapman (2006), and National Center for Education Statistics (2005).

6. For a detailed discussion of the Civil Rights movement and the history of community organizing in Mississippi, see Payne (1995).

7. For Echo's own account of this campaign, see Southern Echo (2004).

8. There were a number of other partners in this action, including the Advancement Project; the law firms of Skadden Arps and Rob McDuff provided legal services.

9. An existing court order on school desegregation that followed the original litigation of the 1960s to desegregate the schools gave the federal court continuing jurisdiction over the school district as long as the federal court desegregation order was in existence.

10. The Mississippi Adequate Education Program establishes a formula for the provision of an adequate education (Level 3 accreditation standard). The program was first passed by the legislature in 1994 and the formula adopted in 1997; the formula to determine funding was first used in 2003. For further information, see the report of the Joint Legislative Committee on Performance Evaluation and Expenditure Review (2002).

11. Data on county funding comes from the National Center for Educational Statistics, available at http://www.nces.ed.gov/ccd.

12. The Mississippi Department of Education defines a child at risk as any child enrolled in school who is eligible for free lunch under US Department of Agriculture regulations. Echo considers this a narrow definition and argues for other contextual factors to be considered; see its discussion of children at risk on the network's Web site at http://southernecho.org/s/?page_id=248.

13. According to Echo, even before meeting, the Legislative Budget Committee agreed there would be full funding for MAEP—the only issue on which they had such an agreement.

Chapter 6

1. Unless otherwise noted, data from this chapter come from the primary author's original fieldwork; specific citations for interview and observational material are available upon request. A fuller treatment of the Logan Square Neighborhood Association can be found in the author's book-length discussion of the group's work, entitled *A Cord of Three Strands: A New Approach to Parent Engagement in Schools* (Hong, 2011).
2. As quoted in "Bilingual Students Forced to Take ISAT Test," from the March 2008 LSNA newsletter, available at http://www.lsna.net/news/13.
3. Ibid.
4. For a further discussion of the migration of Latinos to Chicago, see Padilla (1993).
5. For a further discussion of the origins and development of LSNA's education organizing, see Blanc et al. (2002), Warren (2005), and Warren et al. (2009).
6. Secretary Bennett's comments were made in reference to the release of high school students' scores on the American College Test. Half of Chicago's sixty-four high schools were ranked in the bottom 1 percent of schools that gave the test. See "Schools in Chicago are called the worst by Education Chief," New York *Times*, November 8, 1987.
7. The momentum for this policy change is disputed among those who have studied Chicago school reform—between those who credit business and civic leaders for the policy change and those who credit a grassroots movement of parent and community activists; see Katz, Fine, and Simon (1997), Shipps (1997), Wrigley (1997), and Moore (2001).
8. Details of the 1995 Holistic Plan are based on a press release for LSNA's 32nd Annual Congress, May 1994 and as reported in Blanc, Goldwasser, and Brown (2003).
9. For a discussion of the statewide GYO campaign, see McAlister, Mediratta, and Shah (2010).

Chapter 7

1. Unless otherwise noted, data from this chapter come from the primary authors' original fieldwork; specific citations for interview and observational material are available upon request.
2. Information on the Grier projections and DoE enrollment plans comes from an analysis conducted in 2006 by the Community Involvement Program of the Annenberg Institute for School Reform at Brown University, in partnership with the Coalition, and is available from the Institute's Web site as a PowerPoint presentation entitled "Planning for Failure." Retrieved April 1, 2010 from www.annenberginstitute.org/cip/presentations/planning-for-failure.pdf.
3. These processes can also be understood as *principles* through which the Coalition's decisions are made, as well as *overarching goals* threaded throughout the Coalition's diverse campaigns.
4. See the 2009 report of the NYC Department of Education, *Enrollment—Capacity—Utilization Organizational Report: Bronx.* Retrieved December 3, 2009, from http://schools.nyc.gov/Offices/SCA/Reports/CapPlan/ECURpt08-09OrgEdSchoolDistrict.htm. Note that, in these calculations, a school with more than one building is considered over 100 percent capacity if any one of its buildings is marked as such.
5. See Su (2009, 38).
6. As quoted in *Campaigns and Programs: Improving Public Education,* Northwest Bronx Community and Clergy Coalition (n.d.). Retrieved December 19, 2009 from www.northwestbronx.org/improveedu.html.
7. *John F. Kennedy High School: Accountability and Overview Report 2008.* Retrieved December 19, 2009 from New York State Testing and Accountability Tool Web site at https://www.nystart.gov/publicweb/School.do?county=BRONX&;district=321000010000&school=321000011475&year=2008.

8. Poverty rate estimated by the U.S. Census Bureau; see *Estimate for New York Counties, 2008.* Retrieved December 1, 2009, from http://www.census.gov/cgi-bin/saipe/saipe.cgi.

9. Statistics as reported by the Northwest Bronx Community and Clergy Coalition. (n.d.) *Our Organization: The Northwest Bronx Community.* Retrieved December 3, 2009, from http://www.northwestbronx.org/northwestbronx.html.

10. Ibid.

11. Although the Coalition originally emerged from an Alinsky tradition of organizing, it has evolved over time. At the time of this study, few staff or leaders used this label to describe their present-day work. On the early history of the Coalition, see Ibid. Discussions of the work of the Coalition can also be found in Su (2009), Mediratta, McAlister, and Shah (2009), and Fabricant (2010).

12. Similar to many Alinsky-inspired organizations, the Coalition uses the term "leader" to refer to a community member who volunteers time to organize the community, and "organizer" for paid staff members. We will use these terms in the same way.

13. See Mediratta, McAlister, and Shah (2009) from which this account draws.

14. See the Web site of the Kingsbridge Armory Redevelopment Alliance at http://www.ourarmory.com for more information on this campaign.

15. For further information, see the Coalition's description of the campaign, *NY Seats (Schools Exploding At The Seams),* available on its Web site at http://www.northwestbronx.org/ny-seats.html.

16. See "Group Enlists Council in Battle to Add School Seats," A. Kratz, *Norwood News* August 23–September 5, 2007. Retrieved December 9, 2009 from http://www.bronxmall.com/norwoodnews/news/N70823page3.html.

17. The focus of this chapter is on the Coalition, with SBU analyzed as a part of the Coalition. This aligns with the intergenerational and collaborative nature of the current education campaigns. For a study that looks at the two organizations separately, noting some of the cultural differences and past tensions between SBU and the Coalition, see Su (2009).

18. Quoted from "The Campaign for Community Values." Center for Community Change. Retrieved December 3, 2009, from http://www.communitychange.org/our-projects/communityvalues.

Chapter 8

1. The following project members worked on the analysis presented in chapter 8 (although all project members contributed): Connie K. Chung, Cynthia Gordon, Soo Hong, Ann Ishimaru, Paul Kuttner, Karen Mapp, Meredith Mira, Thomas Nikundiwe, Mara Tieken, and Mark Warren. Mark Warren is the primary author of the chapter.

2. We, of course, have not conducted a comparative study so we cannot say whether less strong or less significant groups also share these features. Nor have we examined a large number of other strong groups to see if other processes are present. In that sense, our work is exploratory and our findings will need to be examined through further research on education organizing. At the same time, we believe we make a compelling case for the importance of these processes by carefully tracing how they work to build capacity for education reform. In addition, the fact that we find these processes shared across a widely diverse set of organizing groups also increases our confidence that we have identified key elements that help explain how strong organizing groups work to improve quality and equity in public education.

3. Celina Su (2009), for example, compares education organizing groups in New York and contrasts what she calls Freirean and Alinskyite approaches. Kristina Smock (2004) presents a typology of community organizing groups.

4. Our discussion of transactional and transformational change draws from James MacGregor Burns's (1978) original contrast between transactional and transformational leadership. Our use is not exactly the same, however, because in transactional leadership, there is a

functional exchange of compliance (from a follower) for lack of sanction (from a leader); for a more recent treatment, see Bass and Riggio (2006). Our discussion also has parallels to Ronald Heifitz's distinction between technical and adaptive leadership (Heifetz, Grashow, and Linsky, 2009).

5. For other treatments of relationship building in organizing, see Shirley (1997, 2002), Warren (2001, 2005), Gold, Simon, and Brown (2002b), Mediratta and Fruchter (2003), and Delgado-Gaitan (2001). For a classic discussion of the relationship between mobilization and formal organization of the poor, see Piven and Cloward (1977).

6. For a further discussion of the development of collective stories as public narrative, see Ganz (2010).

7. For other treatments of leadership development in organizing, see Shirley (1997; 2002), Warren (2001; 2005), Gold, Simon, and Brown (2002b), and Oakes and Rogers (2005).

8. For a classic discussion of the importance of skills and knowledge to civic engagement, see Verba, Schlozman, and Brady (1995). For a further treatment of the importance of knowledge in education organizing, see Mediratta, Shah, and McAlister (2009).

9. For a related discussion of the collaborative nature of relationships between organizers and leaders, see Warren (2001, chapter 8).

10. For a related discussion of authority and participation in community organizing, see Warren (2001).

11. Moreover, many of the groups in our study have undertaken other reform initiatives that we did not have room to include.

12. We have not tried to examine all of the factors that might explain the success or failure of any particular organizing effort. That is not our purpose in this research. Consequently, we do not address important issues such as how groups raise funds or marshal other financial resources. We also do not focus on internal organization structure, decision making, and staffing. We wanted instead to focus on identifying and analyzing what we see as the core processes through which organizing works.

Conclusion

1. By one estimate, low-income students make up 45 percent of public school students in the United States. For further information on socio-economic and racial trends in the student population across the country, see Suitts (2007; 2010).

2. Although schools do not produce inequality on their own, they contribute to this result in a number of ways. A long body of research has shown that, by offering highly unequal opportunity to students, the American education system reproduces racial and class inequality; for a recent treatment, see Lipman (2004). A new body of research, meanwhile, shows how schools differentially prepare students for citizenship, leading to a "civic opportunity gap;" see, for example, Kahne and Middaugh (2008), and Levinson (2007). On American's beliefs in the democratic promise of public education, see Hochschild and Scovronick (2003).

3. For recent discussion of how racism and poverty impact children's development and their education, see Ginwright (2010); see also Duncan and Brooks-Gunn (1997).

4. When we started the research project on which this book is based, we hoped we would be able to articulate a single theory of change that would demonstrate how community organizing leads to improved education in low-income communities. We were unable to do so. Instead, we found a great diversity in the specific ends of education organizing. We concluded this was because organizing is really about process. We analyzed these processes in close detail in the previous chapter. Organizing results in diverse practices and its effects cannot be entirely predetermined. It simply does not fit a precise theory of change as it is normally understood.

5. For a discussion of federal policy on scientific research, see the report of the National Research Council (Shavelson and Towne, 2002). On scaling up in education, see Schneider and McDonald (2007).

6. For a further critique of "scaling up" in education policy, see Coburn (2003). For treatments of the weaknesses of school reform implementation, see Payne (2008), Elmore (2000), Hess 1999, and Farkas (1992). David Tyack and Larry Cuban (1995) characterize such traditional school reform efforts as "tinkering." For a broader discussion of the importance of local knowledge in relation to the universalistic claims of social reformers, see Scott (1998).
7. See Bryk and Schneider (2002).
8. See Bryk et al. (2010, 96).
9. See Designs for Change (2005). For further discussion on building trust in schools, see Tschannen-Moran (2004) and Kochanek (2005).
10. On distributed leadership, see Spillane (2006). On adaptive leadership, see Heifetz, Grashow, and Linsky (2009); for its application to school settings, see Wagner (2006). For a discussion of collaborative leadership, see Rubin (2002).
11. For foundational work on communities of practice, see Wenger, McDermott, and Snyder (2002). On instructional rounds, see City et al. (2009). For a discussion of communities of practice that incorporates issues of race and the community beyond the school, see Murrell (2001).
12. On the importance of instructional practice to school reform, see Elmore (2004); on teacher-student relationships more broadly, see Pianta (1999).
13. For a review of the evidence showing the effects of parent participation on children's learning as well as a discussion of approaches to family and community engagement that stress authentic partnerships, see Henderson et al. (2007). Rudy Crew (2007) articulated the concept of demand parents when he was superintendent of schools in Miami-Dade County, Florida.
14. For a critique of "deficit" views of families in low-income communities of color, see, for example, Olivos (2006).
15. For a further discussion of the importance of "bonding" ties among parents for the ability of parents to participate in powerful ways in schools, see Warren et al. (2009).
16. On the need to address power in building partnerships, see Henderson et al. (2007); see also Olivos (2006). The survey results are reported in Adams, Forsyth, and Mitchell (2009). For qualitative treatments of building trust between parents and teachers, see Warren et al. (2009) and Miretzky (2004).
17. Some groups in our study, like Southern Echo and Padres y Jóvenes Unidos, place issues of race squarely on the table; other groups are intentional about bringing differences out in the open but do not prioritize race in particular.
18. For a further discussion of the role of organizing groups as intermediaries and catalysts for change in school-family relationships, see Warren et al. (2009), and Lopez, Kreider, and Coffman (2005).
19. For an overview of the effects of poverty on children's development, see Duncan and Brooks-Gunn (1997), and also Rothstein (2004).
20. See Bryk et al. (2010, 196).
21. On the need for public schools to collaborate with community organizations to create integrated strategies, see Warren (2005). For a discussion of community schools, see Dryfoos and Quinn (2005). Paul Tough (2008) has written an extensive account of the Harlem Children's Zone. For an examination of effects of HCZ on educational outcomes, see Dobbie and Fryer (2009).
22. For a call for school leadership that incorporates political advocacy, see Anderson (2009). For a further discussion of the role of community organizing in building a political constituency, see Warren (2011).
23. For an assessment of the relationship between test scores and real improvement in student learning, see Koretz (2008); for a critique of standardized tests as the primary means of accountability for schools, see, for example, Ravitch (2010).
24. See Bryk et al. (2010) who identify family and community engagement as one of the five essential pillars of school improvement efforts; see Mediratta, Shah, and McAlister (2009)

for evidence that strong forms of community organizing are associated with increases in a variety of student educational outcomes including test scores.

25. For an assessment of the effectiveness of small schools, see Shear et al. (2008).

26. On the debate over charter schools, see Henig (2008). For a critique of neoliberal reform, see Ross and Gibson (2007); see also Ravitch (2010).

27. For a further discussion of face-to-face accountability through community organizing, see Mediratta and Fruchter (2003); for a broader discussion of collaboration, see Mediratta, Shah, and McAlister (2009).

28. The collaborations we advocate are more political in nature than the typical efforts of school systems to partner with community-based organizations; see, for example, Honig (2004). For a related discussion, see Xavier de Souza Briggs (2008) who has suggested "grasstops" leadership as a new way to understand how experts and policymakers can co-lead with local people at the ground level.

29. The lower budget figure is reported in Warren and Wood (2001) and the higher number in Mediratta and Fruchter (2001).

30. Mediratta and Fruchter (2001) report the 80 percent figure. For a broader examination of foundation giving to social justice, see the report by the Foundation Center (Lawrence, 2005), where the 11 percent figure is reported. The Applied Research Center (Pittz and Sen, 2006) reported the 7 percent figure on foundation giving to communities of color. The CUNY Graduate Center (Howard Samuels Center, 2006) published a study of the funding of community organizing by the Ford Foundation, one of the major sources of foundation funding for organizing.

31. For a discussion of the tensions between social justice organizations and private foundations, see Incite! Women of Color Against Violence (2007).

32. These collaboratives include Communities for Public Education Reform, Interfaith Funders, the Linchpin Campaign at the Center for Community Change, and the Funder's Collaborative for Youth Organizing, among others.

33. For a discussion of the motivations of organizers and other activists, see Warren (2010b).

34. The field has witnessed the growth of a number of intermediaries that support organizing in various ways. For example, the Jewish Fund for Justice offers a Community Organizing Residency program while the Center for Community Change has developed a range of activities designed to help build the field; see www.jewishjustice.org and www.communitychange.org.

35. Marshall Ganz offers an online, distance learning course called Leadership, Organizing and Action: Leading Change through Harvard University's Kennedy School of Government; see http://ksgexecprogram.harvard.edu/Programs/loa/overview.aspx.

36. For an extensive discussion of collaborations between organizing groups and educators, see Mediratta, Shah, and McAlister (2009). For the diverse responses of organizing groups to No Child Left Behind legislation and standardized testing, see Shirley and Evans (2007); see also Rogers (2006). For a discussion of the impact of mayoral control and other developments in the political context of public education on processes of public engagement, see Henig (2010). For a discussion of the impact of privatization, see Simon, Gold, and Cucchiara (2010).

37. See, for example, the report on a meeting of community organizing groups and teachers unions in 2003 (Center for Community Change, 2003).

38. We attribute the phrase "organizing into schools and schools out into organizing" to Ernesto Cortes Jr., the director of the Southwest Industrial Areas Foundation.

39. On Horace Mann and common schools, see Kaestle (1983). For references to the ideas discussed in this section on John Dewey, see *The School and Society* (Dewey, 1915) and *The Public and its Problems* (Dewey, 1991 [1927]); see also *Democracy and Education* (Dewey, 1938 [1916]). The scholarship and commentary on Dewey is voluminous. For one useful treatment, see Westbrook (1991). On the challenge to progressives to engage with social issues, see Counts (1978 [1932]).

40. Oakes and Rogers (2005) also discuss contemporary community organizing from the point of view of Dewey. See also Fung (2004).
41. On the history of African American education, see Williams (2005). While denied to some, public education has been forced on others in ways that have reinforced oppression. For example, boarding schools sponsored by the federal government were used to "Americanize" Native Americans by destroying their indigenous culture, see Hoxie (1984); and see Olsen (1997) on the Americanization experiences of immigrants. Working class children, meanwhile, received a "factory-style" education designed to prepare them for life as blue collar workers, see Bowles and Gintis (1976). On the inherently political nature of struggles surrounding American public education, see Ravitch (1988).
42. This brief account of Freire draws primarily from his *Pedagogy of the Oppressed* (Freire, 2000 [1970]); see also *Education for Critical Consciousness* (Freire, 1998 [1972]).
43. On Freire and critical pedagogy in the classroom, see Shor (1992), and also hooks (1994). On popular education with adults, and the work of the Highlander Center, see Horton and Jacobs (2003), and also Horton and Freire (1990).

Appendix

1. For a useful discussion of the kinds of studies for which qualitative research is appropriate, see Ragin, Nagel, and White (2004). We drew on a variety of texts to help design and conduct our research. In general, we follow the approach to qualitative research design elaborated by Joseph Maxwell (2005). On case study research, we found useful Yin (2003), Stake (1995), Merriam (1998), and George and Bennett (2005). On data collection and analysis, we also drew upon Lofland et al. (2006), Rubin and Rubin (2005), and Weiss (1994).
2. On the building of relationships, see Shirley (1997; 2002), Warren (2001; 2005), Gold, Simon, and Brown (2002), Mediratta and Fruchter (2003), and Delgado-Gaitan (2001), among others. We also drew upon a broader literature concerned with the importance of relationships and trust to parent participation (Mapp 2003; Warren et al. 2009) and to school improvement (Bryk and Schneider, 2002). Robert Putnam's (2000) work on social capital and its application to anti-poverty strategies by Saegert, Thompson, and Warren (2001) were also helpful.
3. On leadership development, see Shirley (1997; 2002), Warren (2001; 2005), Gold, Simon, and Brown (2002), and Oakes and Rogers (2005). We also examined a broader literature on leadership, including Heifetz, Grashow, and Linsky (2009).
4. On alliances in educational organizing, see in particular Mediratta, Shah, and McAlister (2009). For an overview of the research on alliances in social movements and social change, see Della Porta and Diani (2006), and Woolcock (1998).
5. On power in organizing, see Oakes and Rogers (2005), Warren (2005), and also Stone et al. (2001).
6. On culture and community organizing, see Hart (2001), and Wood (2002). On the broader research in social movements on framing and narratives, see Benford and Snow (2000); on stories and narrative, see Polletta (2006), and Ganz (2010).
7. On the influence of context on community organizing, see Warren (2009).
8. In addition to the studies listed above, we also reviewed a broader array of research on community organizing for education reform, including case studies of organizing efforts in New York City (Fabricant, 2010; Mediratta and Karp, 2003; Su, 2009; Zachary and olatoya, 2001), Philadelphia (Mediratta et al. 2001; Rhodes and Gold, 2002), Baltimore (Baum, 2003; Orr, 1999), and California (McLaughlin et al. 2009; Rogers, 2006); as well as a national study of ACORN (Beam and Irani, 2003) and several broader overviews of the field (Mediratta, 2004; Mediratta and Fruchter, 2001). We also examined the growing literature on youth organizing, including, for example, the collection in Ginwright,

Noguera, and Cammarota (2006), as well as Shah and Mediratta (2008), and Warren, Mira, and Nikundiwe (2008).

9. Data collection for the chapter on the Logan Square Neighborhood Association (LSNA) in Chicago was conducted somewhat differently than the rest. Soo Hong worked alone as she had already begun collecting data on LSNA for her dissertation. She took several additional data collection trips during 2007–2008, however, to make sure she collected comparable data with the rest of the project, based upon the project's conceptual framework. Otherwise, data analysis and write-up for the LSNA case proceeded in the same way as the rest of the cases.

10. See Maxwell (2004) for a discussion of causal explanation in qualitative research.

11. While cross-case analysis often stresses differences, multicase studies can also produce more synthetic accounts like ours; see, for example, Sara Lawrence-Lightfoot's (1983) treatment of the shared features of effective high schools.

12. There is a growing body of scholarship that explores the dynamics of collaborative relationships in community-based research; see, for example, Strand et al. (2003).

13. For a broader discussion of researcher positionality and reflexivity in education research, see the collection in Luttrell (2010).

14. We found H. Richard Milner's (2007) discussion of race and positionality particularly useful. We drew upon features of portraiture methodology (Lawrence-Lightfoot and Davis, 1997) to develop our approach to research relationships and to many other facets of our data collection and analysis and the writing of case studies.

References

Adams, Curt M., Forsyth, Patrick B., and Mitchell, Roxanne M. 2009. The formation of parent-school trust: A multilevel analysis. *Educational Administration Quarterly* 45: 4–33.

Alinsky, Saul D. 1969 [1946]. *Reveille for radicals*. New York: Vintage Books.

Alinsky, Saul D. 1971. *Rules for radicals: A practical primer for realistic radicals*. New York: Random House.

Anderson, Gary L. 2009. *Advocacy leadership: Toward a post-reform agenda in education*. New York: Routledge.

Anderson, James D. 1988. *The education of Blacks in the South, 1860–1935*. Chapel Hill: University of North Carolina Press.

Anyon, Jean. 1997. *Ghetto schooling: A political economy of urban educational reform*. New York: Teachers College Press.

Anyon, Jean. 2005. *Radical possibilities: Public policy, urban education, and a new social movement*. New York: Routledge.

Atlas, John. 2010. *Seeds of change: The story of ACORN, America's most controversial antipoverty community organizing group*. Nashville, TN: Vanderbilt University Press.

Barton, Angela Calabrese, Drake, Corey, Perez, Jose Gustavo, St. Louis, Kathleen, and George, Magnia. 2004. Ecologies of parental engagement in urban education. *Educational Researcher* 33(4): 3–12.

Bass, Bernard M., and Riggio, Ronald E. 2006. *Transformational leadership*. Mahwah: Lawrence Erlbaum Associates.

Baum, Howell S. 2003. *Community action for school reform*. Albany: State University of New York Press.

Beam, John M., and Irani, Sharmeen. 2003. *ACORN education reform organizing: Evolution of a model*. New York: National Center for Schools and Communities.

Benford, Robert D., and Snow, David A. 2000. Framing processes and social movements: An overview and assessment. *Annual Review of Sociology* 26: 611–639.

Berger, Peter L., and Neuhaus, Richard John. 1977. *To empower people: The role of mediating structures in public policy*. Washington, DC: American Enterprise Institute.

Biddle, Bruce J., and Berliner, David C. 2003. *What research says about unequal funding for schools in America*. San Francisco: WestEd.

Blanc, Suzanne, Brown, Joanna, Nevarez-La Torre, Aida, and Brown, Chris. 2002. *Case Study: Logan Square Neighborhood Association*. Chicago: Cross City Campaign for Urban School Reform.

Blanc, Suzanne, Goldwasser, Matthew, and Brown, Joanna. 2003. *From the ground up: The Logan Square Neighborhood Association's approach to building community capacity*. Philadelphia: Research for Action.

Bolton, Charles C. 2009. The last stand of massive resistance: Mississippi public school integration, 1970 [Electronic Version]. *Mississippi History Now.* Retrieved April 1, 2010 from http://mshistory.k12.ms.us/articles/305/the-last-stand-of-massive-resistance-1970.

Bowles, Samuel, and Gintis, Herbert. 1976. *Schooling in capitalist America: Educational reform and the contradictions of economic life.* New York: Basic Books.

Briggs, Xavier de Souza. 1998. Brown kids in white suburbs: Housing mobility and the many faces of social capital. *Housing Policy Debate* 9(1): 177–221.

Briggs, Xavier de Souza. 2008. *Democracy as problem solving: Civic capacity in communities across the globe.* Cambridge: MIT Press.

Briggs, Xavier de Souza, Mueller, Elizabeth J., and Sullivan, Mercer. 1997. *From neighborhood to community: Evidence on the social effects of community development.* New York: Community Development Research Center, New School for Social Research.

Brodkin, Karen. 2007. *Making democracy matter: Identity and activism in Los Angeles.* New Brunswick: Rutgers University Press.

Bryk, Anthony S., and Schneider, Barbara. 2002. *Trust in schools: A core resource for improvement.* New York: Russell Sage Foundation Press.

Bryk, Anthony S., Sebring, Penny Bender, Allensworth, Elaine, Luppescu, Stuart, and Easton, John Q. 2010. *Organizing schools for improvement: Lessons from Chicago.* Chicago: University of Chicago Press.

Burns, James MacGregor. 1978. *Leadership.* New York: Harper & Row.

Center for Community Change. 2003. Partnerships for change. *Education Organizing* 13 (Summer): 1–20.

Chambers, Edward T. 2003. *Roots for radicals: Organizing for power, action, and justice.* New York: Continuum.

City, Elizabeth A., Elmore, Richard F., Fiarman, Sarah, and Teitel, Lee. 2009. *Instructional rounds in education: A network approach to improving teaching and learning.* Cambridge: Harvard Education Press.

Coburn, Cynthia E. 2003. Rethinking scale: Moving beyond numbers to deep and lasting change. *Educational Researcher* 32 (6): 3–12.

Cohen, Anthony P. 1985. *The symbolic construction of community.* London: Tavistock Publications.

Cohen, Cathy J. 1999. *The boundaries of blackness: AIDS and the breakdown of Black politics.* Chicago: University of Chicago Press.

Coleman, James S. 1988. Social capital in the creation of human capital. *American Journal of Sociology* 94 (Supplement): S95–S120.

Coleman, James S., and Hoffer, Thomas. 1987. *Public and private high schools: The impact of communities.* New York: Basic Books.

Collins, Patricia Hill. 2000. *Black feminist thought: Knowledge, consciousness, and the politics of empowerment.* 2nd ed. New York: Routledge.

Cortes, Ernesto, Jr. 1993. Reweaving the fabric: The iron rule and the IAF strategy for power and politics. In *Interwoven destinies,* ed. Henry G. Cisneros, 294–319. New York: W. W. Norton.

Counts, George S. 1978 [1932]. *Dare the school build a new social order?* Carbondale: Southern Illinois University Press.

Crew, Rudy. 2007. *Only connect: The way to save our schools.* New York: Farrar, Straus and Giroux.

Cutler, William W., III. 2000. *Parents and schools: The 150-year struggle for control in American education.* Chicago: University of Chicago Press.

Dahl, Robert. 1961. *Who governs?: Democracy and power in an American city.* New Haven: Yale University Press.

Darling-Hammond, Linda. 2010. *The flat world and education: How America's commitment to equity will determine our future.* New York: Teachers College Press.

Day, Graham. 2006. *Community and everyday life.* London: Routledge.

DeFilippis, James, Fisher, Robert, and Shragge, Eric. 2010. *Contesting community: The limits and potential of local organizing.* New Brunswick: Rutgers University Press.

Delanty, Gerard. 2010. *Community.* 2nd ed. London: Routledge.

Delgado, Gary. 1997. *Beyond the politics of place: New directions in community organizing in the 1990s.* Oakland, CA: Applied Research Center.

Delgado-Gaitan, Concha. 2001. *The power of community: Mobilizing for family and schooling.* Lanham, MD: Rowman & Littlefield.

Della Porta, Donatella, and Diani, Mario. 2006. *Social movements: An introduction.* Oxford: Blackwell.

Designs for Change. 2005. *The big picture: School initiated reforms, centrally initiated reforms, and elementary school achievement in Chicago (1990–2005).* Chicago: Designs for Change.

Dewey, John. 1915. *The school and society.* Chicago: University of Chicago Press.

Dewey, John. 1938 [1916]. *Democracy and education: An introduction to the philosophy of education.* New York: MacMillan.

Dewey, John. 1991 [1927]. *The public and its problems.* Athens: Swallow Press, Ohio University Press.

Diamond, John, and Gomez, Kimberly. 2004. African American parents' educational orientations: The importance of social class and parents' perceptions of schools. *Education and Urban Society* 36 (4): 383–427.

Dobbie, Will, and Fryer, Roland. 2009. *Are high quality schools enough to close the achievement gap? Evidence from a social experiment in Harlem.* NBER Working Paper No. 15473. Cambridge: National Bureau of Economic Research.

Dryfoos, Joy G., and Quinn, Jane. 2005. *Community schools: A strategy for integrating youth development and school reform.* San Francisco: Jossey-Bass.

Duncan, Greg J., and Brooks-Gunn, Jeanne. 1997. *Consequences of growing up poor.* New York: Russell Sage Foundation Press.

Elmore, Richard F. 2000. *Building a new structure for school leadership.* Washington, DC: Albert Shanker Institute.

Elmore, Richard F. 2004. *School reform from the inside out: Policy, practice, and performance.* Cambridge: Harvard Education Press.

Fabricant, Michael. 2010. *Organizing for educational justice: The campaign for public school reform in the South Bronx.* Minneapolis: University of Minnesota Press.

Farkas, Steve. 1992. *Education reform: The players and the politics.* New York: The Public Agenda Foundation.

Fine, Janice. 2006. *Worker centers: Organizing communities at the edge of the dream.* Ithaca: ILR Press.

Fine, Michelle. 1993. [Ap]parent involvement: Reflections on parents, power and urban public schools. *Teachers College Record* 94 (4): 682–710.

Fisher, Robert. 1994. *Let the people decide: Neighborhood organizing in America.* Updated ed. New York: Twayne Publishers.

Fisher, Robert, ed. 2009. *The people shall rule: ACORN, community organizing, and the struggle for economic justice.* Nashville: Vanderbilt University Press.

Flaherty, Mary Ann, and Wood, Richard L. 2004. *Faith and public life: Faith-based community organizing and the development of congregations.* New York: Interfaith Funders.

Follett, Mary Parker. 1924. *Creative experience.* New York: Longmans, Green.

Follett, Mary Parker. 1942. *Dynamic administration.* New York: Harper and Brothers.

Fowler, Robert Booth. 1991. *The dance with community: The contemporary debate in American political thought.* Lawrence: University Press of Kansas.

Freire, Paulo. 1998 [1972]. *Education for critical consciousness.* New York: Continuum.

Freire, Paulo. 2000 [1970]. *Pedagogy of the oppressed.* Trans. Myra Bergman Ramos. New York: Continuum.

Fung, Archon. 2004. *Empowered participation: Reinventing urban democracy.* Princeton: Princeton University Press.

Ganz, Marshall. 2009. *Why David sometimes wins: Leadership, organization, and strategy in the California farm worker movement.* New York: Oxford University Press.

Ganz, Marshall. 2010. Leading change: Leadership, organizations and social movements. In *Handbook of leadership theory and practice,* ed. Nitin Nohria and Rakesh Khurana, 527–568. Boston: Harvard Business School Press.

Gaventa, John. 1980. *Power and powerlessness: Quiescence and rebellion in an Appalachian valley.* Urbana: University of Illinois Press.

Gendron, Richard. 2006. Forging collective capacity for urban redevelopment: "Power to," "power over," or both? *City and Community* 5 (1): 5–22.

George, Alexander L., and Bennett, Andrew. 2005. *Case studies and theory development in the social sciences.* Cambridge: MIT Press.

Ginwright, Shawn A. 2010. *Black youth rising: Activism and radical healing in urban America.* New York: Teachers College Press.

Ginwright, Shawn, Noguera, Pedro, and Cammarota, Julio. 2006. *Beyond resistance: Youth resistance and community change: New democratic possibilities for practice and policy for America's youth.* New York: Routledge.

Gittell, Ross, and Vidal, Avis. 1998. *Community organizing: Building social capital as a development strategy.* Thousand Oaks, CA: Sage.

Gold, Eva, Simon, Elaine, and Brown, Chris. 2002a. *Case study: Oakland Community Organizations.* Chicago: Cross City Campaign for Urban School Reform.

Gold, Eva, Simon, Elaine, and Brown, Chris. 2002b. *Successful community organizing for school reform.* Chicago: Cross City Campaign for Urban School Reform.

Guinier, Lani, and Torres, Gerald. 2002. *The miner's canary: Enlisting race, resisting power, transforming democracy.* Cambridge: Harvard University Press.

Hart, Stephen. 2001. *Cultural dilemmas of progressive politics: Styles of engagement among grassroots activists.* Chicago: University of Chicago Press.

Heifetz, Ronald A., Grashow, Alexander, and Linsky, Martin. 2009. *The practice of adaptive leadership: Tools and tactics for changing your organization and the world.* Boston: Harvard Business Press.

Henderson, Anne T., Mapp, Karen L., Johnson, Vivian R., and Davies, Don. 2007. *Beyond the bake sale: The essential guide to family-school partnerships.* New York: The New Press.

Henig, Jeffrey R. 2008. *Spin cycle: How research is used in policy debates: The case of charter schools.* New York: Russell Sage Foundation Press.

Henig, Jeffrey R. 2010. The contemporary context of public engagement: The new political grid. In *Public engagement for public education: Joining forces to revitalize democracy and equalize schools,* ed. Marion Orr and John Rogers, 52–85. Palo Alto: Stanford University Press.

Henig, Jeffrey R., Hula, Richard C., Orr, Marion, and Pedelescleaux, Desiree S. 1999. *The color of school reform: Race, politics and the challenge of urban education.* Princeton: Princeton University Press.

Hess, Frederick M. 1999. *Spinning wheels: The politics of urban school reform.* Washington, DC: Brookings Institution Press.

Hillery, George A., Jr. 1955. Definitions of community: Areas of agreement. *Rural Sociology* 20: 111–123.

Hochschild, Jennifer L., and Scovronick, Nathan. 2003. *The American dream and the public schools.* New York: Oxford University Press.

Hong, Soo. 2011. *A cord of three strands: A new approach to parent engagement in schools.* Cambridge: Harvard Education Press.

Honig, Meredith. 2004. The new middle management: Intermediary organizations in education policy implementation. *Educational Evaluation and Policy Analysis* 26 (1): 65–87.

hooks, bell. 1994. *Teaching to transgress: Education as the practice of freedom.* New York: Routledge.

Horton, Myles, and Freire, Paulo. 1990. *We make the road by walking: Conversations on education and social change.* Philadelphia: Temple University Press.

Horton, Myles, and Jacobs, Dale. 2003. *The Myles Horton reader: Education for social change.* Knoxville: University of Tennessee Press.

Horvat, Erin McNamara, Weininger, Elliot B., and Lareau, Annette. 2003. From social ties to social capital: Class differences in the relations between schools and parent networks. *American Educational Research Journal* 40 (2): 319–351.

Horwitt, Sanford D. 1989. *Let them call me rebel: Saul Alinsky, his life and legacy.* New York: Knopf.

Howard Samuels Center. 2006. *Assessing community change: An evaluation of the Ford Foundation's community organizing initiative, 2000–2004.* New York: CUNY Graduate Center.

Hoxie, Frederick E. 1984. *A final promise: The campaign to assimilate the Indians, 1880–1920.* Lincoln: University of Nebraska Press.

Incite! Women of Color Against Violence. 2007. *The revolution will not be funded: Beyond the nonprofit industrial complex.* Cambridge: South End Press.

Jayaraman, Sarumathi, and Ness, Immanuel, eds. 2005. *The new urban immigrant workforce: Innovative models for labor organizing.* Armonk: M.E. Sharpe.

Joint Legislative Committee on Performance Evaluation and Expenditure Review. 2002. *A review of the Mississippi Adequate Education Program funding process.* Jackson: Joint Legislative Committee on Performance Evaluation and Expenditure Review.

Kaestle, Carl. 1983. *Pillars of the republic: Common Schools and American society, 1780–1860.* New York: Hill and Wang.

Kahne, Joseph, and Middaugh, Ellen. 2008. *Democracy for some: The civic opportunity gap in high school.* Washington, DC: The Center for Information and Research on Civic Learning (CIRCLE).

Katz, Michael B., Fine, Michelle, and Simon, Elaine. 1997. Poking around: Outsiders view Chicago school reform. *Teachers College Record* 99 (1): 117–157.

Keller, Suzanne. 2003. *Community: Pursuing the dream, living the reality.* Princeton: Princeton University Press.

Kochanek, Julie Reed. 2005. *Building trust for better schools: Research-based practices.* Thousand Oaks: Corwin Press.

Koretz, Daniel. 2008. *Measuring up: What educational testing really tells us.* Cambridge: Harvard University Press.

Kozol, Jonathan. 1991. *Savage inequalities: Children in America's schools.* New York: Crown.

Kreisberg, Seth. 1992. *Transforming power: Domination, empowerment, and education.* Albany: University of New York Press.

Krishna, Anirudh. 2002. *Active social capital: Tracing the roots of development and democracy.* New York: Columbia University Press.

Laird, Jennifer, DeBell, Matthew, and Chapman, Chris. 2006. *Dropout rates in the United States: 2004.* Washington, DC: U.S. Department of Education.

Lawrence-Lightfoot, Sara. 1983. *The good high school: Portraits of character and culture.* New York: Basic Books.

Lawrence-Lightfoot, Sara, and Davis, Jessica Hoffman. 1997. *The art and science of portraiture.* San Francisco: Jossey-Bass.

Lawrence, Steven. 2005. *Social justice grantmaking: A report on foundation trends.* New York: Foundation Center.

Levinson, Meira. 2007. *The civic achievement gap.* Washington, DC: The Center for Information and Research on Civic Learning (CIRCLE).

Lipman, Pauline. 2004. *High stakes education: Inequality, globalization, and urban school reform.* New York: Routledge.

Lofland, John, Snow, David A., Anderson, Leon, and Lofland, Lyn H. 2006. *Analyzing social settings: A guide to qualitative observation and analysis.* 4th ed. Belmont: Wadsworth.

Loomer, Bernard. 1976. Two conceptions of power. *Criterion* 15 (1): 11–29.

Lopez, M. Elena, Kreider, Holly, and Coffman, Julia. 2005. Intermediary organizations as capacity builders in family educational involvement. *Urban Education* 40 (1): 78–105.

Luttrell, Wendy, ed. 2010. *Qualitative educational research: Readings in reflexive methodology and transformative practice.* New York: Routledge.

Mapp, Karen L. 2003. Having their say: Parents describe why and how they are engaged in their children's learning. *The School Community Journal* 13 (1): 35–64.

Maxwell, Joseph A. 2004. Causal explanation, qualitative research, and scientific inquiry in education. *Educational Researcher* 33: 3–11.

Maxwell, Joseph A. 2005. *Qualitative research design: An interactive approach.* 2nd ed. Thousand Oaks: Sage.

McAlister, Sara, Mediratta, Kavitha, and Shah, Seema. 2010. Improving teacher quality through public engagement in Chicago. In *Public engagement for public education: Joining forces to revitalize democracy and equalize schools*, ed. Marion Orr and John Rogers, 201–226. Palo Alto: Stanford University Press.

McCourt, Kathleen. 1977. *Working-class women and grass-roots politics*. Bloomington: Indiana University Press.

McLaughlin, Milbrey W., Scott, W. Richard, Deschenes, Sarah, and Hopkins, Kathryn. 2009. *Between movement and establishment: Organizations advocating for youth*. Palo Alto: Stanford University Press.

Mediratta, Kavitha. 2004. *Constituents of change: Community organizations and public education reform*. New York: Institute for Education and Social Policy, New York University.

Mediratta, Kavitha, and Fruchter, Norm. 2001. *Mapping the field of organizing for school improvement*. New York: Institute for Education and Social Policy, New York University.

Mediratta, Kavitha, and Fruchter, Norm. 2003. *From governance to accountability: Building relationships that make schools work*. New York: Institute for Education and Social Policy, New York University.

Mediratta, Kavitha, Fruchter, Norm, Gross, Barbara, Keller, Christine Donis, and Bonilla, Mili. 2001. *Community organizing for school reform in Philadelphia*. New York: Institute for Education and Social Policy, New York University.

Mediratta, Kavitha, and Karp, Jessica. 2003. *Parent power and urban school reform: The story of Mothers on the Move*. New York: Institute for Education and Social Policy, New York University.

Mediratta, Kavitha, McAlister, Sara, and Shah, Seema. 2009. *Improving schools through youth leadership and action*. Providence: Annenberg Institute for School Reform.

Mediratta, Kavitha, Shah, Seema, and McAlister, Sara. 2009. *Community organizing for stronger schools: Strategies and successes*. Cambridge: Harvard Education Press.

Meier, Deborah. 1995. *The power of their ideas: Lessons for America from a small school in Harlem*. Boston: Beacon Press.

Merriam, Sharan B. 1998. *Qualitative research and case study applications in education*. San Francisco: Jossey-Bass.

Milkman, Ruth, ed. 2000. *Organizing immigrants: The challenge for unions in contemporary California*. Ithaca: ILR Press.

Miller, Jean Baker. 1982. *Women and power. Work in progress #82–01*. Wellesley, MA: Stone Center Working Paper Series.

Milner, H. Richard, IV. 2007. Race, culture, and researcher positionality: Working through dangers seen, unseen, and unforeseen. *Educational Researcher* 36 (7): 388–400.

Miretzky, Debra. 2004. The communication requirements of democratic schools: Parent-teacher perspectives on their relationships. *Teachers College Record* 106: 814–851.

Moll, Louis C., Amanti, Cathy, Neff, Deborah, and Gonzalez, Norma. 1992. Funds of knowledge for teaching: Using a qualitative approach to connect homes and classrooms. *Theory into Practice* 31 (2): 132–141.

Moore, Donald R. 2001. Changing the ground rules. [Electronic version] *Shelterforce*, July/August, Retrieved March 15, 2011 from http://www.nhi.org/online/issues/118/Moore.html.

Morgen, Sandra, and Bookman, Ann. 1988. *Women and the politics of empowerment*. Philadelphia: Temple University Press.

Morris, Aldon, and Braine, Naomi. 2001. Social movements and oppositional consciousness. In *Oppositional consciousness: The subjective roots of social protest*, ed. Jane Mansbridge and Aldon Morris, 20–37. Chicago: University of Chicago Press.

Morris, Aldon D. 1984. *The origins of the Civil Rights movement: Black communities organizing for change*. New York: Free Press.

Moses, Robert P., and Cobb, Charles E., Jr. 2001. *Radical equations: Math literacy and civil rights*. Boston: Beacon Press.

Munford, Luther. 1973. White flight from desegregation in Mississippi. *Equity and Excellence in Education* 11 (3): 12–26.

Munoz, Carlos, Jr. 2007. *Youth, identity, power: The Chicano movement*. Rev. ed. New York: Verso.

Murrell, Peter C. 2001. *The community teacher: A new framework for effective urban teaching.* New York: Teachers College Press.

Naples, Nancy A., ed. 1998a. *Community activism and feminist politics: Organizing across race, class and gender.* New York: Routledge.

Naples, Nancy A. 1998b. *Grassroots warriors: Activist mothering, community work, and the War on Poverty.* New York: Routledge.

National Center for Education Statistics. 2005. *The nation's report card: Reading 2005.* Washington, DC: U.S. Department of Education.

Neckerman, Kathryn M. 2007. *Schools betrayed: Roots of failure in inner-city education.* Chicago: University of Chicago Press.

Noguera, Pedro. 2001. Transforming urban schools through investments in the social capital of parents. In *Social capital and poor communities,* ed. Susan Saegert, J. Phillip Thompson and Mark R. Warren, 189–212. New York: Russell Sage Foundation Press.

Nyberg, David. 1981. *Power over power.* Ithaca: Cornell University Press.

Oakes, Jeannie, and Rogers, John. 2005. *Learning power: Organizing for education and justice.* New York: Teachers College Press.

Olivos, Edward M. 2006. *The power of parents: A critical perspective of bicultural parent involvement in public schools.* New York: Peter Lang.

Olsen, Laurie. 1997. *Made in America: Immigrant students in our public schools.* New York: New Press.

Orfield, Gary, Losen, Daniel, Wald, Johanna, and Swanson, Christopher B. 2004. *Losing our future: How minority youth are being left behind by the graduation rate crisis.* Cambridge: The Civil Rights Project at Harvard University.

Orr, Marion. 1999. *Black social capital: The politics of school reform in Baltimore, 1986–1998.* Lawrence: University Press of Kansas.

Orr, Marion, ed. 2007. *Transforming the city: Community organizing and the challenge of political change.* Lawrence: University Press of Kansas.

Osterman, Paul. 2002. *Gathering power: The future of progressive politics in America.* Boston: Beacon Press.

Padilla, Felix M. 1993. The quest for community: Puerto Ricans in Chicago. In *In the barrios: Latinos and the underclass debate,* ed. Joan Moore and Raquel Pinderhughes, 129–148. New York: Russell Sage Foundation Press.

Pardo, Mary S. 1998. *Mexican American women activists: Identity and resistance in two Los Angeles communities.* Philadelphia: Temple University Press.

Payne, Charles M. 1995. *I've got the light of freedom: The organizing tradition and the Mississippi freedom struggle.* Berkeley: University of California Press.

Payne, Charles M. 2008. *So much reform, so little change: The persistence of failure in urban schools.* Cambridge: Harvard Education Press.

Payne, Charles M., and Strickland, Carol Sills. 2008. *Teach freedom: Education for liberation in the African-American tradition.* New York: Teachers College Press.

Perry, Theresa. 2003. Freedom for literacy and literacy for freedom: The African-American philosophy of education. In *Young, gifted and Black: Promoting high achievement among African-American students,* ed. Theresa Perry, Claude Steele, and Asa G. Hilliard III, 11–51. Boston: Beacon Press.

Pianta, Robert C. 1999. *Enhancing relationships between children and teachers.* Washington, DC: American Psychological Association.

Pittz, Will, and Sen, Rinku. 2006. *Short changed: Foundation giving and communities of color.* Oakland: Applied Research Center.

Piven, Frances Fox, and Cloward, Richard A. 1977. *Poor people's movements: Why they succeed, how they fail.* New York: Pantheon Books.

Polletta, Francesca. 2006. *It was like a fever: Storytelling in protest and politics.* Chicago: University of Chicago Press.

Polsby, Nelson W. 1963. *Community power and political theory.* New Haven: Yale University Press.

Putnam, Robert D. 1993. *Making democracy work: Civic traditions in modern Italy.* Princeton: Princeton University Press.

Putnam, Robert D. 2000. *Bowling alone: The collapse and revival of American community.* New York: Simon and Schuster.

Ragin, Charles C., Nagel, Joane, and White, Patricia. 2004. *Report of the Workshop on Scientific Foundations of Qualitative Research.* Washington, DC: National Science Foundation.

Ravitch, Diane. 1988. *The great school wars: A history of the New York City public schools.* New York: Basic Books.

Ravitch, Diane. 2010. *The death and life of the great American school system: How testing and choice are undermining education.* New York: Basic Books.

Reitzes, Donald C., and Reitzes, Dietrich C. 1987. *The Alinsky legacy: Alive and kicking.* Greenwood, CT: JAI Press.

Rhodes, Amy, and Gold, Eva. 2002. *Lessons learned about parent organizing: A case study.* Chicago: Research for Action, The Philadelphia Education Fund.

Robnett, Belinda. 1997. *How long? How long? African-American women in the struggle for civil rights.* New York: Oxford University Press.

Rogers, John. 2006. Forces of accountability? The power of poor parents in NCLB. *Harvard Educational Review* 76 (4): 611–641.

Ross, E. Wayne, and Gibson, Rich. 2007. *Neoliberalism and education reform.* Cresskill: Hampton Press.

Rothstein, Richard. 2004. *Class and schools: Using social, economic and educational reform to close the black-white achievement gap.* Washington, DC: Economic Policy Institute.

Rubin, Hank. 2002. *Collaborative leadership: Developing effective partnerships in communities and schools.* Thousand Oaks: Corwin Press.

Rubin, Herbert J., and Rubin, Irene S. 2005. *Qualitative interviewing: The art of hearing data.* 2nd ed. Thousand Oaks: Sage.

Rucht, Dieter. 2004. Movement allies, adversaries, and third parties. In *The Blackwell companion to social movements,* ed. David A. Snow, Sarah A. Soule, and Haspeter Kriesi, 197–216. Malden, MA: Blackwell.

Rusch, Lara. 2009. Rethinking bridging: Risk and trust in multiracial community organizing. *Urban Affairs Review* 45 (4): 483–506.

Saegert, Susan, Thompson, J. Phillip, and Warren, Mark R., eds. 2001. *Social capital and poor communities.* New York: Russell Sage Foundation Press.

Sampson, Robert J., McAdam, Doug, MacIndoe, Heather, and Weffer-Elizondo, Simon. 2005. Civil society reconsidered: The durable nature and community structure of collective civic action. *American Journal of Sociology* 111 (3): 673–714.

Sampson, Robert J., Morenoff, Jeffrey D., and Earls, Felton. 1999. Beyond social capital: Spatial dynamics of collective efficacy for children. *American Sociological Review* 64: 633–660.

Santow, Mark. 2007. Running in place: Saul Alinsky, race, and community organizing. In *Transforming the city: Community organizing and the challenge of political change,* ed. Marion Orr, 28–55. Lawrence: University Press of Kansas.

Schneider, Barbara L., and McDonald, Sarah-Kathryn, eds. 2007. *Scale-up in education.* Lanham, MD: Rowman & Littlefield.

Scott, James C. 1998. *Seeing like a state: How certain schemes to improve the human condition have failed.* New Haven: Yale University Press.

Scott, W. Richard, and Davis, Gerald F. 2007. *Organizations and organizing: Rational, natural, and open systems perspectives.* Upper Saddle River, NJ: Pearson Prentice Hall.

Shah, Seema, and Mediratta, Kavitha. 2008. Negotiating reform: Young people's leadership in the educational arena. *New Directions for Youth Development* 117: 43–59.

Shavelson, Richard J., and Towne, Lisa, eds. 2002. *Scientific research in education.* Washington, DC: National Academy Press.

Shear, Linda, Means, Barbara, Mitchell, Karen, House, Ann, Gorges, Torie, Joshi, Aasha, Smerdon, Becky, and Shkolnik, Jamie. 2008. Contrasting paths to small-school reform: Results of a

5-year evaluation of the Bill and Melinda Gates Foundation's National High School Initiative. *Teachers College Record* 110 (9): 1986–2039.

Shipps, Dorothy. 1997. The invisible hand: Big business and Chicago school reform. *Teachers College Record* 99 (1): 73–116.

Shirley, Dennis. 1997. *Community organizing for urban school reform.* Austin: University of Texas Press.

Shirley, Dennis. 2002. *Valley Interfaith and school reform.* Austin: University of Texas Press.

Shirley, Dennis, and Evans, Michael. 2007. Community organizing and No Child Left Behind. In *Transforming the city: Community organizing and the challenge of political change,* ed. Marion Orr, 109–133. Lawrence: University Press of Kansas.

Shor, Ira. 1992. *Empowering education: Critical teaching for social change.* Chicago: University of Chicago Press.

Simon, Elaine, and Gold, Eva. 2002. *Case Study: Austin Interfaith.* Chicago: Cross City Campaign for Urban School Reform.

Simon, Elaine, Gold, Eva, and Cucchiara, Maia. 2010. The prospects for public engagement in a market-oriented public education system: A case study of Philadelphia, 2001–2007. In *Public engagement for public education: Joining forces to revitalize democracy and equalize schools,* ed. Marion Orr and John Rogers, 276–300. Palo Alto: Stanford University Press.

Skocpol, Theda. 1992. *Protecting soldiers and mothers: The political origins of social policy in the United States.* Cambridge: Harvard University Press.

Skocpol, Theda. 2003. *Diminished democracy: From membership to management in American civic life.* Norman: University of Oklahoma Press.

Skocpol, Theda, Ganz, Marshall, and Munson, Ziad. 2000. A nation of organizers: The institutional origins of civic voluntarism in the United States. *American Political Science Review* 94 (3): 527–546.

Skocpol, Theda, Liazos, Ariane, and Ganz, Marshall. 2006. *What a mighty power we can be: African American fraternal groups and the struggle for racial equality.* Princeton: Princeton University Press.

Smock, Kristina. 2004. *Democracy in action: Community organizing and urban change.* New York: Columbia University Press.

Snow, David A., Rochford, Jr., E. Burke, Worden, Steven K., and Benford, Robert D. 1986. Frame alignment processes, micromobilization and movement participation. *American Sociological Review* 51: 464–481.

Southern Echo. 2004. *A thousand spider webs linked together: Using community organizing as an antidote to the 3rd stage of domination and control—How African Americans worked to empower the grassroots community on the Mississippi front: A 15 year report by Southern Echo.* Jackson: Southern Echo.

Speer, Paul, and Hughey, Joseph. 1995. Community organizing: An ecological route to empowerment. *American Journal of Community Psychology* 23 (5): 729–749.

Spillane, James P. 2006. *Distributed leadership.* San Francisco: Jossey-Bass.

Stake, Robert E. 1995. *The art of case study research.* Thousand Oaks: Sage.

Stall, Susan, and Stoecker, Randy. 1998. Community organizing or organizing community? Gender and the crafts of empowerment. *Gender and Society* 12: 729–756.

Stone, Clarence, Doherty, Kathryn, Jones, Cheryl, and Ross, Timothy. 1999. Schools and disadvantaged neighborhoods: The community development challenge. In *Urban problems and community development,* ed. Ronald F. Ferguson and William T. Dickens, 339–380. Washington, DC: Brookings Institution Press.

Stone, Clarence N., Henig, Jeffrey R., Jones, Bryan D., and Pierannunzi, Carol. 2001. *Building civic capacity: The politics of reforming urban schools.* Lawrence: University Press of Kansas.

Strand, Kerry J., Cutforth, Nicholas, Stoecker, Randy, and Marullo, Sam. 2003. *Community-based research and higher education: Principles and practices.* San Francisco: Jossey-Bass.

Su, Celina. 2009. *Streetwise for book smarts: Grassroots organizing and education reform in the Bronx.* Ithaca: Cornell University Press.

Suitts, Steve. 2007. *A new majority: Low income students in the South's public schools*. Atlanta: Southern Education Foundation.

Suitts, Steve. 2010. *A new diverse majority: Students of color in the South's public schools*. Atlanta: Southern Education Foundation.

Sum, Andrew, Khatiwada, Ishwar, and McLaughlin, Joseph. 2009. *The consequences of dropping out of high school*. Boston: Northeastern University Center for Labor Market Studies.

Swarts, Heidi J. 2008. *Organizing urban America: Secular and faith-based progressive movements*. Minneapolis: University of Minnesota Press.

Taylor, Charles. 1989. *Sources of the self: The making of the modern identity*. Cambridge: Harvard University Press.

Thompson, Becky. 2001. *A promise and a way of life: White antiracist activism*. Minneapolis: University of Minnesota Press.

Tough, Paul. 2008. *Whatever it takes: Geoffrey Canada's quest to change Harlem and America*. Boston: Houghton Mifflin.

Tschannen-Moran, Megan. 2004. *Trust matters: Leadership for successful schools*. San Francisco: Jossey-Bass.

Tyack, David B., and Cuban, Larry. 1995. *Tinkering toward utopia: A century of public school reform*. Cambridge: Harvard University Press.

Valenzuela, Angela. 1999. *Subtractive schooling: U.S.-Mexican youth and the politics of caring*. Albany: State University of New York Press.

Valenzuela, Richard R., and Black, Mary S. 2002. "Mexican Americans don't value education!" On the basis of the myth, mythmaking and debunking. *Journal of Latinos and Education* 1 (2): 81–103.

Verba, Sidney, Schlozman, Kay Lehman, and Brady, Henry E. 1995. *Voice and equality: Civic voluntarism in American politics*. Cambridge: Harvard University Press.

Wagner, Tony. 2006. *Change leadership: A practical guide to transforming our schools*. San Francisco: Jossey-Bass.

Warren, Mark R. 2001. *Dry bones rattling: Community building to revitalize American democracy*. Princeton: Princeton University Press.

Warren, Mark R. 2005. Communities and schools: A new view of urban education reform. *Harvard Educational Review* 75 (2): 133–173.

Warren, Mark R. 2009. Community organizing in Britain: The political engagement of faith-based social capital. *City and Community* 8 (2): 99–127.

Warren, Mark R. 2010a. Community organizing for education reform. In *Public engagement for public education: Joining forces to revitalize democracy and equalize schools*, ed. Marion Orr and John Rogers, 139–172. Palo Alto: Stanford University Press.

Warren, Mark R. 2010b. *Fire in the heart: How white activists embrace racial justice*. New York: Oxford University Press.

Warren, Mark R. 2011. Building a political constituency for urban school reform. *Urban Education* 46 (3): 484–512.

Warren, Mark R., Hong, Soo, Rubin, Carolyn Leung, and Uy, Phitsamay Sychitkokhong. 2009. Beyond the bake sale: A community-based, relational approach to parent engagement in schools. *Teachers College Record* 111 (9): 2209–2254.

Warren, Mark R., Mira, Meredith, and Nikundiwe, Thomas. 2008. Youth organizing: From youth development to school reform. *New Directions in Youth Development*. 117: 27–42.

Warren, Mark R., Thompson, J. Phillip, and Saegert, Susan. 2001. The role of social capital in combating poverty. In *Social capital and poor communities*, ed. Susan Saegert, J. Phillip Thompson, and Mark R. Warren, 1–28. New York: Russell Sage Foundation Press.

Warren, Mark R., and Wood, Richard L. 2001. *Faith based community organizing: The state of the field*. Jericho, NY: Interfaith Funders.

Weber, Max. 1946. Class, status, party. In *From Max Weber: Essays in sociology*, ed. H.H. Gerth and C. Wright Mills, 180–195. New York: Oxford University Press.

Weiss, Robert S. 1994. *Learning from strangers: The art and method of qualitative interview studies*. New York: Free Press.

Wenger, Etienne, McDermott, Richard A., and Snyder, William. 2002. *Cultivating communities of practice: A guide to managing knowledge.* Boston: Harvard Business School Press.

Westbrook, Robert B. 1991. *John Dewey and American democracy.* Ithaca: Cornell University Press.

Williams, Heather Andrea. 2005. *Self-taught: African American education in slavery and freedom.* Chapel Hill: University of North Carolina Press.

Wilson, William J. 1999. *The bridge over the racial divide: Rising inequality and coalition politics.* Berkeley: University of California Press.

Wolin, Sheldon S. 1989. *The presence of the past: Essays on the state and the Constitution.* Baltimore: Johns Hopkins University Press.

Wood, Richard L. 2002. *Faith in action: Religion, race and democratic organizing in America.* Chicago: University of Chicago Press.

Wood, Richard L., and Warren, Mark R. 2002. A different face of faith-based politics: Social capital and community organizing in the public arena. *International Journal of Sociology and Social Policy* 22 (9/10): 6–54.

Woolcock, Michael. 1998. Social capital and economic development: Toward a theoretical synthesis and policy framework. *Theory and Society* 27: 151–208.

Wrigley, Julia. 1997. Chicago school reform: Business control or open democracy? *Teachers College Record* 99 (1): 158–161.

Yin, Robert K. 2003. *Case study research: Design and methods.* Thousand Oaks: Sage Publications.

Zachary, Eric, and olatoya, shola. 2001. *Community organizing for school improvement in the South Bronx.* New York: Institute for Education and Social Policy, New York University.

Zimmerman, Marc A. 2000. Empowerment theory: Psychological, organizational and community levels of analysis. In *Handbook of community psychology*, ed. Julian Rappaport and Edward Seidman. New York: Plenum Press.

Index

Page numbers like **p2** indicate the photo plates that follow page 167. Page numbers in bold indicate figures.

314   *Index*